THE SEVEN DEADLY SINS

nakaba suzuki presents

14

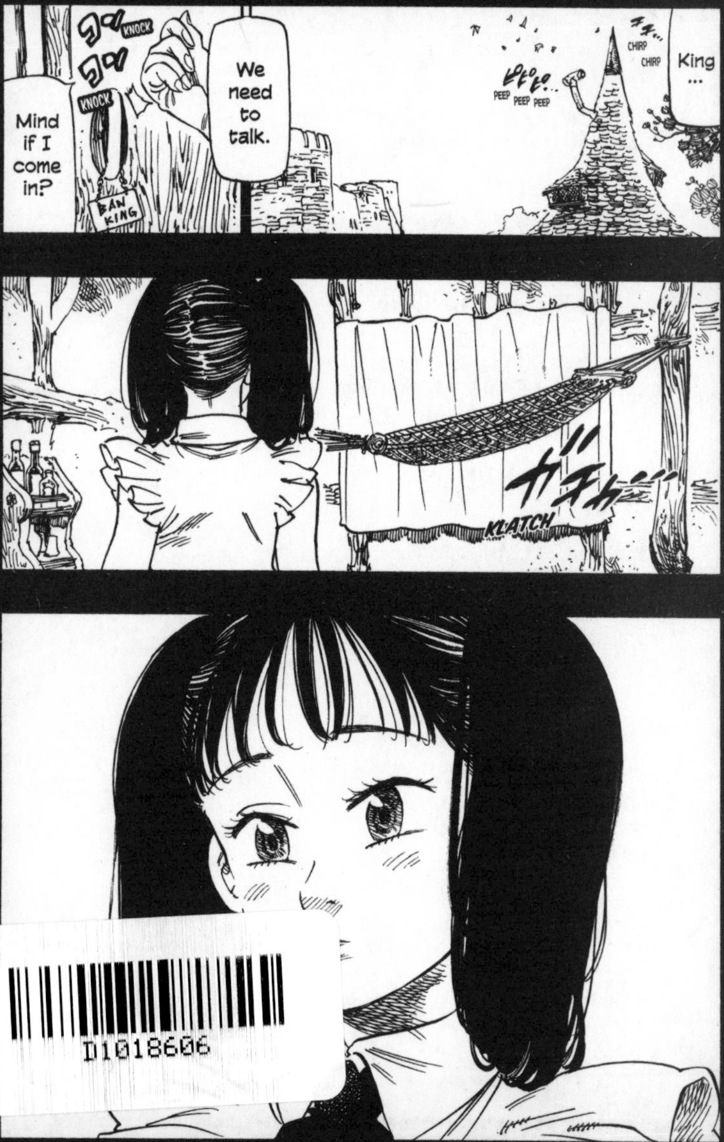
King ...
CHIRP CHIRP
PEEP PEEP PEEP
We need to talk.
KNOCK KNOCK
Mind if I come in?
BAN KING
KLATCH

CONTENTS

BOAR HAT

The Seven Deadly Sins

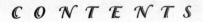

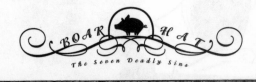

Chapter 105 - The Nobody

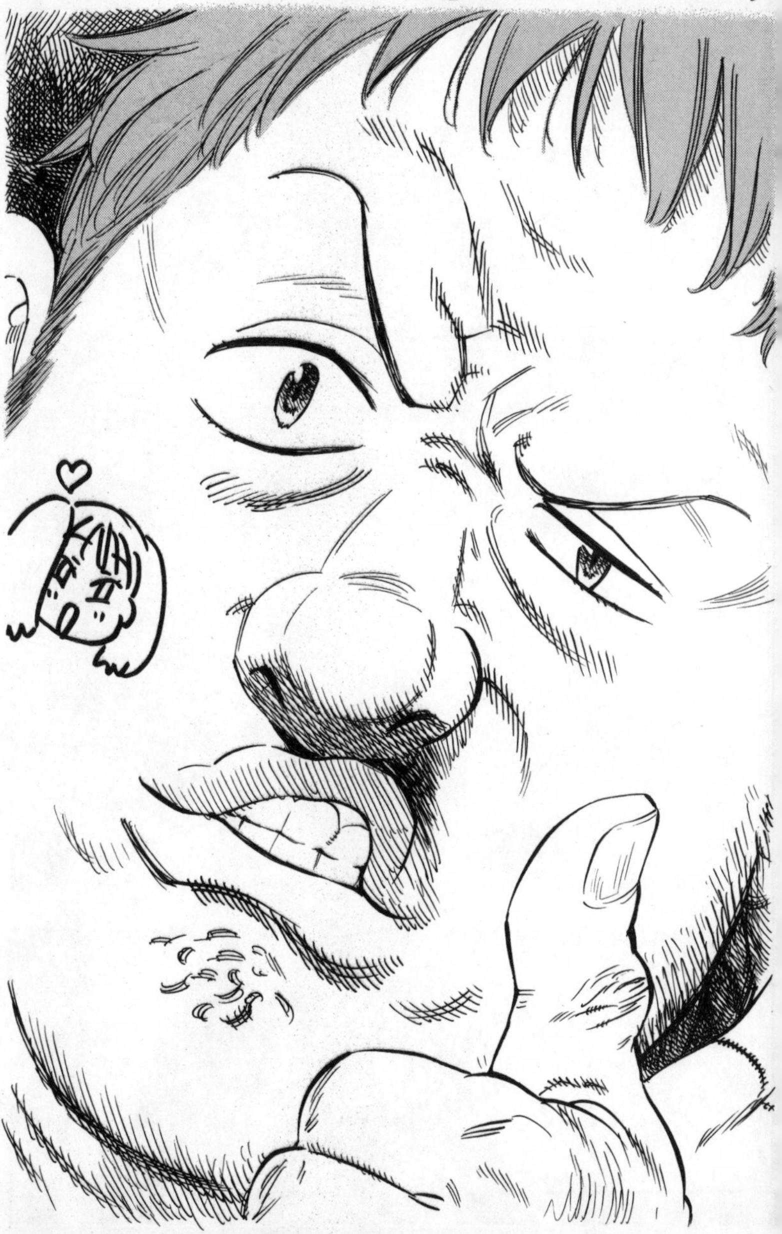

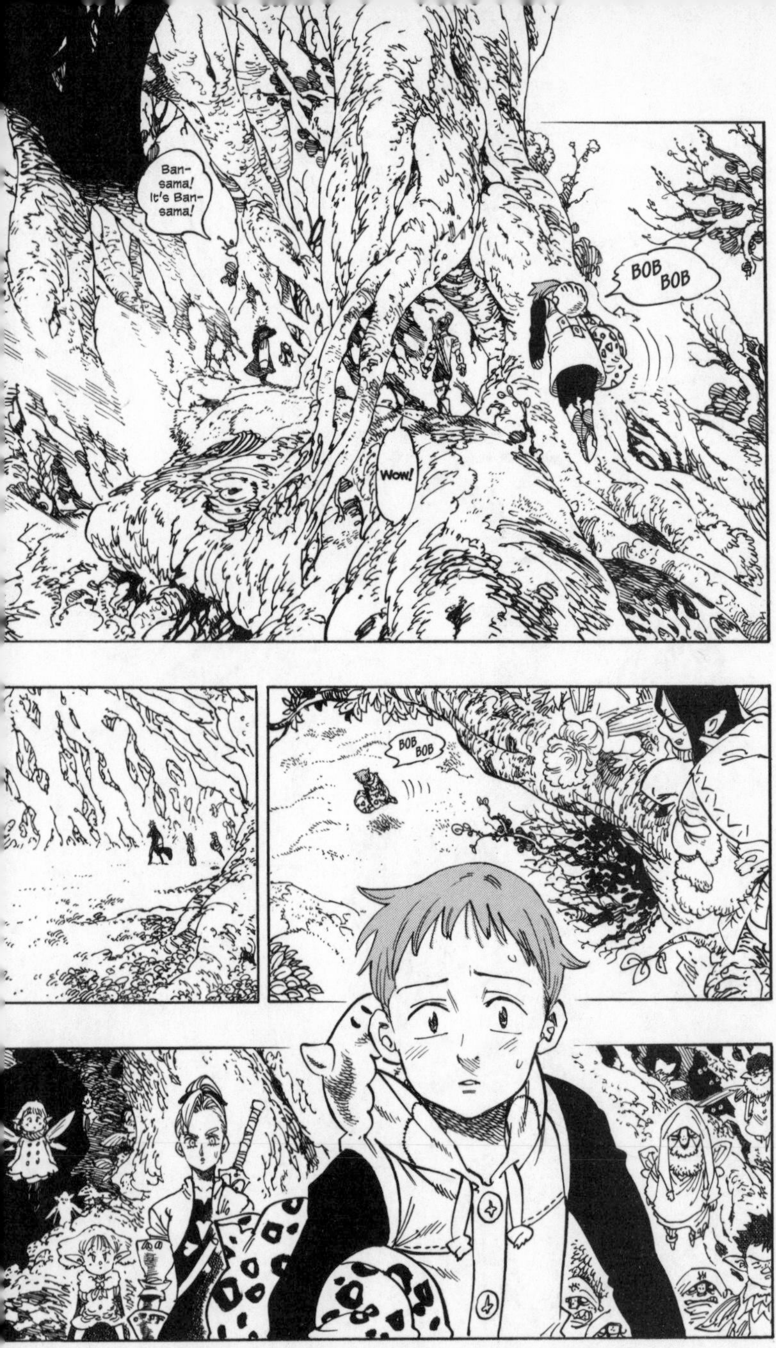
BOB BOB
WOW!
Ban-sama! It's Ban-sama!
BOB BOB

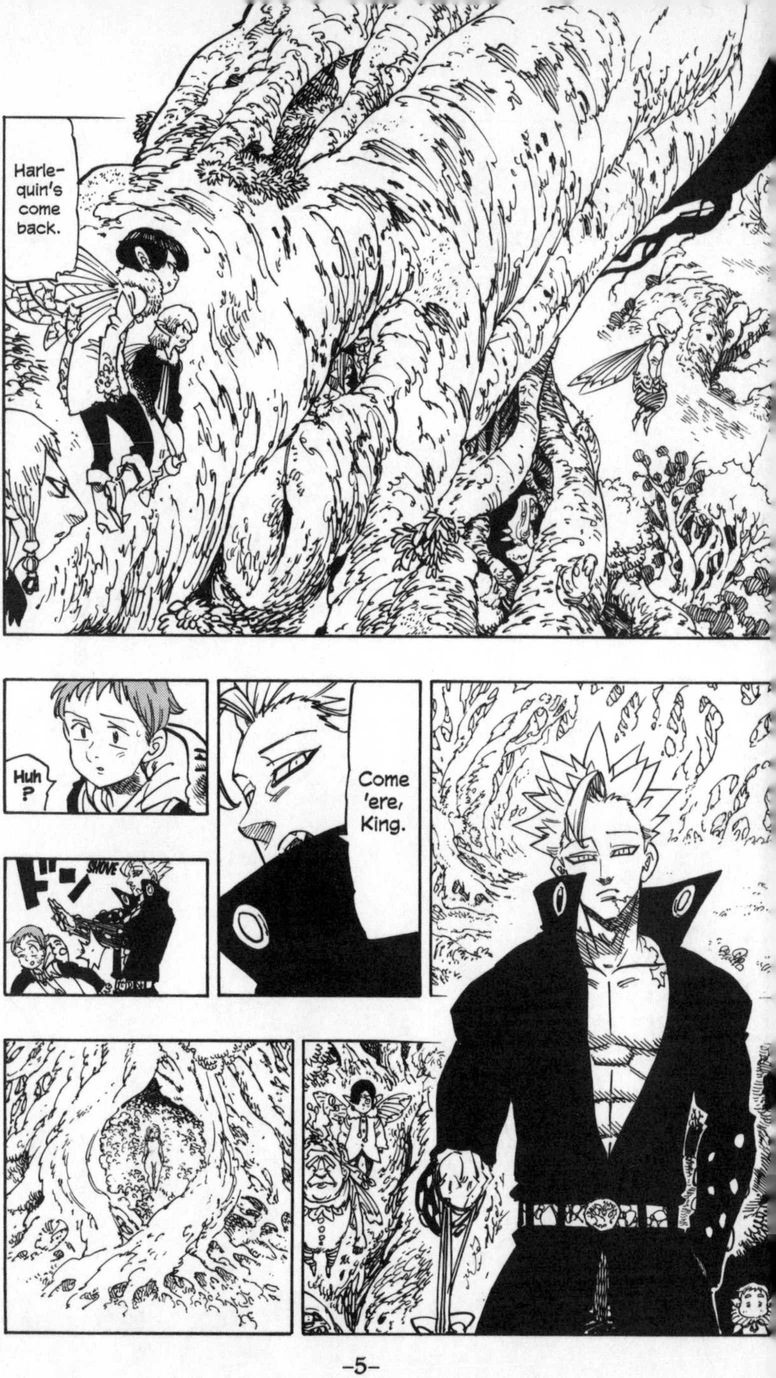
Harle-quin's come back.
Come 'ere, King.
Huh?
SHOVE

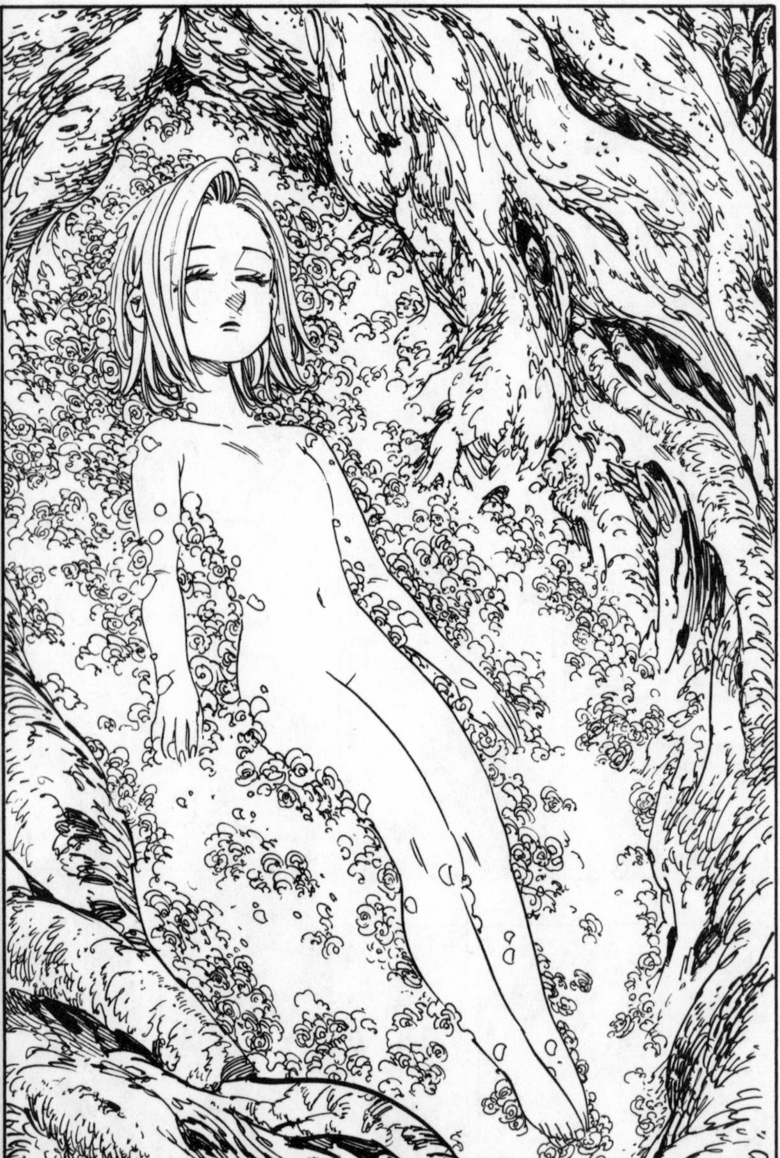

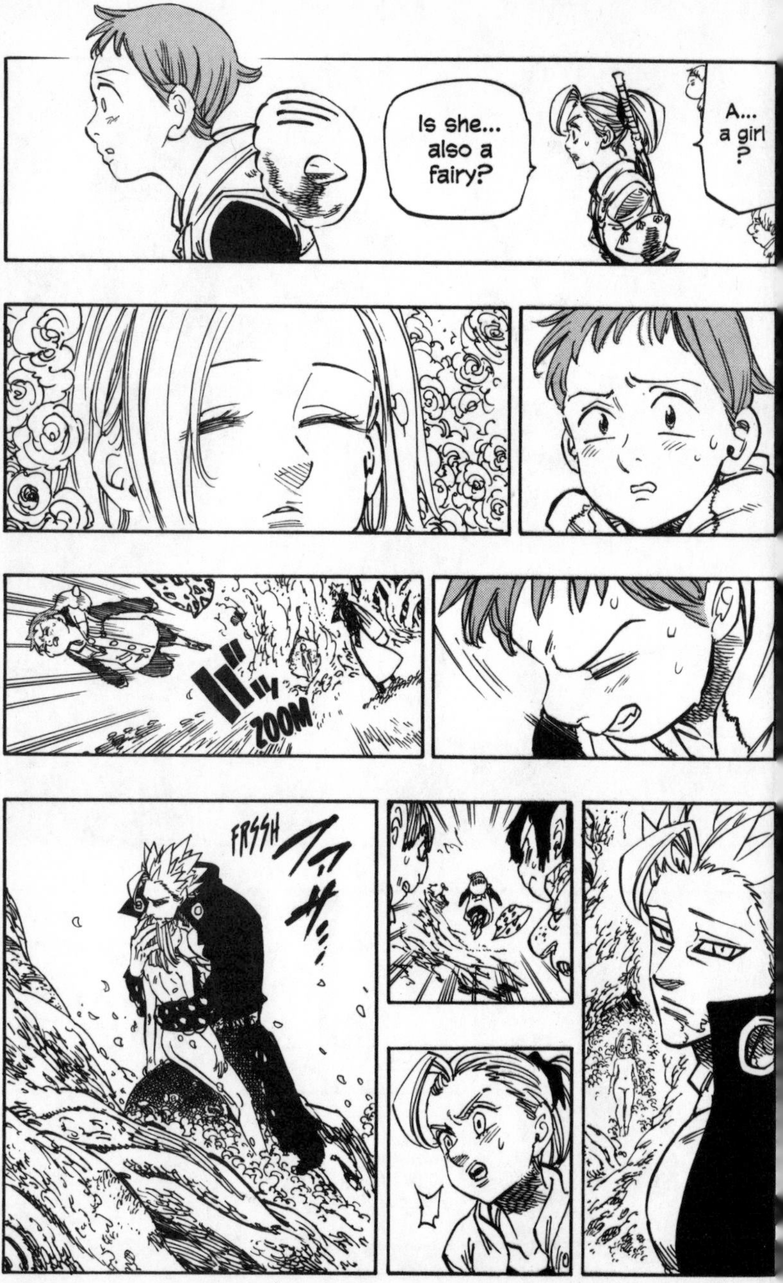
A... a girl?
Is she... also a fairy?
ZOOM
FRSSH

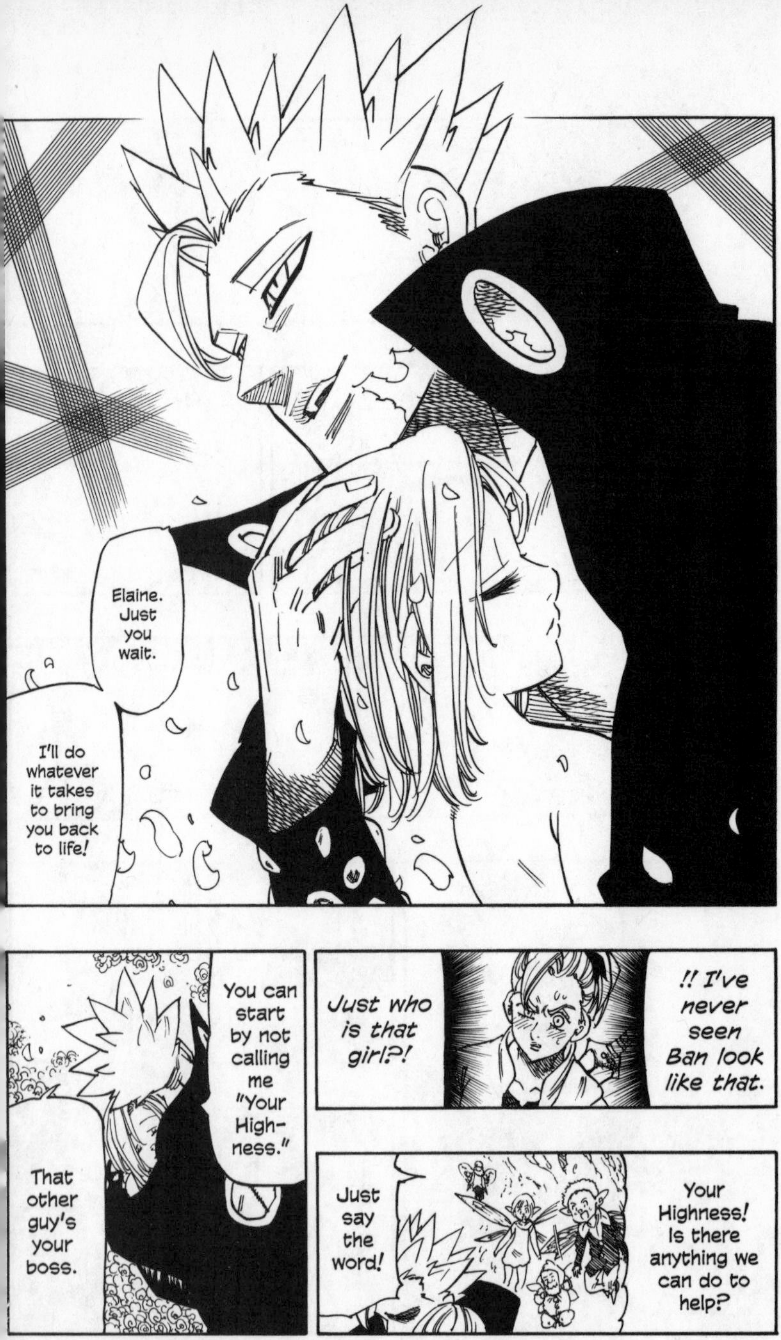
Elaine. Just you wait.
I'll do whatever it takes to bring you back to life!
!! I've never seen Ban look like that.
Just who is that girl?!
Your Highness! Is there anything we can do to help?
Just say the word!
You can start by not calling me "Your High-ness."
That other guy's your boss.

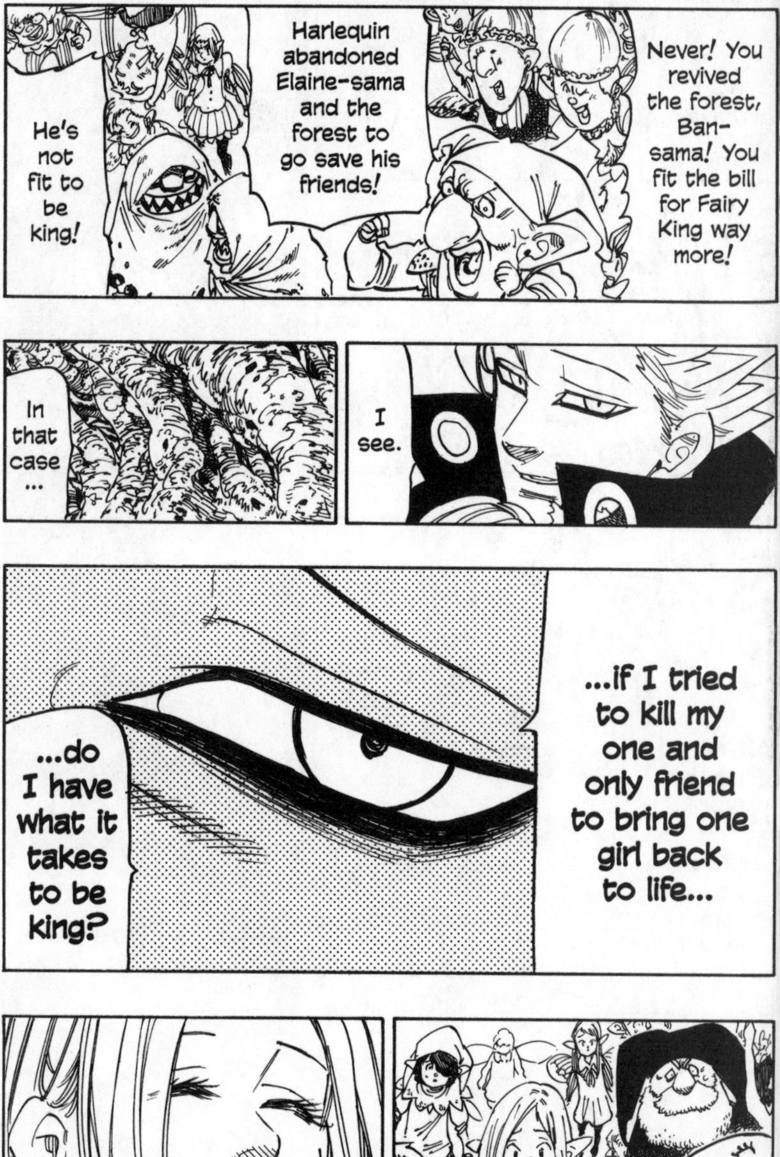

Never! You revived the forest, Ban-sama! You fit the bill for Fairy King way more!
Harlequin abandoned Elaine-sama and the forest to go save his friends!
He's not fit to be king!
I see.
In that case...
...if I tried to kill my one and only friend to bring one girl back to life...
...do I have what it takes to be king?

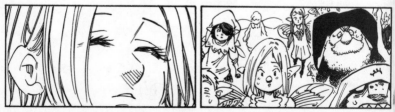

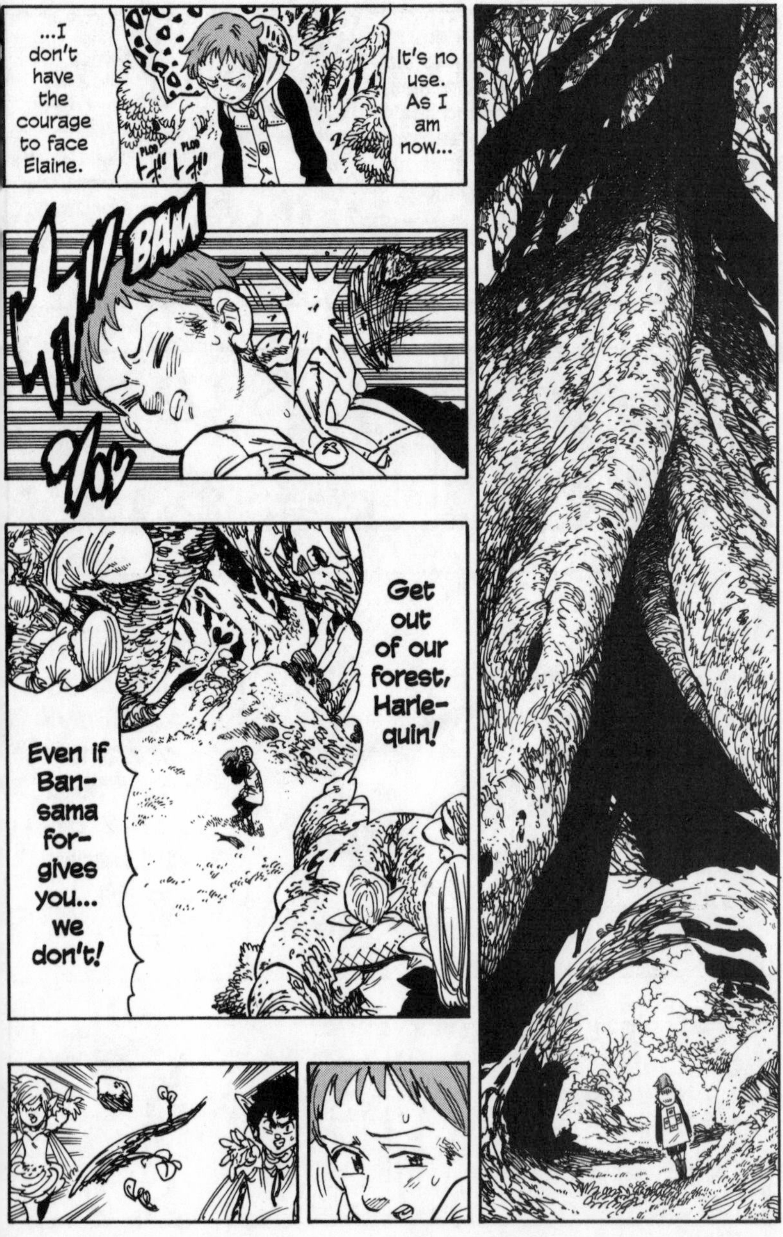
It's no use. As I am now...
...I don't have the courage to face Elaine.
PLOD PLOD
BAM
Get out of our forest, Harlequin!
Even if Ban-sama forgives you... we don't!

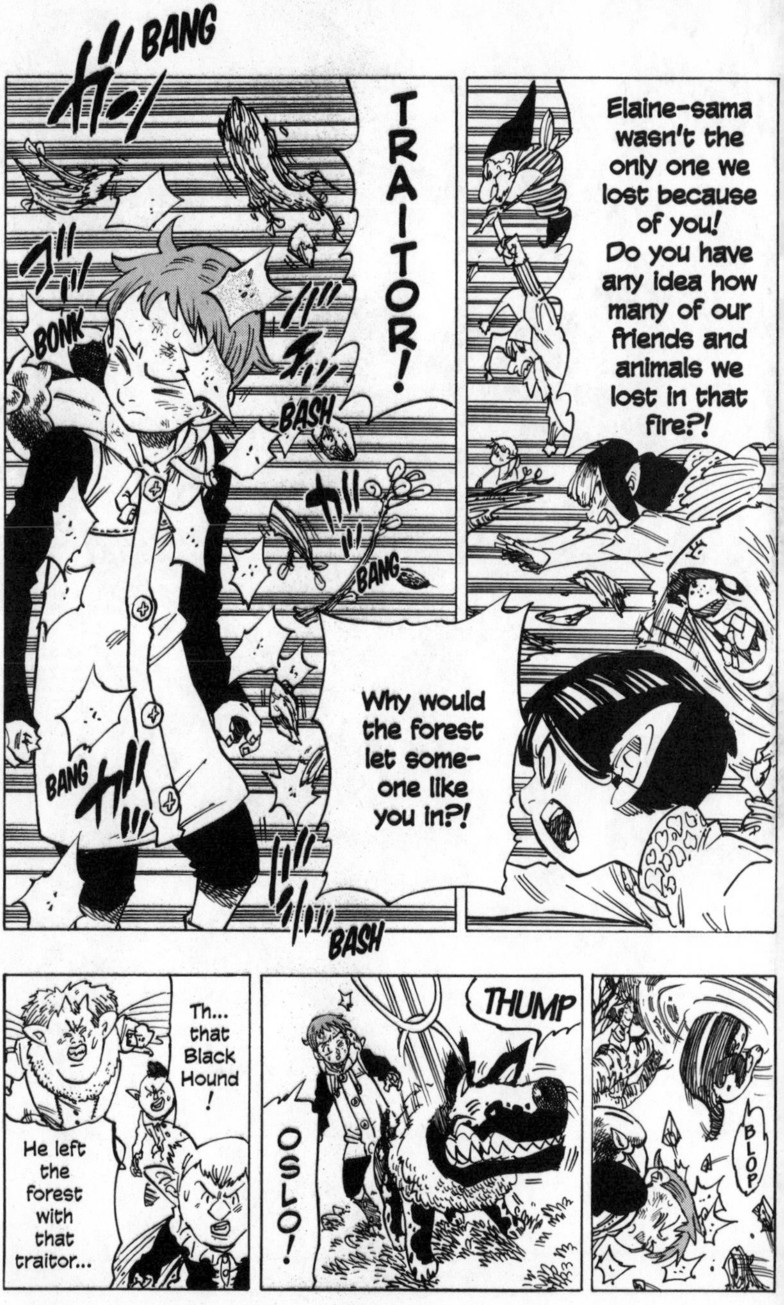

Elaine-sama wasn't the only one we lost because of you! Do you have any idea how many of our friends and animals we lost in that fire?!
Why would the forest let some-one like you in?!
BANG
TRAITOR!
BONK
BASH
BANG
BANG
BASH
BLOP
THUMP
OSLO!
Th... that Black Hound!
He left the forest with that traitor...

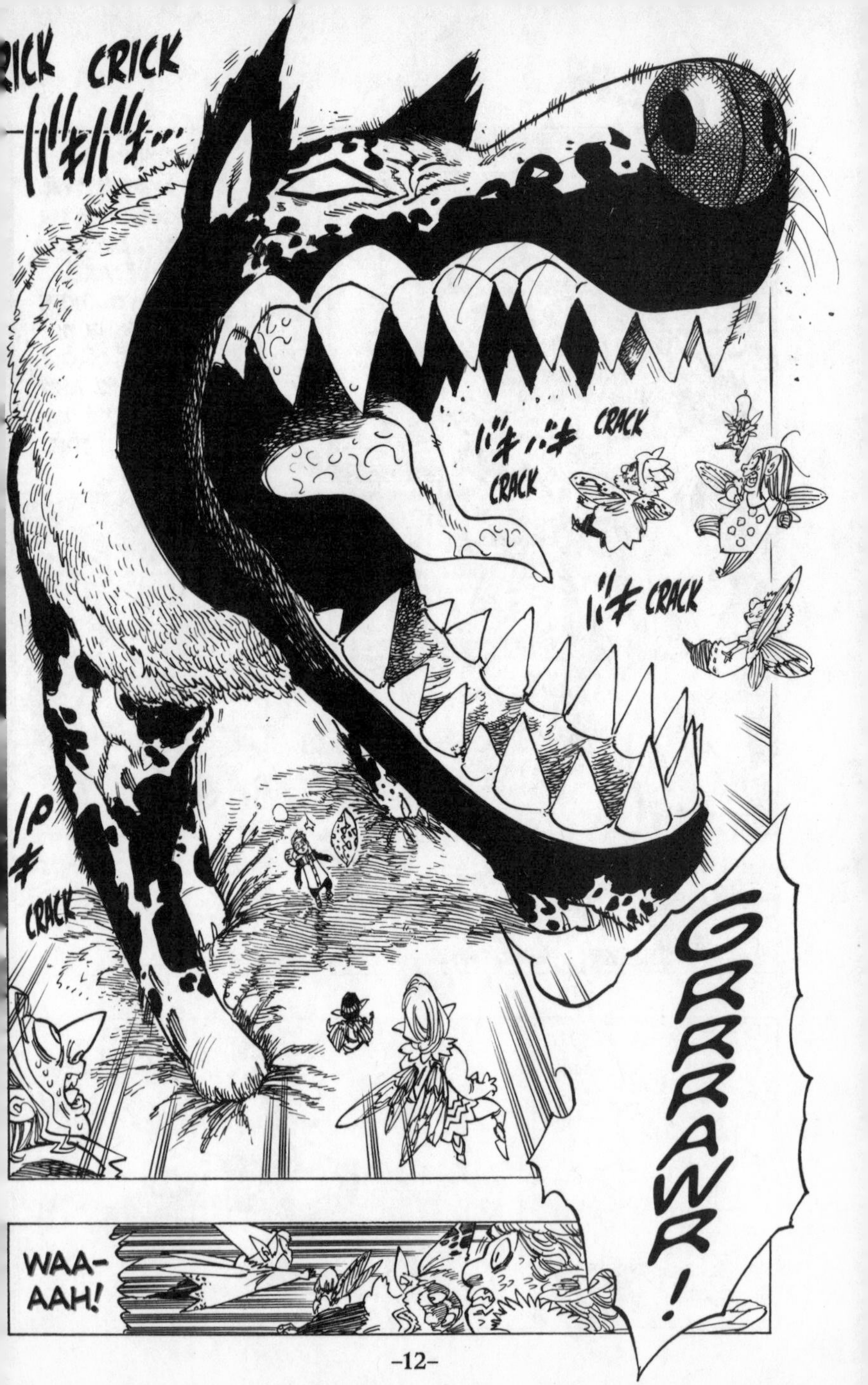
CRICK CRICK
CRACK
CRACK
CRACK
GRRRAWR!
CRACK
WAA-AAH!

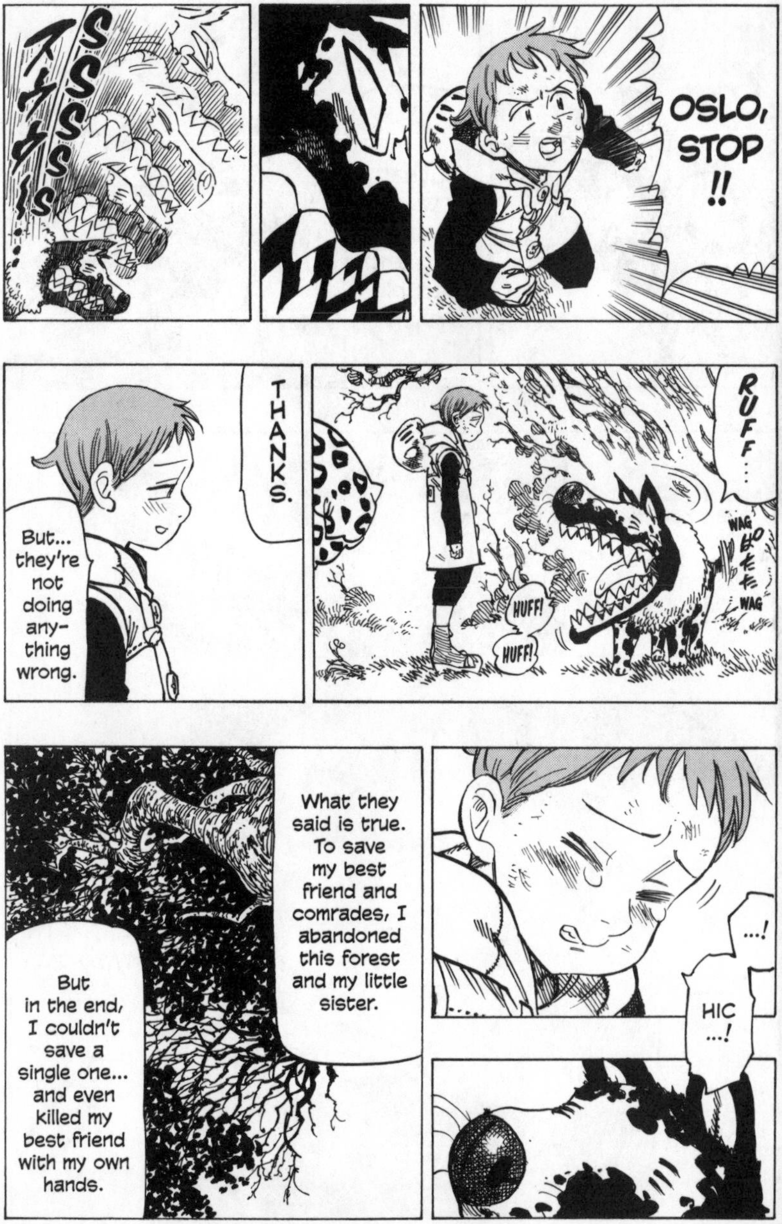
OSLO, STOP!!
SSSSS...
RUFF...
WAG WAG
HUFF!
HUFF!
THANKS.
But... they're not doing anything wrong.
...!
HIC...!
What they said is true. To save my best friend and comrades, I abandoned this forest and my little sister.
But in the end, I couldn't save a single one... and even killed my best friend with my own hands.

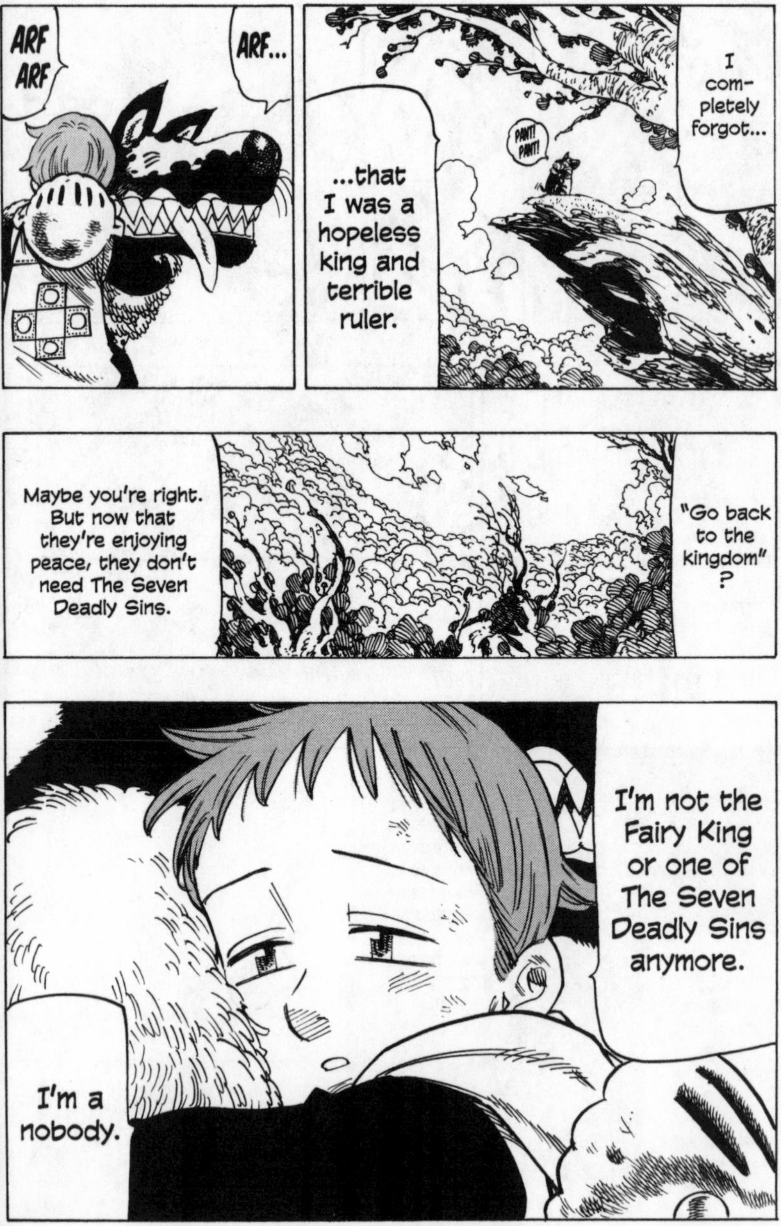
I completely forgot...
PANT! PANT!
...that I was a hopeless king and terrible ruler.
ARF...
ARF ARF
"Go back to the kingdom"?
Maybe you're right. But now that they're enjoying peace, they don't need The Seven Deadly Sins.
I'm not the Fairy King or one of The Seven Deadly Sins anymore.
I'm a nobody.

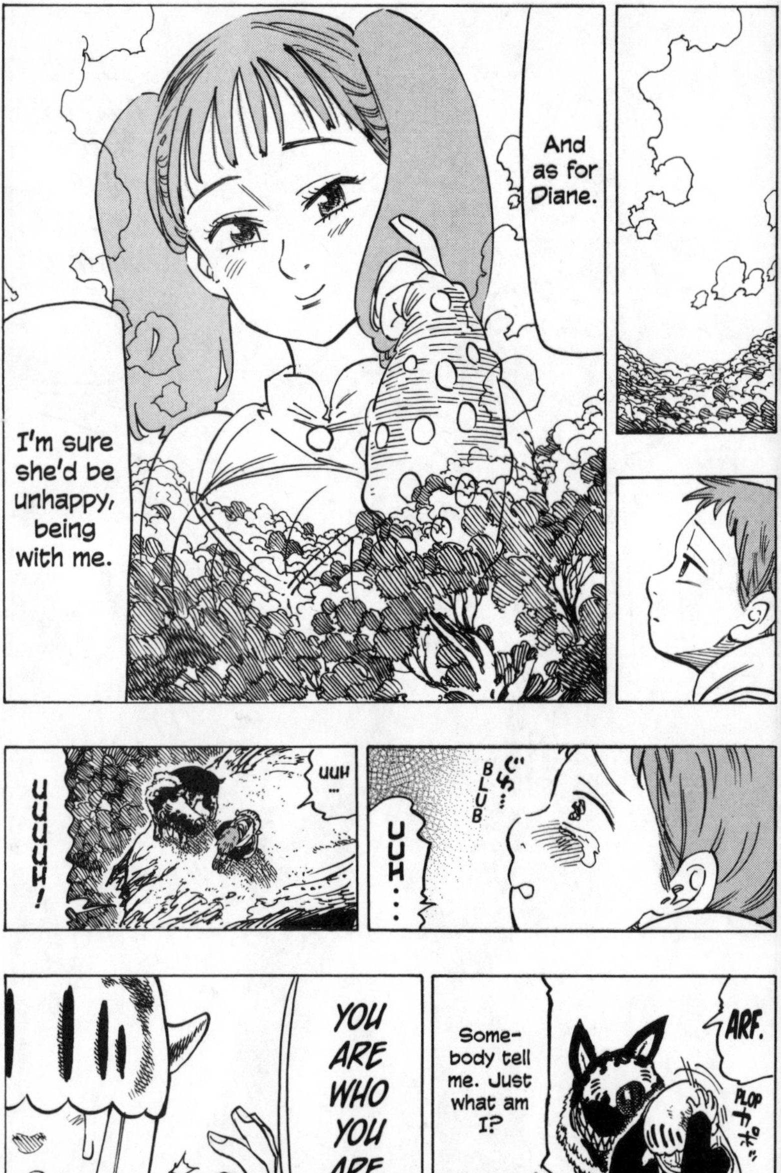

And as for Diane.
I'm sure she'd be unhappy, being with me.
BLUB
UUH...
UUH ...
UUUUUH!
ARF.
PLOP
Some-body tell me. Just what am I?
YOU ARE WHO YOU ARE.

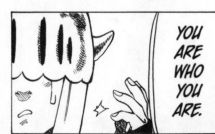

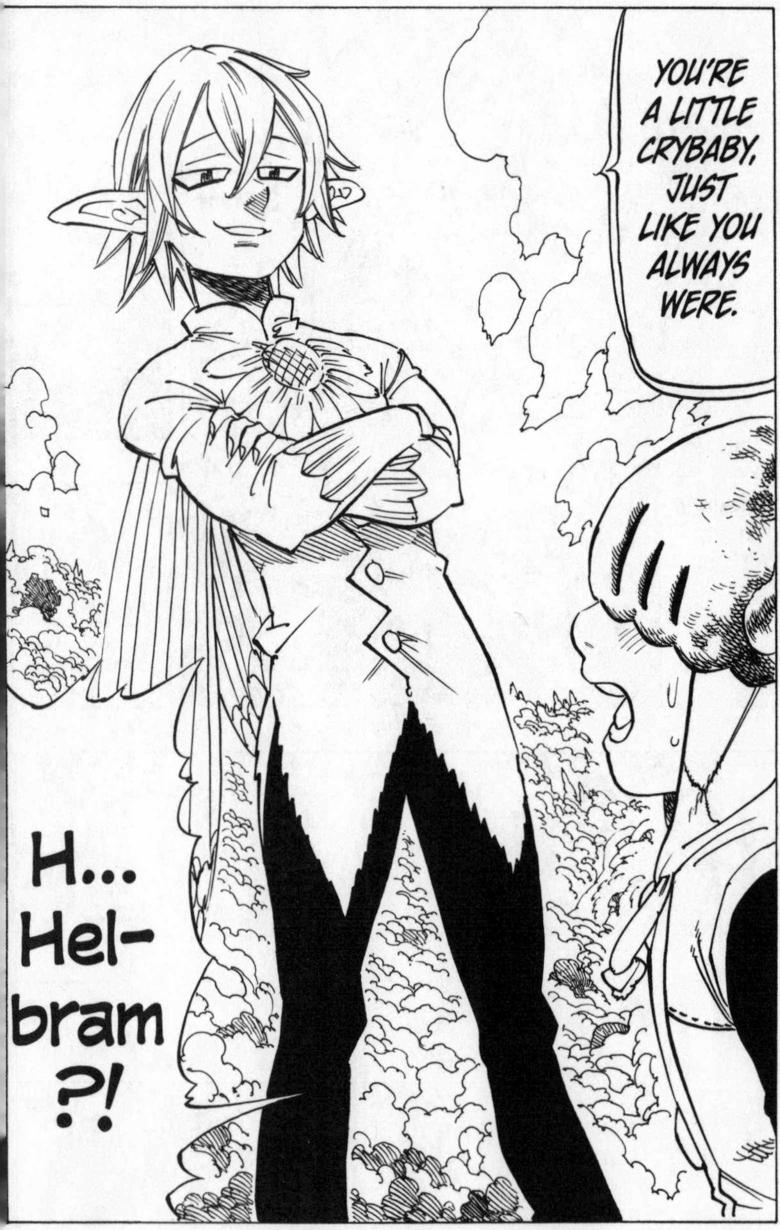
YOU'RE A LITTLE CRYBABY, JUST LIKE YOU ALWAYS WERE.
H... Hel-bram?!

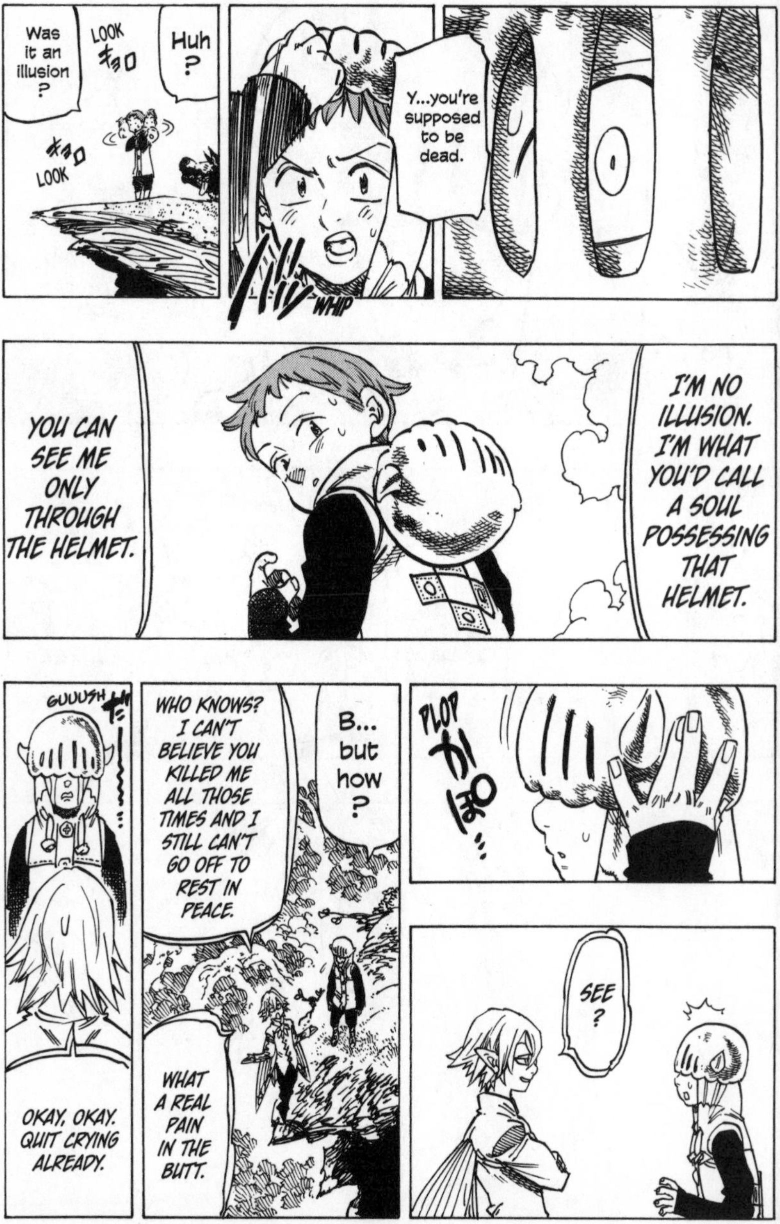
Y...you're supposed to be dead.
WHIP
Huh?
LOOK キョロ
Was it an illusion?
キョロ LOOK
I'M NO ILLUSION. I'M WHAT YOU'D CALL A SOUL POSSESSING THAT HELMET.
YOU CAN SEE ME ONLY THROUGH THE HELMET.
PLOP かぽ
SEE?
B... but how?
WHO KNOWS? I CAN'T BELIEVE YOU KILLED ME ALL THOSE TIMES AND I STILL CAN'T GO OFF TO REST IN PEACE.
WHAT A REAL PAIN IN THE BUTT.
GUUUSH
OKAY, OKAY. QUIT CRYING ALREADY.

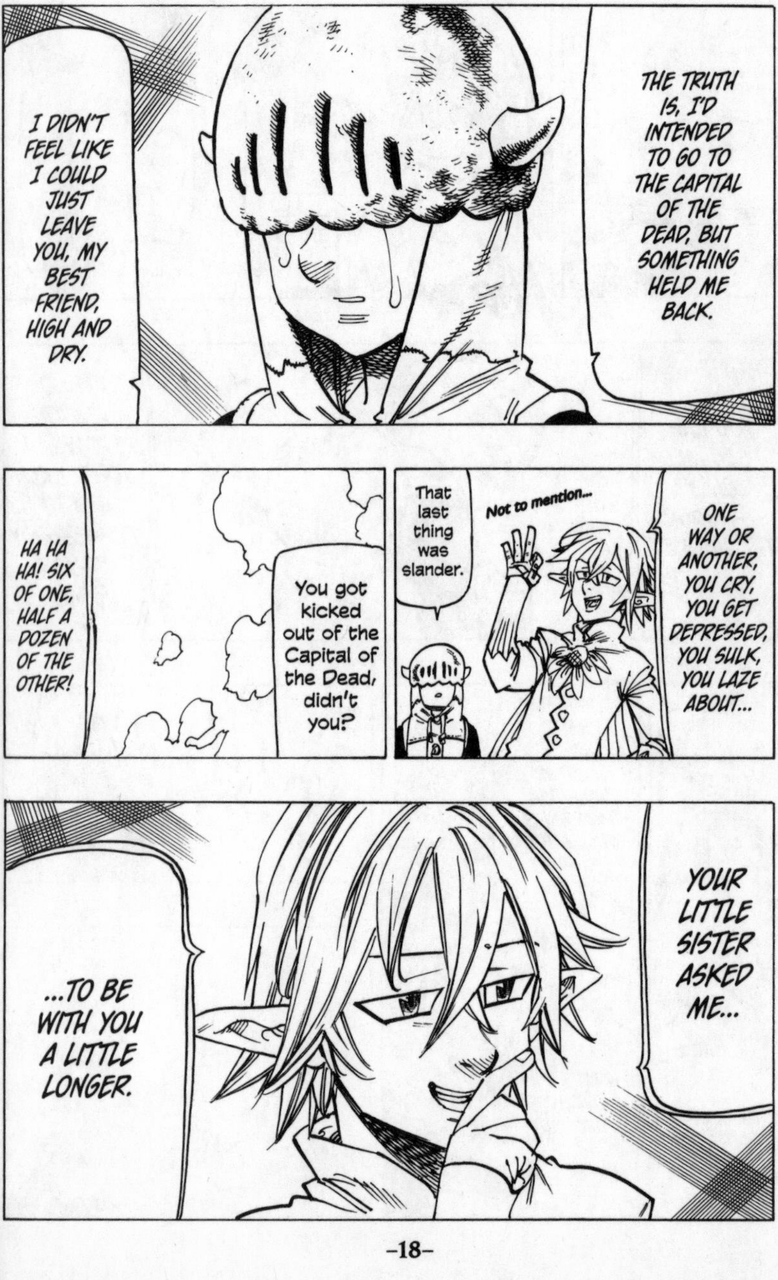
THE TRUTH IS, I'D INTENDED TO GO TO THE CAPITAL OF THE DEAD, BUT SOMETHING HELD ME BACK.
I DIDN'T FEEL LIKE I COULD JUST LEAVE YOU, MY BEST FRIEND, HIGH AND DRY.
ONE WAY OR ANOTHER, YOU CRY, YOU GET DEPRESSED, YOU SULK, YOU LAZE ABOUT...
Not to mention...
That last thing was slander.
You got kicked out of the Capital of the Dead, didn't you?
HA HA HA! SIX OF ONE, HALF A DOZEN OF THE OTHER!
YOUR LITTLE SISTER ASKED ME...
...TO BE WITH YOU A LITTLE LONGER.

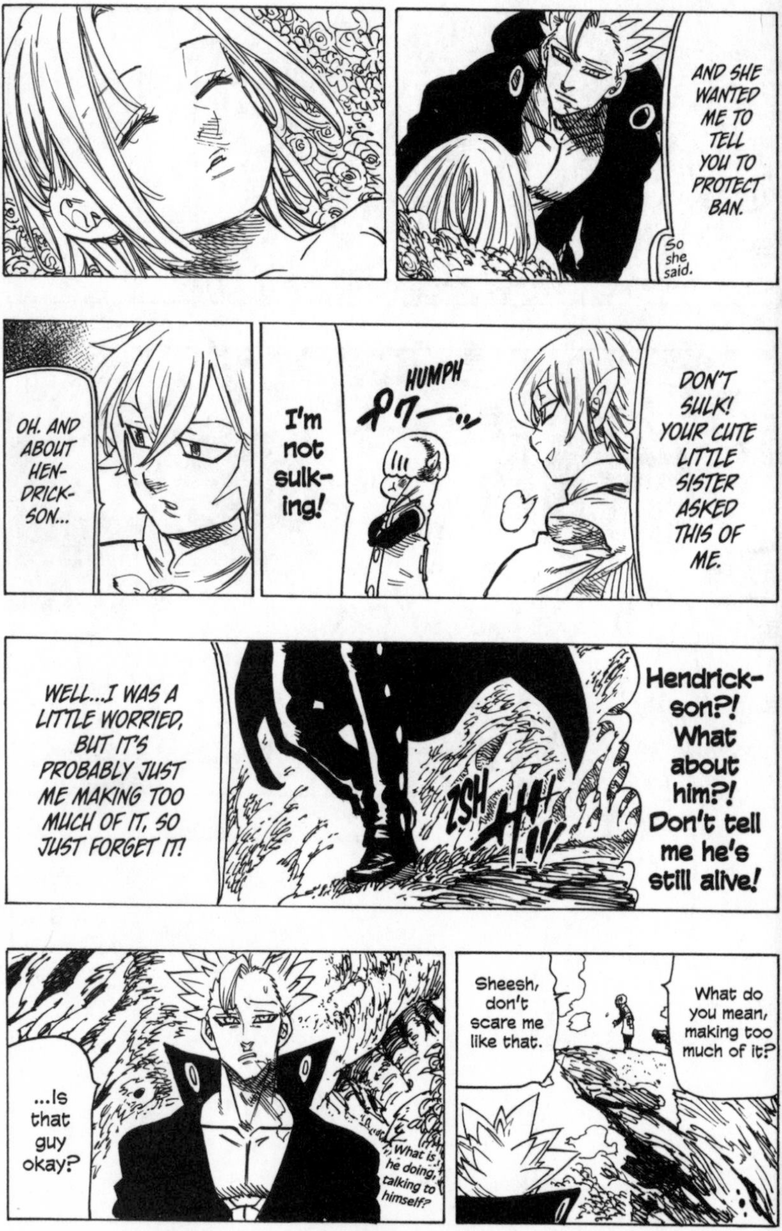
AND SHE WANTED ME TO TELL YOU TO PROTECT BAN.
So she said.
DON'T SULK! YOUR CUTE LITTLE SISTER ASKED THIS OF ME.
HUMPH
I'm not sulk-ing!
OH. AND ABOUT HEN-DRICK-SON...
Hendrick-son?! What about him?! Don't tell me he's still alive!
ZSHH
WELL...I WAS A LITTLE WORRIED, BUT IT'S PROBABLY JUST ME MAKING TOO MUCH OF IT, SO JUST FORGET IT!
What do you mean, making too much of it?
Sheesh, don't scare me like that.
What is he doing, talking to himself?
...Is that guy okay?

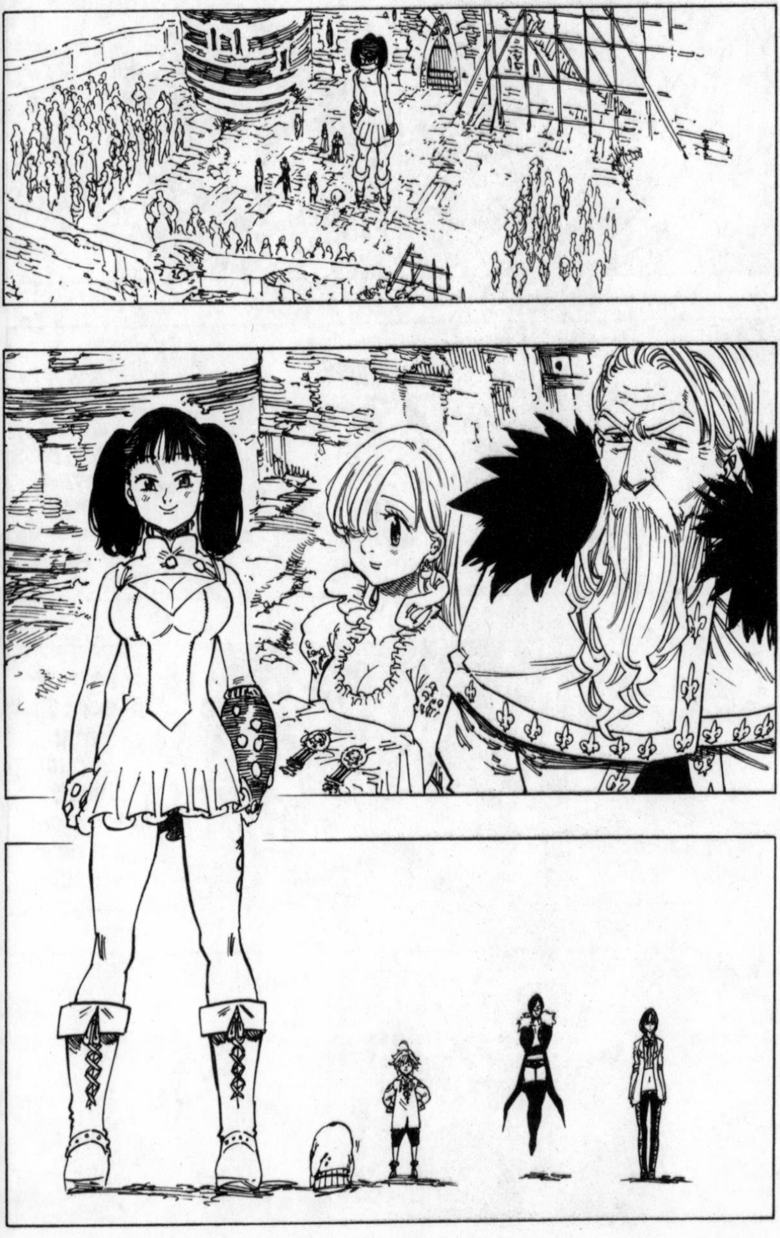

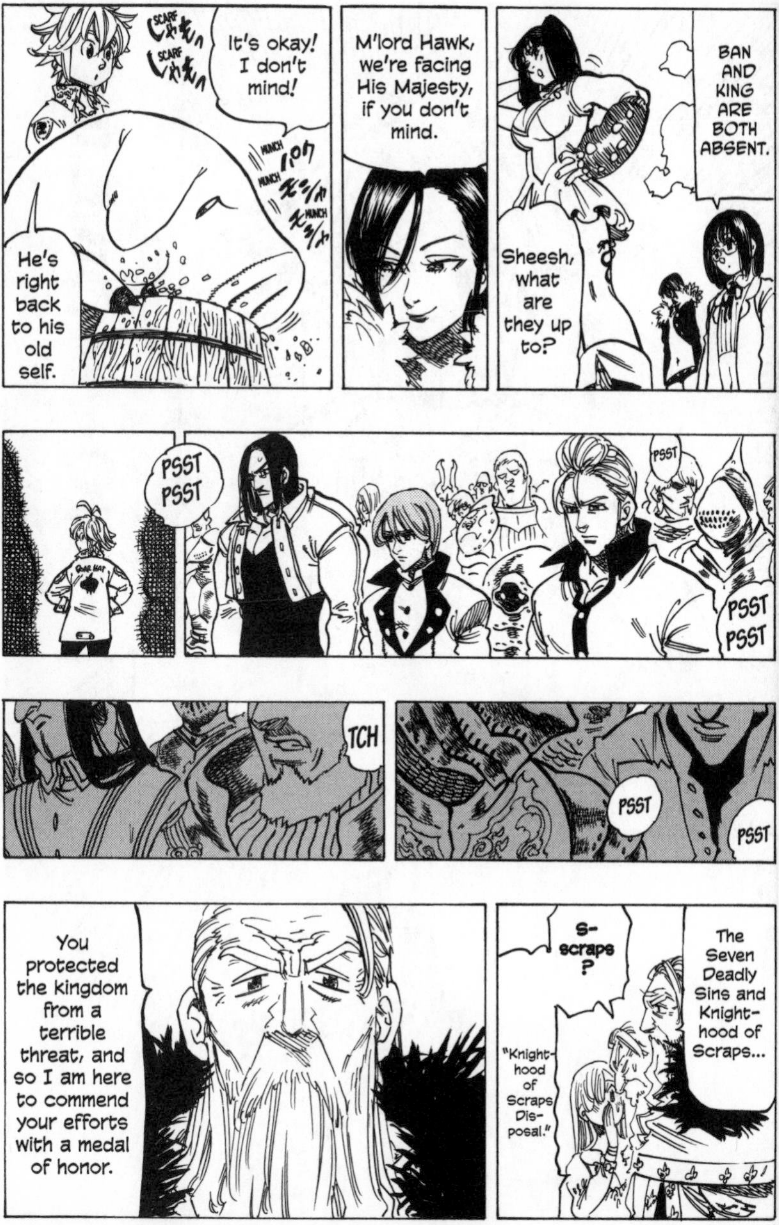
BAN AND KING ARE BOTH ABSENT.
Sheesh, what are they up to?
M'lord Hawk, we're facing His Majesty, if you don't mind.
SCARF
SCARF
It's okay! I don't mind!
MUNCH
MUNCH
MUNCH
He's right back to his old self.
PSST
PSST PSST
PSST PSST
PSST
PSST
TCH
The Seven Deadly Sins and Knighthood of Scraps...
S-scraps?
"Knighthood of Scraps Disposal."
You protected the kingdom from a terrible threat, and so I am here to commend your efforts with a medal of honor.

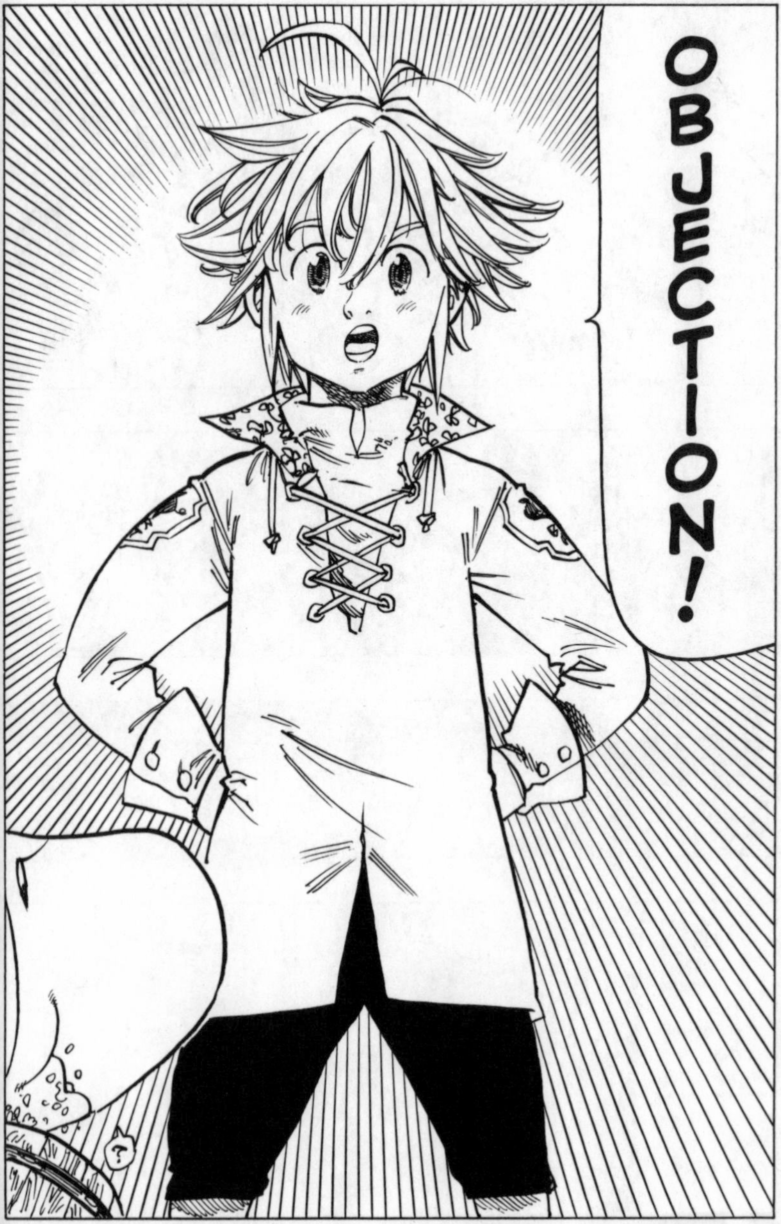
OBJECTION!
?

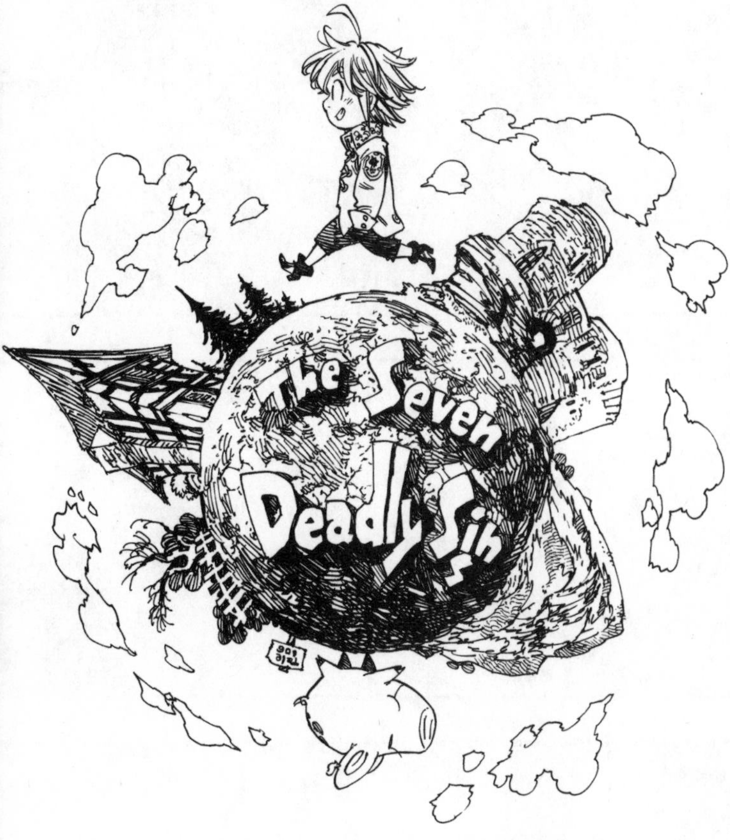
The Seven Deadly Sins

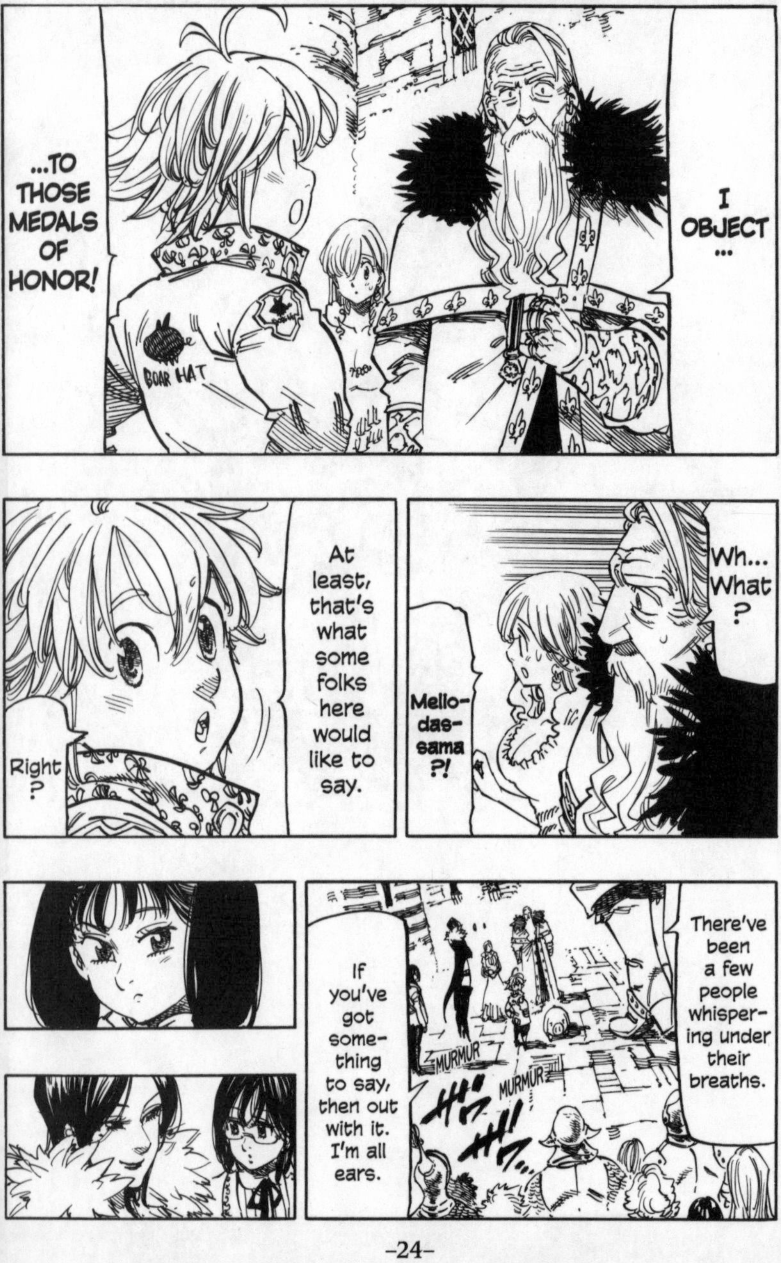
I OBJECT ...
...TO THOSE MEDALS OF HONOR!
BOAR HAT
Wh... What?
Mello-das-sama?!
At least, that's what some folks here would like to say.
Right?
There've been a few people whispering under their breaths.
If you've got something to say, then out with it. I'm all ears.
MURMUR
MURMUR

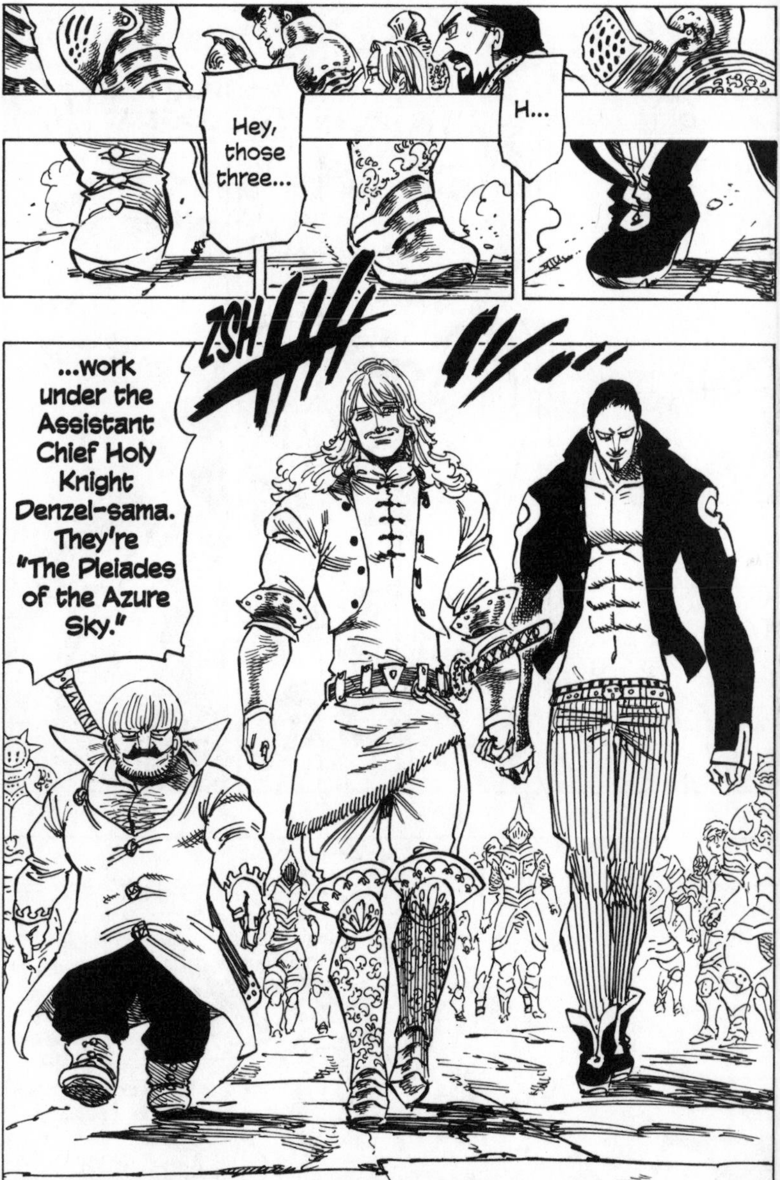
H...
Hey, those three...
ZSH
...work under the Assistant Chief Holy Knight Denzel-sama. They're "The Pleiades of the Azure Sky."

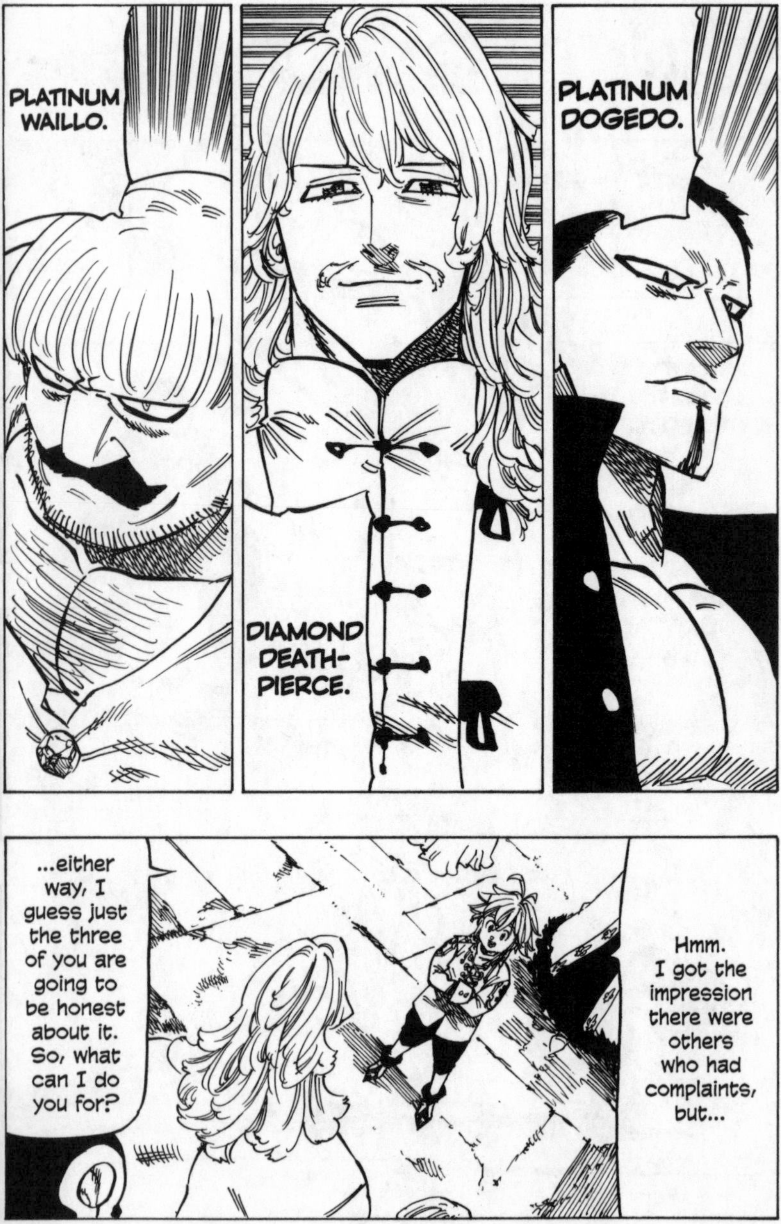
PLATINUM DOGEDO.
DIAMOND DEATH-PIERCE.
PLATINUM WAILLO.
Hmm. I got the impression there were others who had complaints, but...
...either way, I guess just the three of you are going to be honest about it. So, what can I do you for?

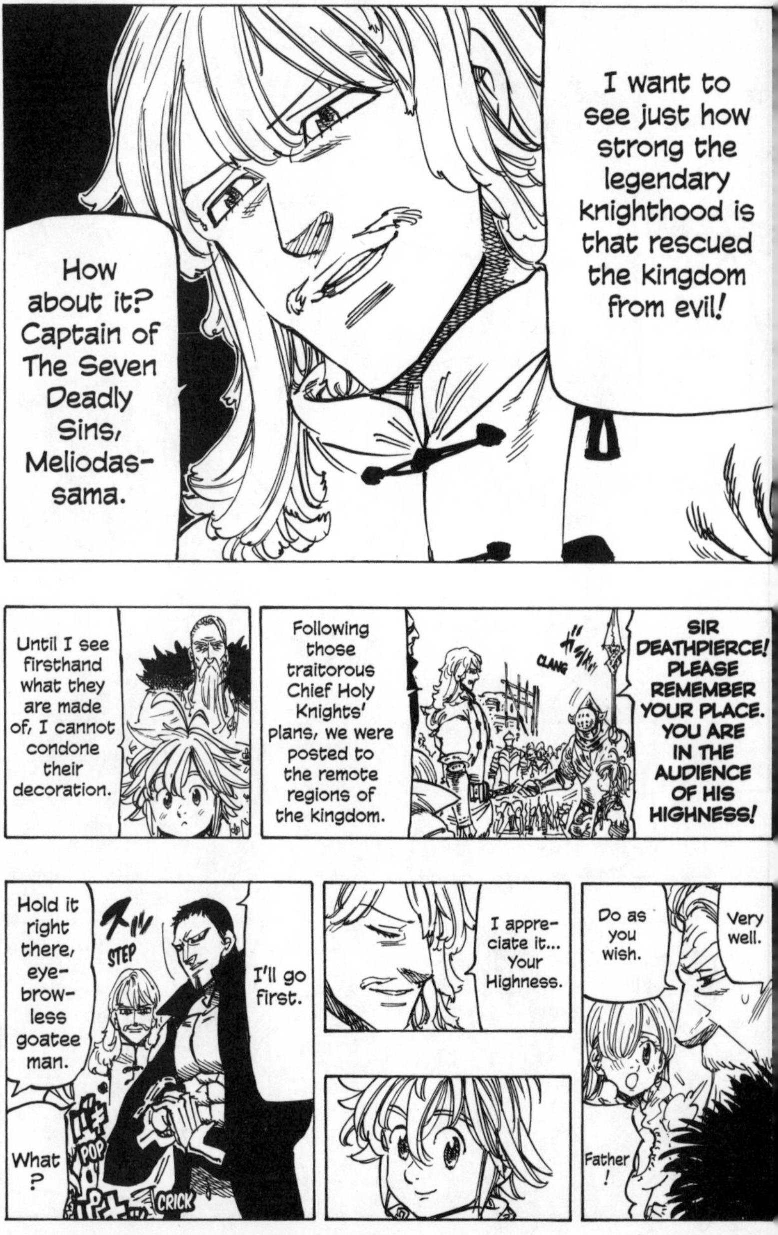
I want to see just how strong the legendary knighthood is that rescued the kingdom from evil!
How about it? Captain of The Seven Deadly Sins, Meliodas-sama.
SIR DEATHPIERCE! PLEASE REMEMBER YOUR PLACE. YOU ARE IN THE AUDIENCE OF HIS HIGHNESS!
CLANG
Following those traitorous Chief Holy Knights' plans, we were posted to the remote regions of the kingdom.
Until I see firsthand what they are made of, I cannot condone their decoration.
Very well.
Do as you wish.
Father!
I appreciate it... Your Highness.
I'll go first.
STEP
Hold it right there, eye-brow-less goatee man.
What?
POP
CRICK

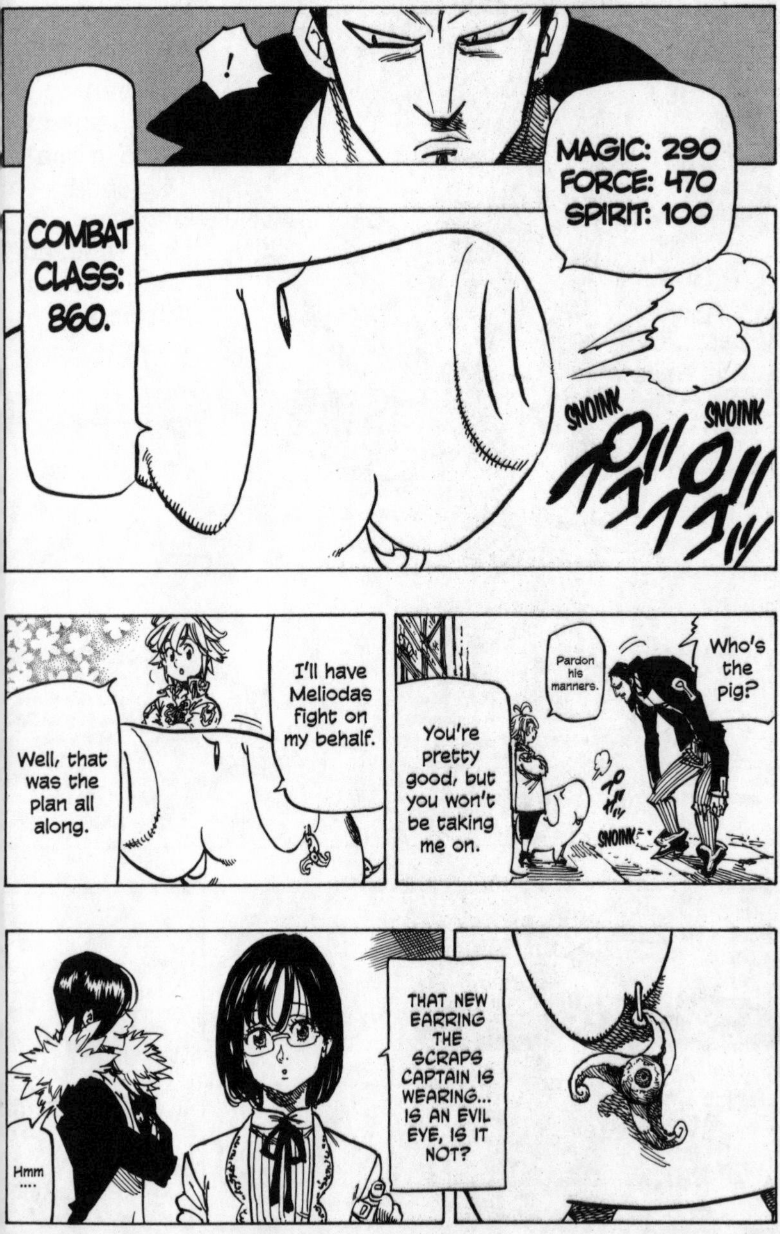
!
MAGIC: 290
FORCE: 470
SPIRIT: 100
COMBAT CLASS: 860.
SNOINK
SNOINK
Who's the pig?
Pardon his manners.
You're pretty good, but you won't be taking me on.
SNOINK
I'll have Meliodas fight on my behalf.
Well, that was the plan all along.
THAT NEW EARRING THE SCRAPS CAPTAIN IS WEARING... IS AN EVIL EYE, IS IT NOT?
Hmm....

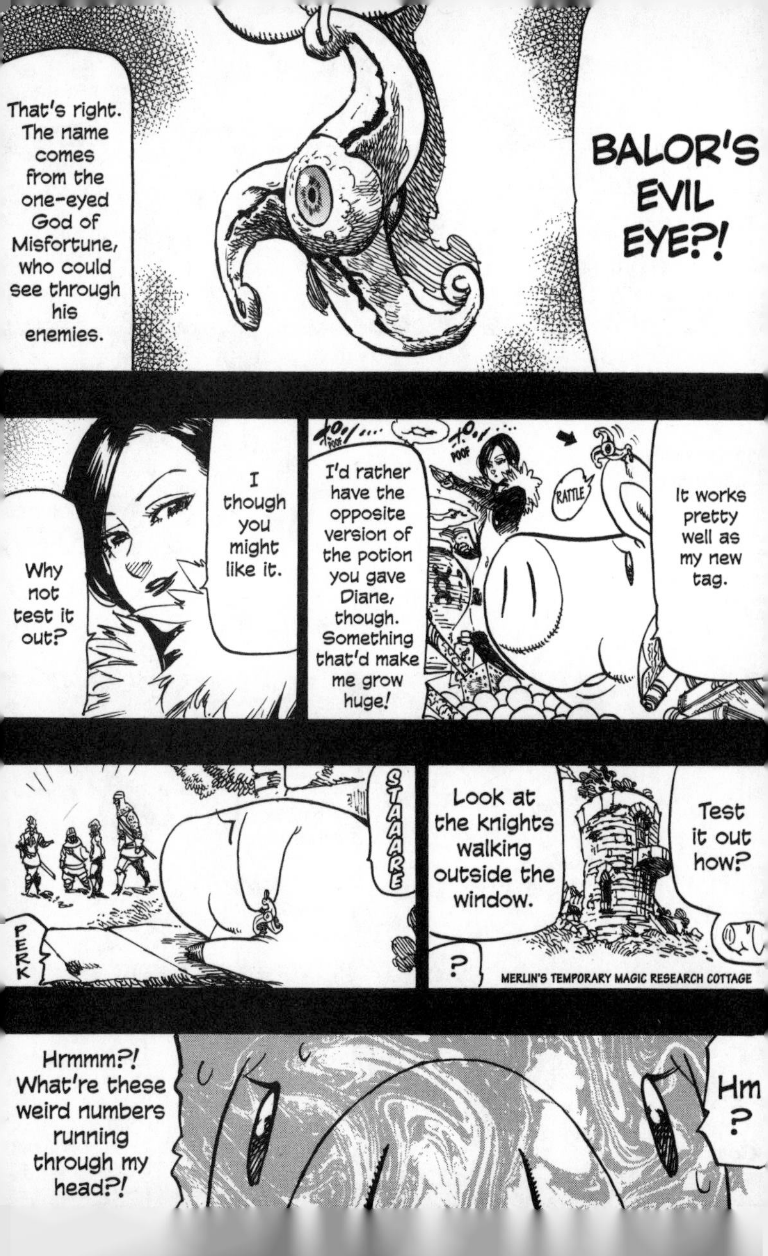
BALOR'S EVIL EYE?!
That's right. The name comes from the one-eyed God of Misfortune, who could see through his enemies.
It works pretty well as my new tag.
RATTLE
POOF
I'd rather have the opposite version of the potion you gave Diane, though. Something that'd make me grow huge!
POOF
I though you might like it.
Why not test it out?
Test it out how?
Look at the knights walking outside the window.
?
MERLIN'S TEMPORARY MAGIC RESEARCH COTTAGE
STAAAARE
PERK
Hm?
Hrmmm?! What're these weird numbers running through my head?!

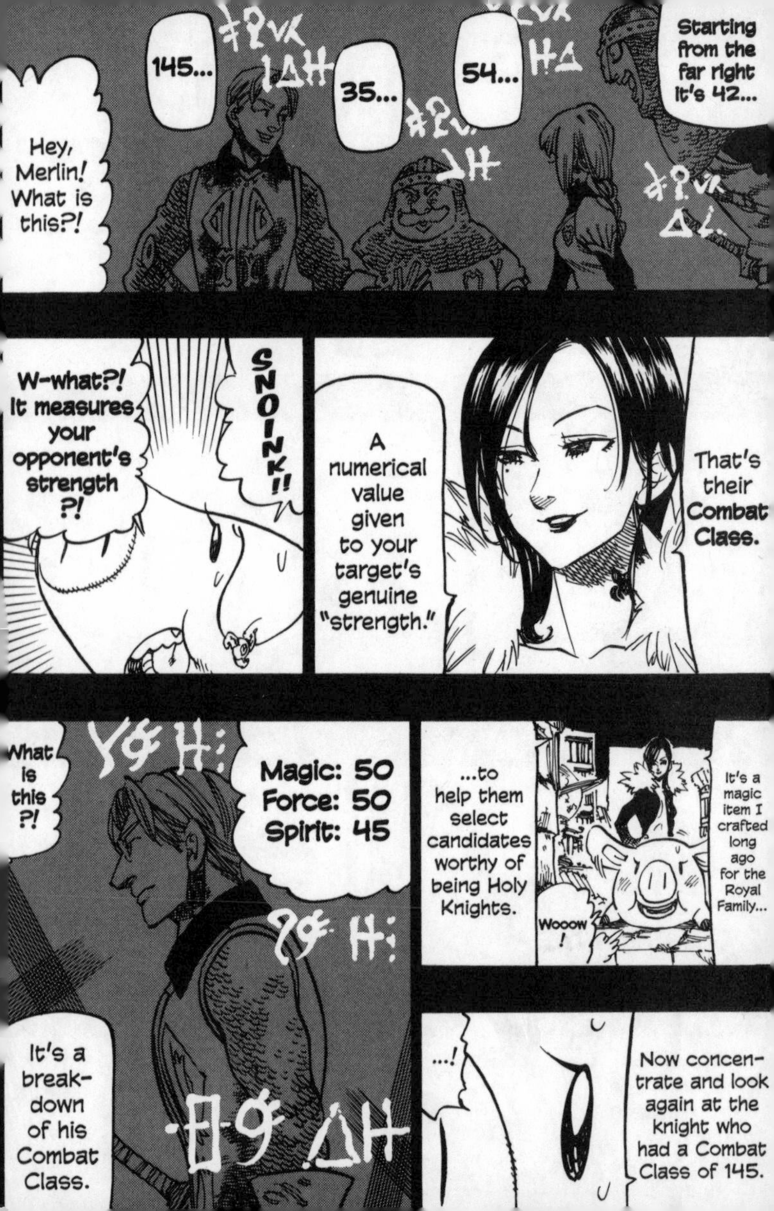
Starting from the far right it's 42...
54...
35...
145...
Hey, Merlin! What is this?!
That's their Combat Class.
A numerical value given to your target's genuine "strength."
SNOINK!!
W-what?! It measures your opponent's strength?!
It's a magic item I crafted long ago for the Royal Family...
Wooow!
...to help them select candidates worthy of being Holy Knights.
Now concentrate and look again at the knight who had a Combat Class of 145.
...!
What is this?!
Magic: 50
Force: 50
Spirit: 45
It's a breakdown of his Combat Class.

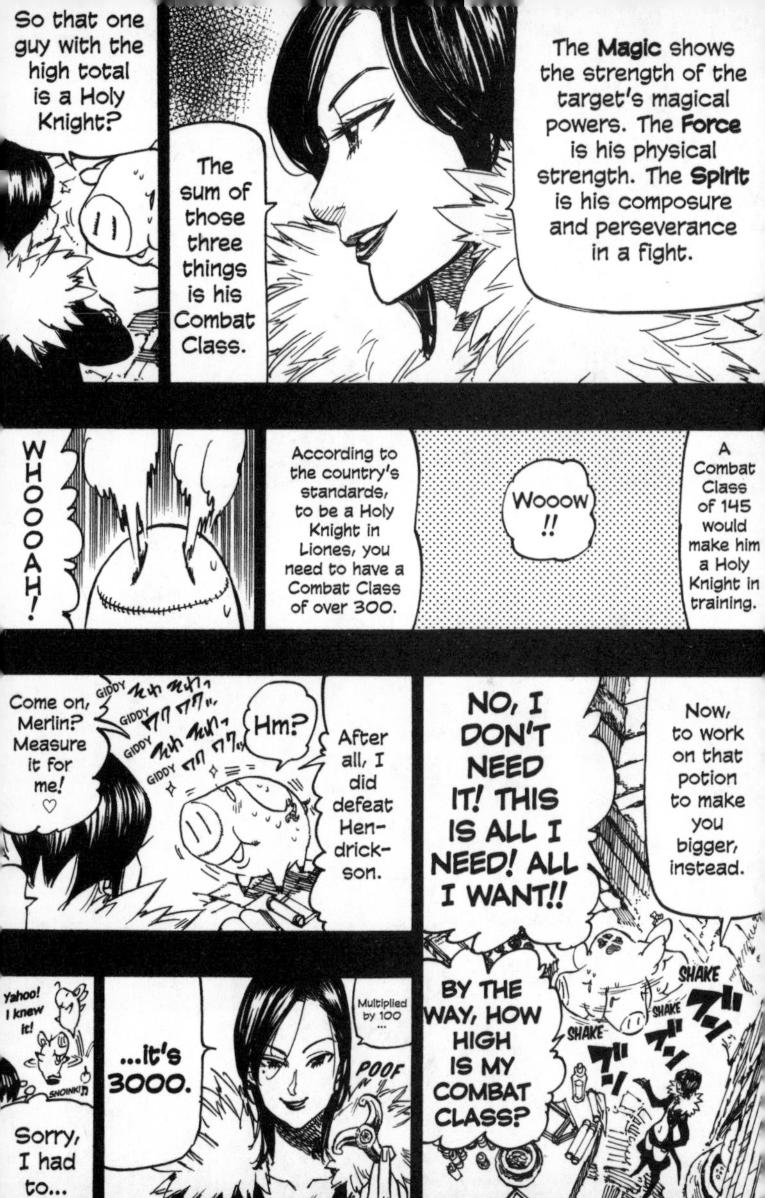
The Magic shows the strength of the target's magical powers. The Force is his physical strength. The Spirit is his composure and perseverance in a fight.
The sum of those three things is his Combat Class.
So that one guy with the high total is a Holy Knight?
A Combat Class of 145 would make him a Holy Knight in training.
Wooow!!
According to the country's standards, to be a Holy Knight in Liones, you need to have a Combat Class of over 300.
WHOOOOAH!
Now, to work on that potion to make you bigger, instead.
NO, I DON'T NEED IT! THIS IS ALL I NEED! ALL I WANT!!
After all, I did defeat Hendrickson.
Hm?
GIDDY GIDDY GIDDY GIDDY
Come on, Merlin? Measure it for me! ♡
BY THE WAY, HOW HIGH IS MY COMBAT CLASS?
SHAKE SHAKE SHAKE
Multiplied by 100...
POOF
...it's 3000.
Yahoo! I knew it!
SNOINK!♪
Sorry, I had to...

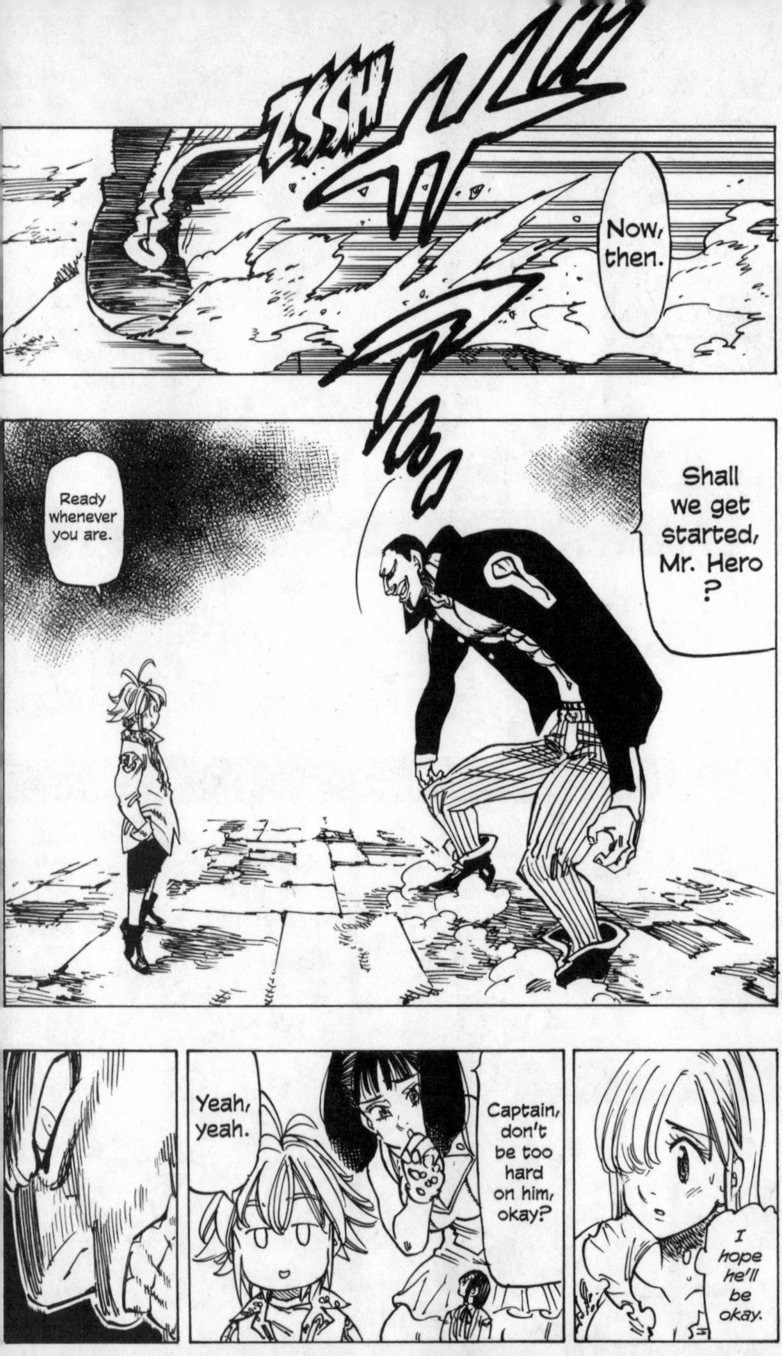
ZSSH
Now, then.
Shall we get started, Mr. Hero?
Ready whenever you are.
I hope he'll be okay.
Captain, don't be too hard on him, okay?
Yeah, yeah.

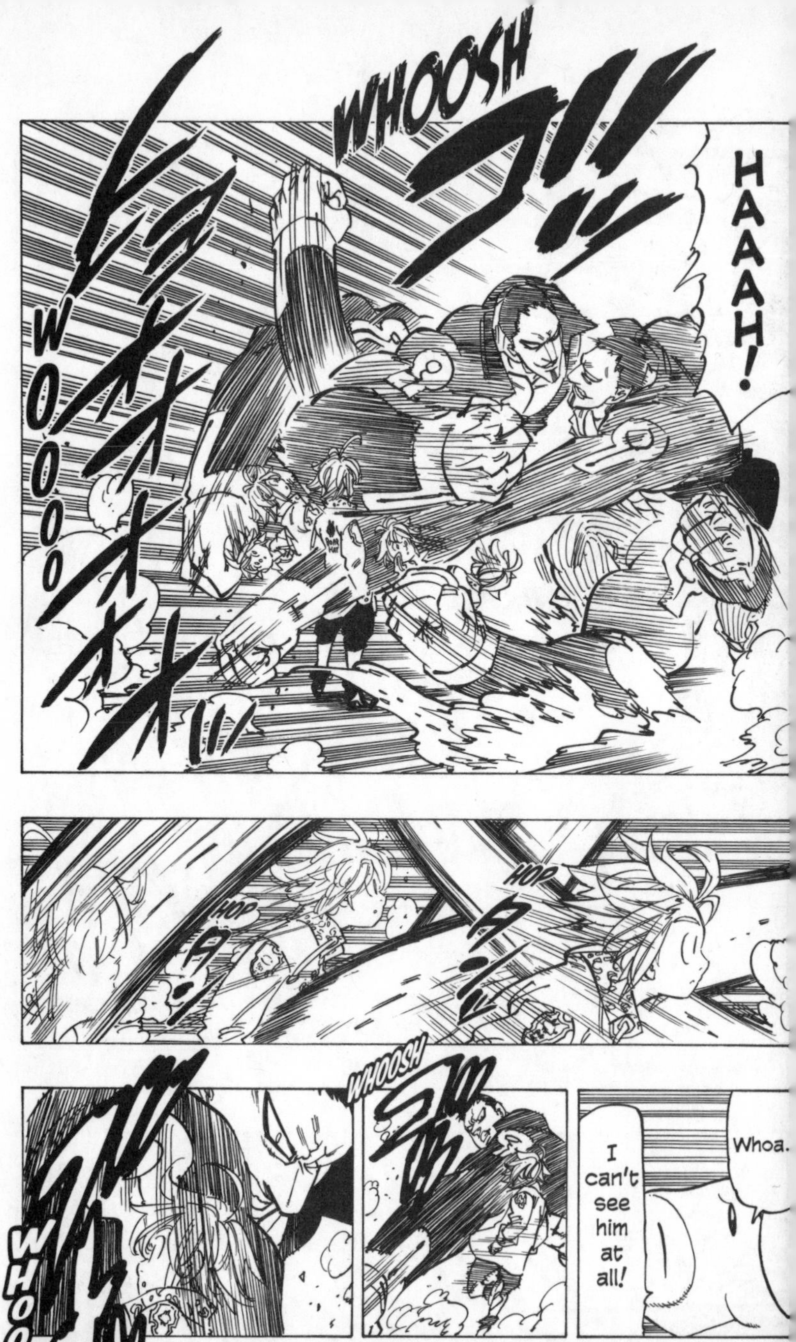
HAAAH!
WHOOSH
WOOOOOO
HOP
HOP
Whoa.
I can't see him at all!
WHOOSH
WHOOSH

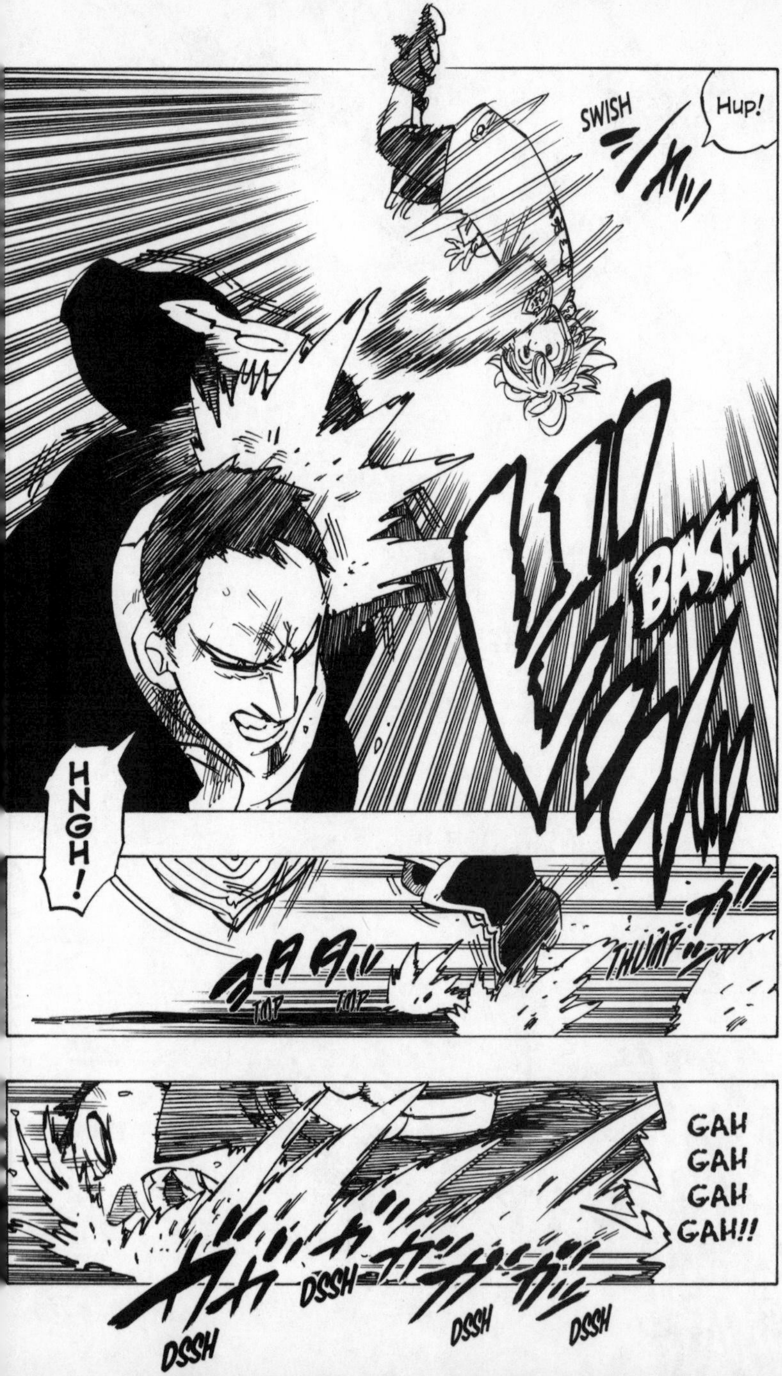

Hup!
SWISH
BASH
HNGH!
THUMP
TAP
TAP
GAH
GAH
GAH
GAH!!
DSSH
DSSH
DSSH
DSSH

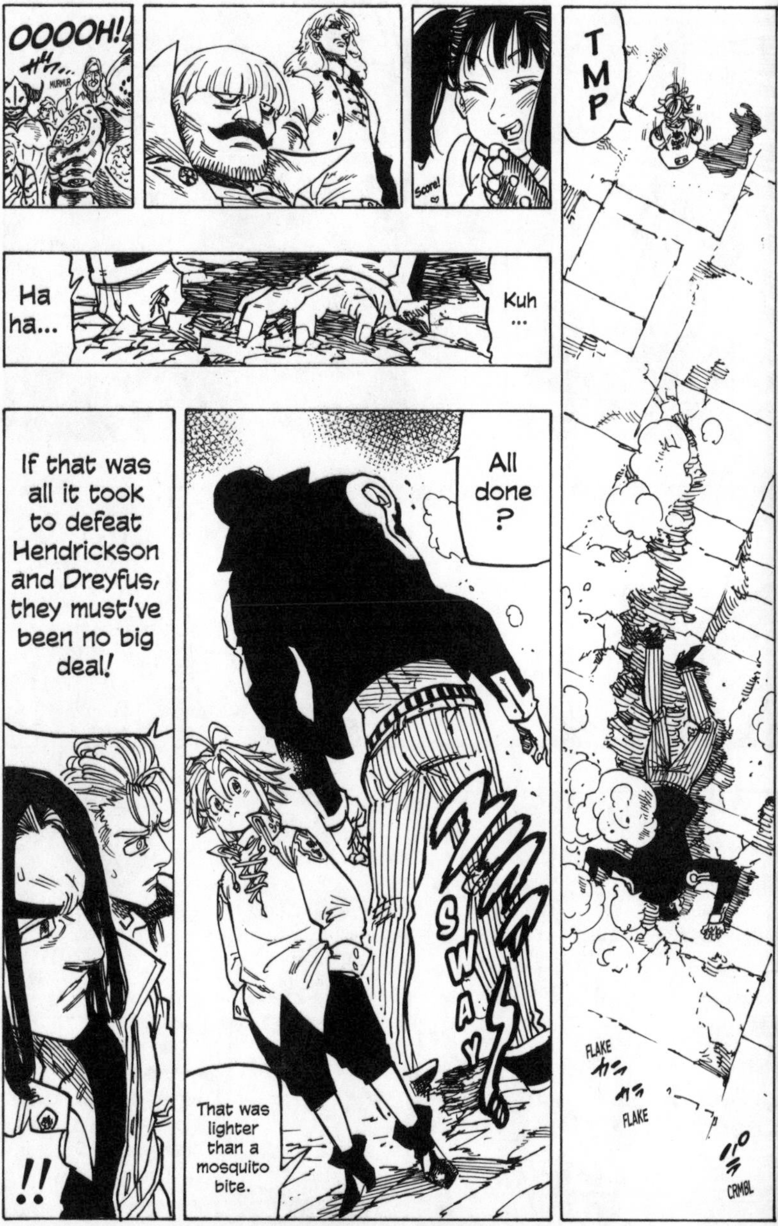
TMP
FLAKE
FLAKE
CRMBL
Score!
OOOOH!
MURMUR
Kuh ...
Ha ha...
All done ?
SWAY
That was lighter than a mosquito bite.
If that was all it took to defeat Hendrickson and Dreyfus, they must've been no big deal!
!!

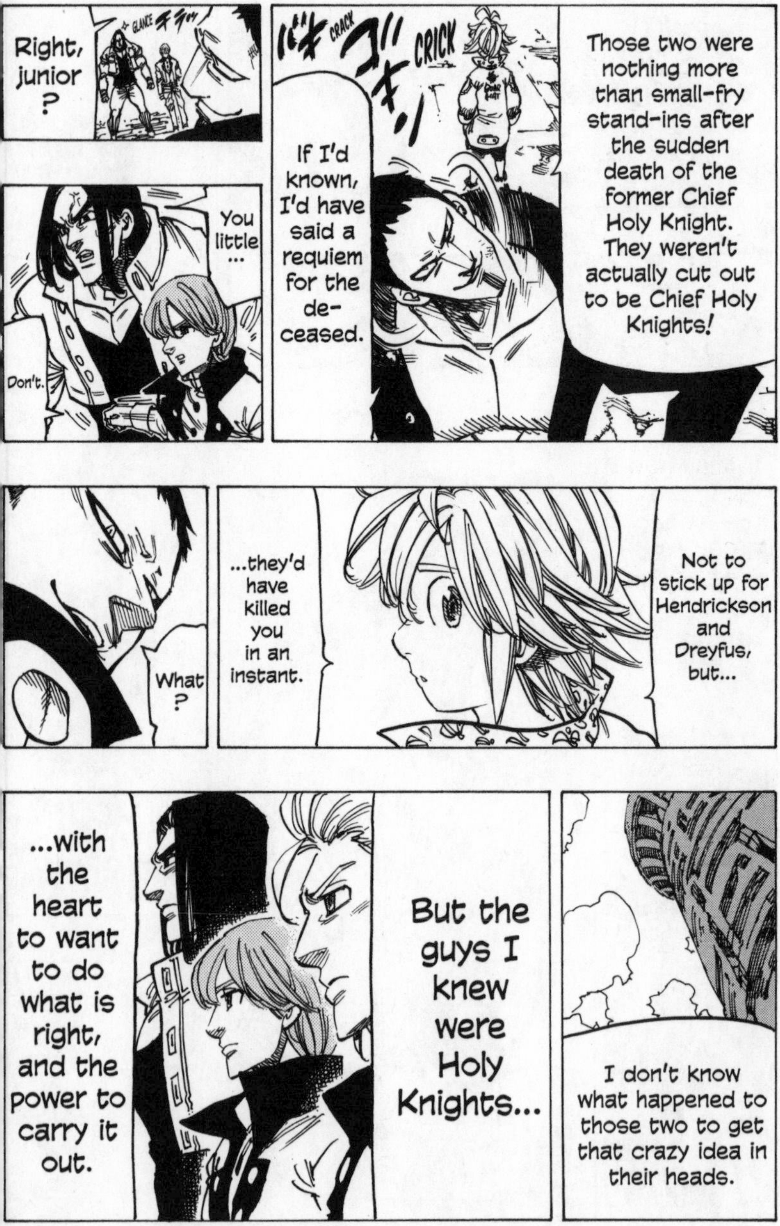
Those two were nothing more than small-fry stand-ins after the sudden death of the former Chief Holy Knight. They weren't actually cut out to be Chief Holy Knights!
バキ CRACK
ゴキッ CRICK
If I'd known, I'd have said a requiem for the deceased.
GLANCE チラッ
Right, junior?
You little...
Don't.
Not to stick up for Hendrickson and Dreyfus, but...
...they'd have killed you in an instant.
What?
I don't know what happened to those two to get that crazy idea in their heads.
But the guys I knew were Holy Knights...
...with the heart to want to do what is right, and the power to carry it out.

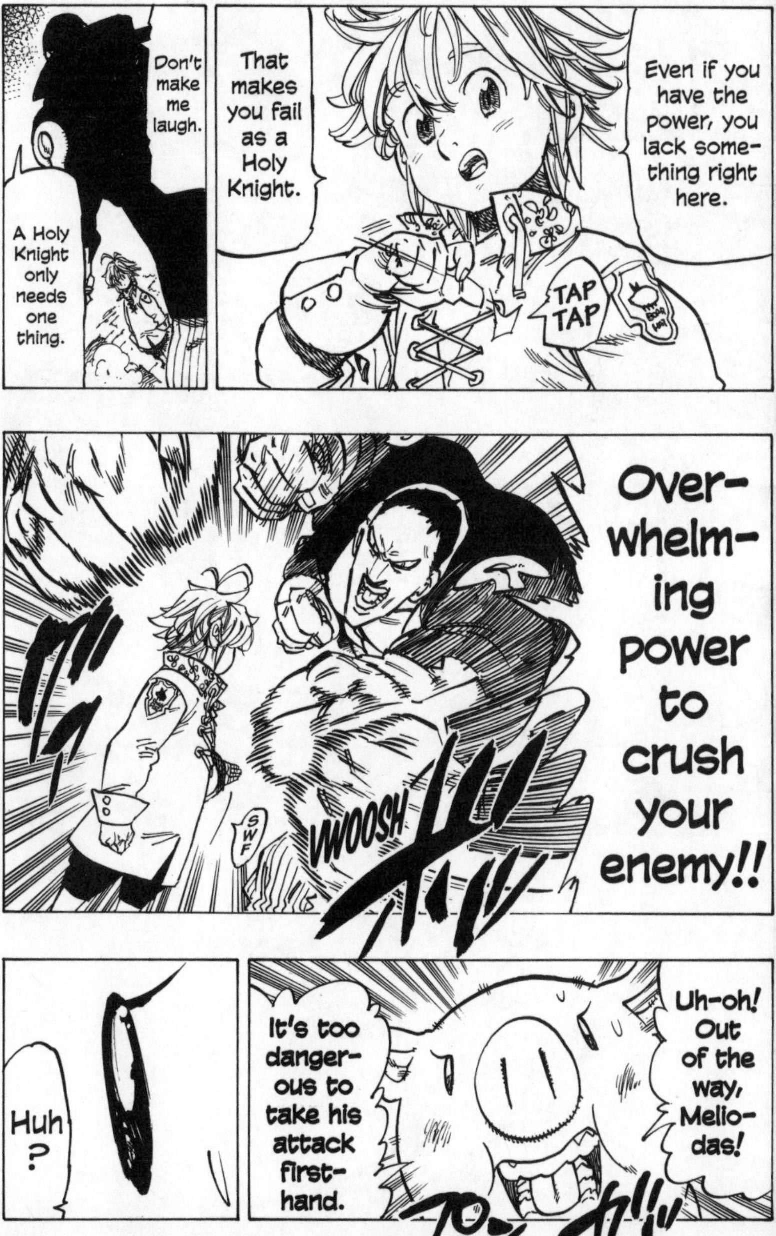
Even if you have the power, you lack some-thing right here.
TAP TAP
That makes you fail as a Holy Knight.
Don't make me laugh.
A Holy Knight only needs one thing.
Over-whelm-ing power to crush your enemy!!
VWOOSH
SWF
Uh-oh! Out of the way, Melio-das!
It's too danger-ous to take his attack first-hand.
SNOINK!
Huh?

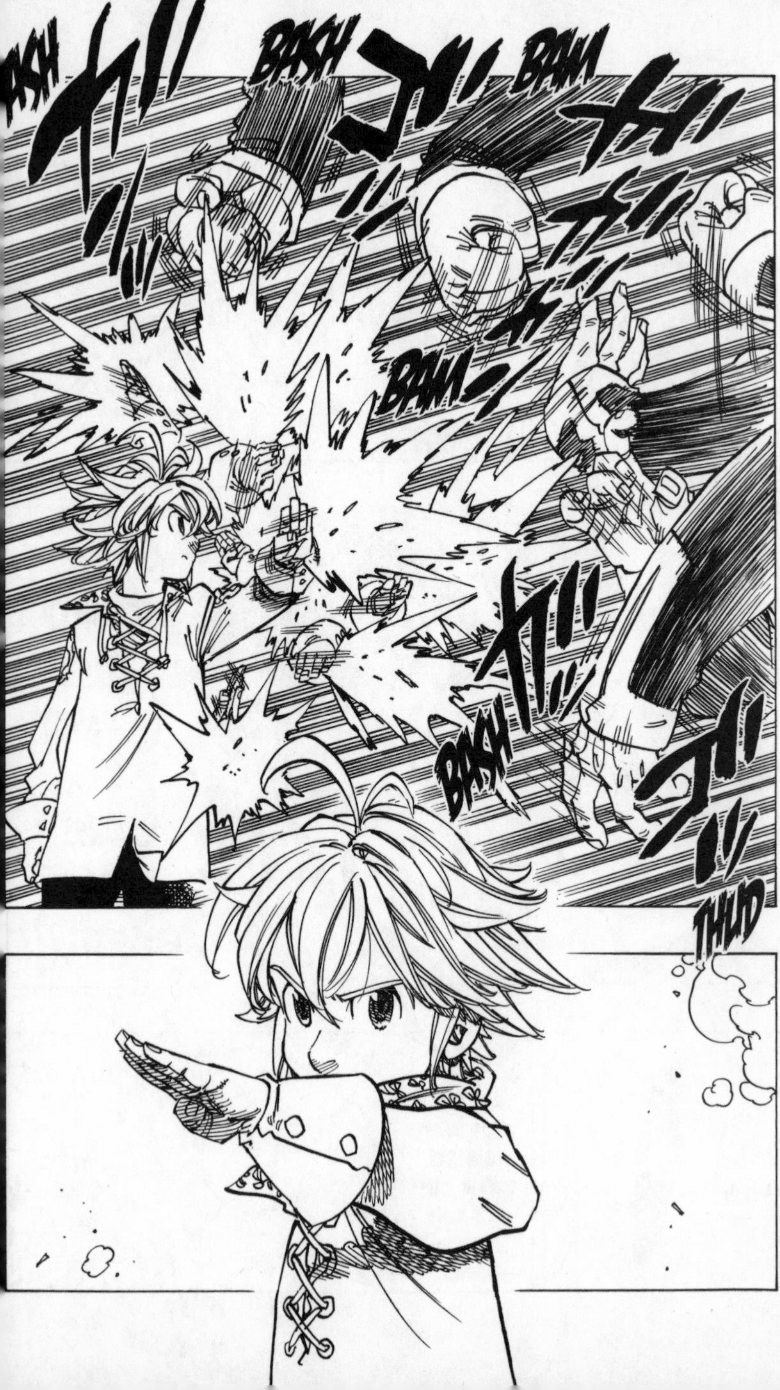
BAM
BASH
BASH
BAM
BASH
THUD

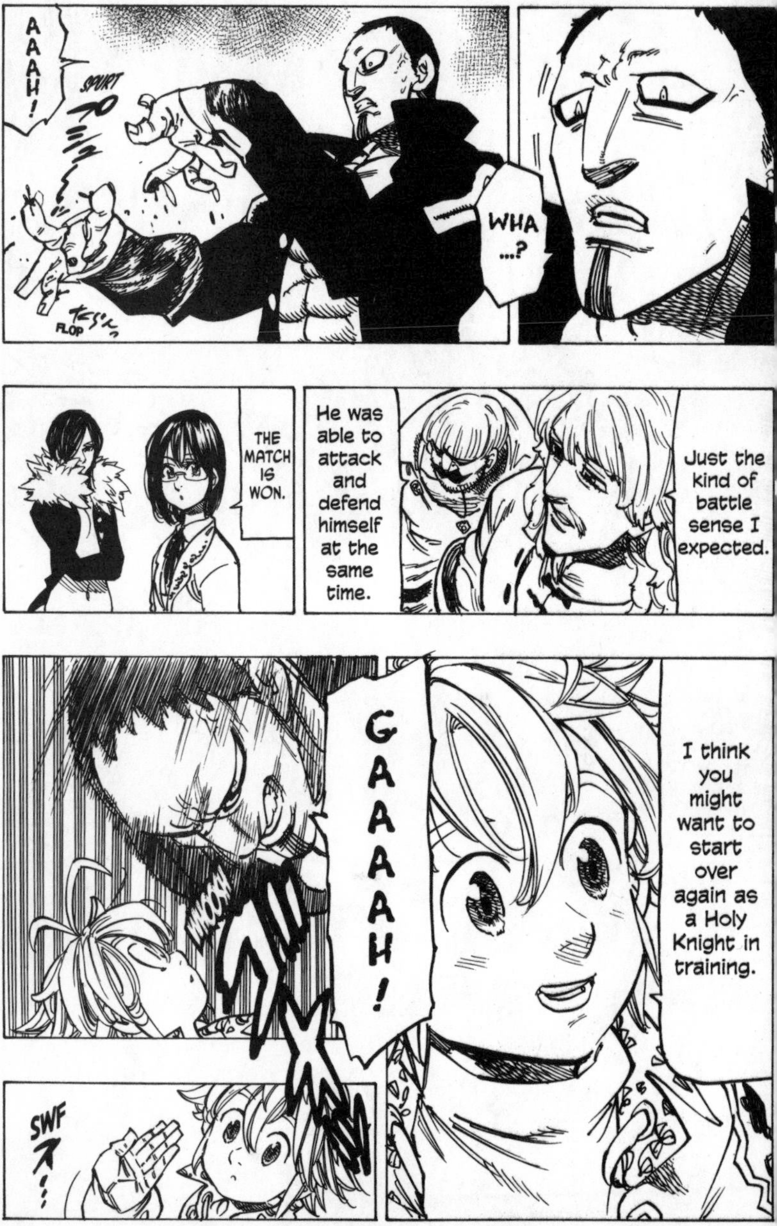
WHA ...?
AAAAH!
SPURT
FLOP
Just the kind of battle sense I expected.
He was able to attack and defend himself at the same time.
THE MATCH IS WON.
I think you might want to start over again as a Holy Knight in training.
GAAAAAH!
SWF

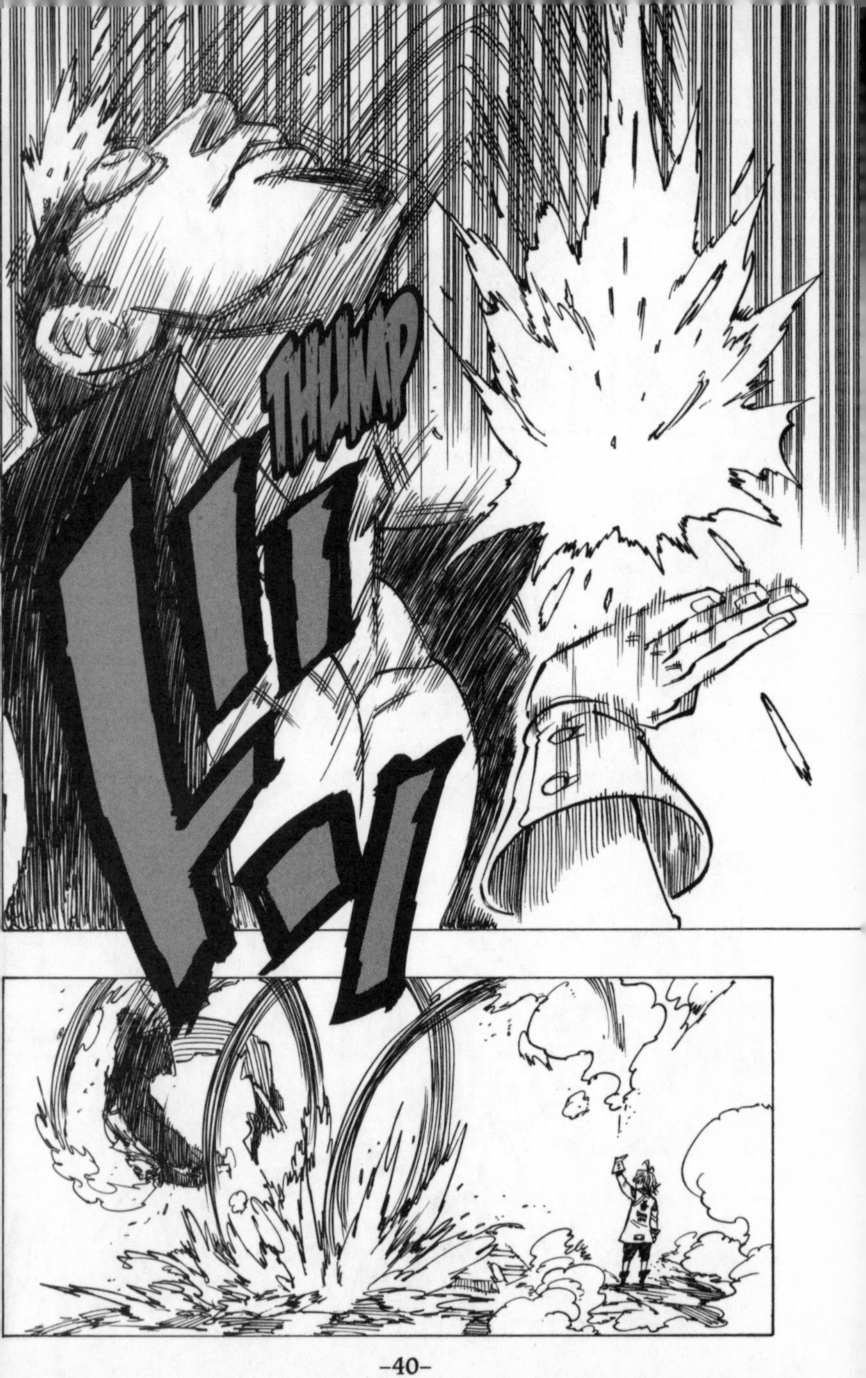
THUMP

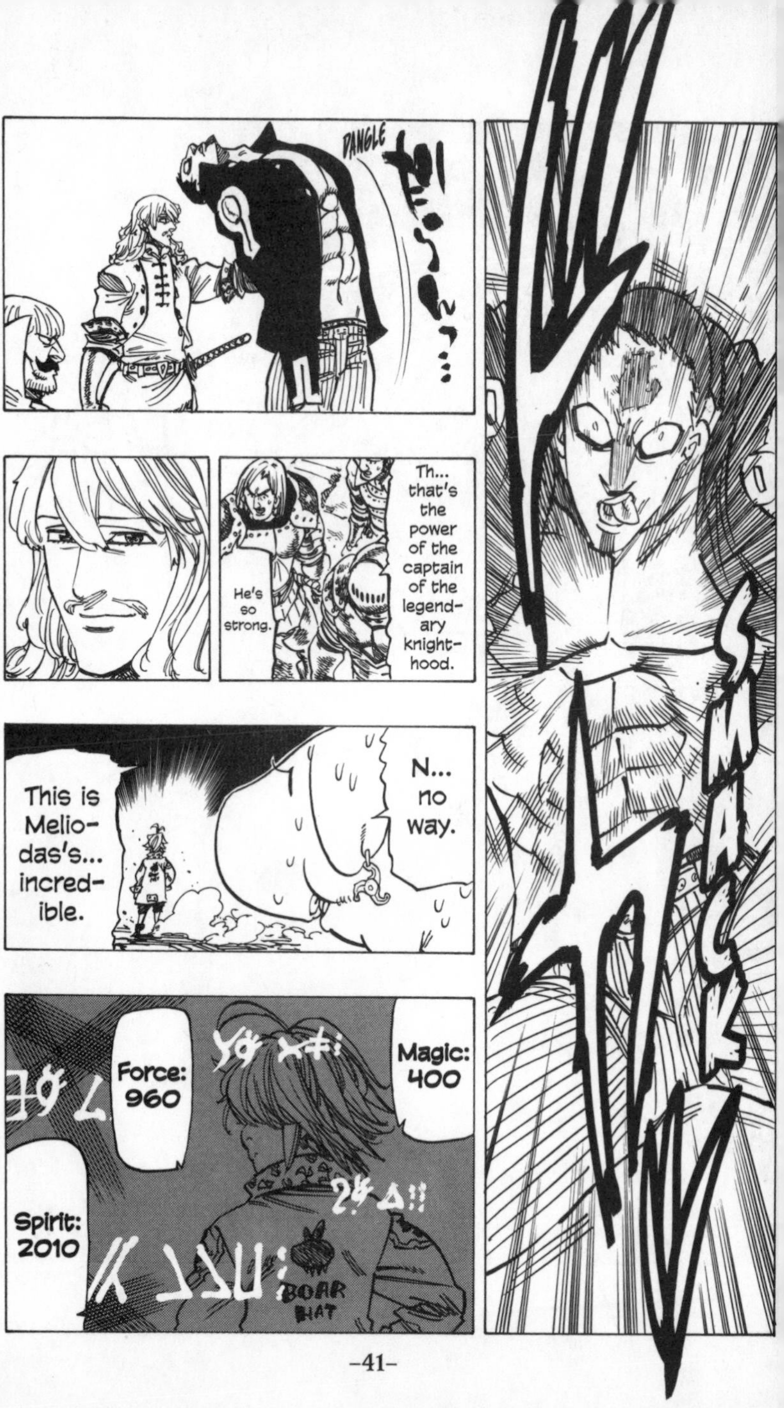
SMACK
DANGLE
Th... that's the power of the captain of the legendary knighthood.
He's so strong.
N... no way.
This is Meliodas's... incredible.
Magic: 400
Force: 960
Spirit: 2010
BOAR HAT

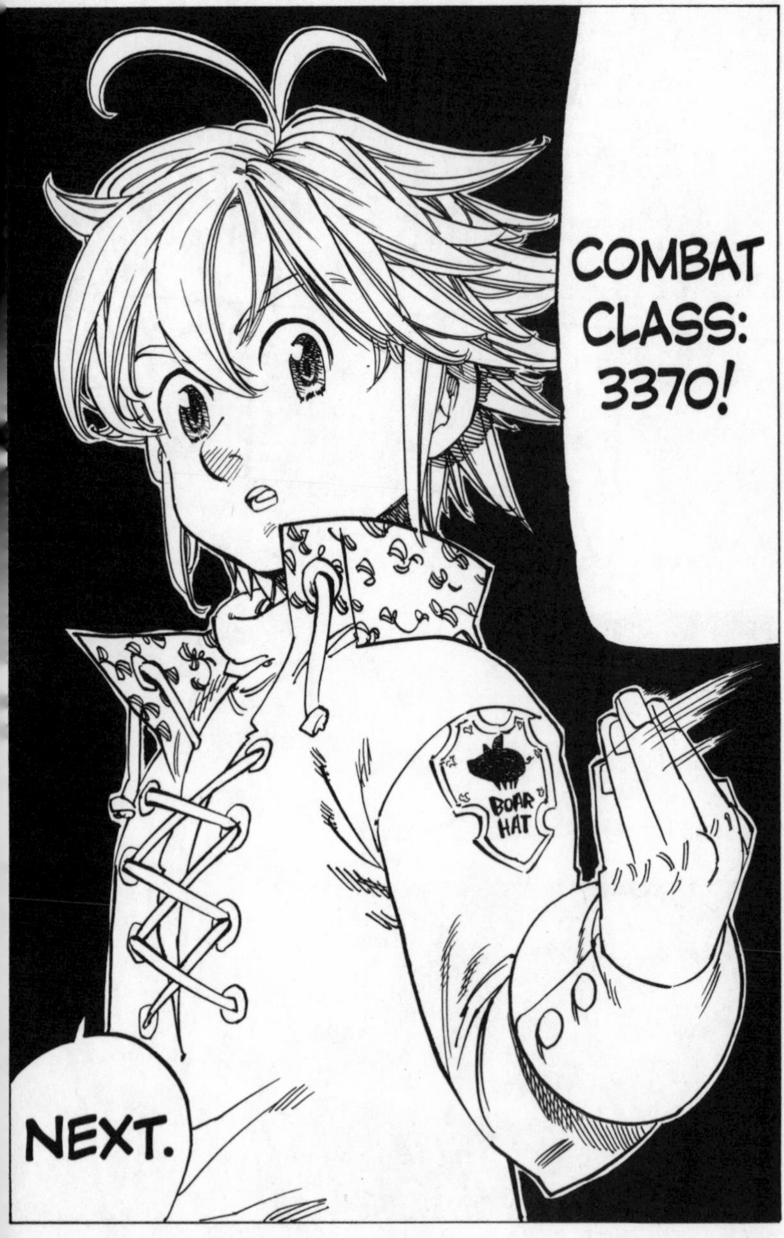
COMBAT CLASS: 3370!
BOAR HAT
NEXT.

THE SEVEN DEADLY SINS

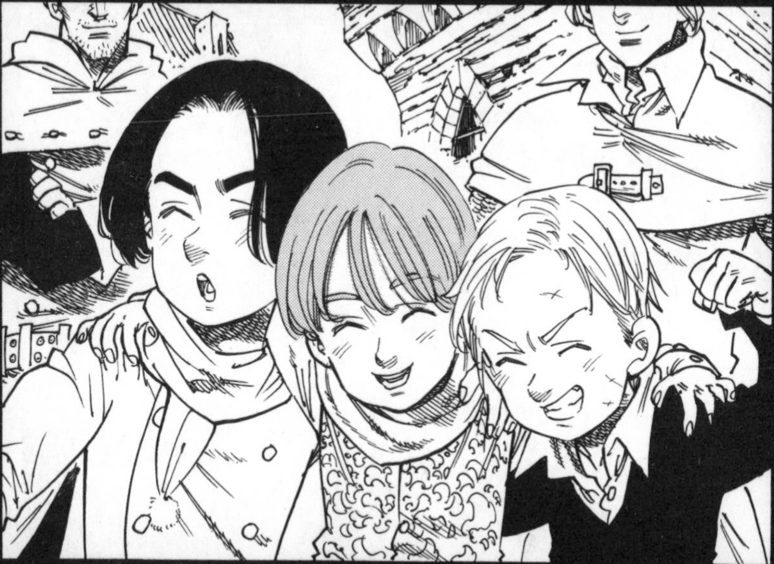

Chapter 107 - Seek the Truth

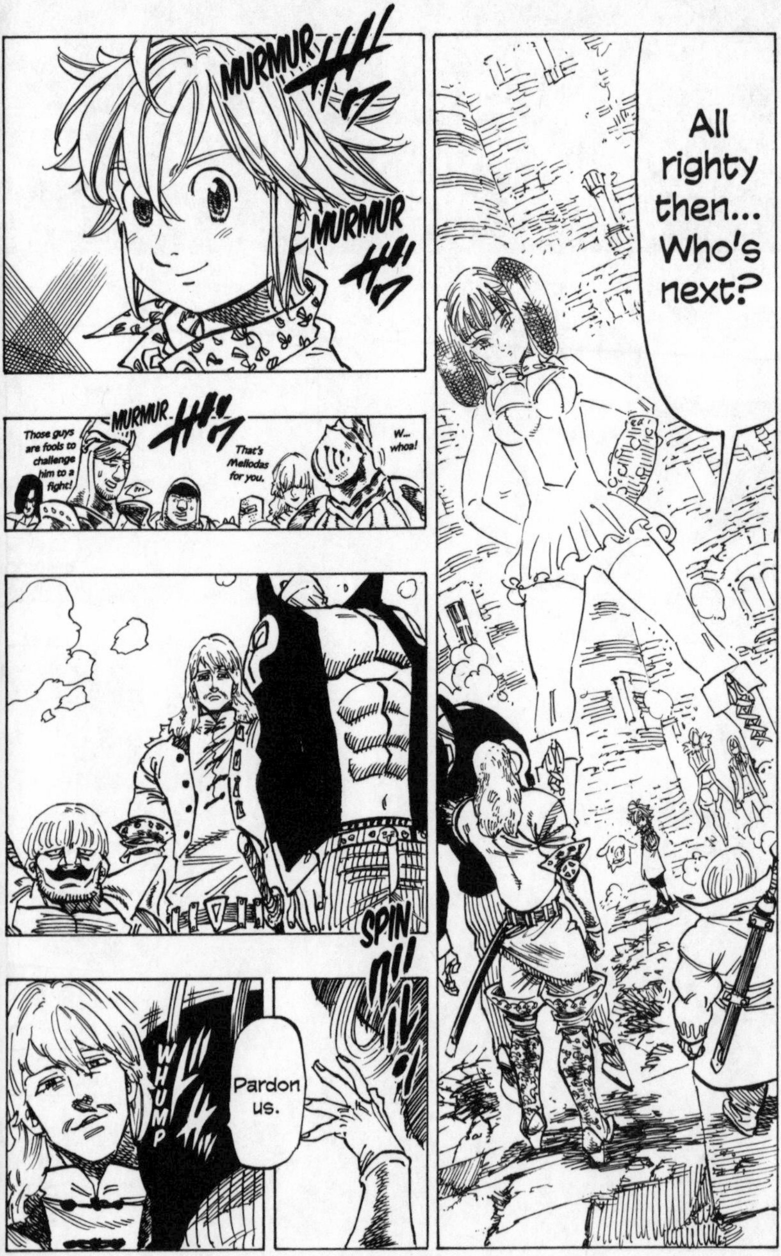
All righty then... Who's next?
MURMUR
MURMUR
MURMUR
W... whoa!
That's Meliodas for you.
Those guys are fools to challenge him to a fight!
SPIN
Pardon us.
WHUMP

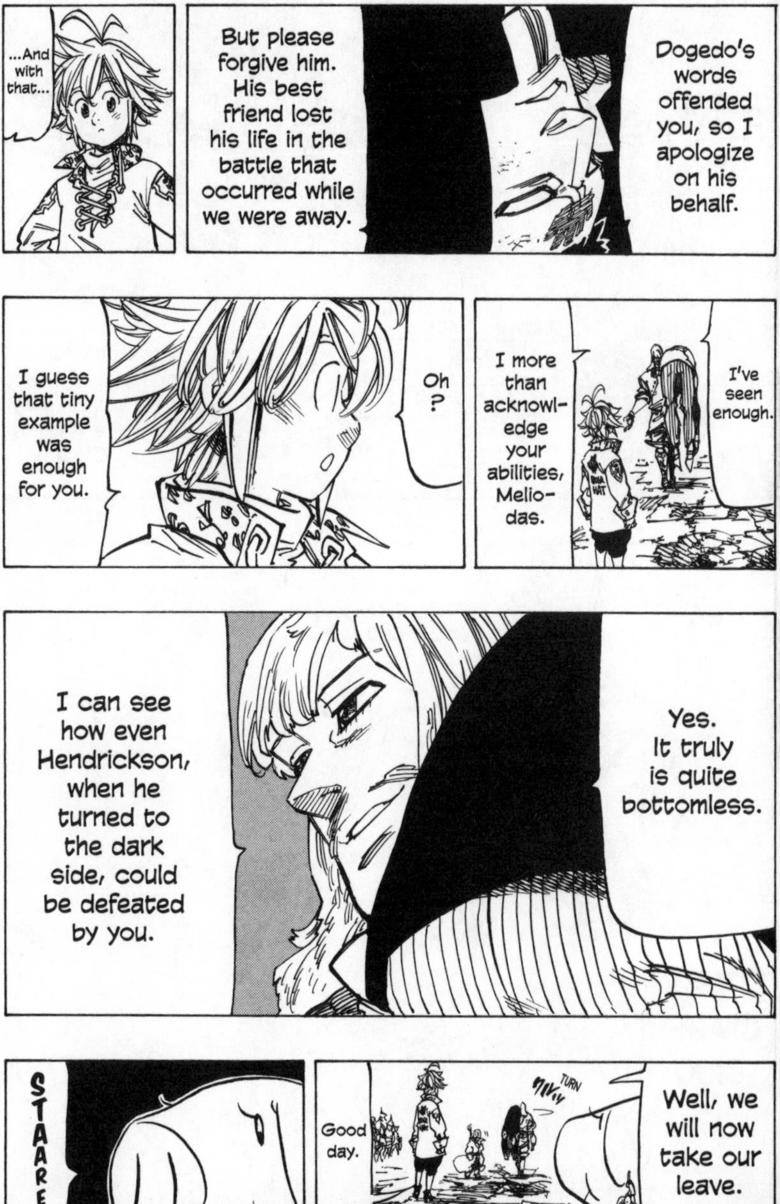
Dogedo's words offended you, so I apologize on his behalf.
But please forgive him. His best friend lost his life in the battle that occurred while we were away.
...And with that...
I've seen enough.
I more than acknowledge your abilities, Melio-das.
Oh?
I guess that tiny example was enough for you.
Yes. It truly is quite bottomless.
I can see how even Hendrickson, when he turned to the dark side, could be defeated by you.
Well, we will now take our leave.
TURN
Good day.
STAARE

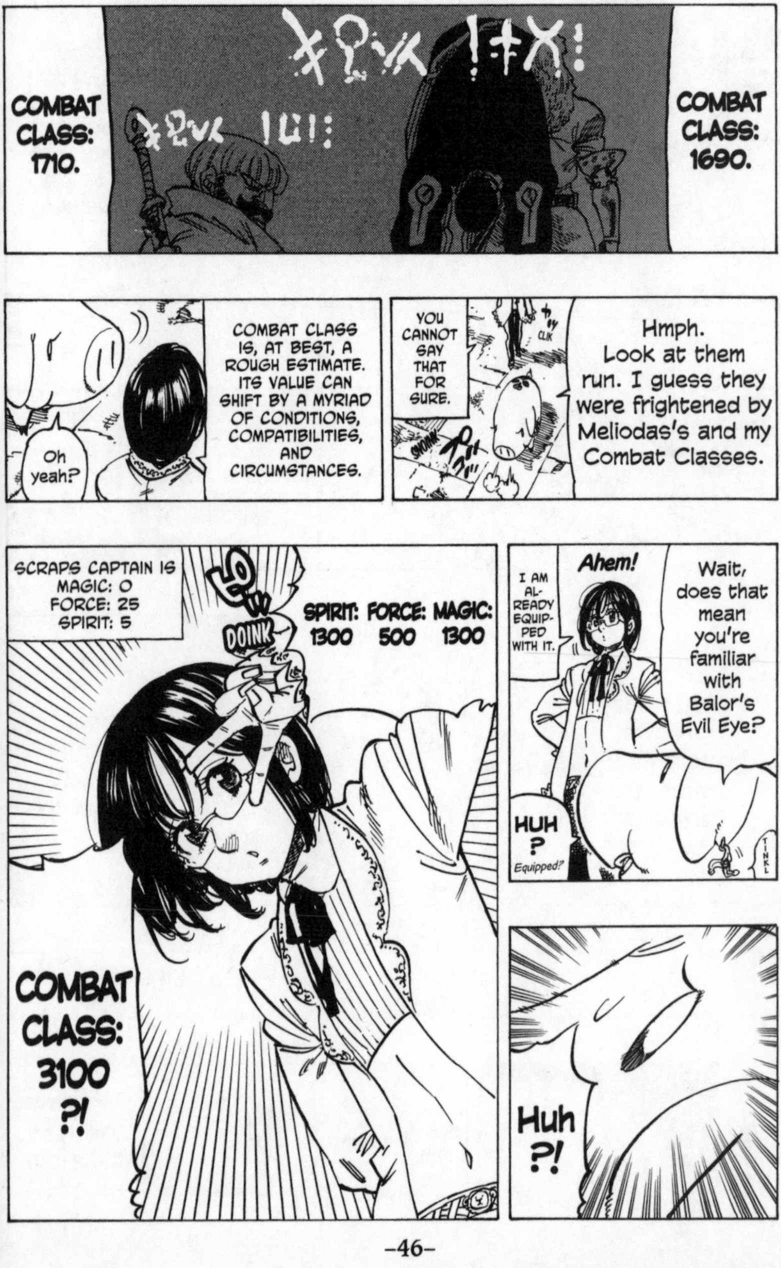
COMBAT CLASS: 1690.
COMBAT CLASS: 1710.
Hmph. Look at them run. I guess they were frightened by Meliodas's and my Combat Classes.
CLIK
YOU CANNOT SAY THAT FOR SURE.
COMBAT CLASS IS, AT BEST, A ROUGH ESTIMATE. ITS VALUE CAN SHIFT BY A MYRIAD OF CONDITIONS, COMPATIBILITIES, AND CIRCUMSTANCES.
Oh yeah?
Wait, does that mean you're familiar with Balor's Evil Eye?
Ahem!
I AM AL-READY EQUIP-PED WITH IT.
HUH?
Equipped?
TINKL
Huh?!
SCRAPS CAPTAIN IS MAGIC: 0 FORCE: 25 SPIRIT: 5
DOINK
SPIRIT: 1300 FORCE: 500 MAGIC: 1300
COMBAT CLASS: 3100?!

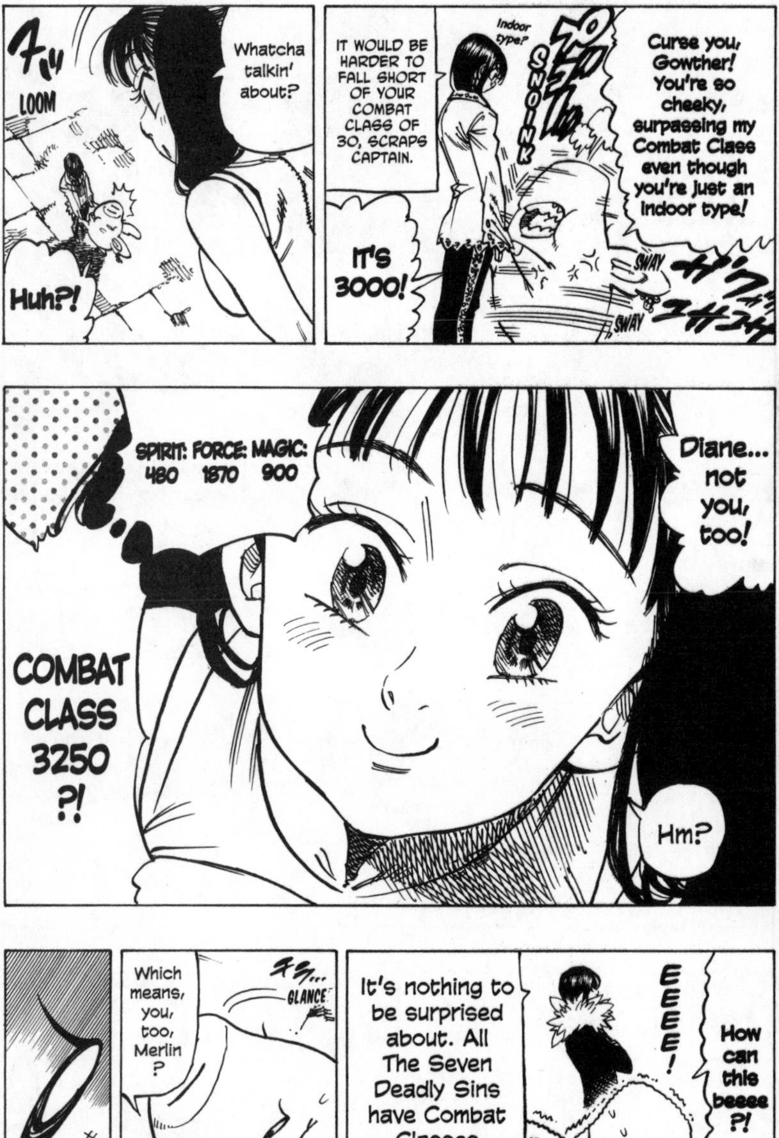

Curse you, Gowther! You're so cheeky, surpassing my Combat Class even though you're just an indoor type!
SNOINK
Indoor type?
IT WOULD BE HARDER TO FALL SHORT OF YOUR COMBAT CLASS OF 30, SCRAPS CAPTAIN.
SWAY
SWAY
IT'S 3000!
Whatcha talkin' about?
LOOM
Huh?!
Diane... not you, too!
SPIRIT: 480
FORCE: 1870
MAGIC: 900
COMBAT CLASS 3250 ?!
Hm?
How can this beeee ?!
EEEE!
It's nothing to be surprised about. All The Seven Deadly Sins have Combat Classes that exceed 3000.
GLANCE
Which means, you, too, Merlin ?

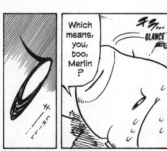

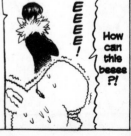

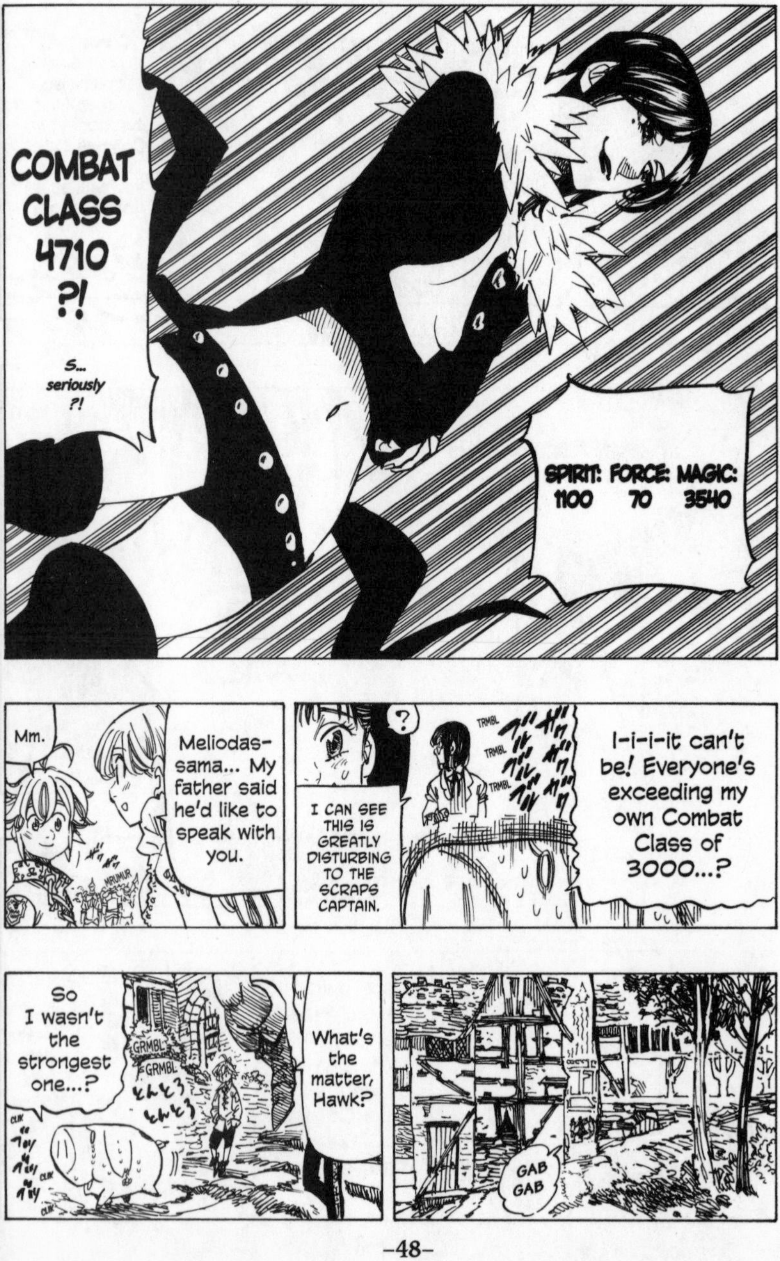
SPIRIT: FORCE: MAGIC: 1100 70 3540
COMBAT CLASS 4710 ?!
S... seriously ?!
I-i-i-it can't be! Everyone's exceeding my own Combat Class of 3000...?
TRMBL TRMBL TRMBL
?
I CAN SEE THIS IS GREATLY DISTURBING TO THE SCRAPS CAPTAIN.
Meliodas-sama... My father said he'd like to speak with you.
Mm.
MRUMUR
GAB GAB
What's the matter, Hawk?
So I wasn't the strongest one...?
GRMBL GRMBL
とんとろ とんとろ
CLIK CLIK CLIK

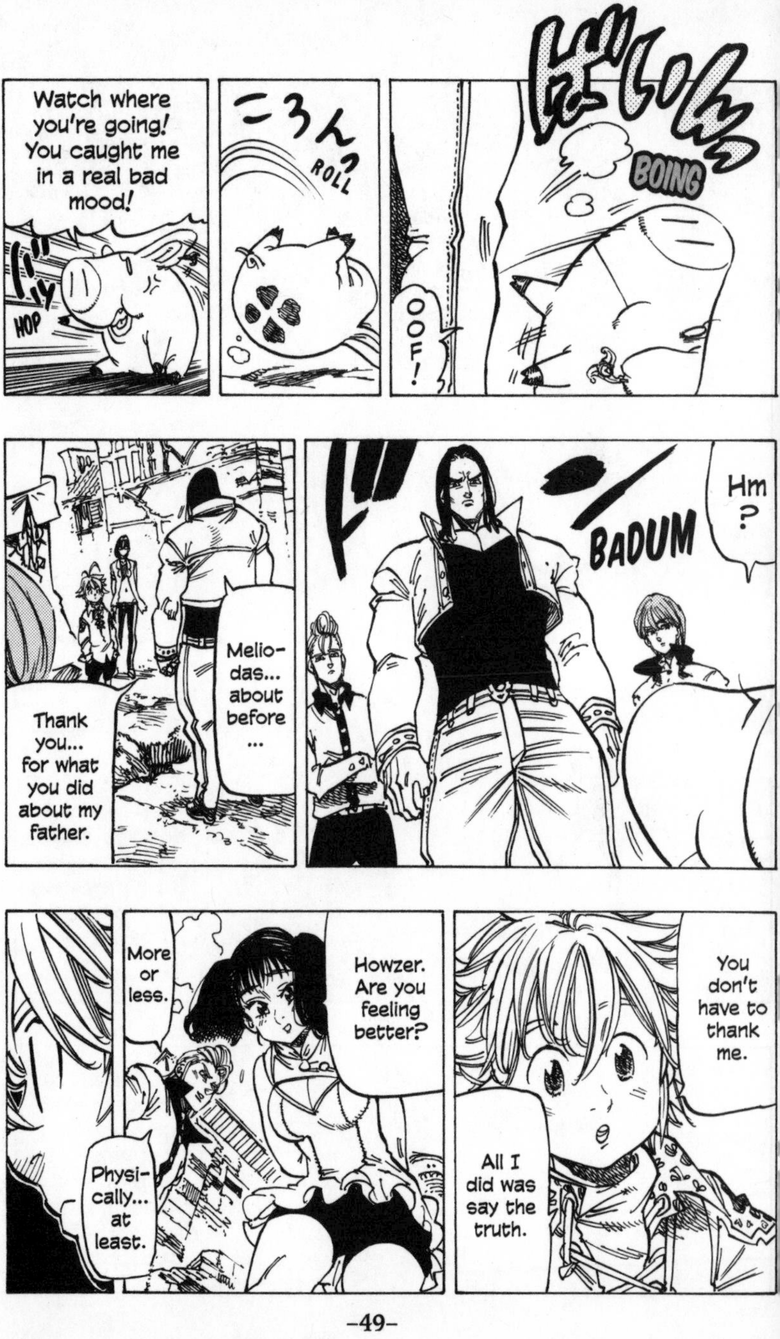
BOING
OOF!
こ ろ ん
ROLL
Watch where you're going! You caught me in a real bad mood!
HOP
Hm?
BADUM
Melio-das... about before...
Thank you... for what you did about my father.
You don't have to thank me.
All I did was say the truth.
Howzer. Are you feeling better?
More or less.
Physi-cally... at least.

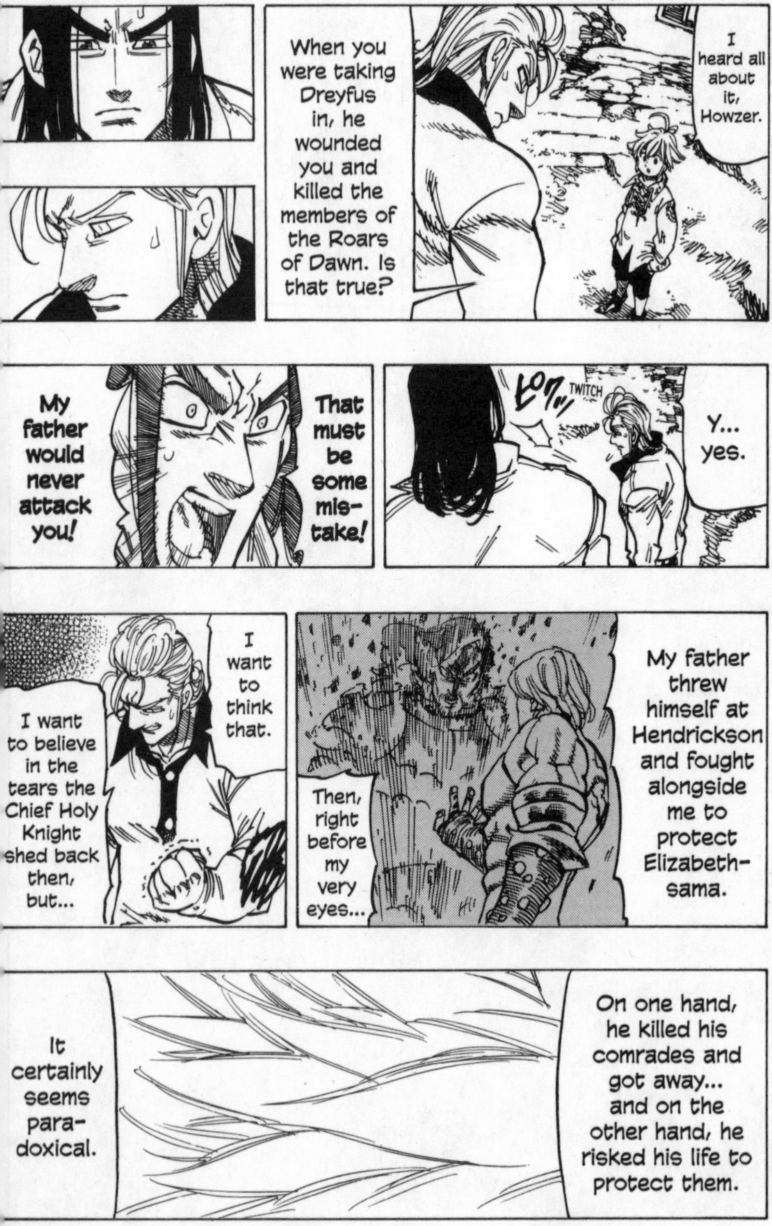
I heard all about it, Howzer.
When you were taking Dreyfus in, he wounded you and killed the members of the Roars of Dawn. Is that true?
TWITCH
Y... yes.
That must be some mistake!
My father would never attack you!
My father threw himself at Hendrickson and fought alongside me to protect Elizabeth-sama.
Then, right before my very eyes...
I want to think that.
I want to believe in the tears the Chief Holy Knight shed back then, but...
On one hand, he killed his comrades and got away... and on the other hand, he risked his life to protect them.
It certainly seems paradoxical.

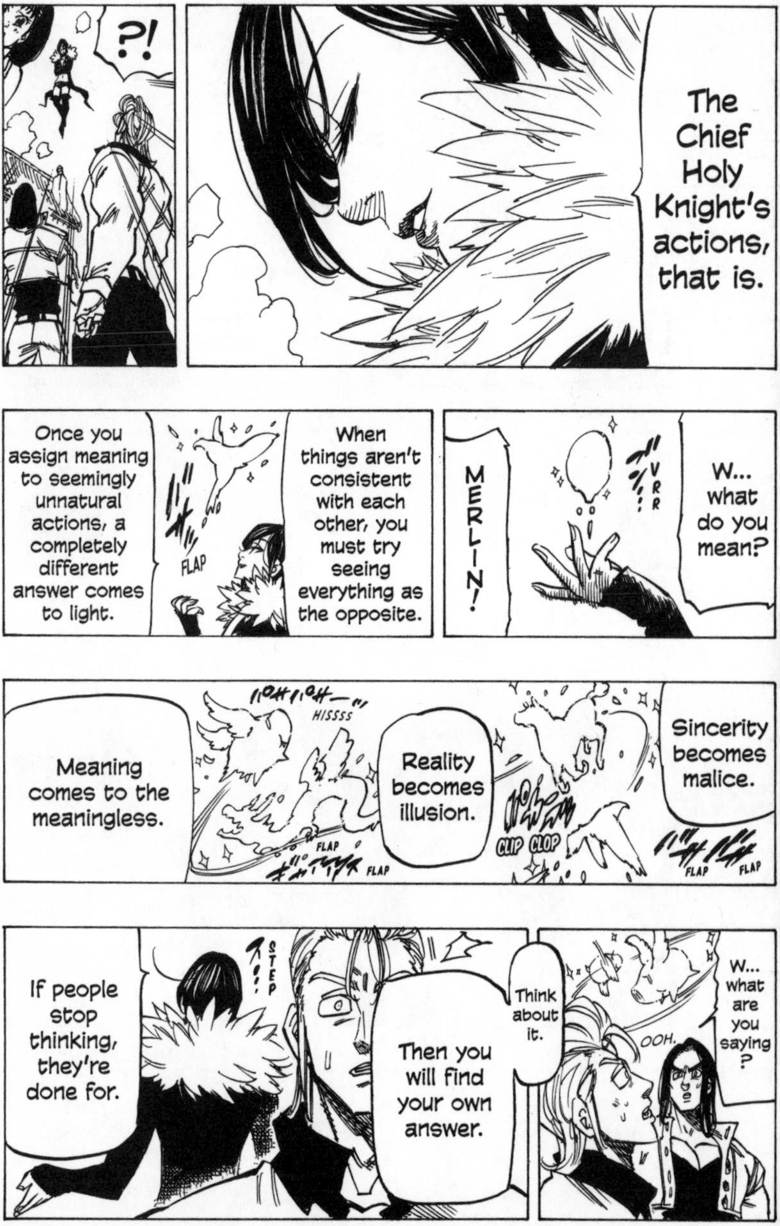

The Chief Holy Knight's actions, that is.
?!
W... what do you mean?
VRR
MERLIN!
When things aren't consistent with each other, you must try seeing everything as the opposite.
FLAP
Once you assign meaning to seemingly unnatural actions, a completely different answer comes to light.
Sincerity becomes malice.
FLAP FLAP
CLIP CLOP
Reality becomes illusion.
HISSSS
FLAP FLAP
Meaning comes to the meaningless.
W... what are you saying?
OOH.
Think about it.
Then you will find your own answer.
STEP
If people stop thinking, they're done for.

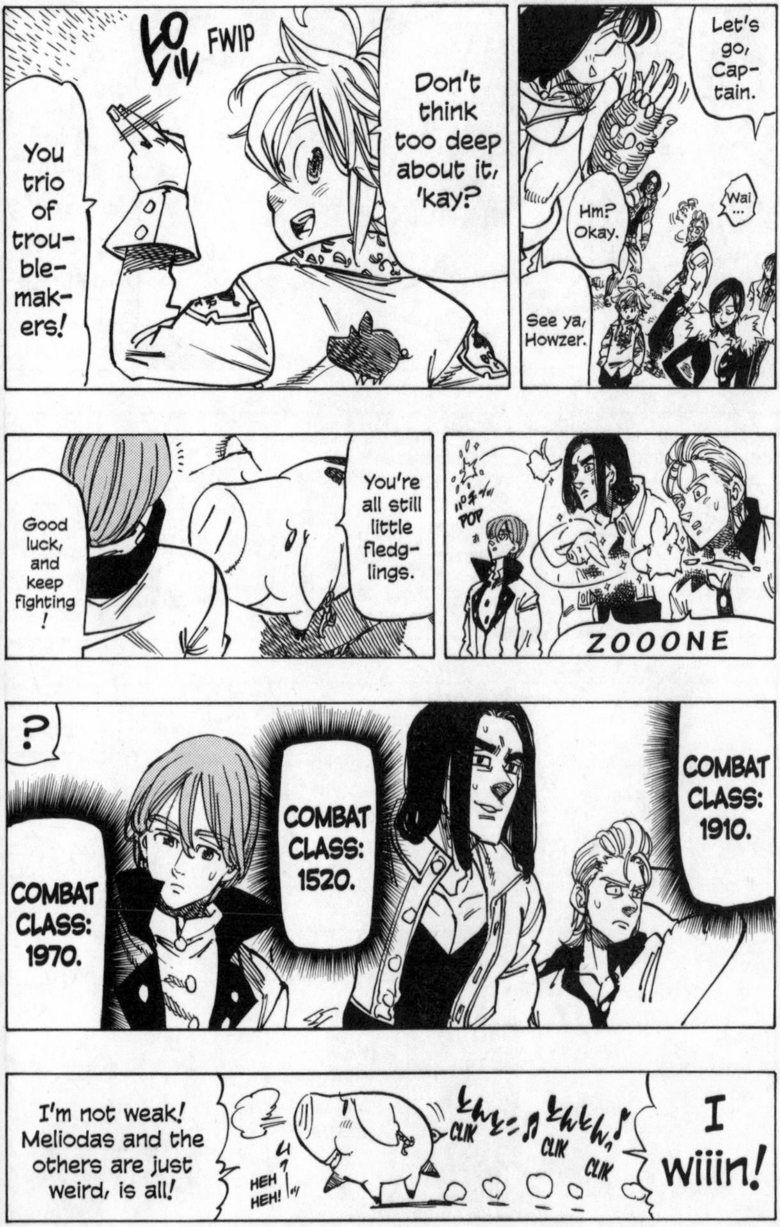

Let's go, Captain.
Wai...
Hm? Okay.
See ya, Howzer.
Don't think too deep about it, 'kay?
FWIP
You trio of trouble-makers!
POP
ZOOONE
You're all still little fledglings.
Good luck, and keep fighting!
COMBAT CLASS: 1910.
COMBAT CLASS: 1520.
?
COMBAT CLASS: 1970.
I wiiin!
CLIK
CLIK
CLIK
HEH HEH!
I'm not weak! Meliodas and the others are just weird, is all!

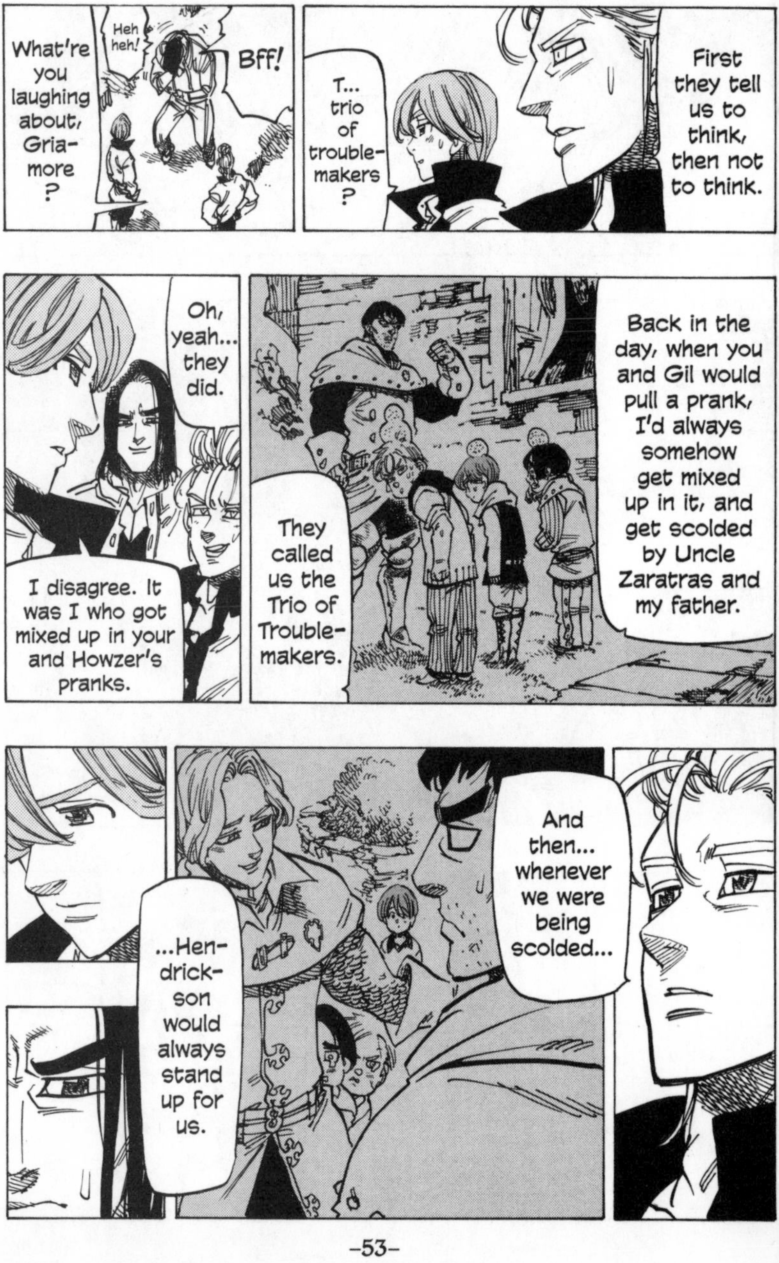
First they tell us to think, then not to think.
T... trio of trouble-makers?
Bff!
Heh heh!
What're you laughing about, Gria-more?
Back in the day, when you and Gil would pull a prank, I'd always somehow get mixed up in it, and get scolded by Uncle Zaratras and my father.
They called us the Trio of Trouble-makers.
Oh, yeah... they did.
I disagree. It was I who got mixed up in your and Howzer's pranks.
And then... whenever we were being scolded...
...Hen-drick-son would always stand up for us.

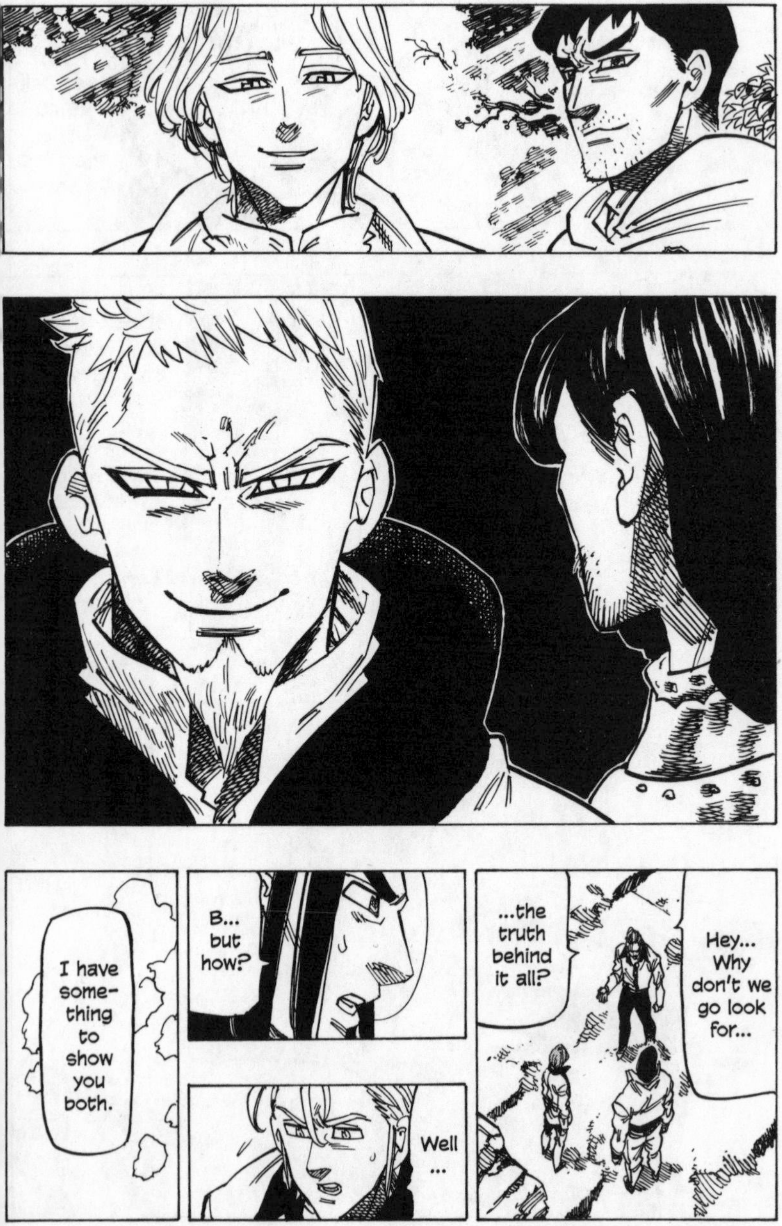
Hey... Why don't we go look for...
...the truth behind it all?
B... but how?
Well ...
I have some-thing to show you both.

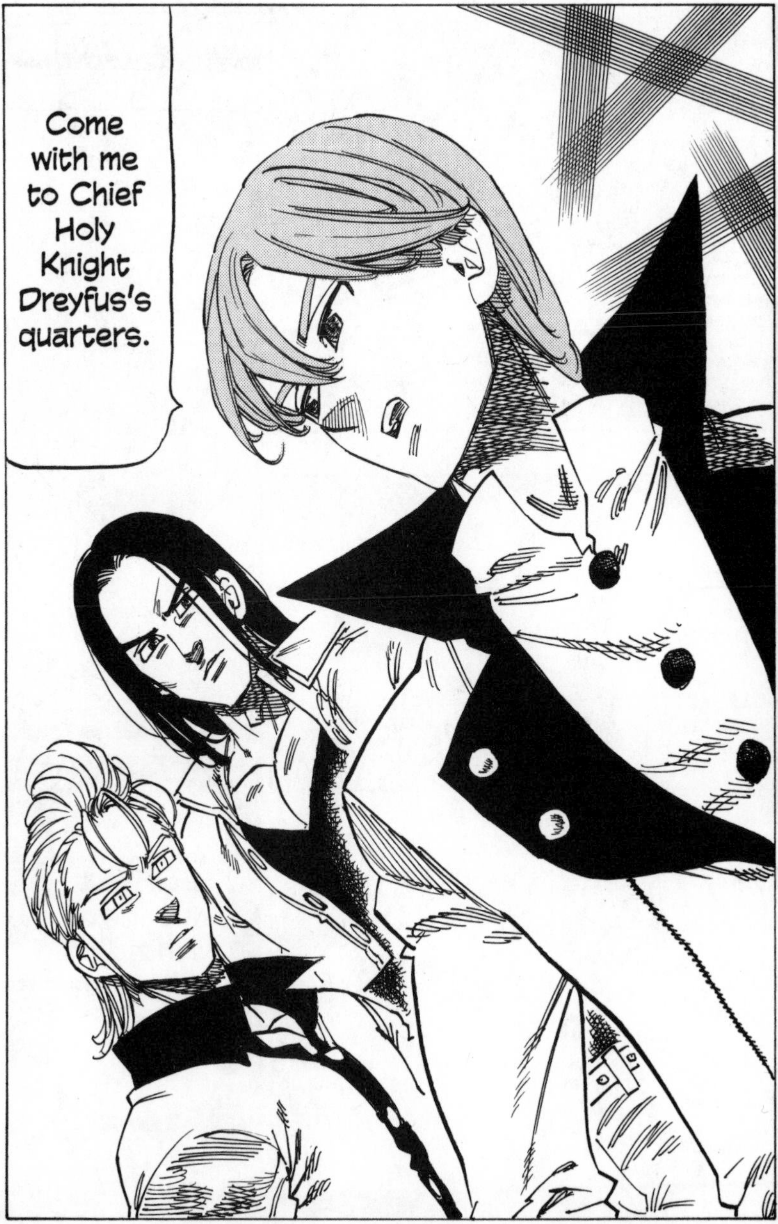
Come with me to Chief Holy Knight Dreyfus's quarters.

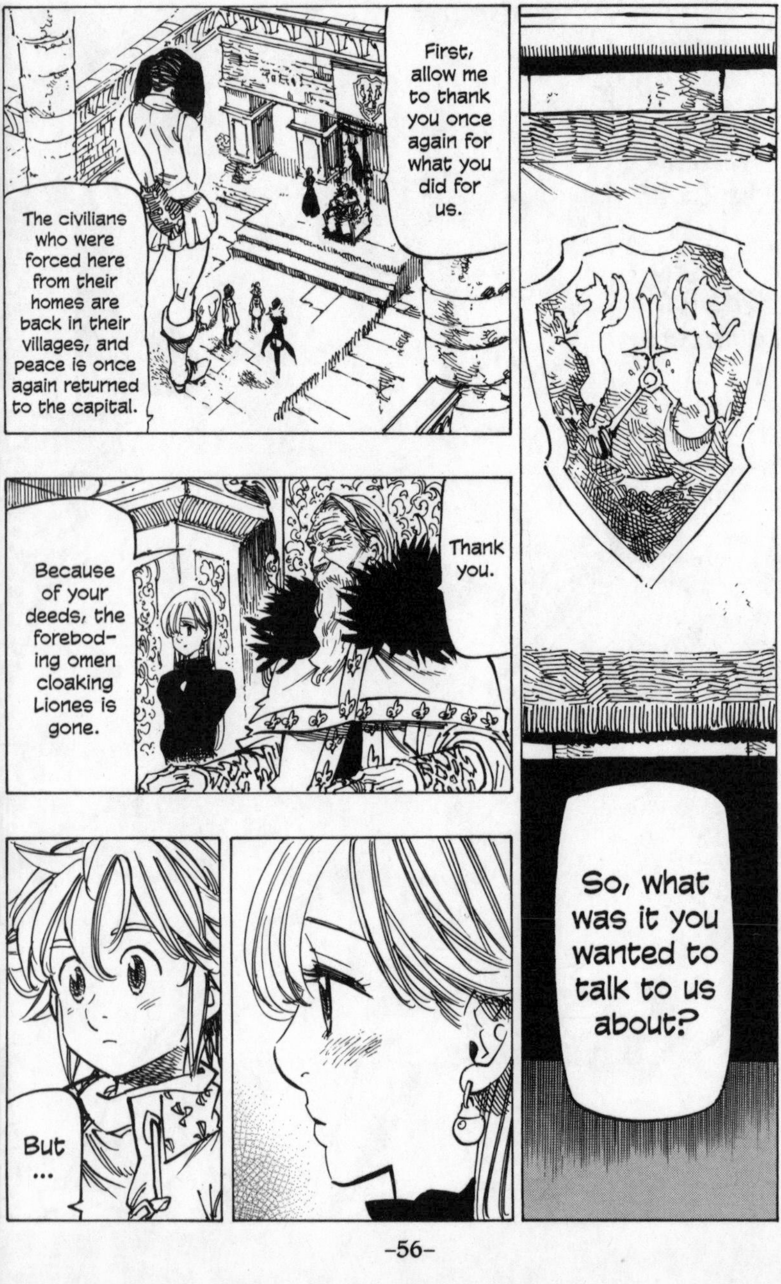
First, allow me to thank you once again for what you did for us.
The civilians who were forced here from their homes are back in their villages, and peace is once again returned to the capital.
Thank you.
Because of your deeds, the forebod-ing omen cloaking Liones is gone.
But ...
So, what was it you wanted to talk to us about?

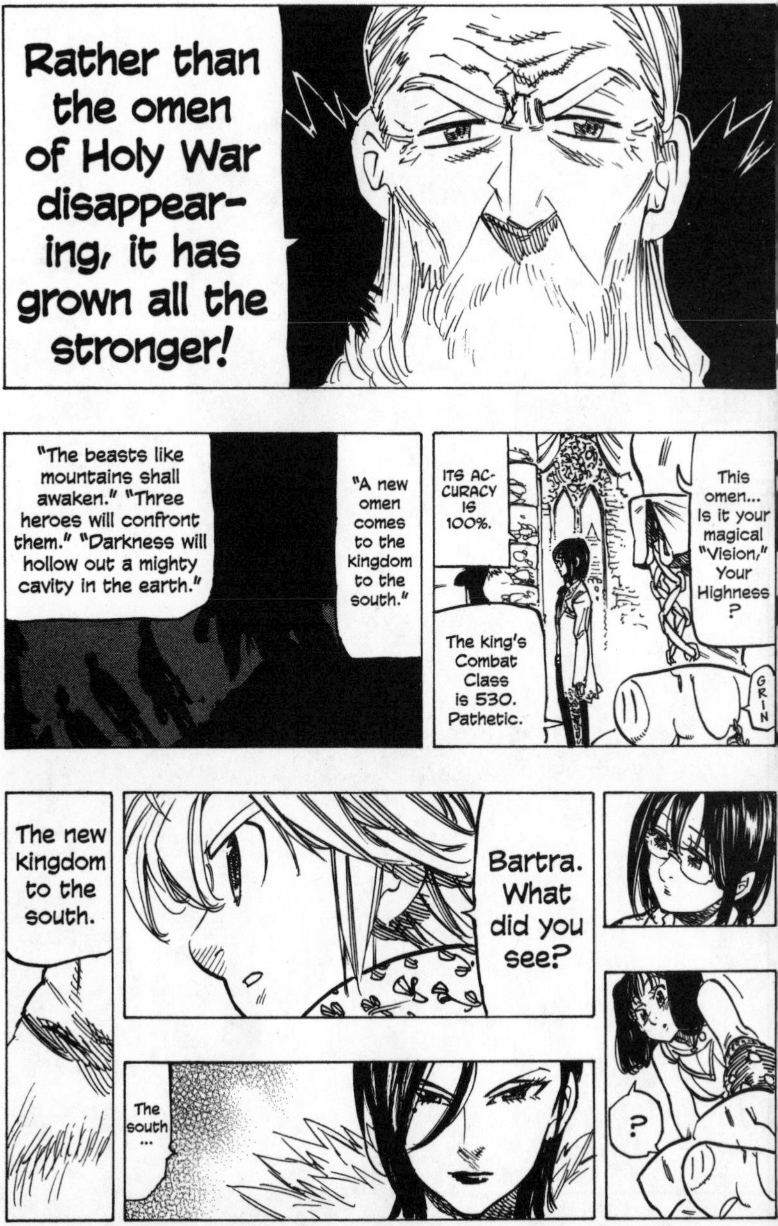
Rather than the omen of Holy War disappearing, it has grown all the stronger!
This omen... Is it your magical "Vision," Your Highness?
ITS ACCURACY IS 100%.
The king's Combat Class is 530. Pathetic.
GRIN
"A new omen comes to the kingdom to the south."
"The beasts like mountains shall awaken." "Three heroes will confront them." "Darkness will hollow out a mighty cavity in the earth."
?
Bartra. What did you see?
The south...
The new kingdom to the south.

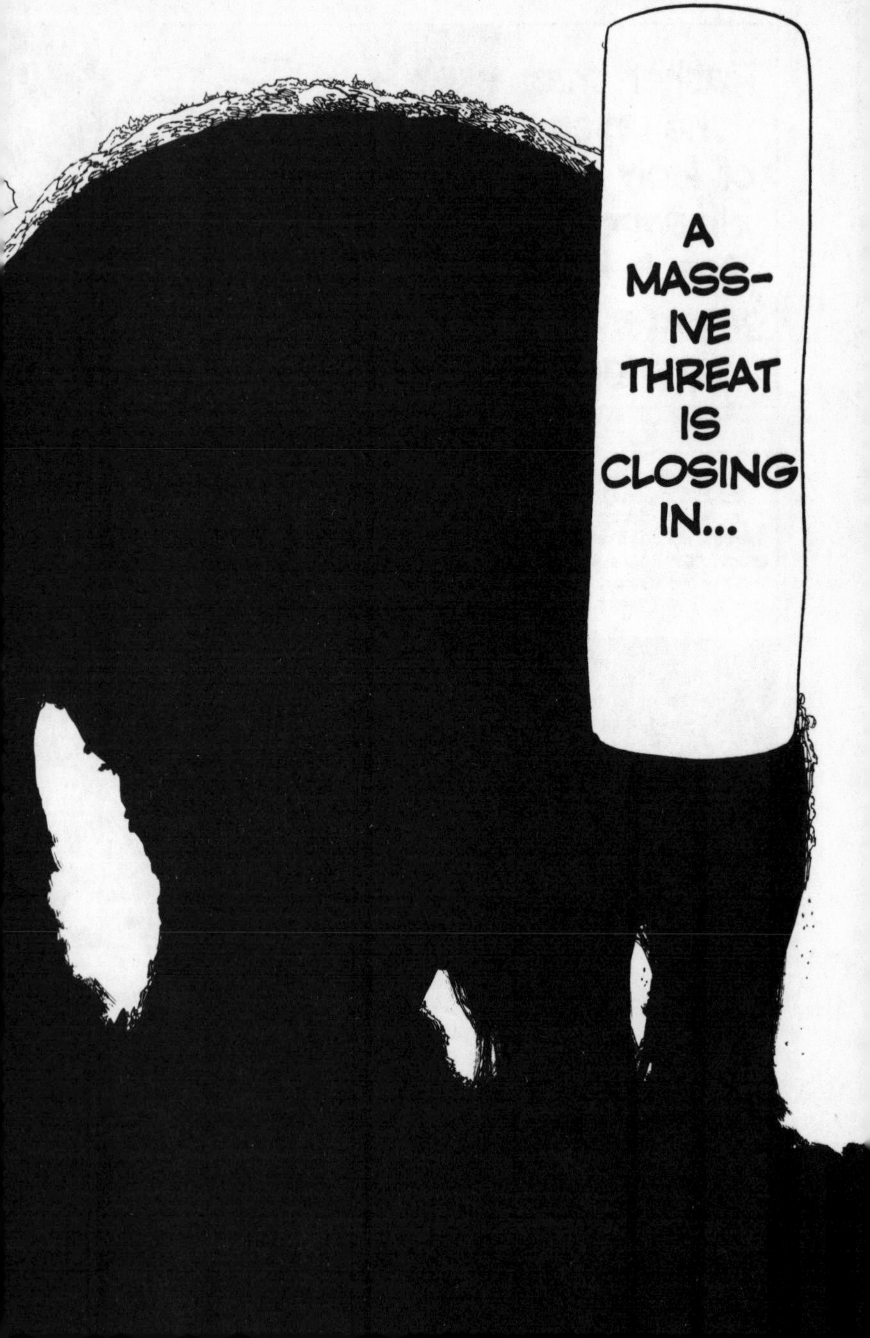
A MASS-IVE THREAT IS CLOSING IN...

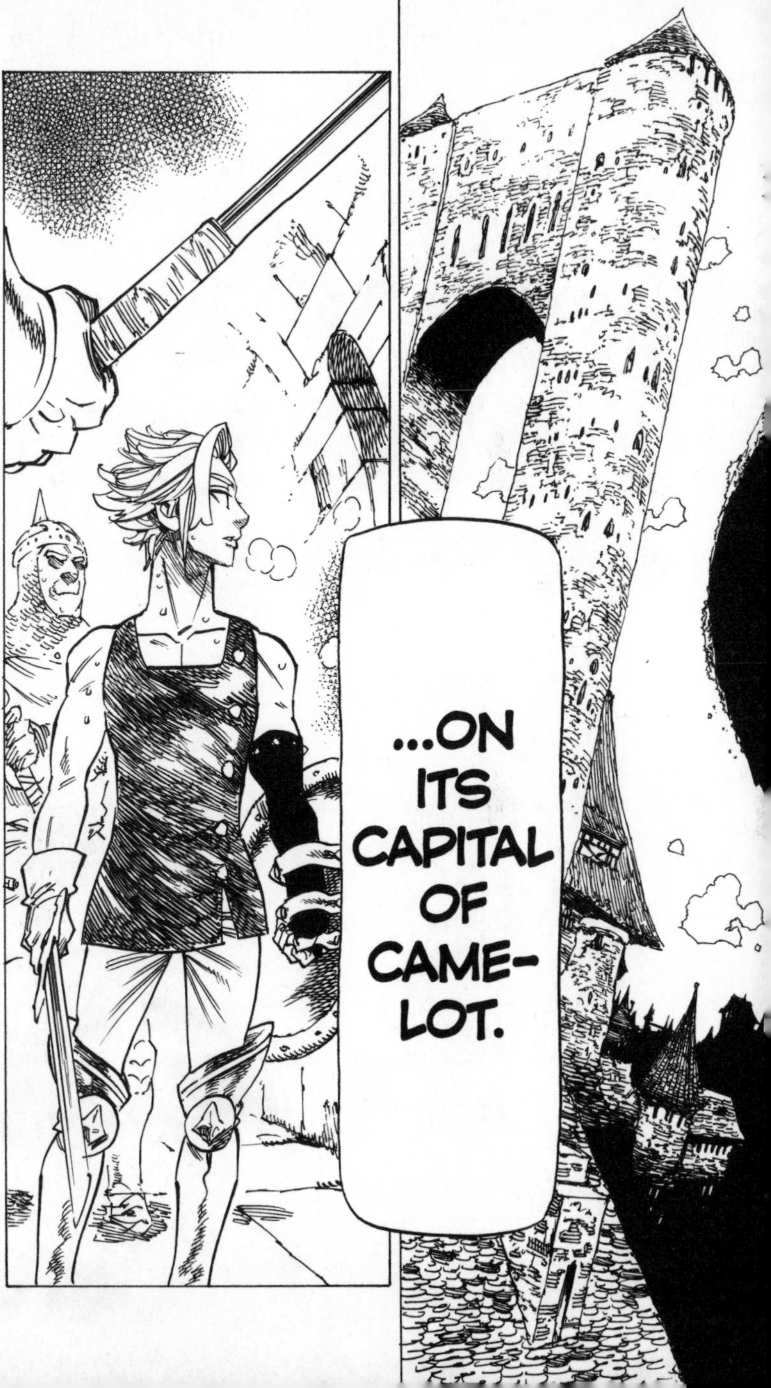
...ON ITS CAPITAL OF CAME- LOT.

Chapter 108 - Gentle Awakening

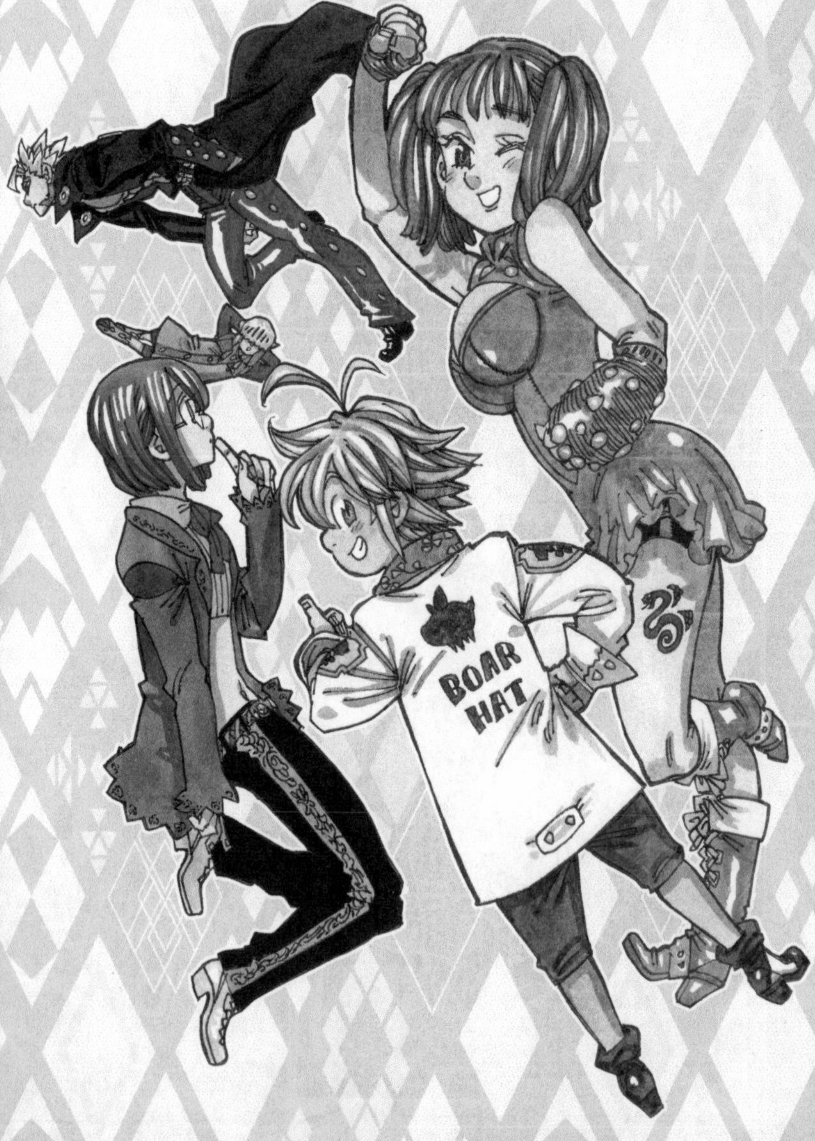
BOAR
HAT

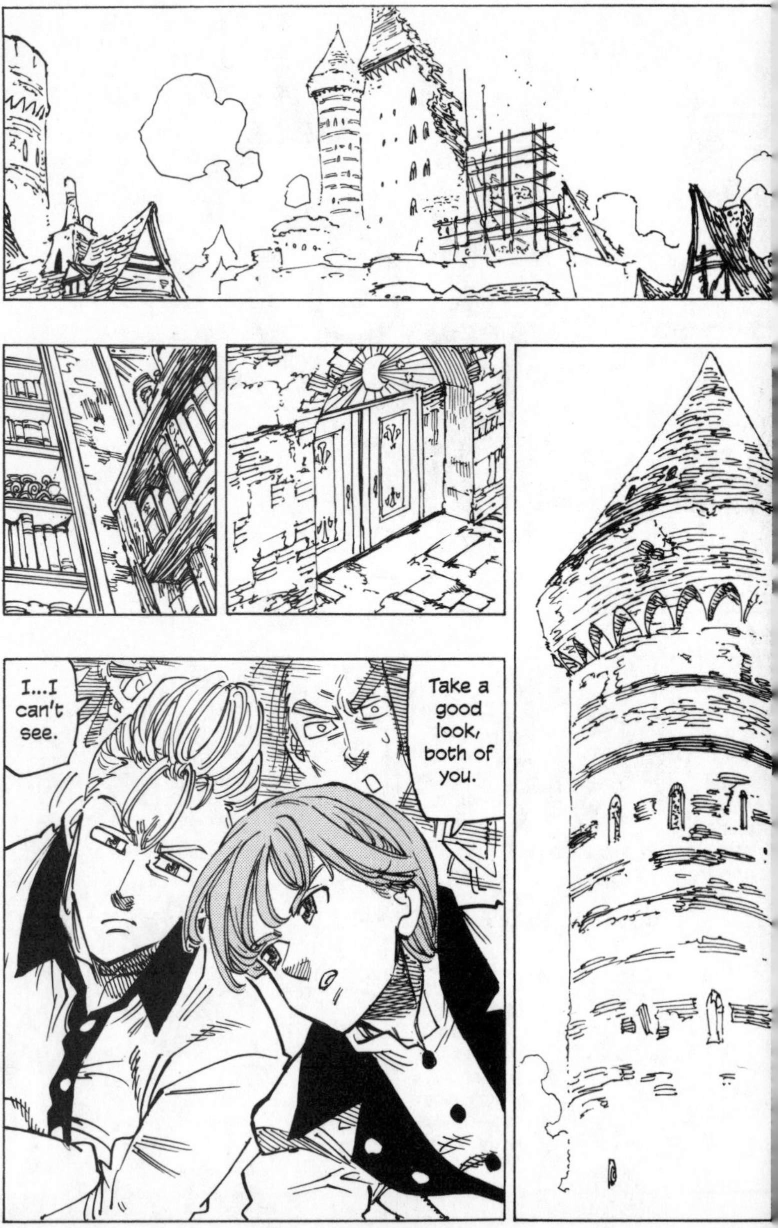
Take a good look, both of you.
I...I can't see.

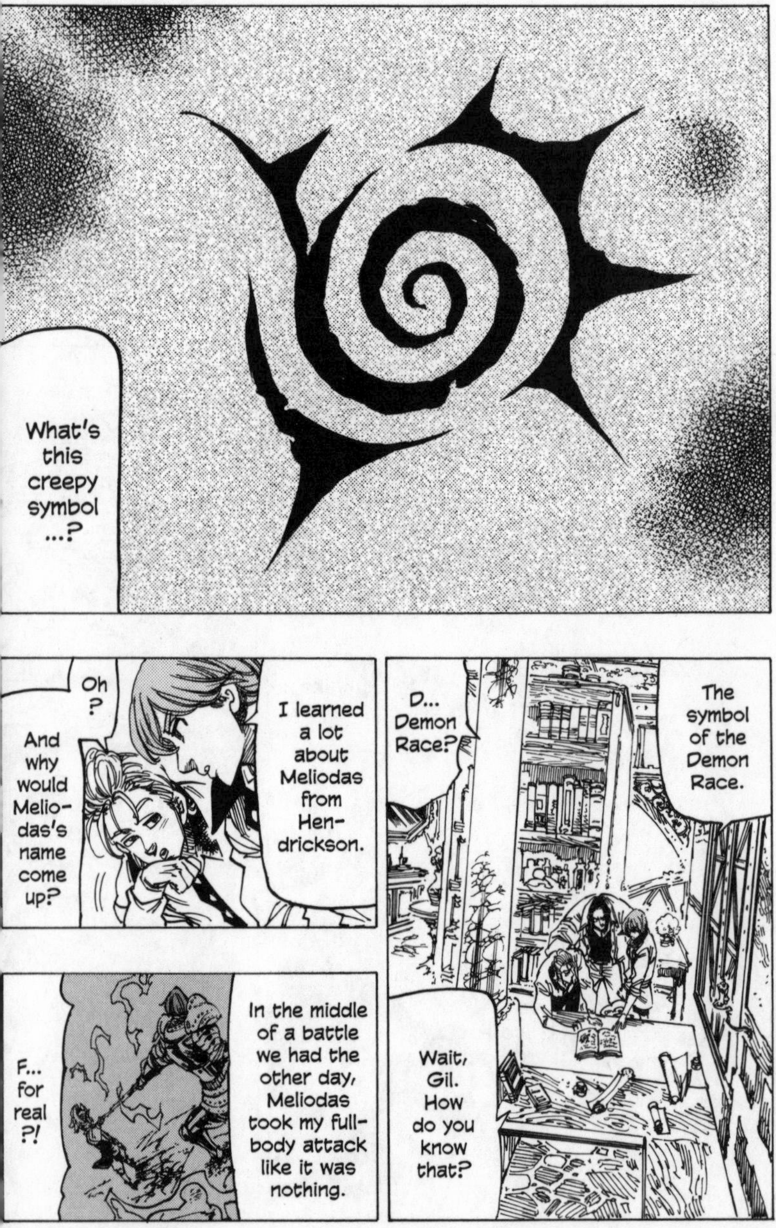
What's this creepy symbol ...?
The symbol of the Demon Race.
D... Demon Race?
Wait, Gil. How do you know that?
I learned a lot about Meliodas from Hen-drickson.
Oh?
And why would Melio-das's name come up?
In the middle of a battle we had the other day, Meliodas took my full-body attack like it was nothing.
F... for real?!

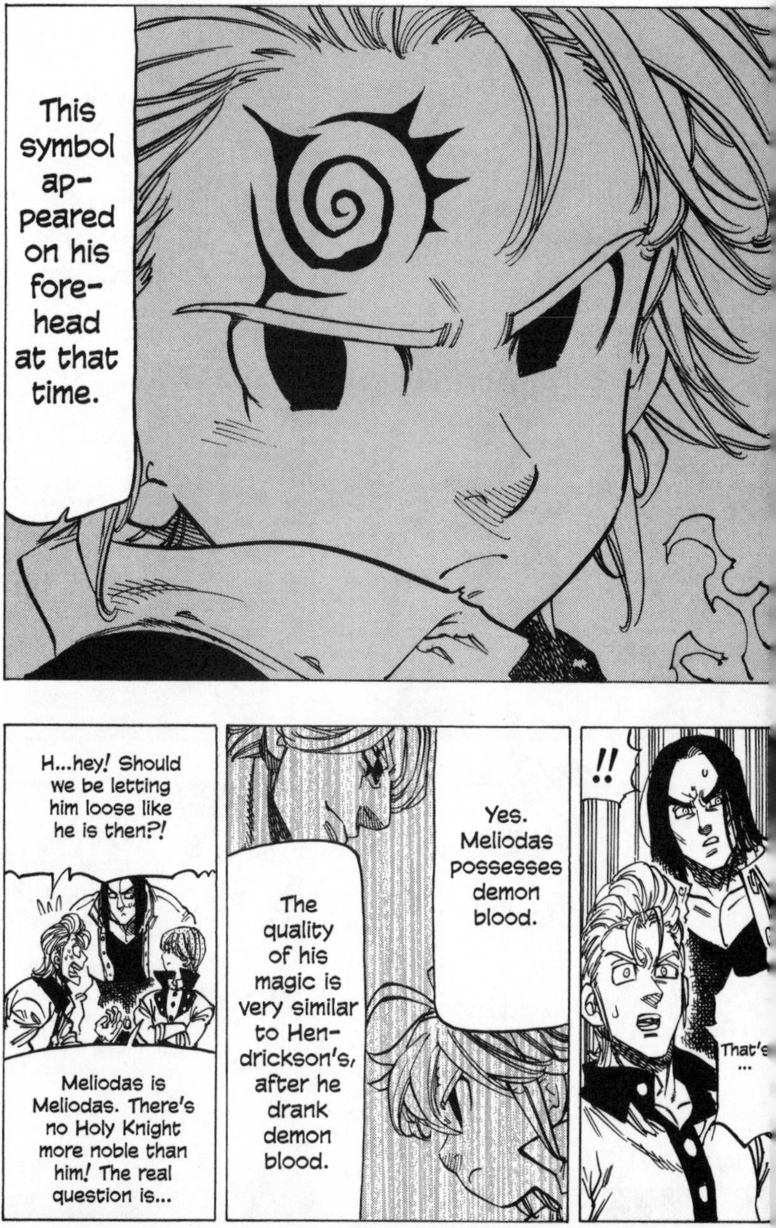

This symbol ap-peared on his fore-head at that time.
!!
That's ...
Yes. Meliodas possesses demon blood.
The quality of his magic is very similar to Hen-drickson's, after he drank demon blood.
H...hey! Should we be letting him loose like he is then?!
Meliodas is Meliodas. There's no Holy Knight more noble than him! The real question is...

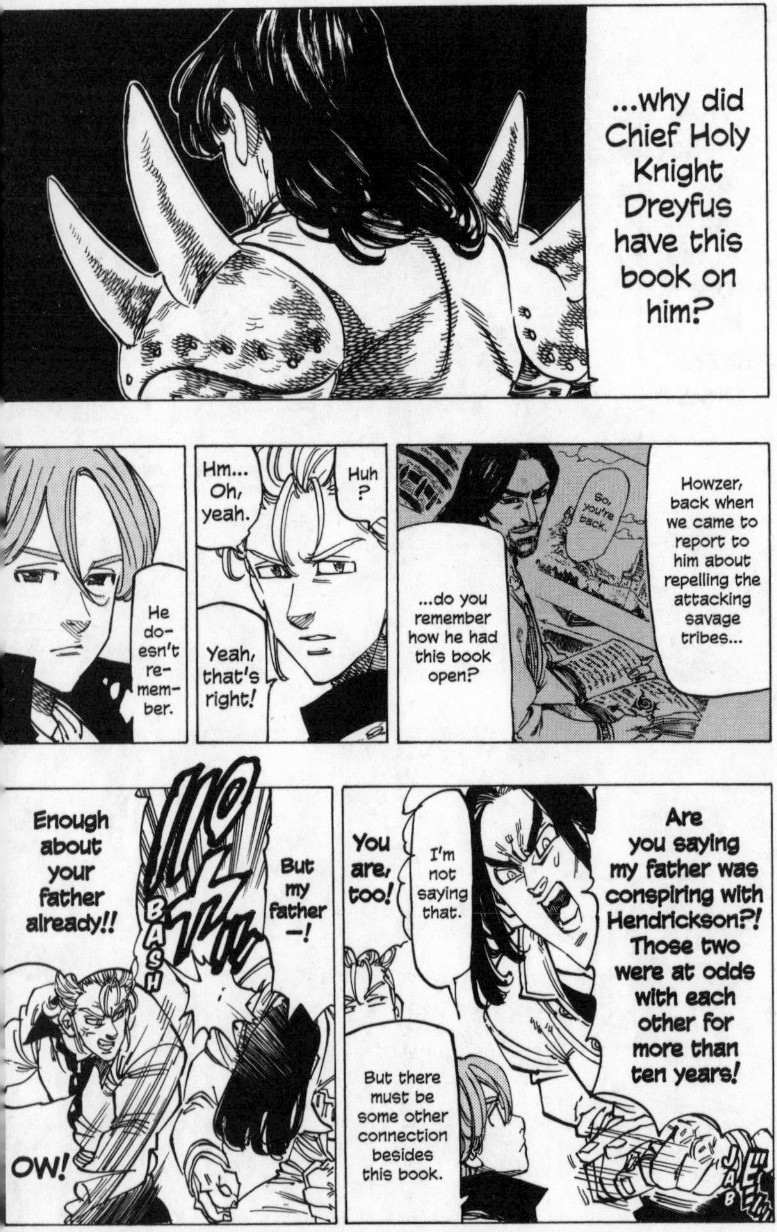
...why did Chief Holy Knight Dreyfus have this book on him?
Howzer, back when we came to report to him about repelling the attacking savage tribes...
So, you're back.
...do you remember how he had this book open?
Huh?
Hm... Oh, yeah.
Yeah, that's right!
He doesn't remember.
Are you saying my father was conspiring with Hendrickson?! Those two were at odds with each other for more than ten years!
I'm not saying that.
You are, too!
But there must be some other connection besides this book.
JAB
But my father—!
BASH
Enough about your father already!!
OW!

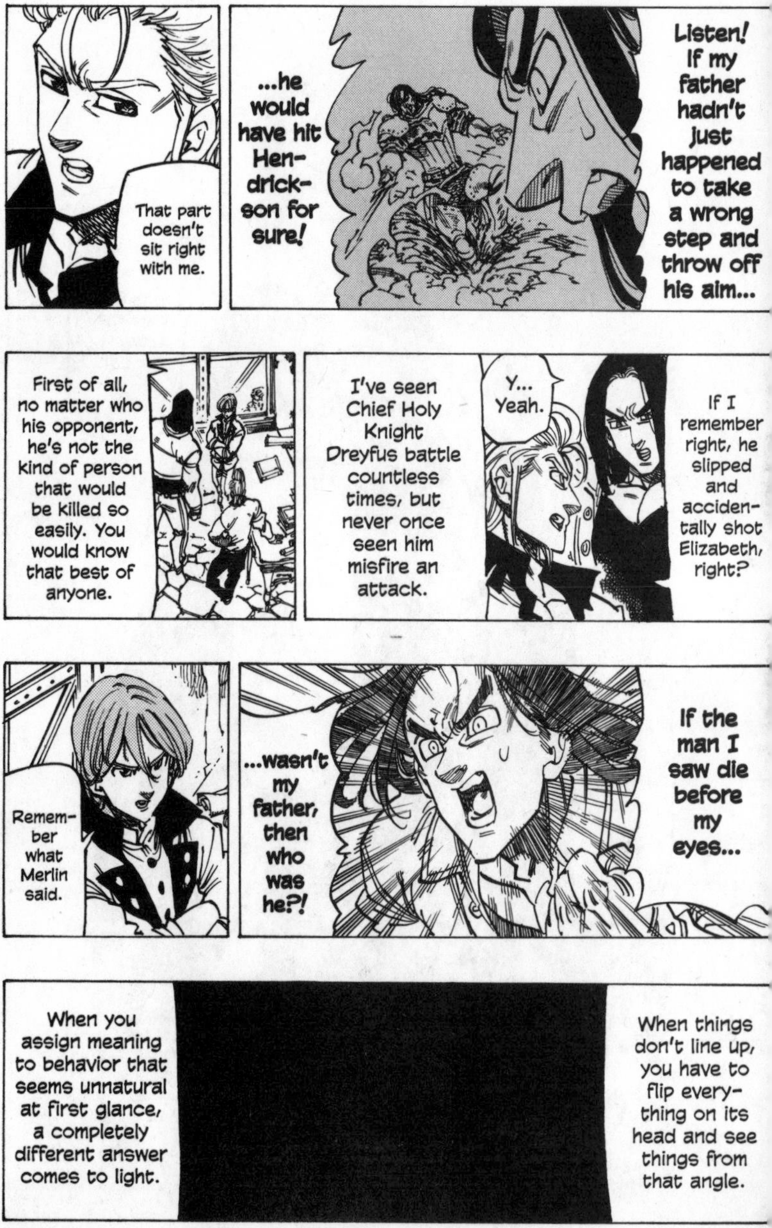

Listen! If my father hadn't just happened to take a wrong step and throw off his aim...
...he would have hit Hen-drick-son for sure!
That part doesn't sit right with me.
If I remember right, he slipped and acciden-tally shot Elizabeth, right?
Y... Yeah.
I've seen Chief Holy Knight Dreyfus battle countless times, but never once seen him misfire an attack.
First of all, no matter who his opponent, he's not the kind of person that would be killed so easily. You would know that best of anyone.
If the man I saw die before my eyes...
...wasn't my father, then who was he?!
Remem-ber what Merlin said.
When things don't line up, you have to flip every-thing on its head and see things from that angle.
When you assign meaning to behavior that seems unnatural at first glance, a completely different answer comes to light.

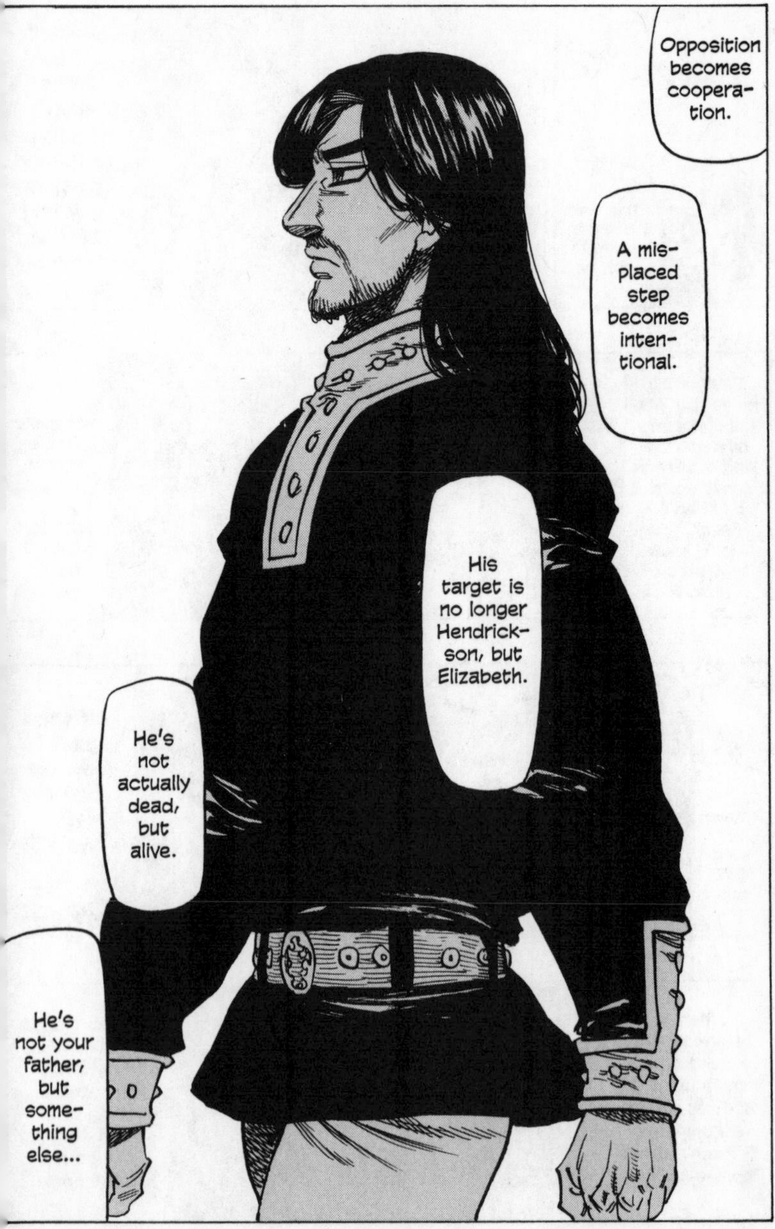
Opposition becomes cooperation.
A misplaced step becomes intentional.
His target is no longer Hendrickson, but Elizabeth.
He's not actually dead, but alive.
He's not your father, but something else...

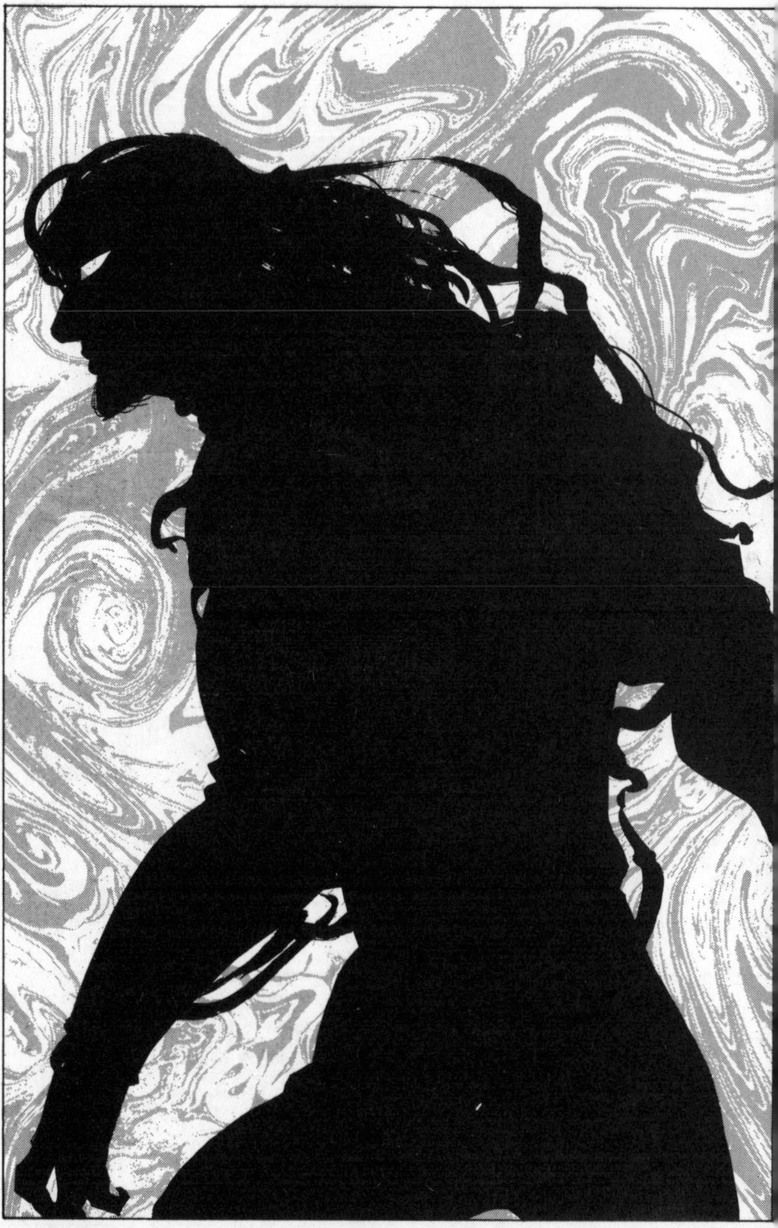

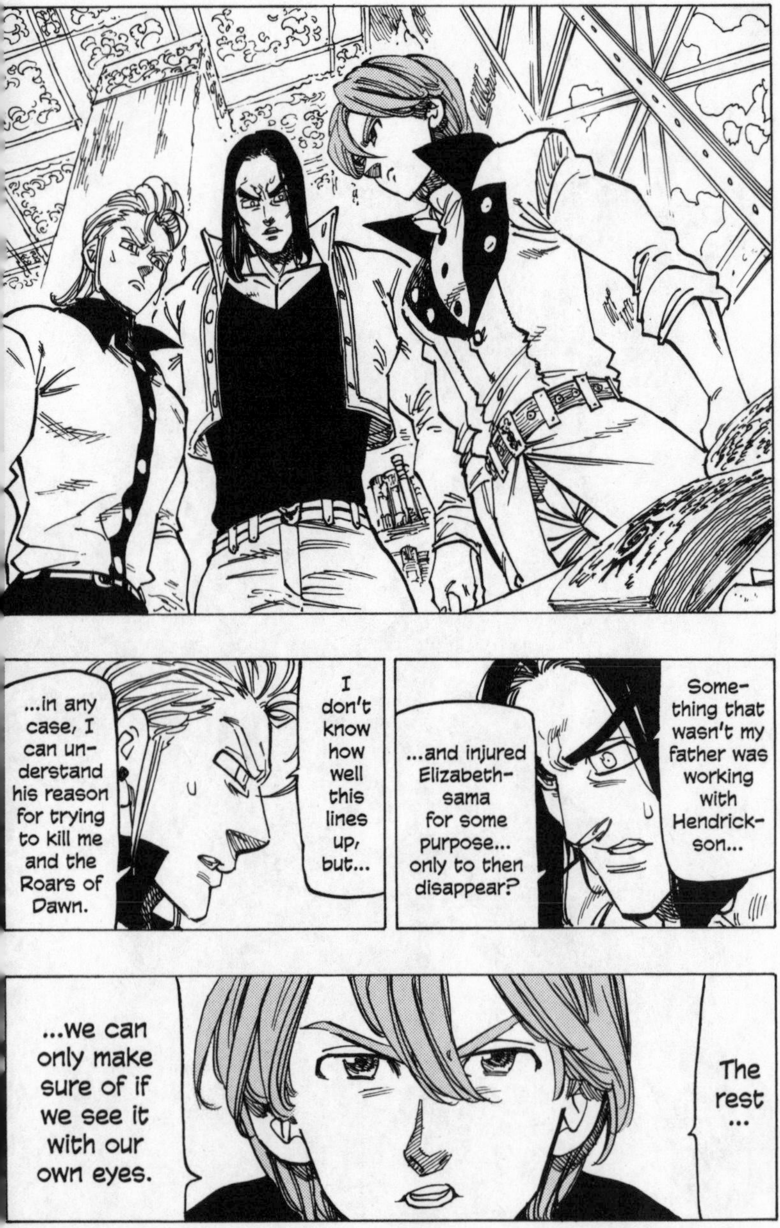
Something that wasn't my father was working with Hendrickson...
...and injured Elizabeth-sama for some purpose... only to then disappear?
I don't know how well this lines up, but...
...in any case, I can understand his reason for trying to kill me and the Roars of Dawn.
The rest...
...we can only make sure of if we see it with our own eyes.

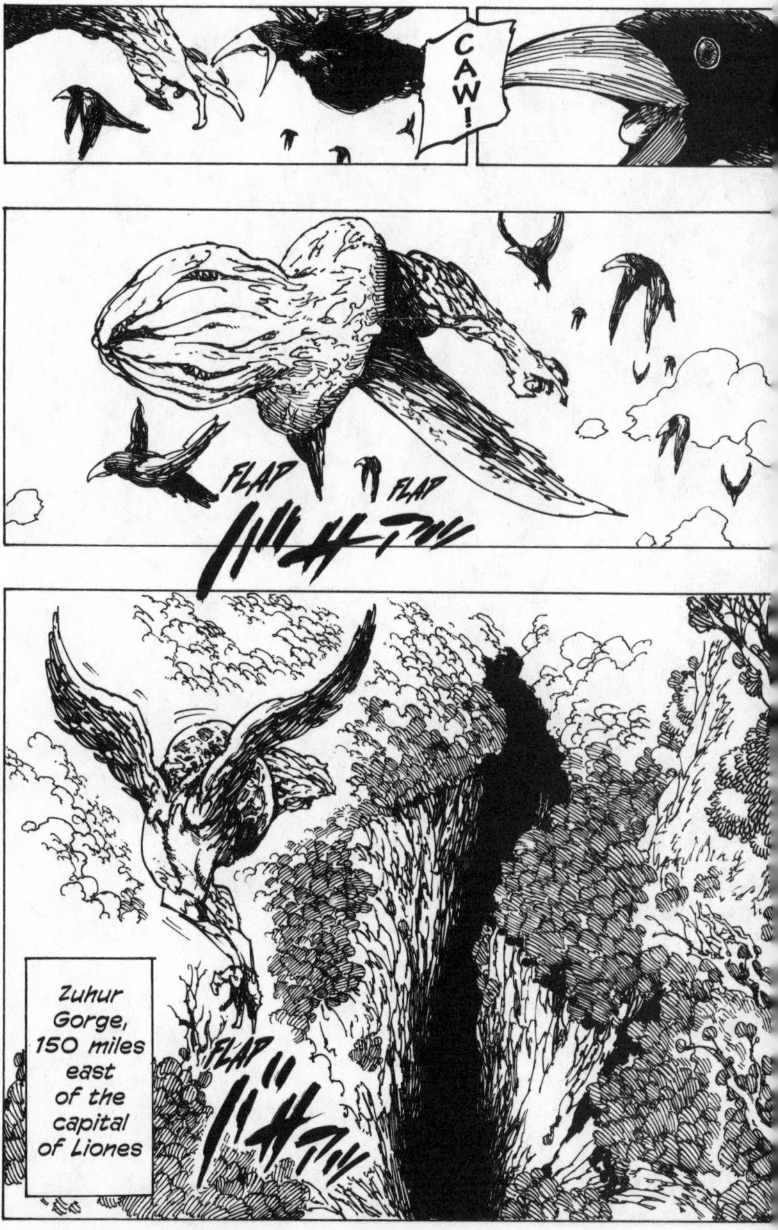
CAW!
FLAP FLAP
バサァッ
Zuhur Gorge, 150 miles east of the capital of Liones
FLAP
バサァッ

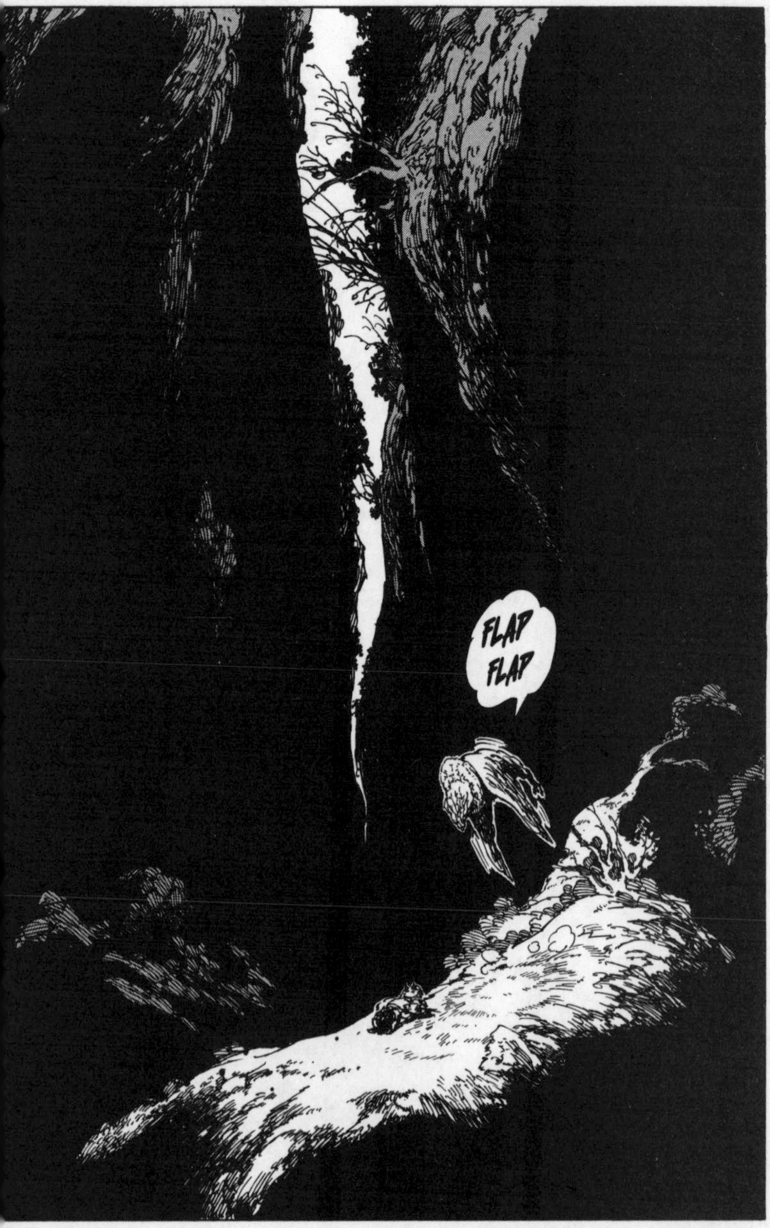
FLAP
FLAP

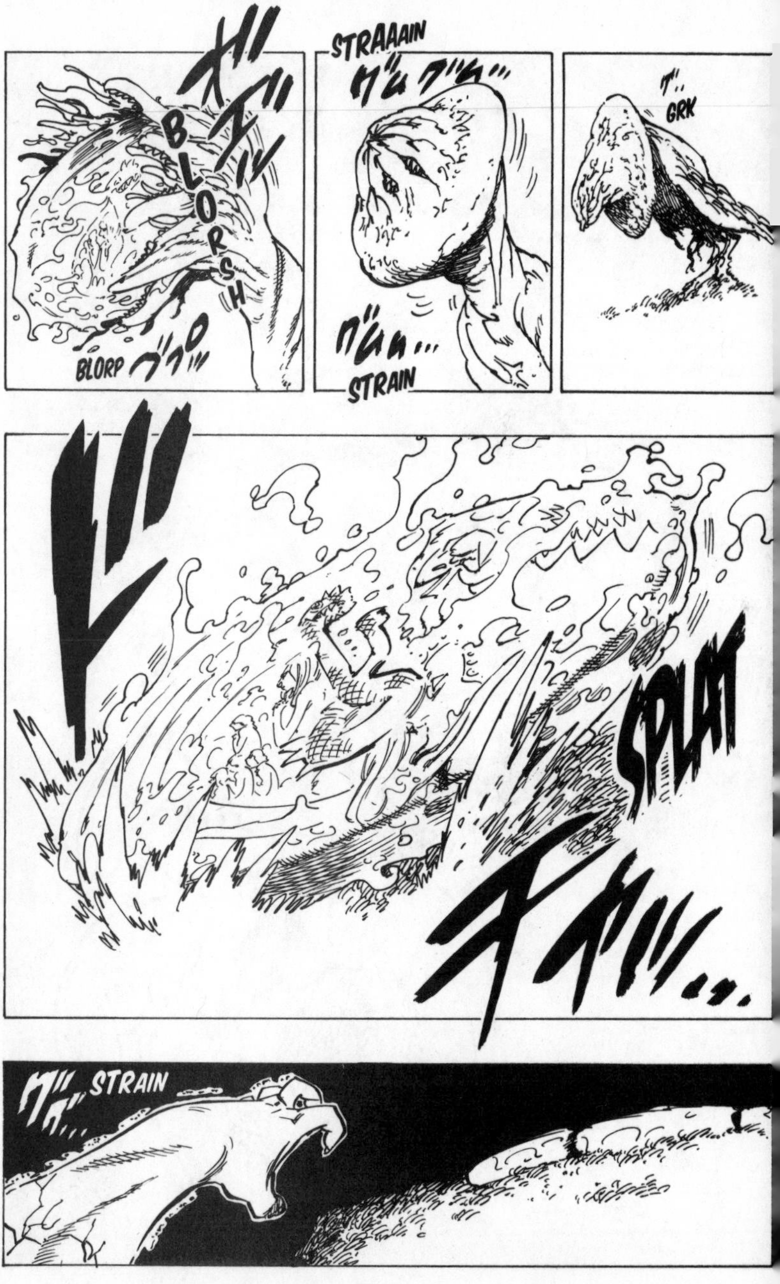
GRK
STRAAAIN
STRAIN
BLORSH
BLORP
SPLAT
STRAIN

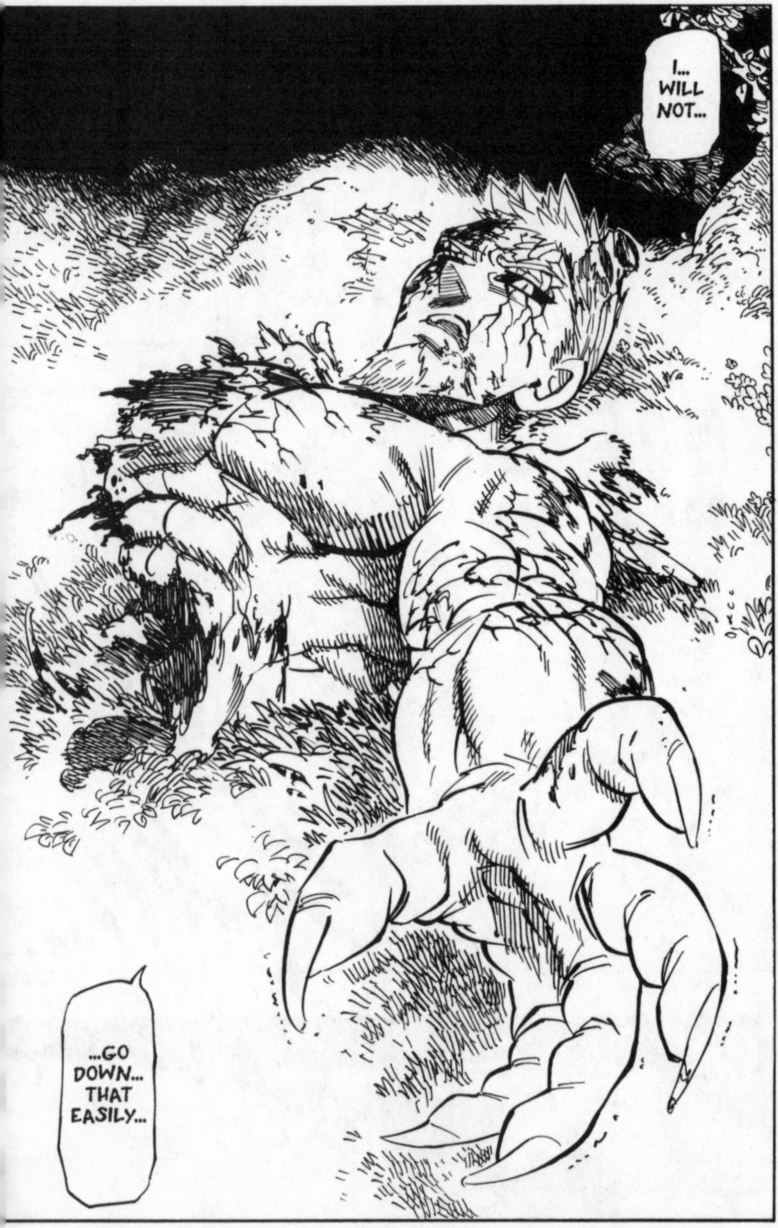
I... WILL NOT...
...GO DOWN... THAT EASILY...

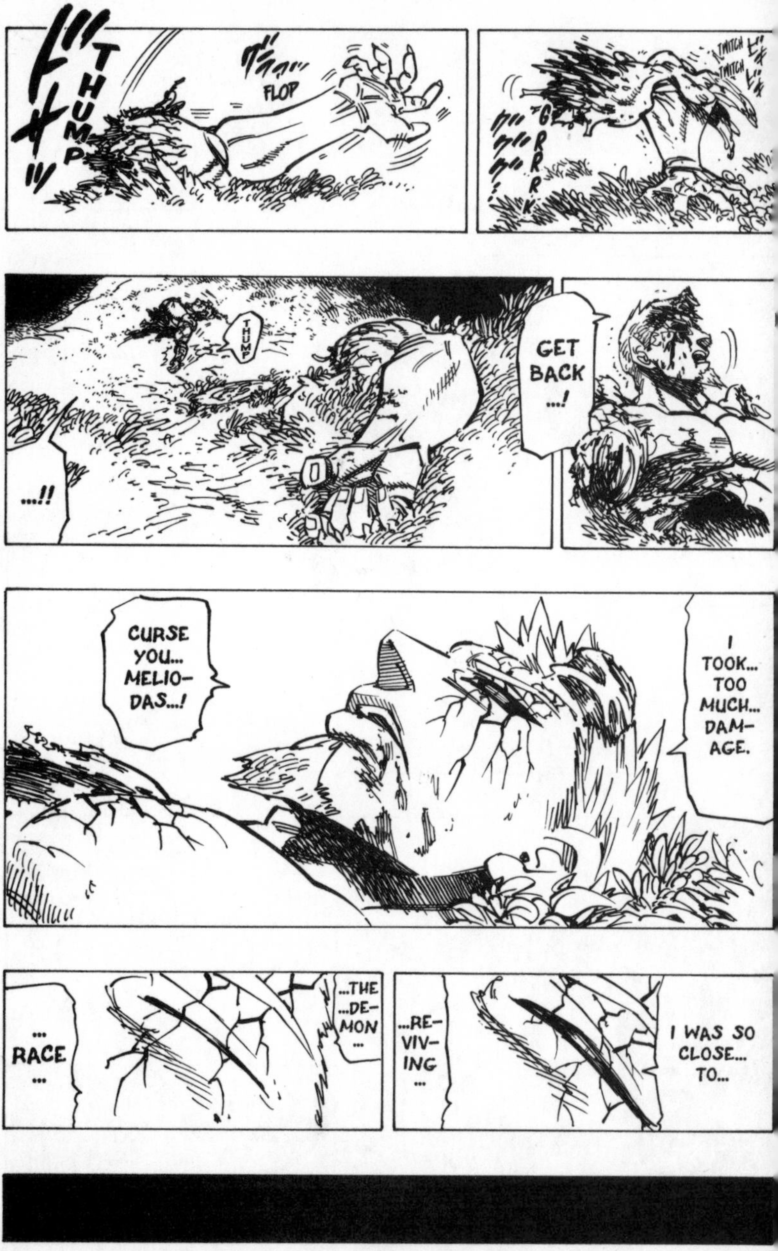
TWITCH
TWITCH
GRRRRK
THUMP
FLOP
GET BACK ...!
THUMP
...!!
I TOOK... TOO MUCH... DAMAGE.
CURSE YOU... MELIODAS...!
I WAS SO CLOSE... TO...
...REVIVING ...
...THE ...DEMON ...
... RACE ...

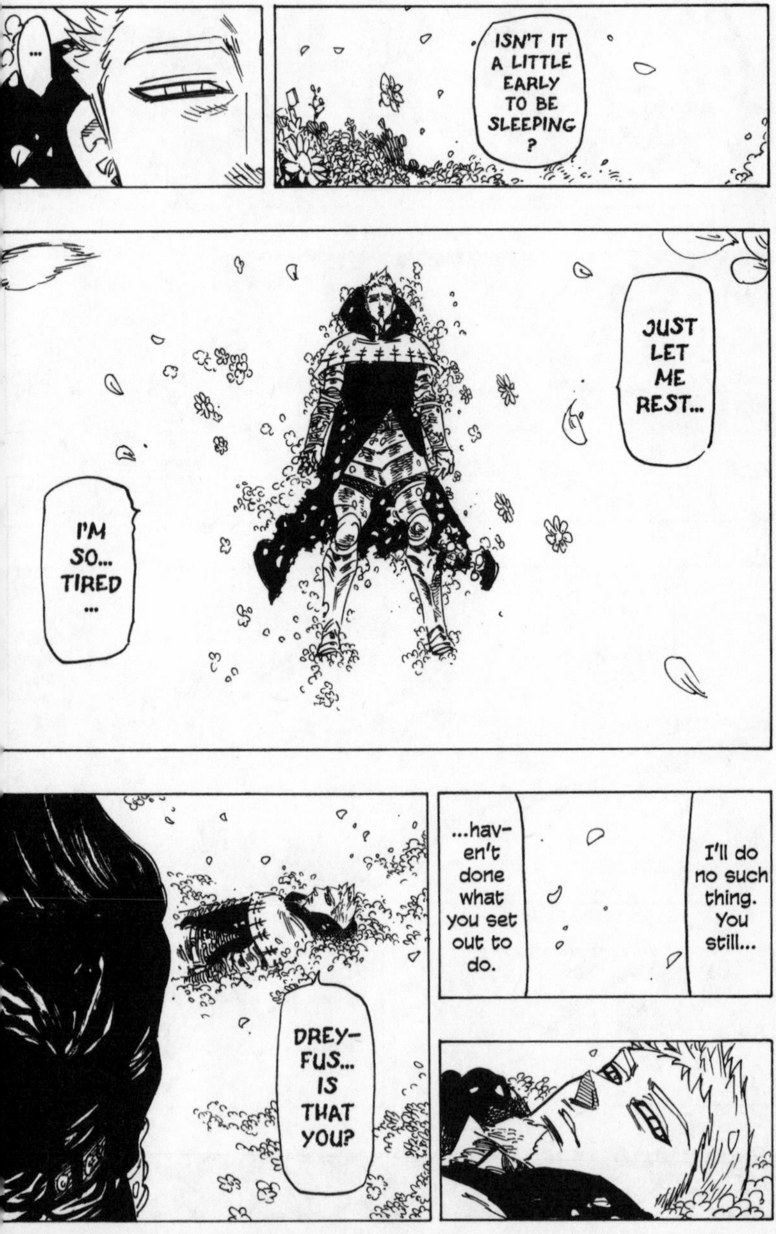
ISN'T IT A LITTLE EARLY TO BE SLEEPING?
...
JUST LET ME REST...
I'M SO... TIRED...
I'll do no such thing. You still...
...hav-en't done what you set out to do.
DREY-FUS... IS THAT YOU?

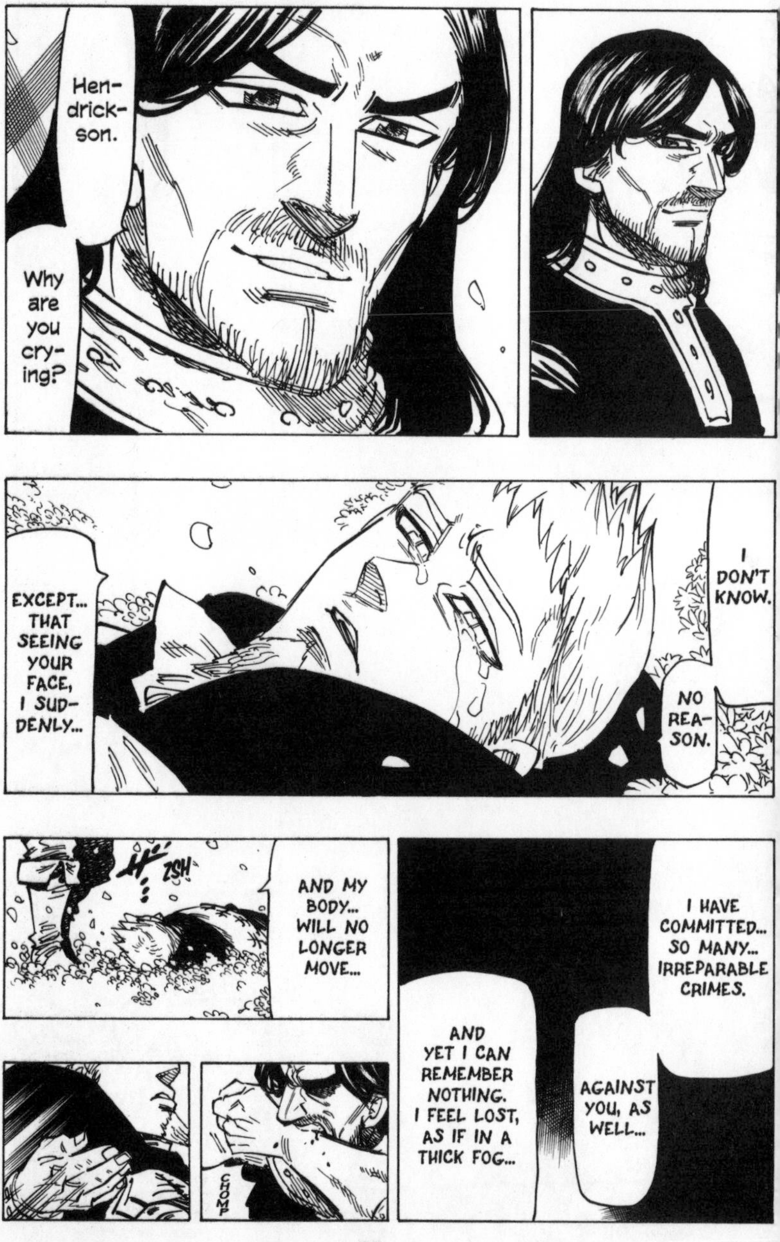
Hendrickson.
Why are you crying?
I DON'T KNOW.
NO REASON.
EXCEPT... THAT SEEING YOUR FACE, I SUDDENLY...
I HAVE COMMITTED... SO MANY... IRREPARABLE CRIMES.
AGAINST YOU, AS WELL...
AND YET I CAN REMEMBER NOTHING. I FEEL LOST, AS IF IN A THICK FOG...
ZSH
AND MY BODY... WILL NO LONGER MOVE...
CHOMP

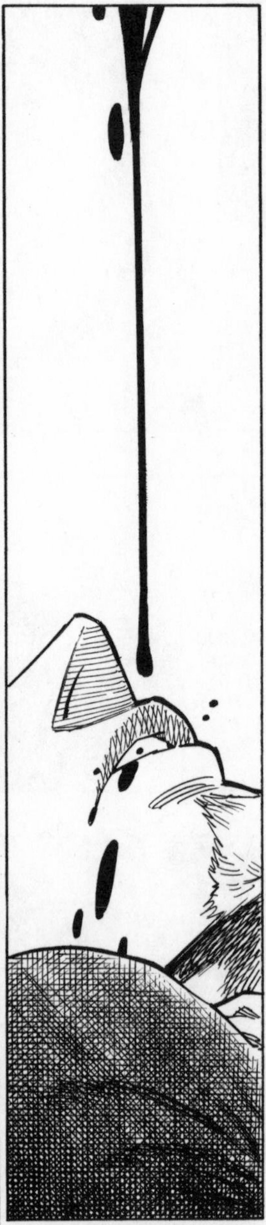
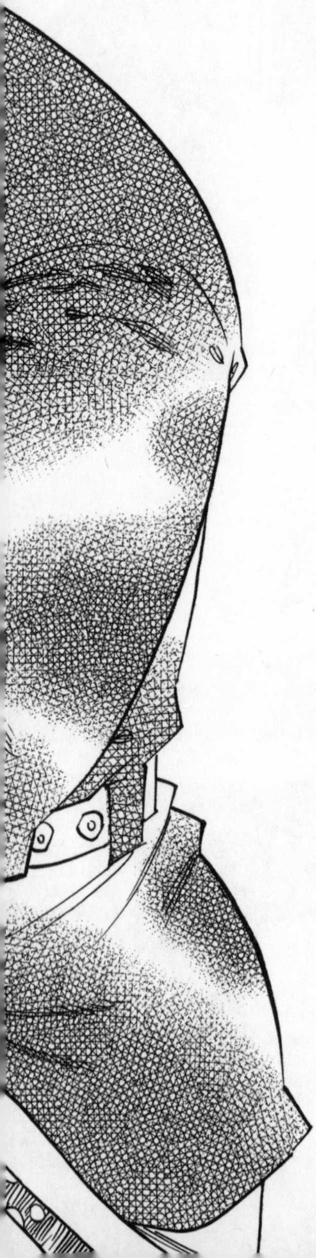

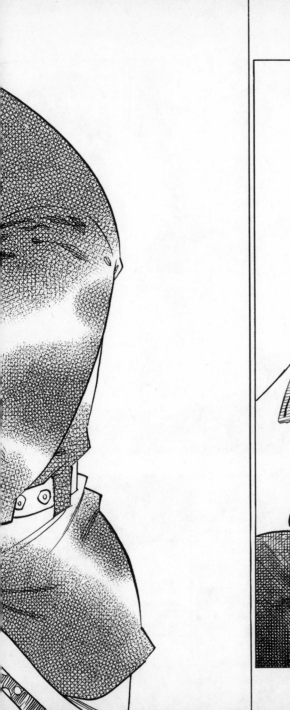

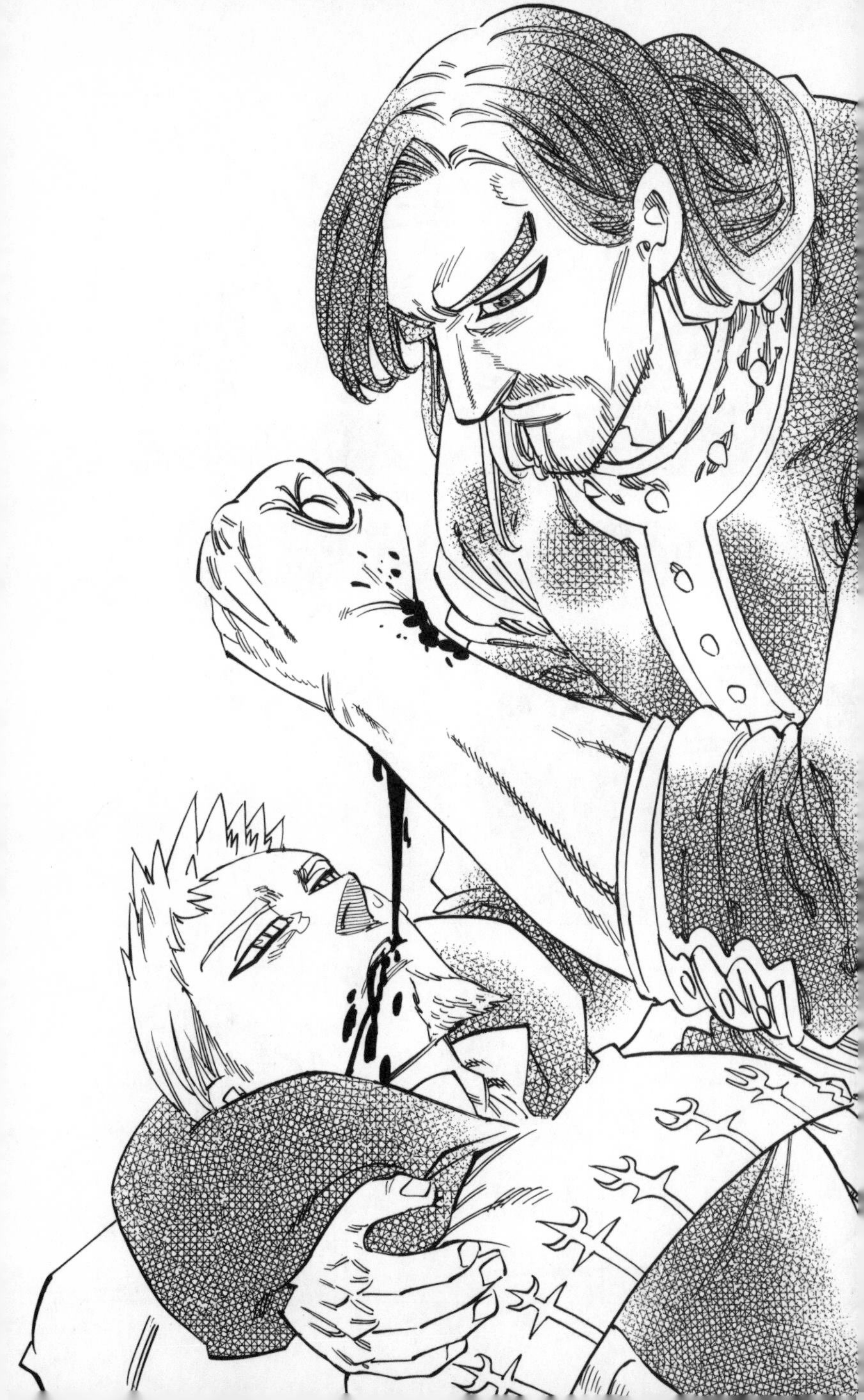

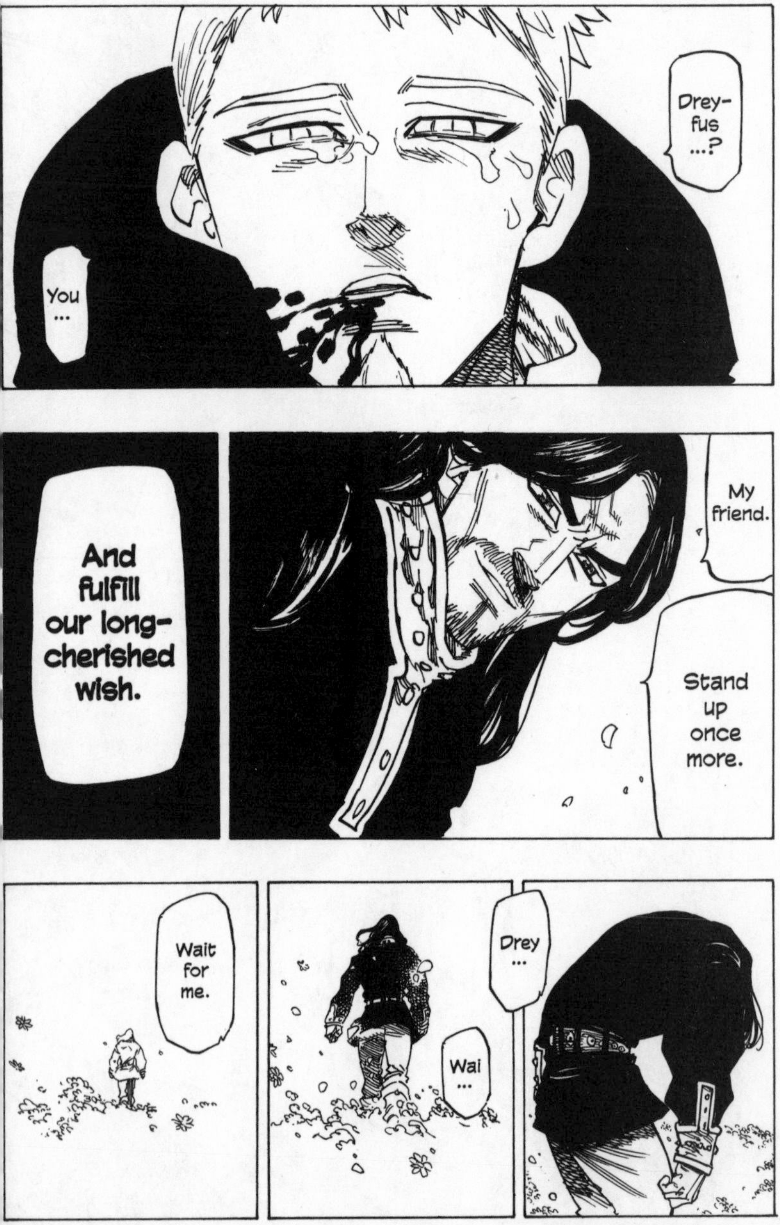
Drey-fus ...?
You ...
My friend.
Stand up once more.
And fulfill our long-cherished wish.
Drey ...
Wai ...
Wait for me.

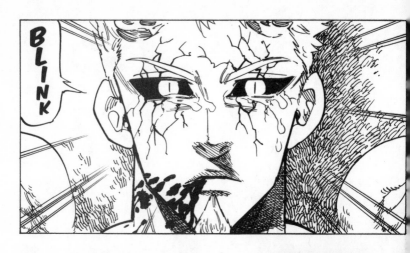

BLINK
I didn't know... I could dream.
RUB
Tears ?
Were those vestiges of my human memories?
...?
My arm's back ...
This is...
BAM

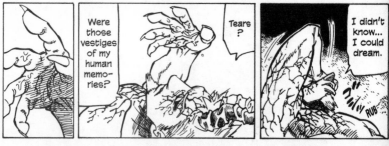

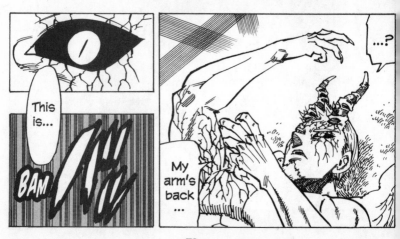

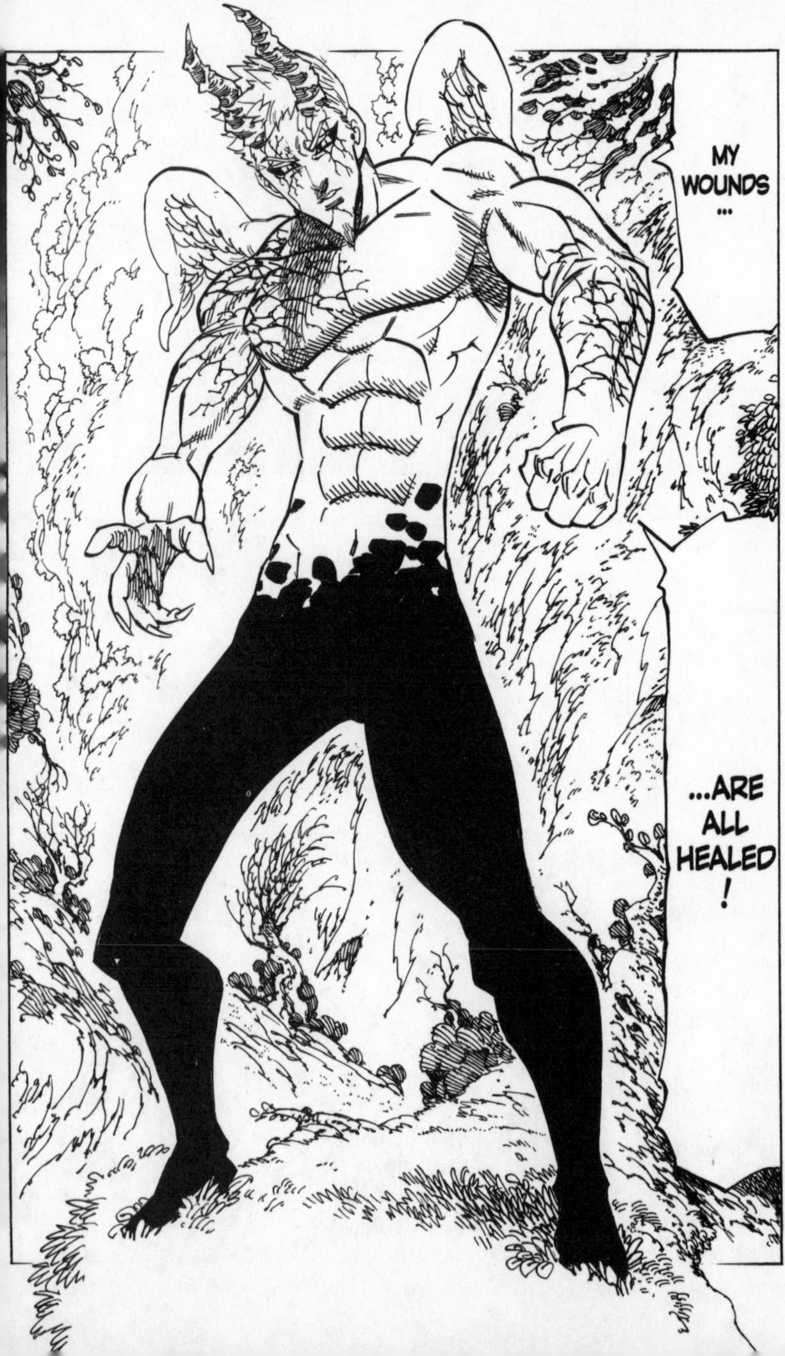
MY WOUNDS ...
...ARE ALL HEALED!

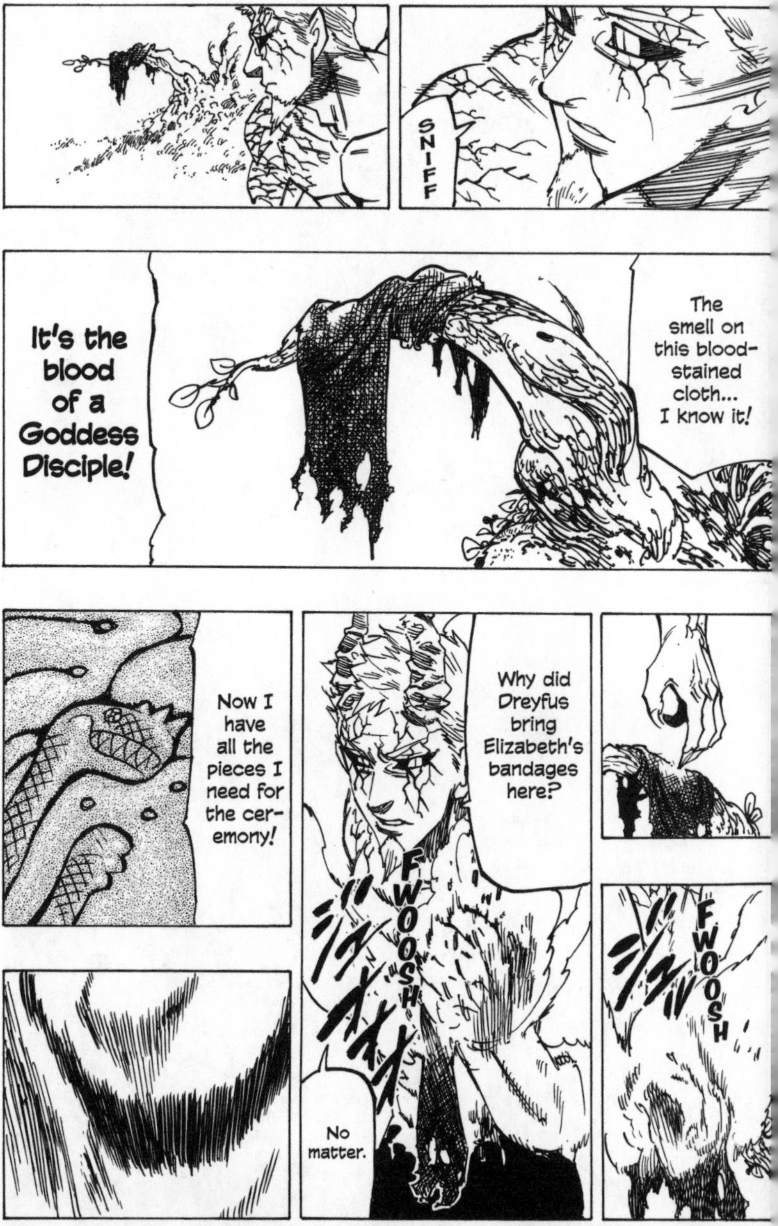
SNIFF
The smell on this blood-stained cloth... I know it!
It's the blood of a Goddess Disciple!
FWOOSH
Why did Dreyfus bring Elizabeth's bandages here?
FWOOSH
No matter.
Now I have all the pieces I need for the ceremony!

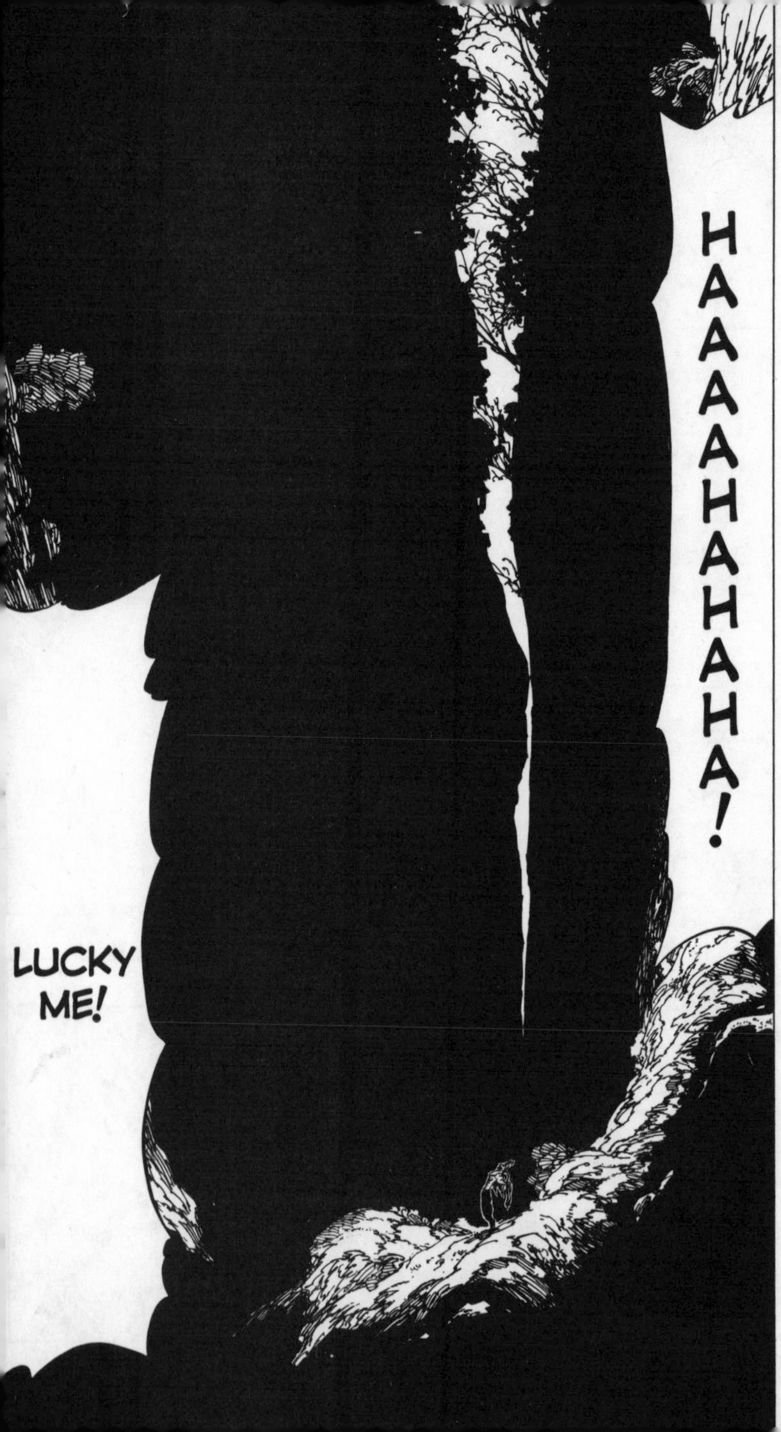
HAAAAHAHAHA!
LUCKY ME!

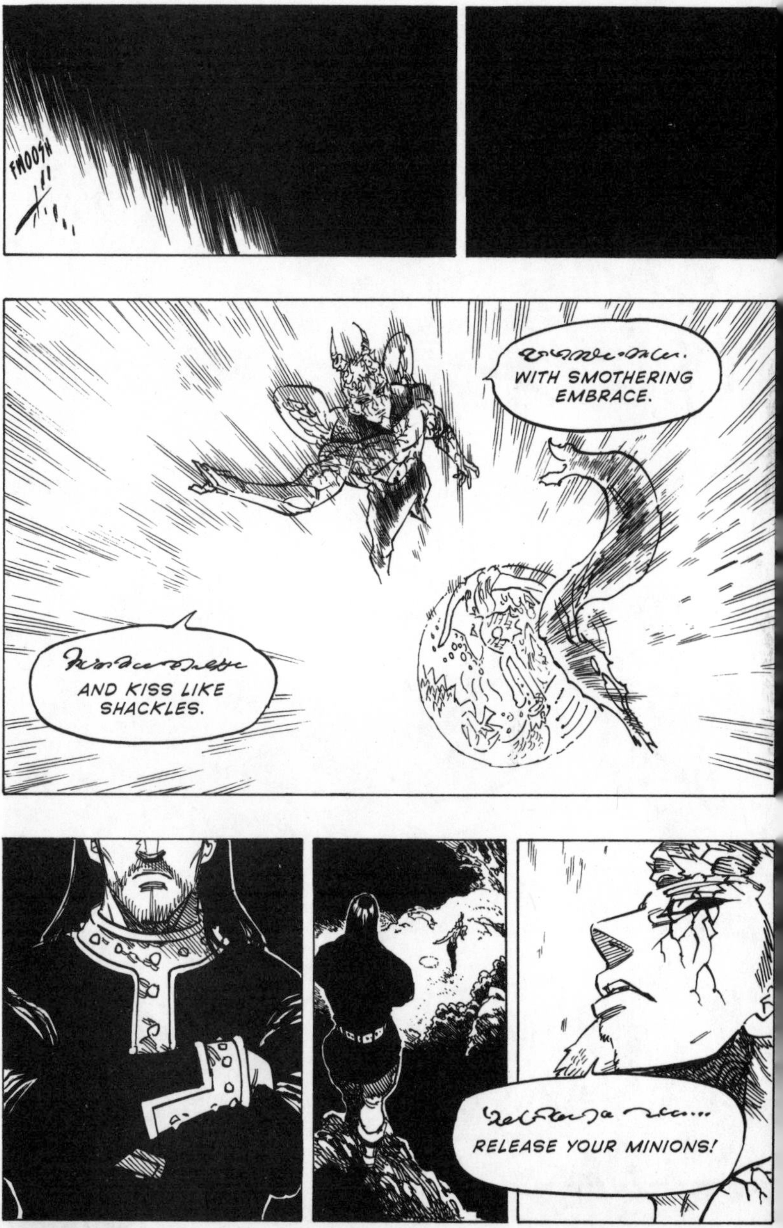
FWOOSH
WITH SMOTHERING EMBRACE.
AND KISS LIKE SHACKLES.
RELEASE YOUR MINIONS!

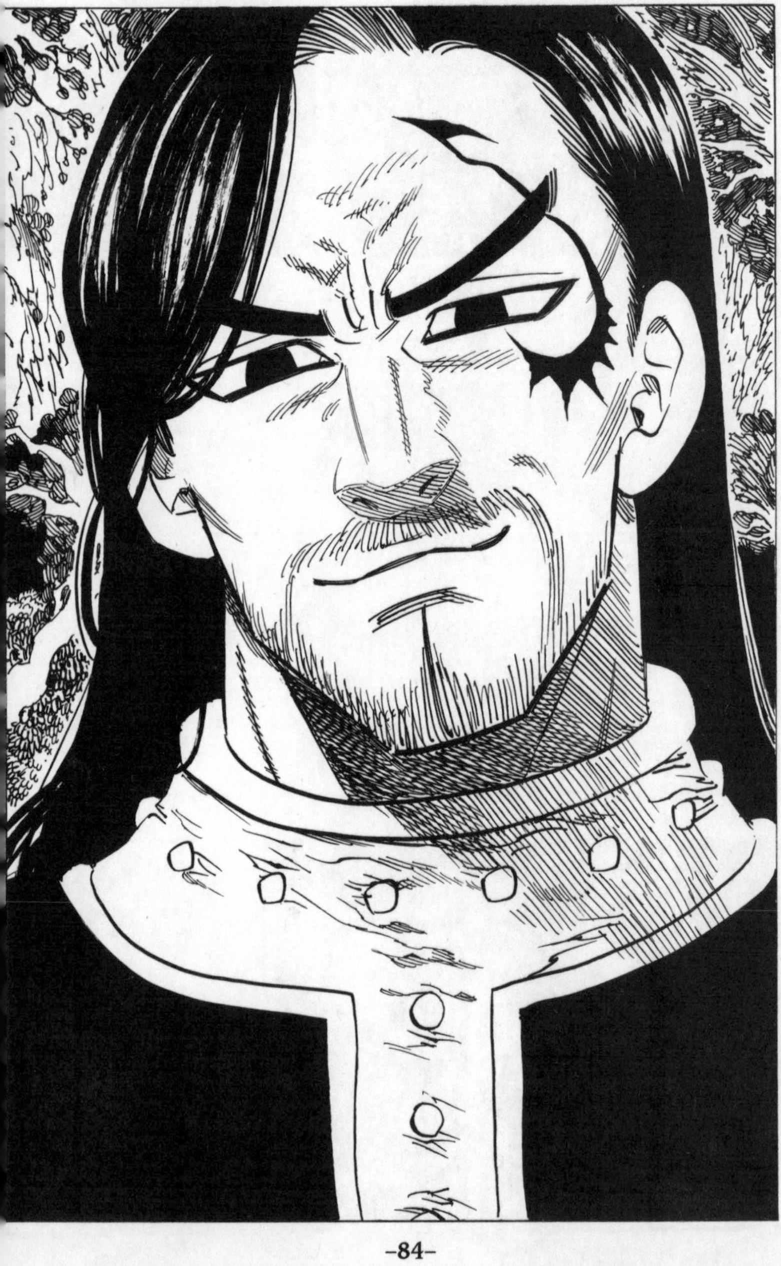

Chapter 109 - Earthquake

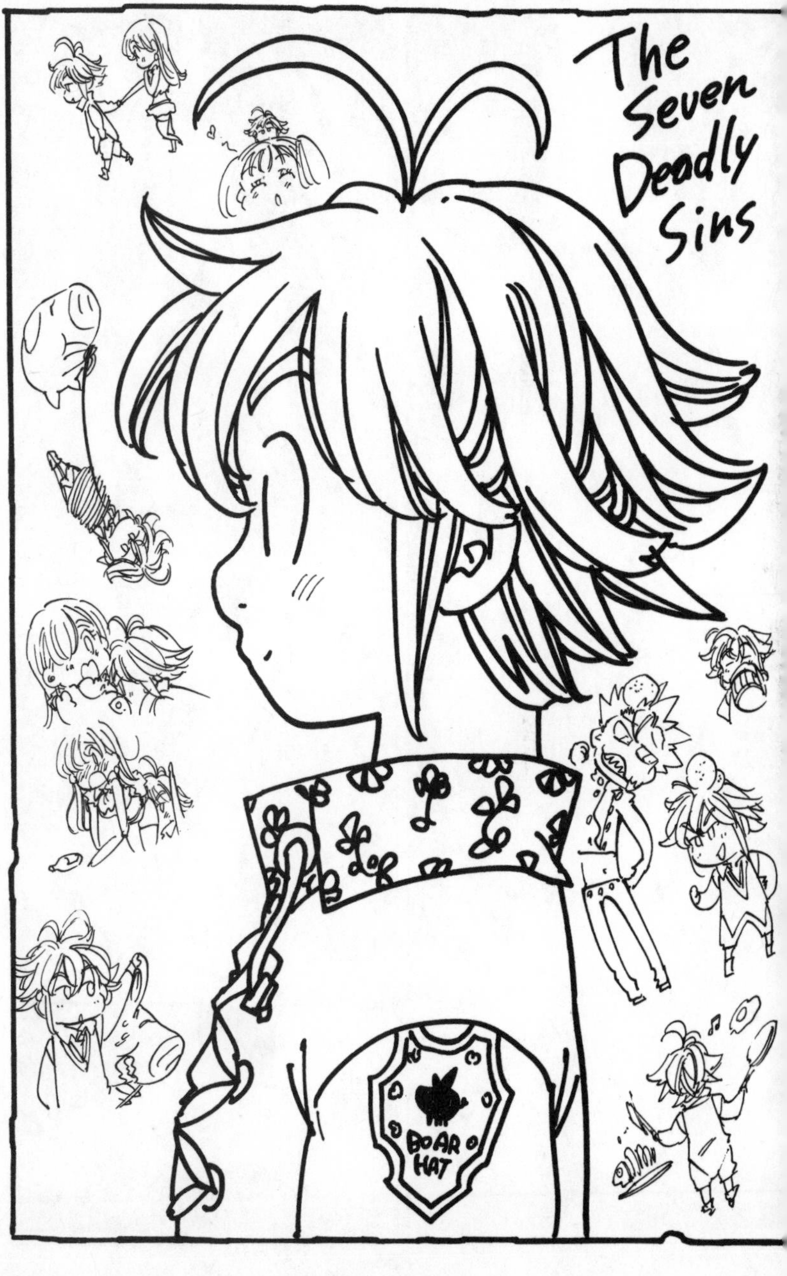
The Seven Deadly Sins
BOAR HAT

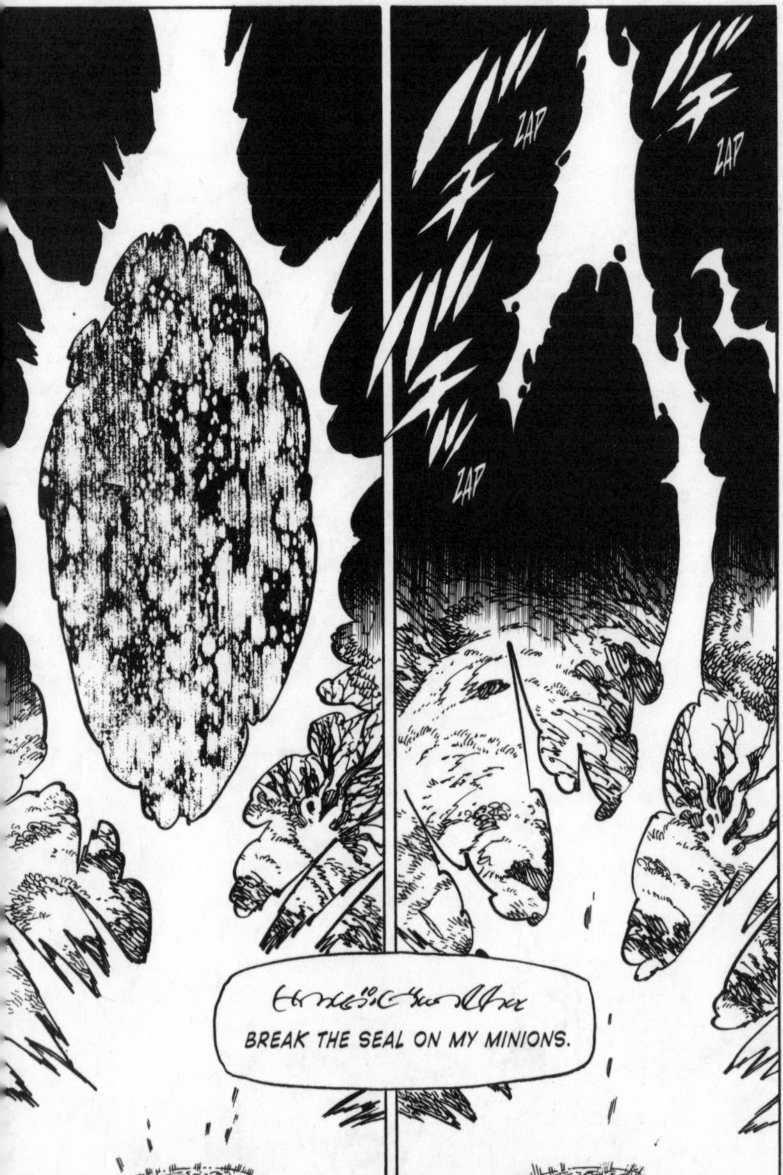
ZAP
ZAP
ZAP
BREAK THE SEAL ON MY MINIONS.

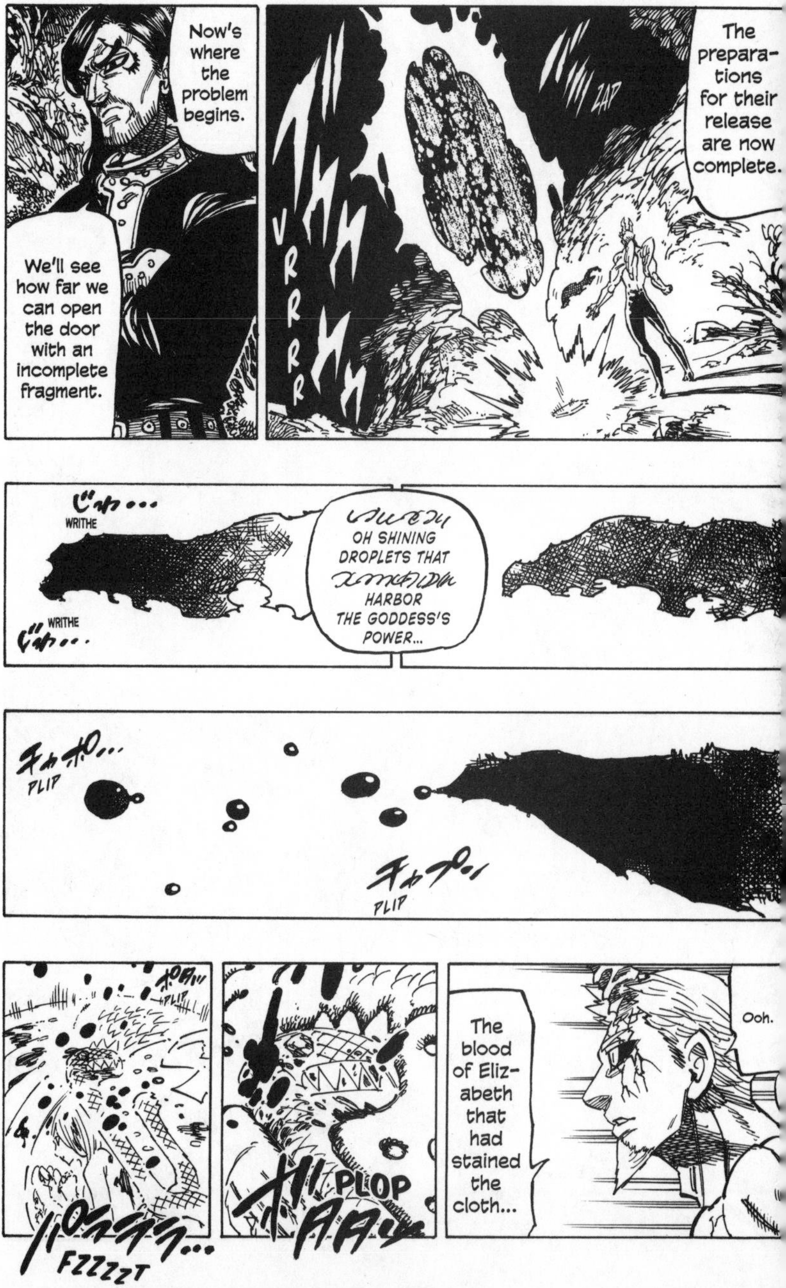
The preparations for their release are now complete.
ZAP
VRRRR
Now's where the problem begins.
We'll see how far we can open the door with an incomplete fragment.
WRITHE
WRITHE
OH SHINING DROPLETS THAT HARBOR THE GODDESS'S POWER...
PLIP
PLIP
Ooh.
The blood of Elizabeth that had stained the cloth...
PLOP
PLIP
FZZZZT

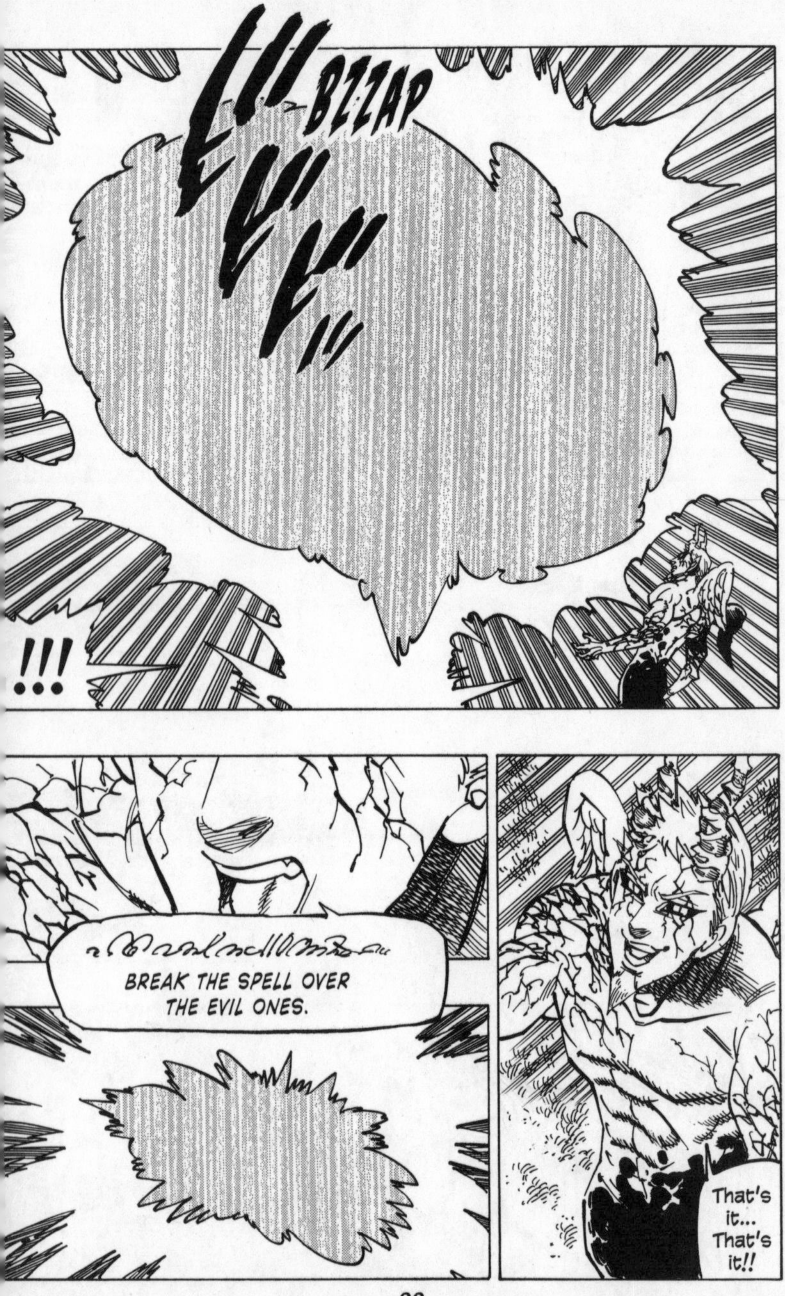
BZZAP
!!!
That's it... That's it!!
BREAK THE SPELL OVER THE EVIL ONES.

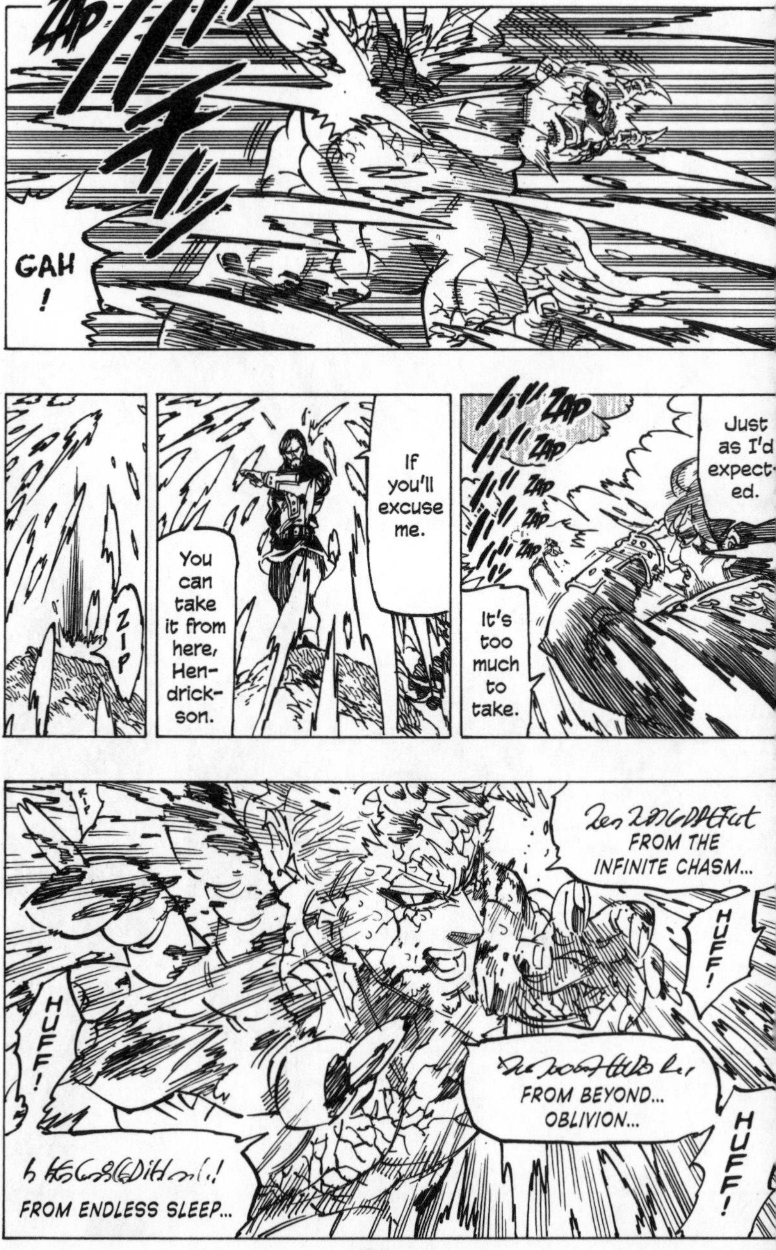
ZAP
GAH!
ZAP
ZAP
ZAP
ZAP
ZAP
Just as I'd expect-ed.
It's too much to take.
If you'll excuse me.
You can take it from here, Hen-drick-son.
ZIP
FROM THE INFINITE CHASM...
HUFF!
HUFF!
FROM BEYOND... OBLIVION...
RIP
HUFF!
FROM ENDLESS SLEEP...

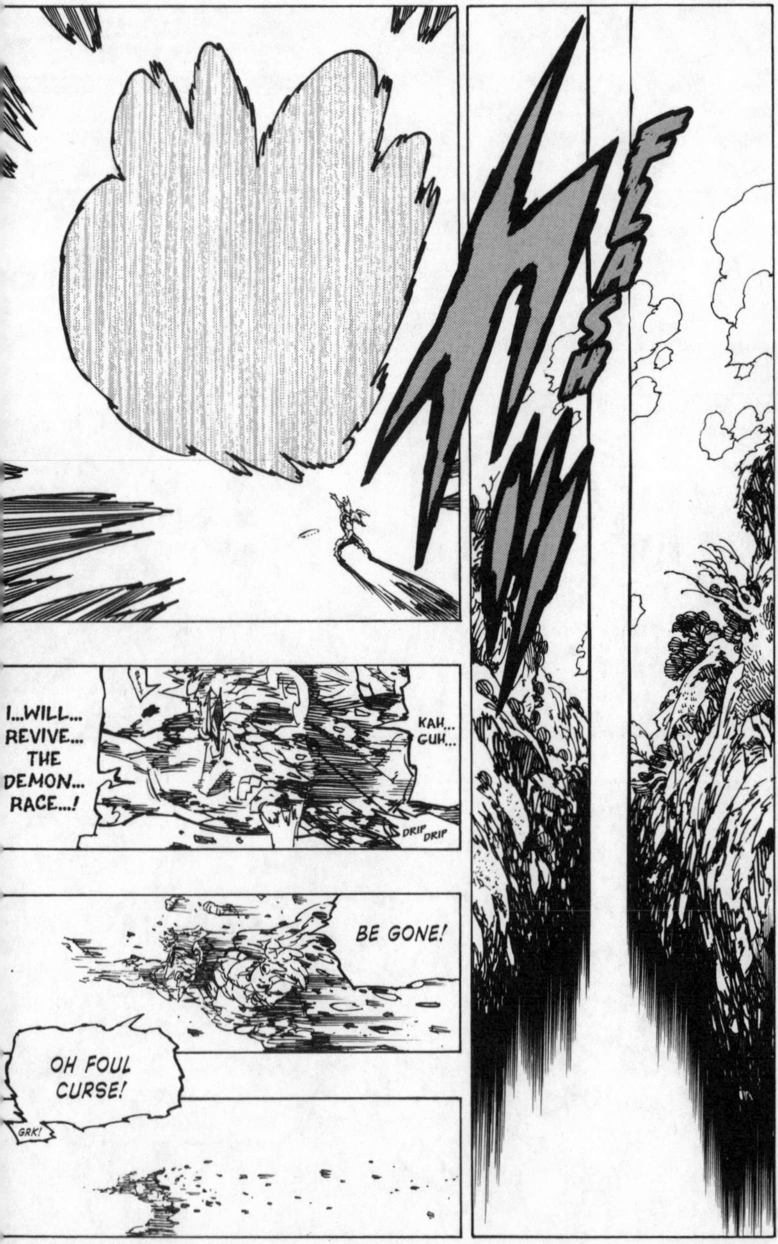
FLASH
KAH... GUH...
I...WILL... REVIVE... THE DEMON... RACE...!
DRIP DRIP
BE GONE!
OH FOUL CURSE!
GRK!

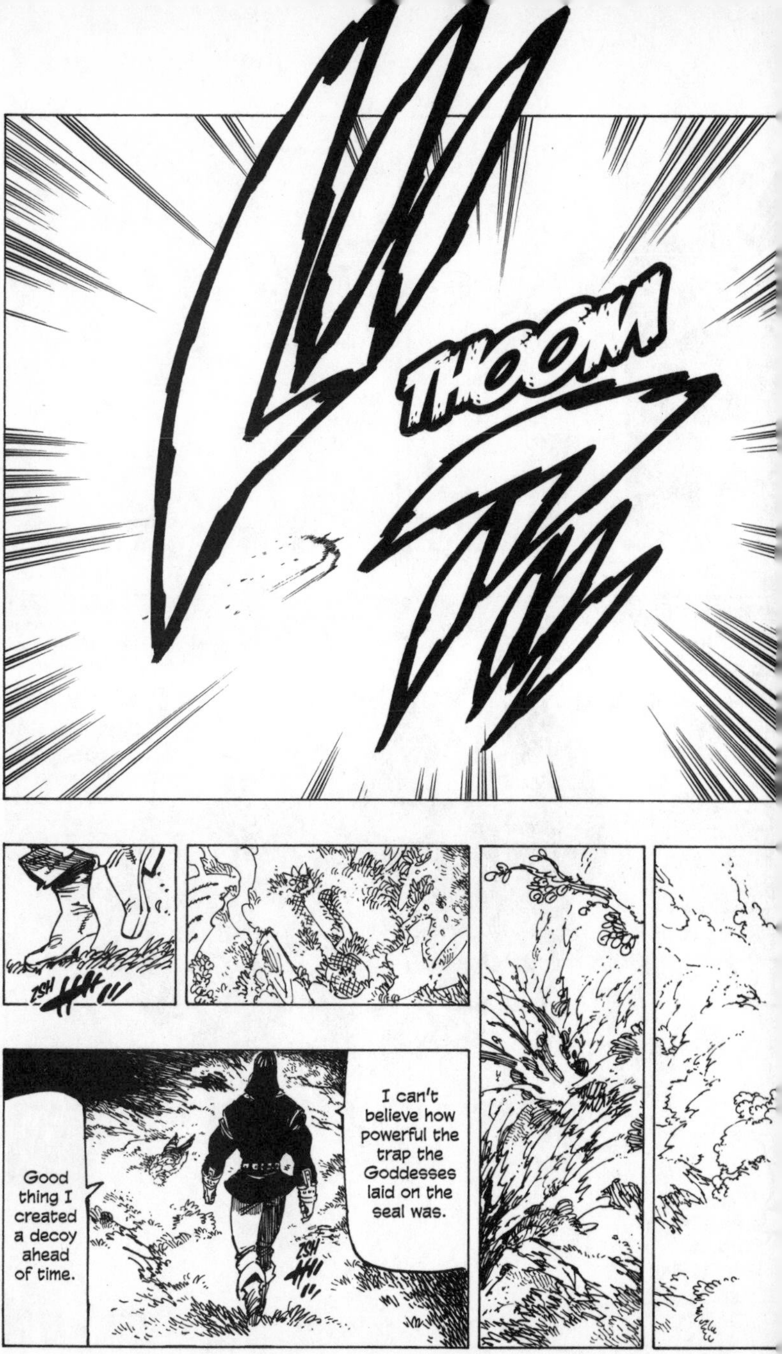
THOOM
ZSH
I can't believe how powerful the trap the Goddesses laid on the seal was.
Good thing I created a decoy ahead of time.
ZSH

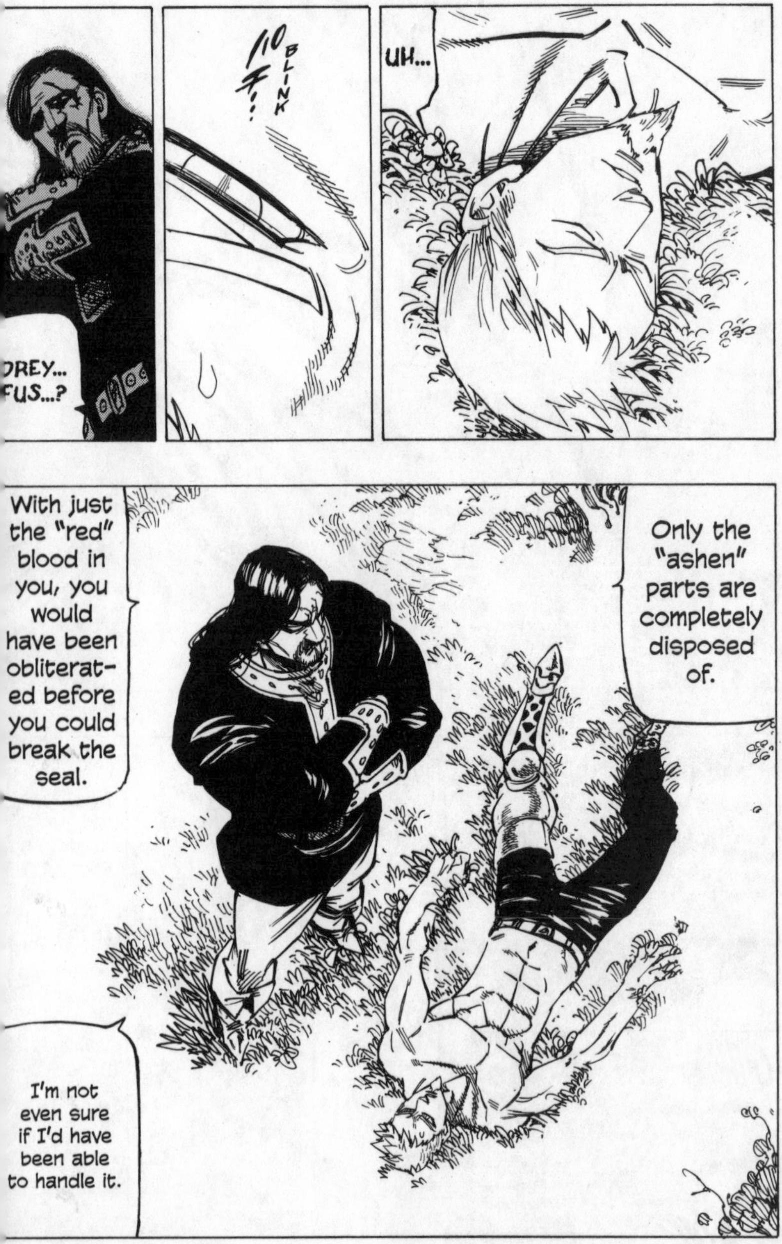
UH...
BLINK
DREY... FUS...?
Only the "ashen" parts are completely disposed of.
With just the "red" blood in you, you would have been obliterat-ed before you could break the seal.
I'm not even sure if I'd have been able to handle it.

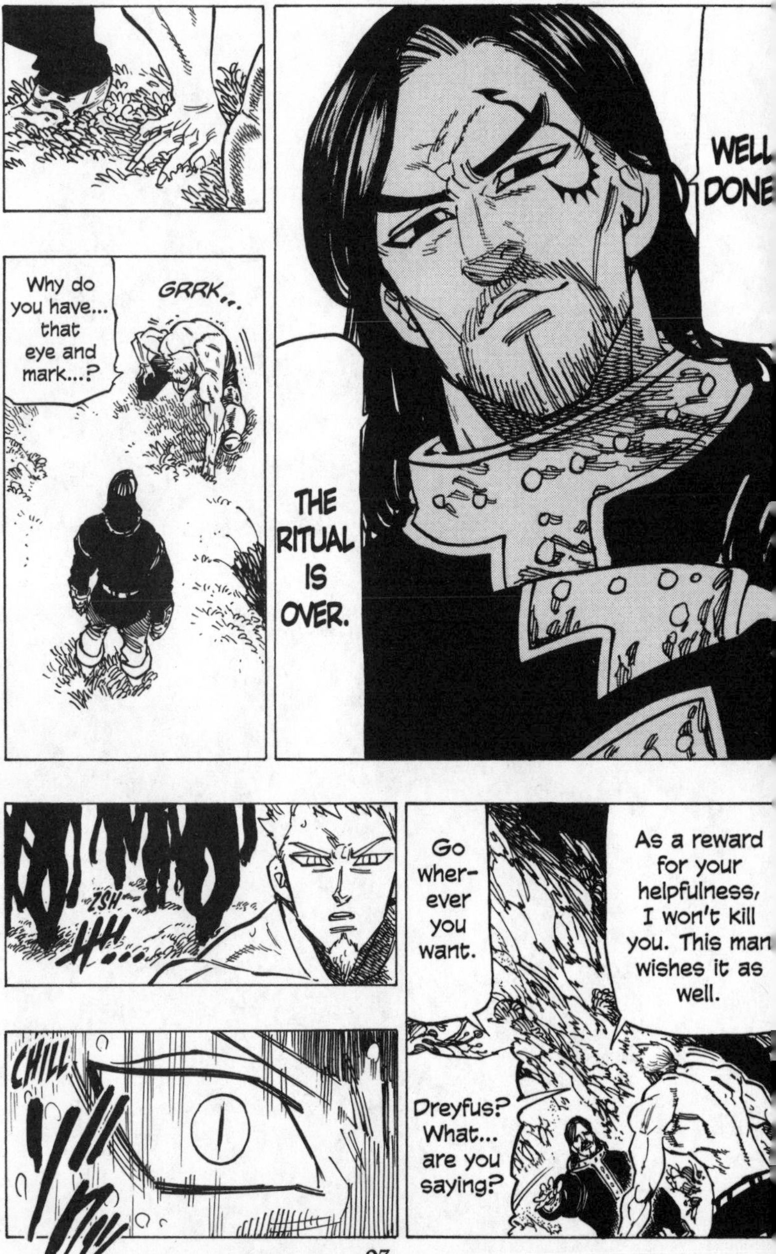
WELL DONE
THE RITUAL IS OVER.
GRRK...
Why do you have... that eye and mark...?
As a reward for your helpfulness, I won't kill you. This man wishes it as well.
Go wher-ever you want.
Dreyfus? What... are you saying?
ZSH...
CHILL

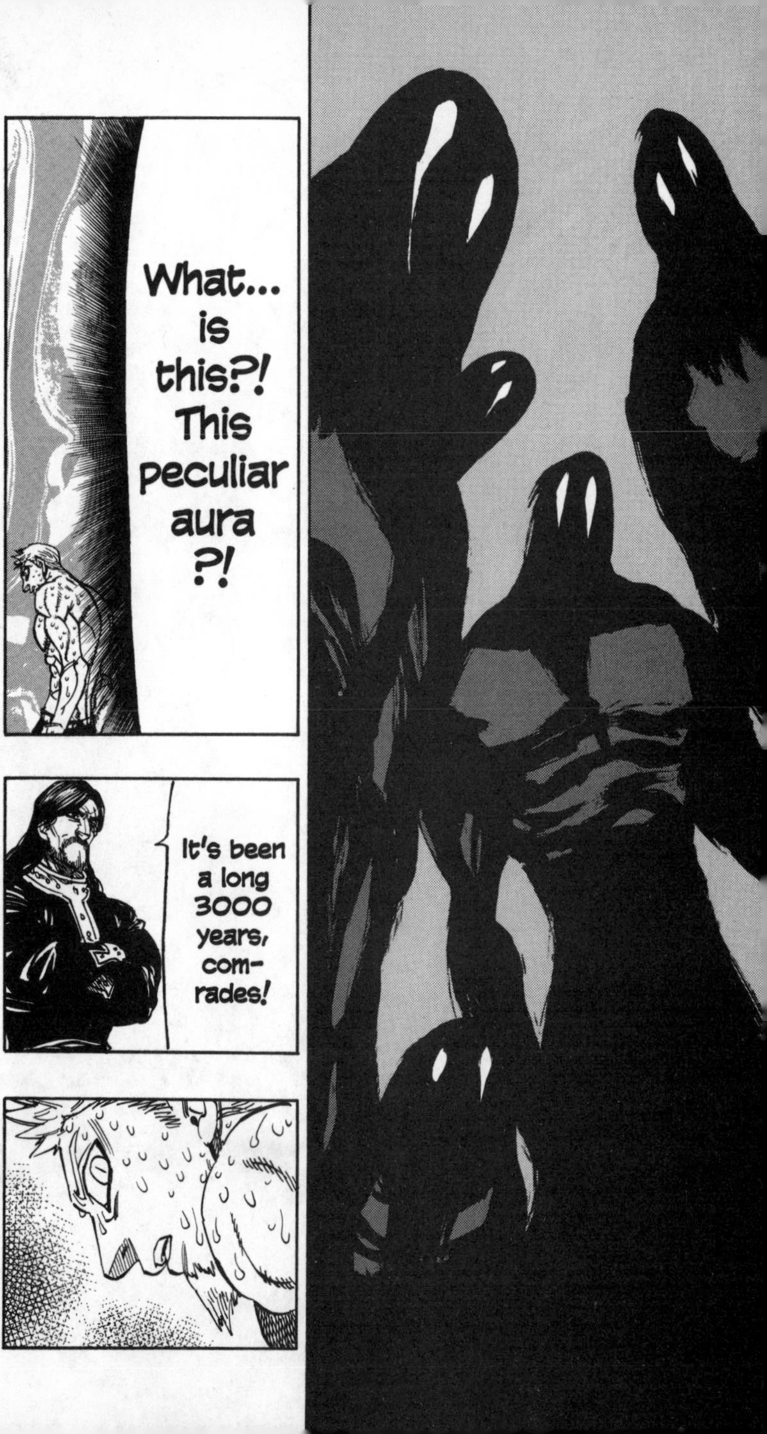
What... is this?! This peculiar aura?!
It's been a long 3000 years, comrades!

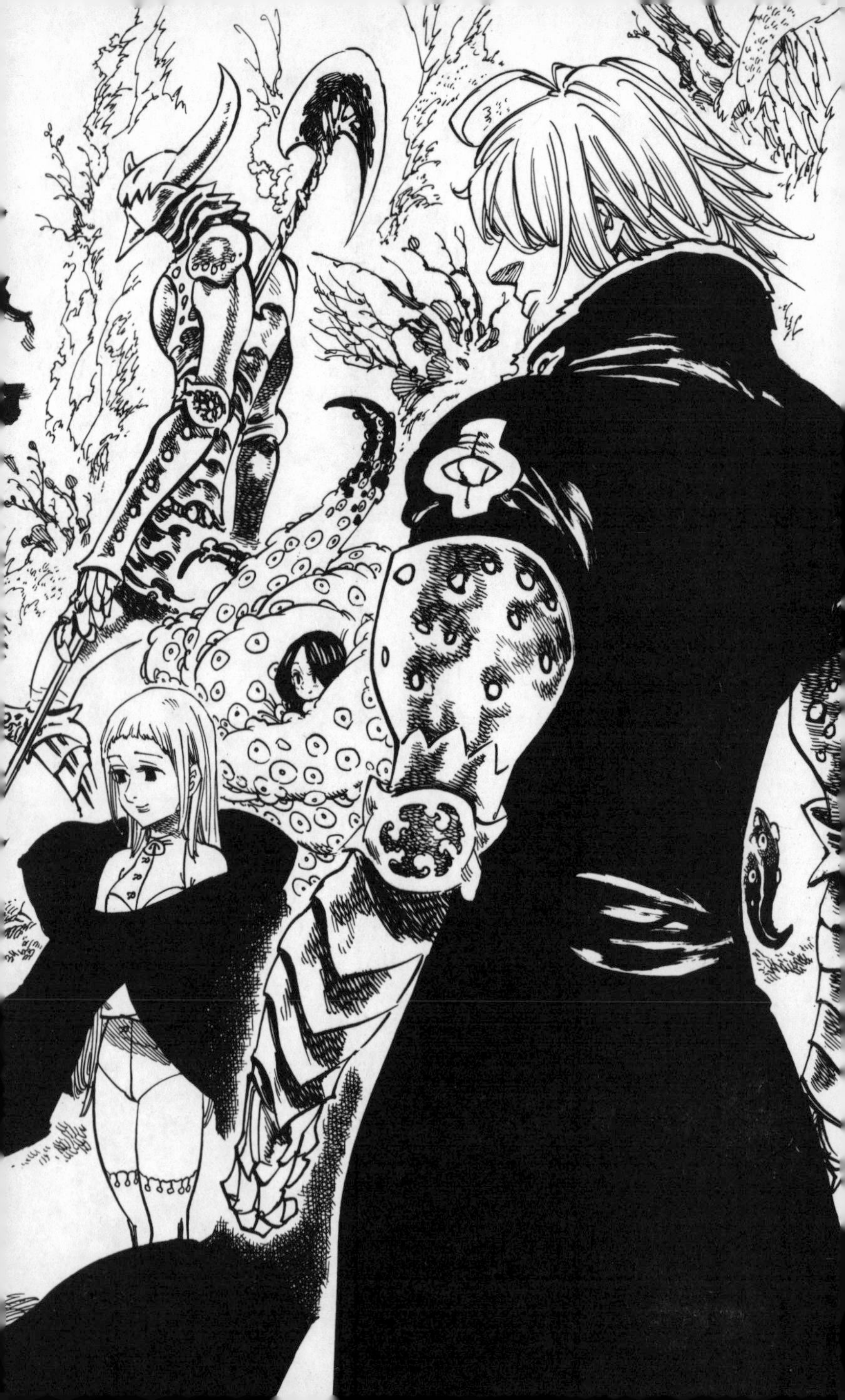

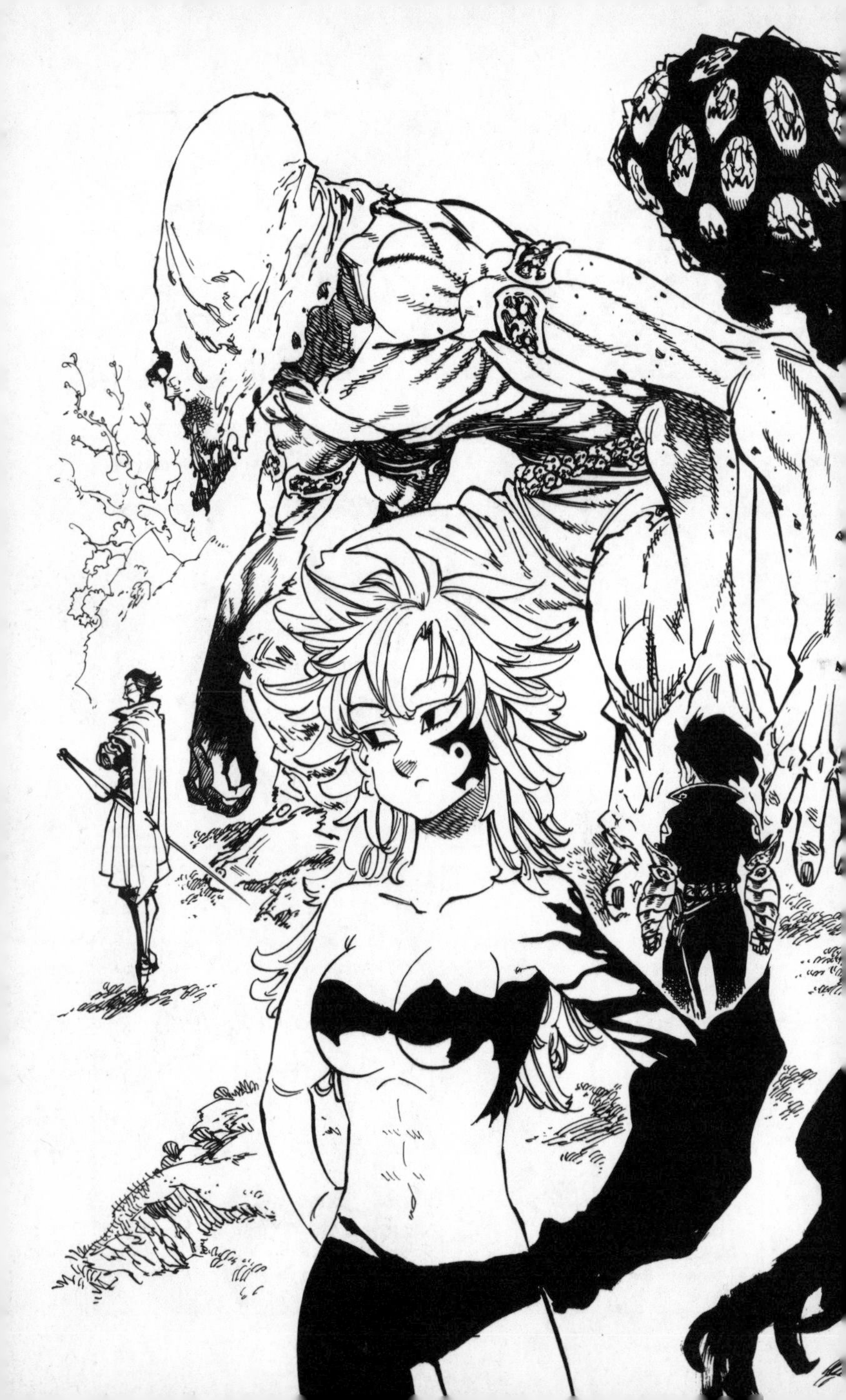

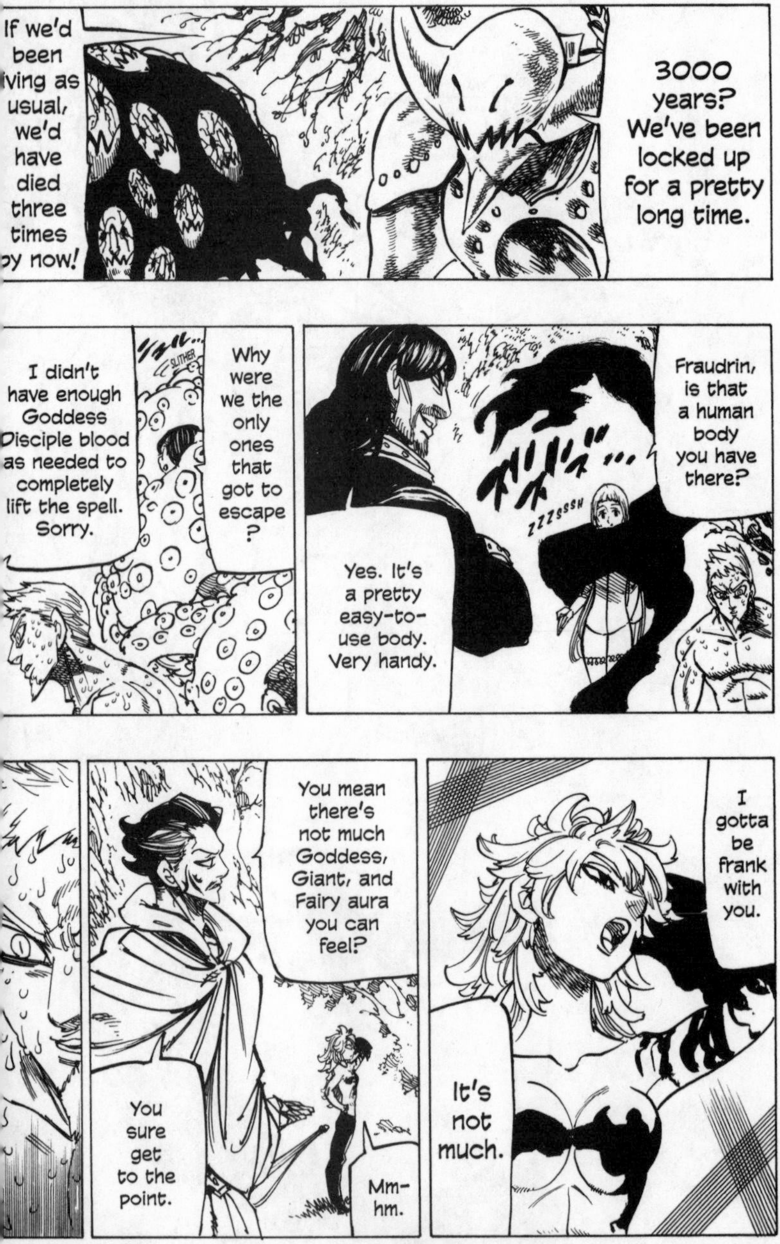
3000 years? We've been locked up for a pretty long time.
If we'd been ving as usual, we'd have died three times y now!
Fraudrin, is that a human body you have there?
ZZZSSSH
Yes. It's a pretty easy-to-use body. Very handy.
Why were we the only ones that got to escape?
SLITHER
I didn't have enough Goddess Disciple blood as needed to completely lift the spell. Sorry.
I gotta be frank with you.
It's not much.
You mean there's not much Goddess, Giant, and Fairy aura you can feel?
Mm-hm.
You sure get to the point.

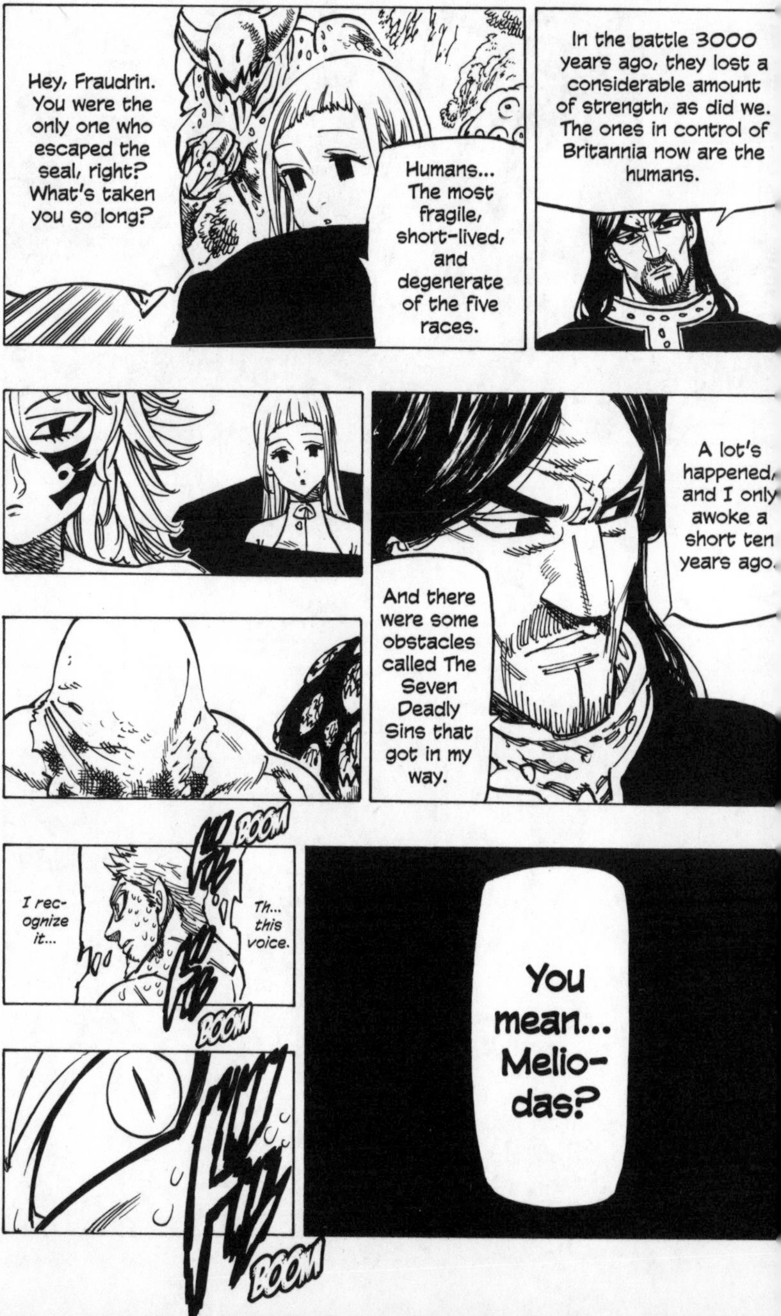
Hey, Fraudrin. You were the only one who escaped the seal, right? What's taken you so long?
Humans... The most fragile, short-lived, and degenerate of the five races.
In the battle 3000 years ago, they lost a considerable amount of strength, as did we. The ones in control of Britannia now are the humans.
A lot's happened, and I only awoke a short ten years ago.
And there were some obstacles called The Seven Deadly Sins that got in my way.
BOOM
You mean... Melio-das?
Th... this voice.
I rec-ognize it...
BOOM
BOOM

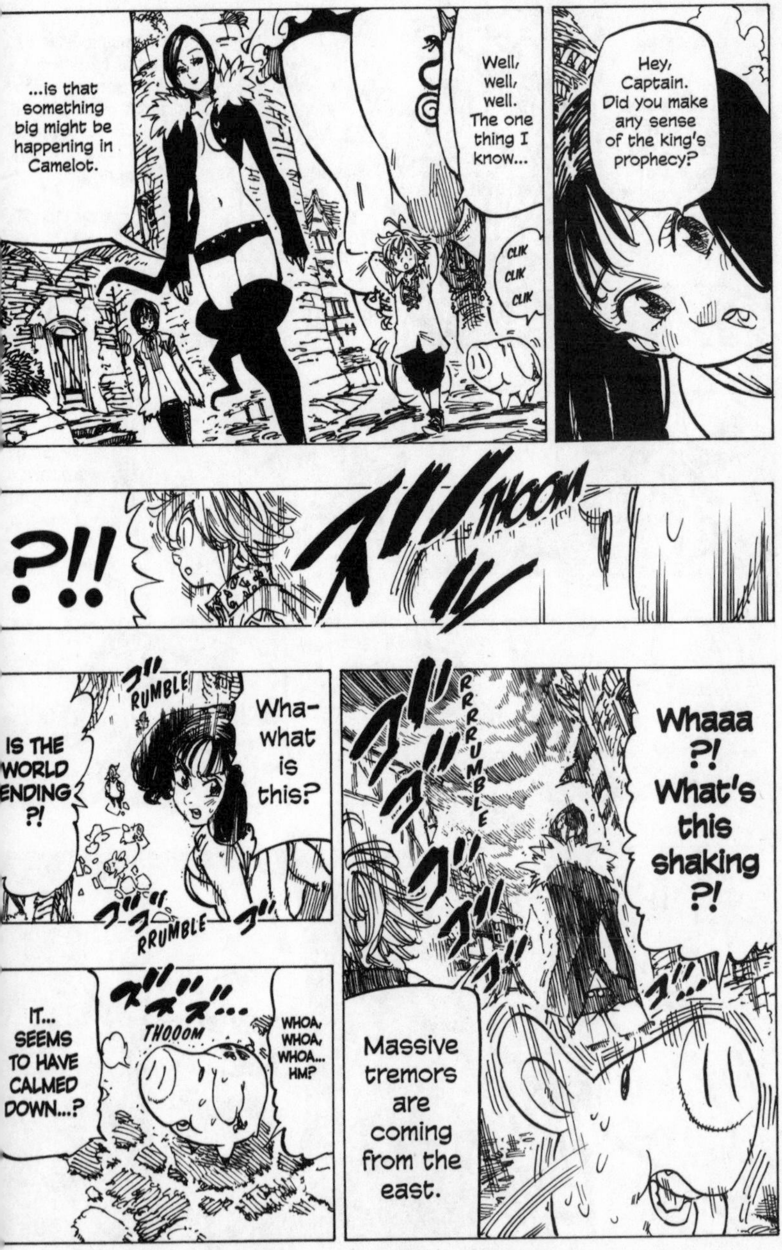

Hey, Captain. Did you make any sense of the king's prophecy?
Well, well, well. The one thing I know...
CLIK CLIK CLIK
...is that something big might be happening in Camelot.
THOOM
?!!
RRRRUMBLE
Whaaa ?! What's this shaking ?!
RUMBLE
Wha- what is this?
IS THE WORLD ENDING ?!
RRUMBLE
THOOOM
WHOA, WHOA, WHOA... HM?
IT... SEEMS TO HAVE CALMED DOWN...?
Massive tremors are coming from the east.

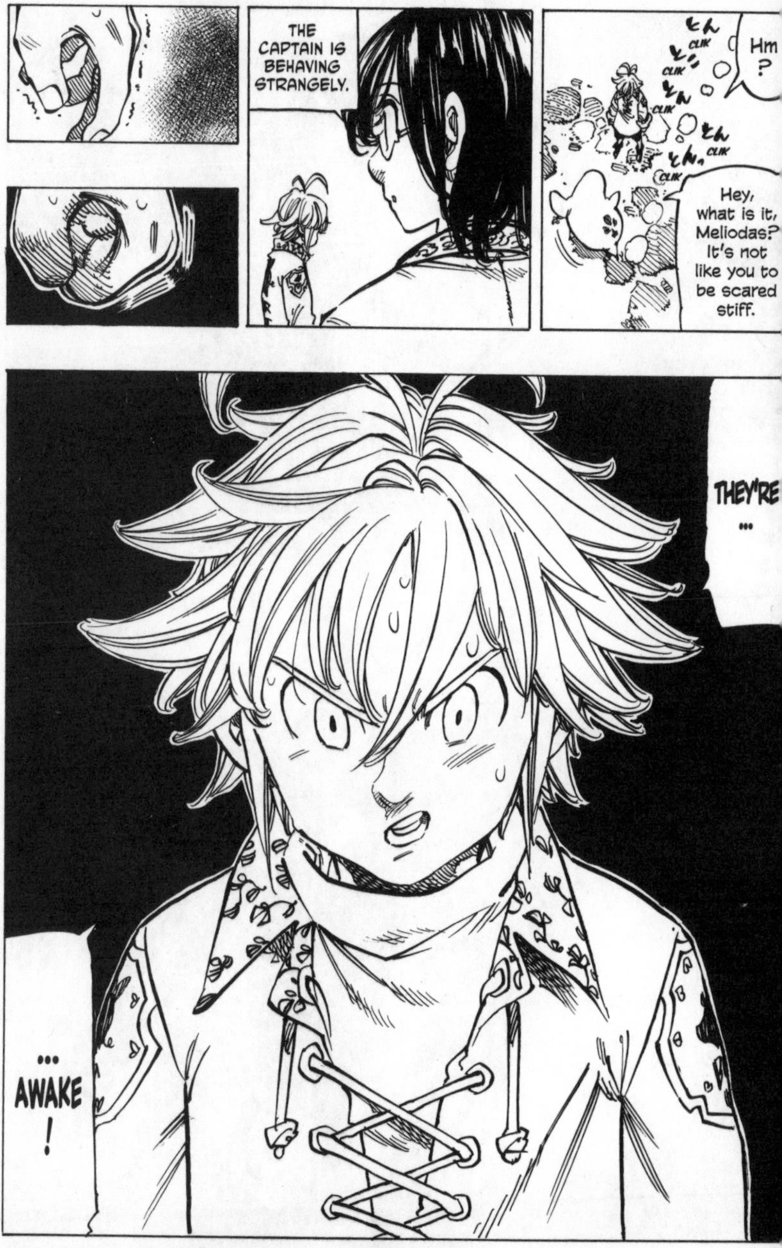
Hm?
とん CLIK
とん CLIK
とん CLIK
とん CLIK
とん CLIK
Hey, what is it, Meliodas? It's not like you to be scared stiff.
THE CAPTAIN IS BEHAVING STRANGELY.
THEY'RE...
...AWAKE!

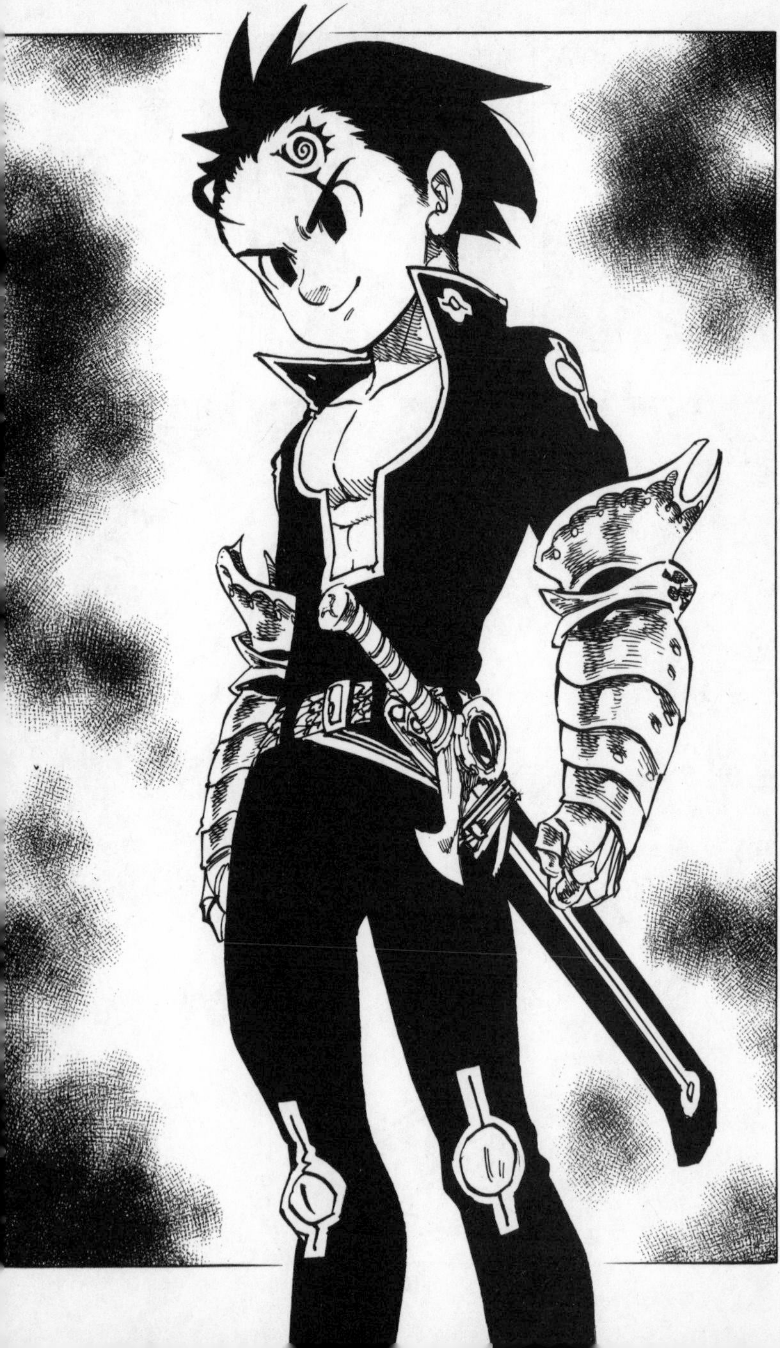

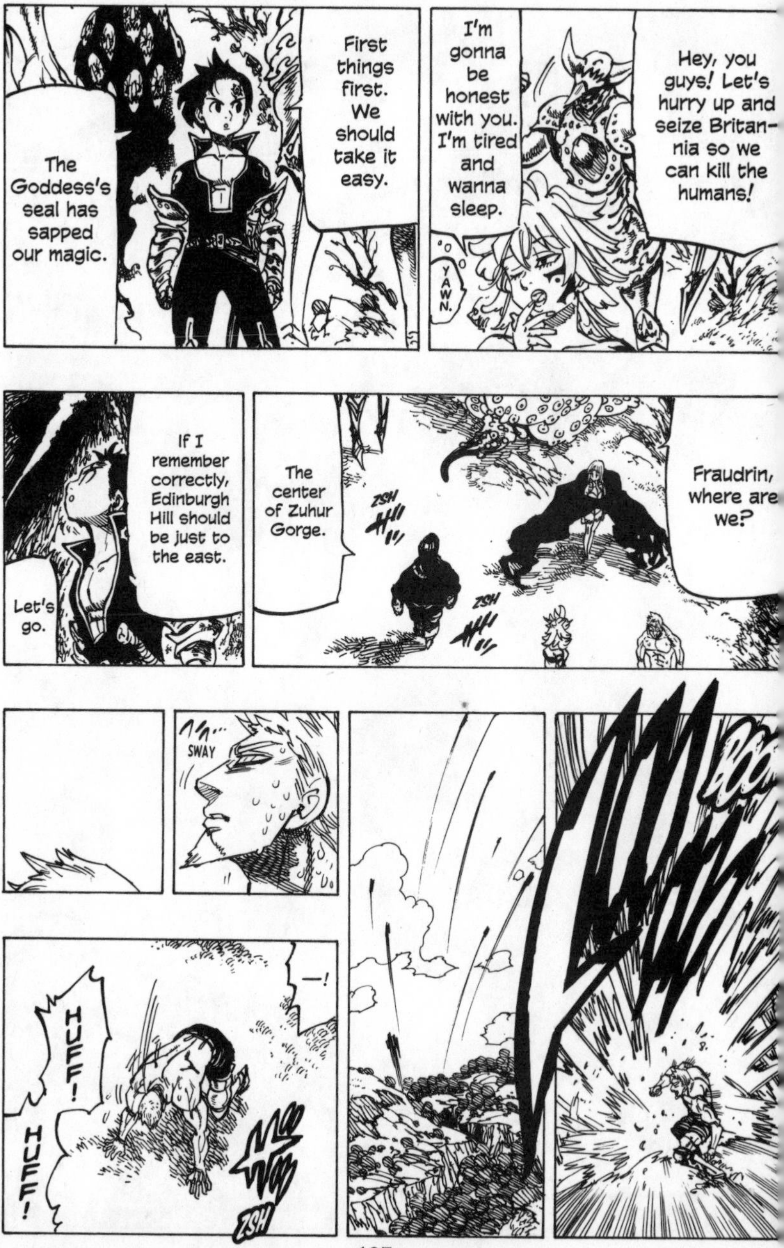

Hey, you guys! Let's hurry up and seize Britannia so we can kill the humans!
I'm gonna be honest with you. I'm tired and wanna sleep.
YAWN.
First things first. We should take it easy.
The Goddess's seal has sapped our magic.
Fraudrin, where are we?
The center of Zuhur Gorge.
ZSH
ZSH
If I remember correctly, Edinburgh Hill should be just to the east.
Let's go.
SWAY
—!
HUFF! HUFF!
ZSH

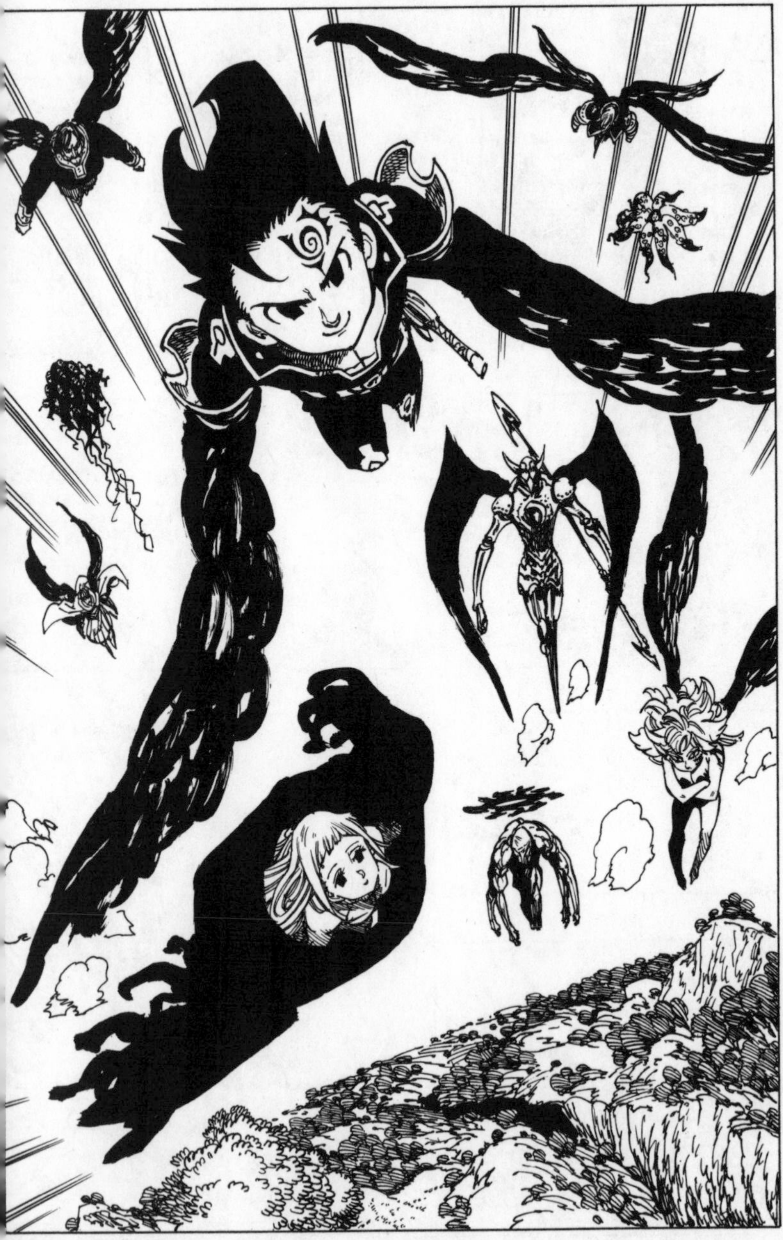

Chapter 110 - Confession

To my precious dear,

How are you doing? Let's go out for delicious food scraps soon. I'm sorry. I have hooves for hands, so I can't write very well

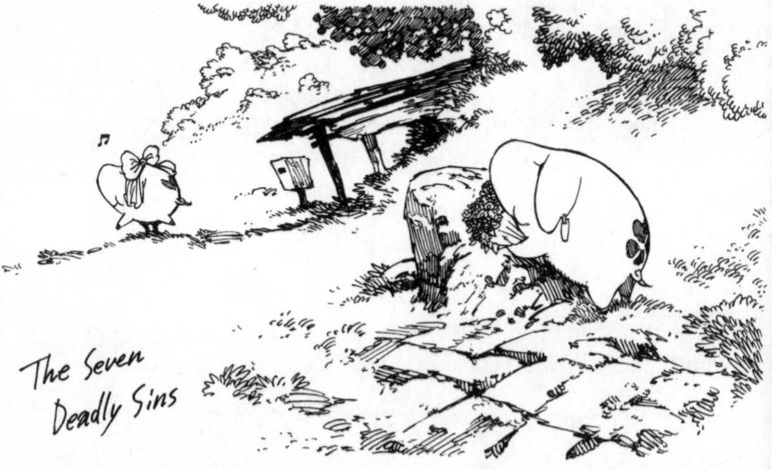
The Seven Deadly Sins

Love, The Strongest Man, Hawk

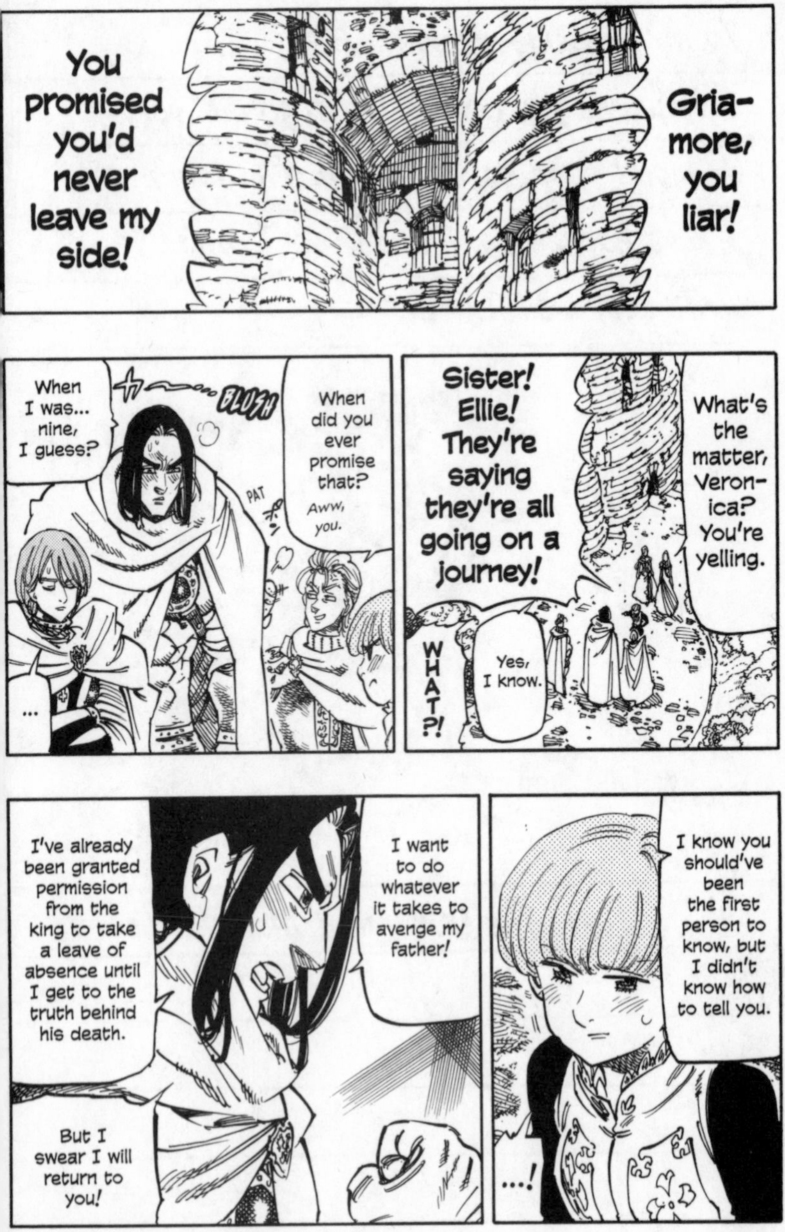
Gria-more, you liar!
You promised you'd never leave my side!
What's the matter, Veronica? You're yelling.
Sister! Ellie! They're saying they're all going on a journey!
Yes, I know.
WHAT?!
When did you ever promise that?
Aww, you.
PAT
BLUSH
When I was... nine, I guess?
...
I know you should've been the first person to know, but I didn't know how to tell you.
...!
I want to do whatever it takes to avenge my father!
I've already been granted permission from the king to take a leave of absence until I get to the truth behind his death.
But I swear I will return to you!

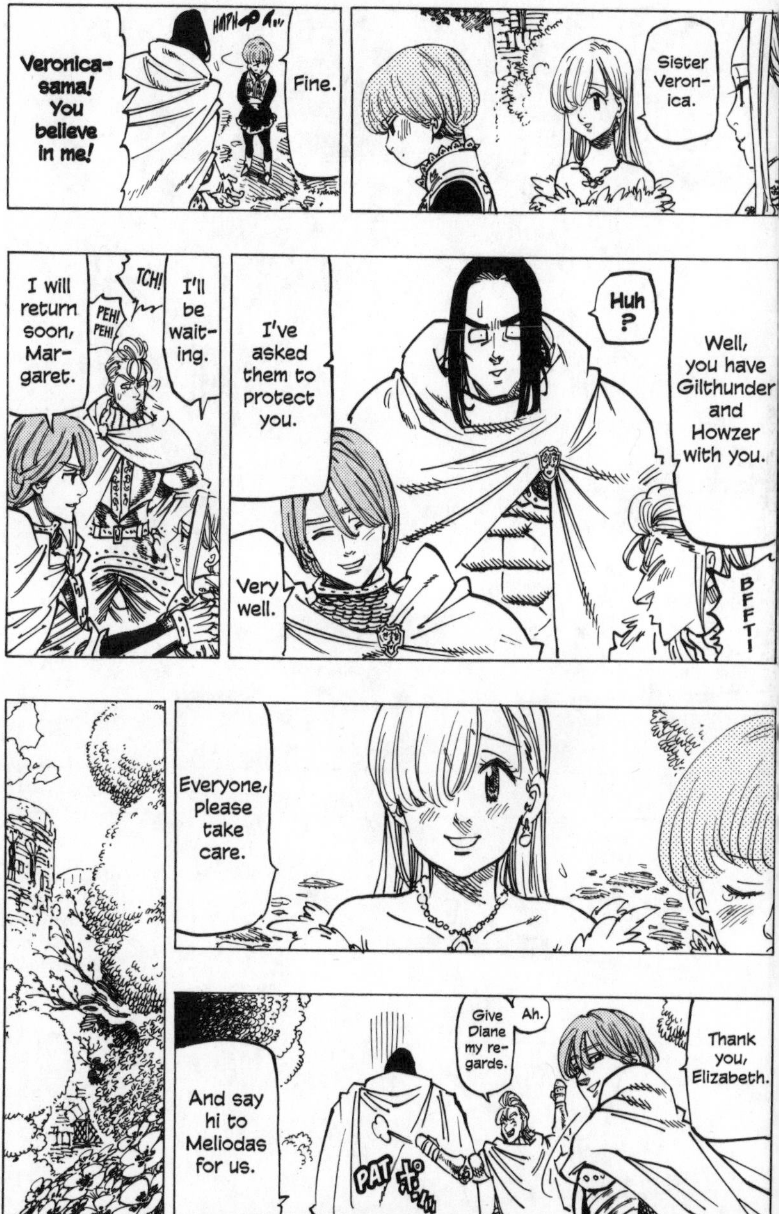
Sister Veronica.
Fine.
HMPH
Veronica-sama! You believe in me!
Well, you have Gilthunder and Howzer with you.
Huh?
BFFT!
I've asked them to protect you.
Very well.
I'll be waiting.
TCH!
PEH! PEH!
I will return soon, Margaret.
Everyone, please take care.
Thank you, Elizabeth.
Ah.
Give Diane my regards.
And say hi to Meliodas for us.
PAT

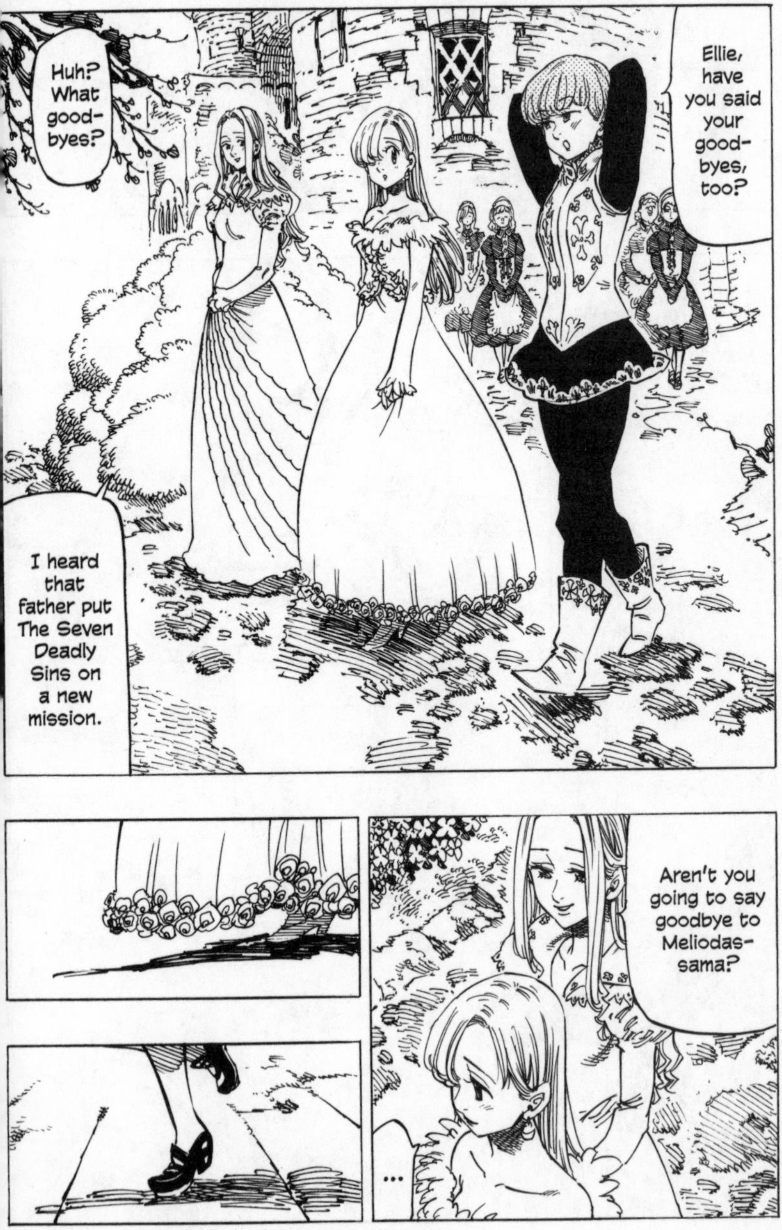
Ellie, have you said your good-byes, too?
Huh? What good-byes?
I heard that father put The Seven Deadly Sins on a new mission.
Aren't you going to say goodbye to Meliodas-sama?
...

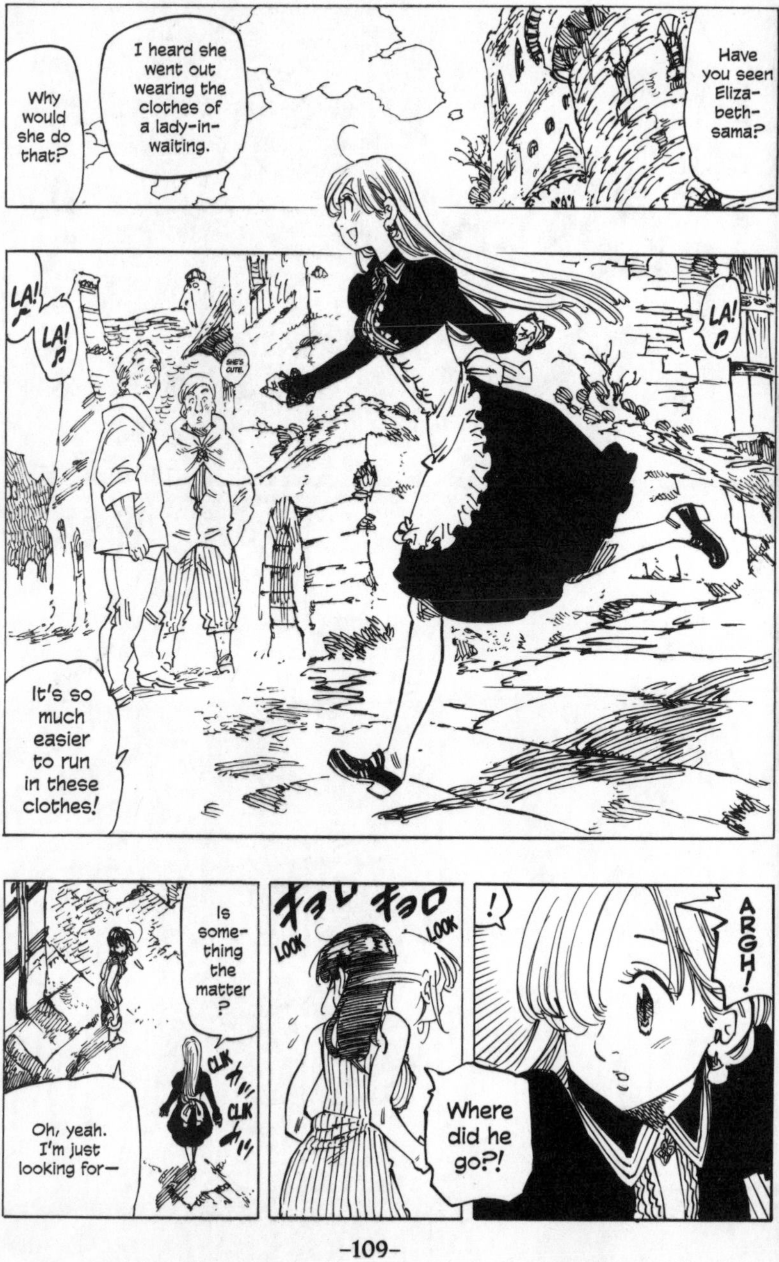

Have you seen Eliza-beth-sama?
I heard she went out wearing the clothes of a lady-in-waiting.
Why would she do that?
LA! ♪
LA! ♪
LA! ♪
SHE'S CUTE.
It's so much easier to run in these clothes!
!
ARGH!
Where did he go?!
LOOK
LOOK
Is some-thing the matter?
CLIK
CLIK
Oh, yeah. I'm just looking for—

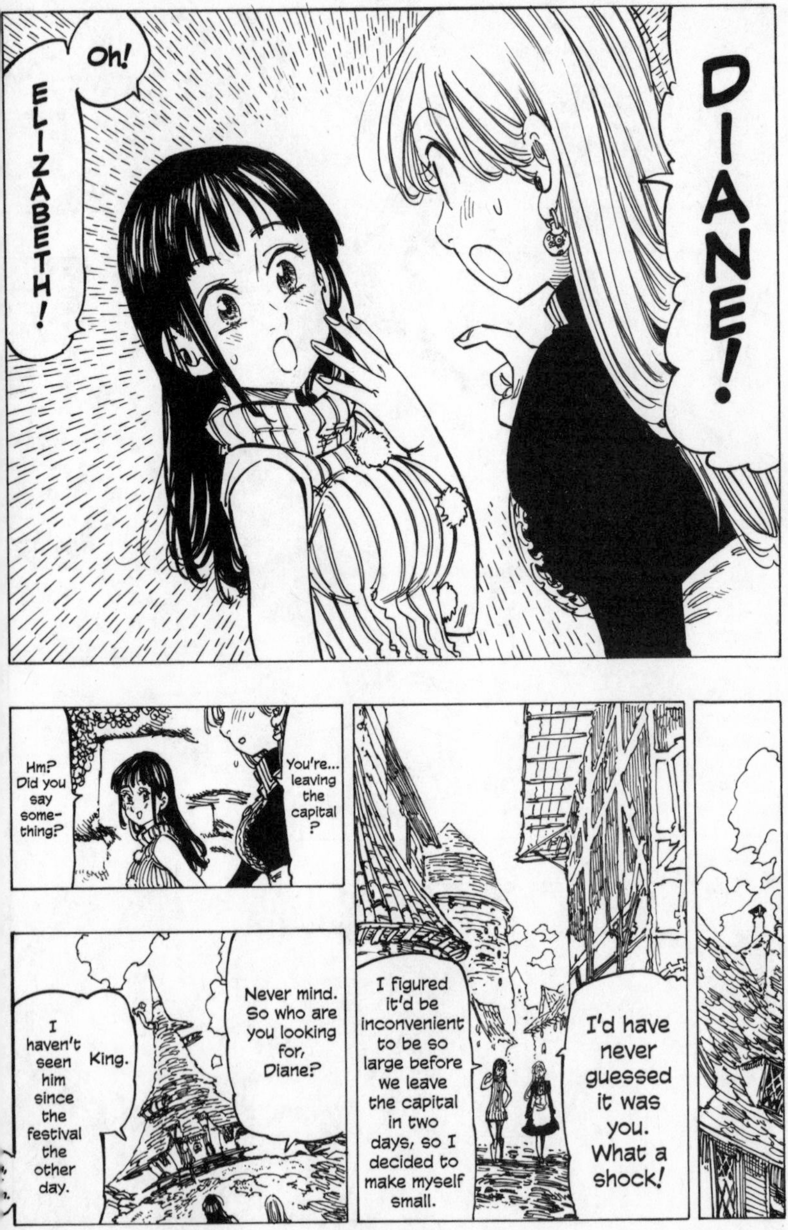
DIANE!
Oh!
ELIZABETH!
I'd have never guessed it was you. What a shock!
I figured it'd be inconvenient to be so large before we leave the capital in two days, so I decided to make myself small.
You're... leaving the capital?
Hm? Did you say something?
Never mind. So who are you looking for, Diane?
King.
I haven't seen him since the festival the other day.

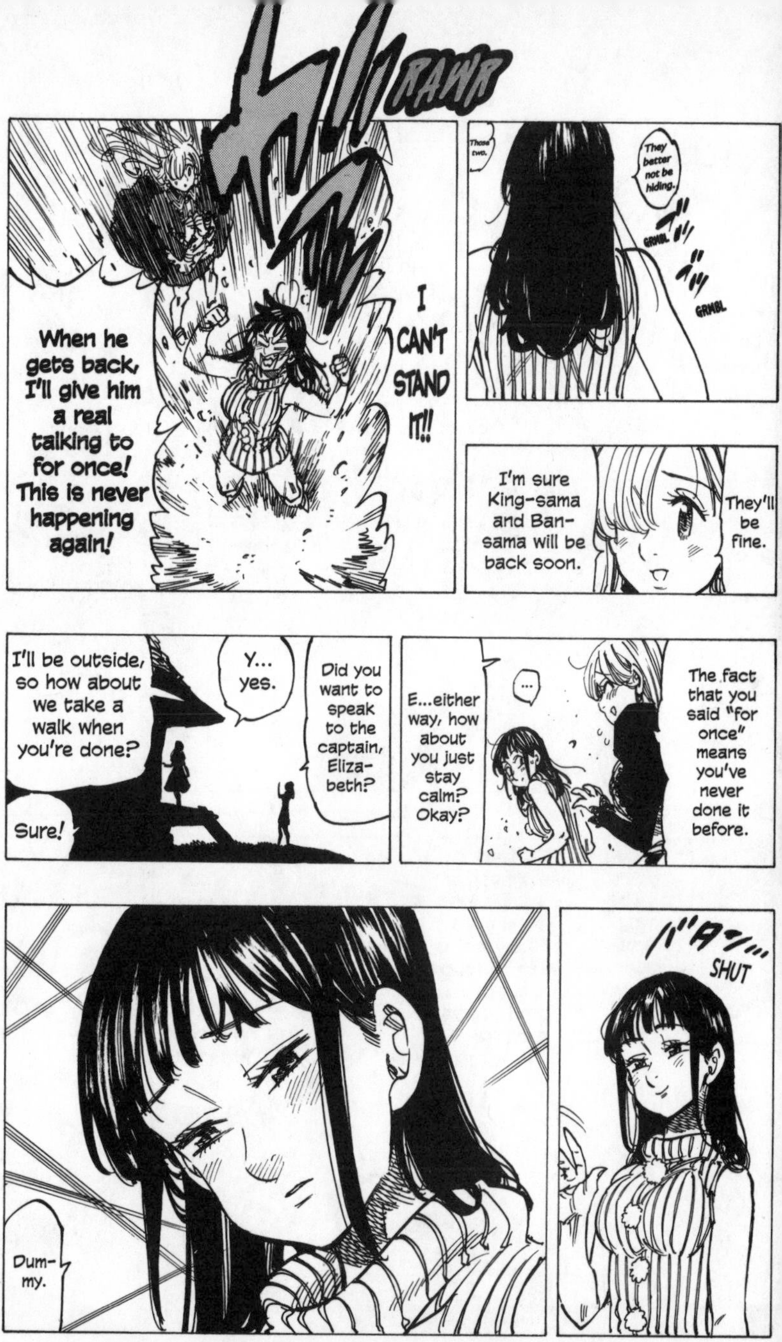
They better not be hiding.
Those two.
GRMBL
GRMBL
They'll be fine.
I'm sure King-sama and Ban-sama will be back soon.
RAWR
I CAN'T STAND IT!!
When he gets back, I'll give him a real talking to for once! This is never happening again!
The fact that you said "for once" means you've never done it before.
...
E...either way, how about you just stay calm? Okay?
Did you want to speak to the captain, Elizabeth?
Y... yes.
I'll be outside, so how about we take a walk when you're done?
Sure!
SHUT
Dum-my.

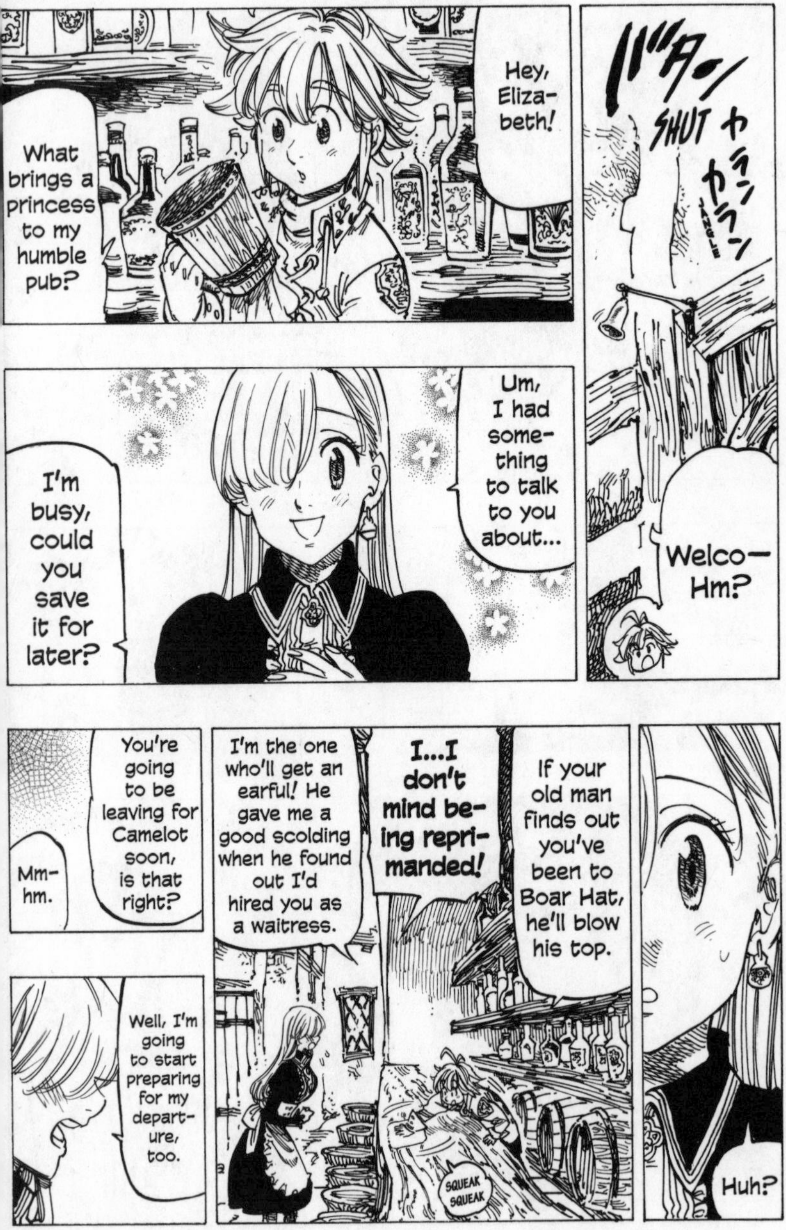
SHUT
JANGLE
Welco— Hm?
Hey, Elizabeth!
What brings a princess to my humble pub?
Um, I had something to talk to you about...
I'm busy, could you save it for later?
Huh?
If your old man finds out you've been to Boar Hat, he'll blow his top.
I...I don't mind being reprimanded!
I'm the one who'll get an earful! He gave me a good scolding when he found out I'd hired you as a waitress.
SQUEAK SQUEAK
You're going to be leaving for Camelot soon, is that right?
Mm-hm.
Well, I'm going to start preparing for my departure, too.

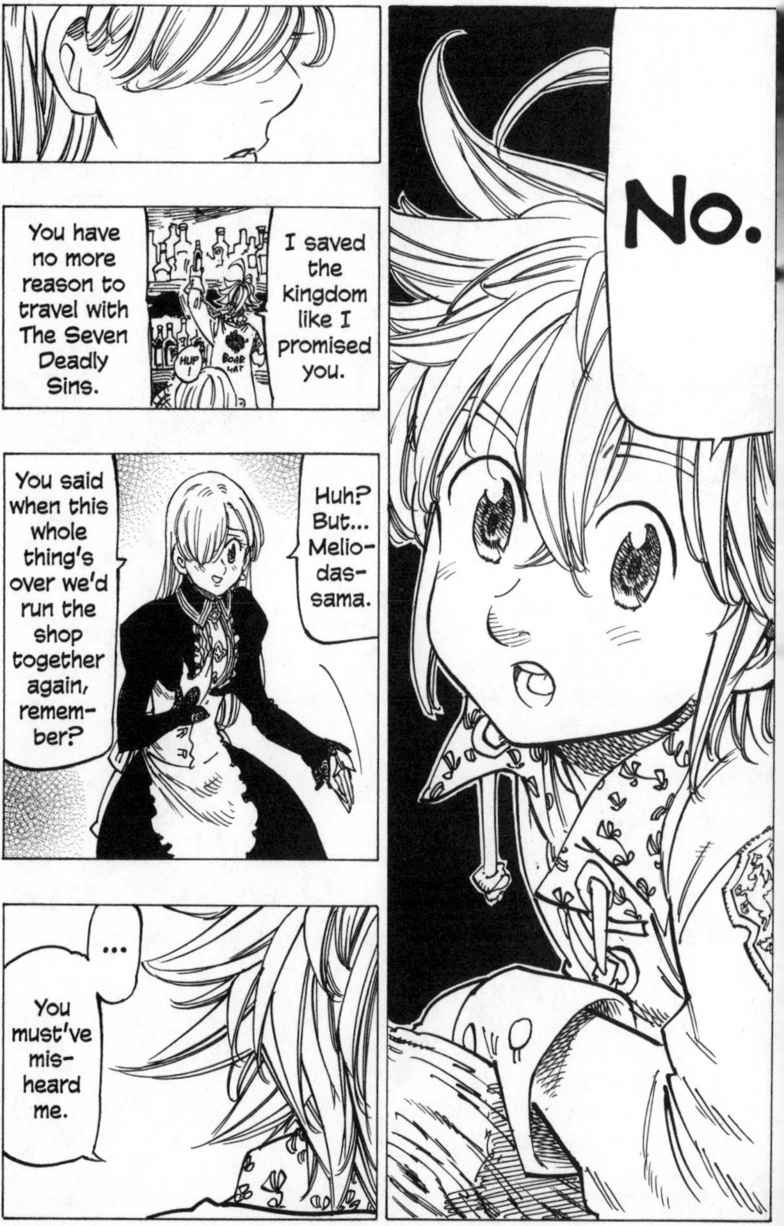
No.
I saved the kingdom like I promised you.
You have no more reason to travel with The Seven Deadly Sins.
BOAR HAT
HUP!
Huh? But... Melio-das-sama.
You said when this whole thing's over we'd run the shop together again, remem-ber?
...
You must've mis-heard me.

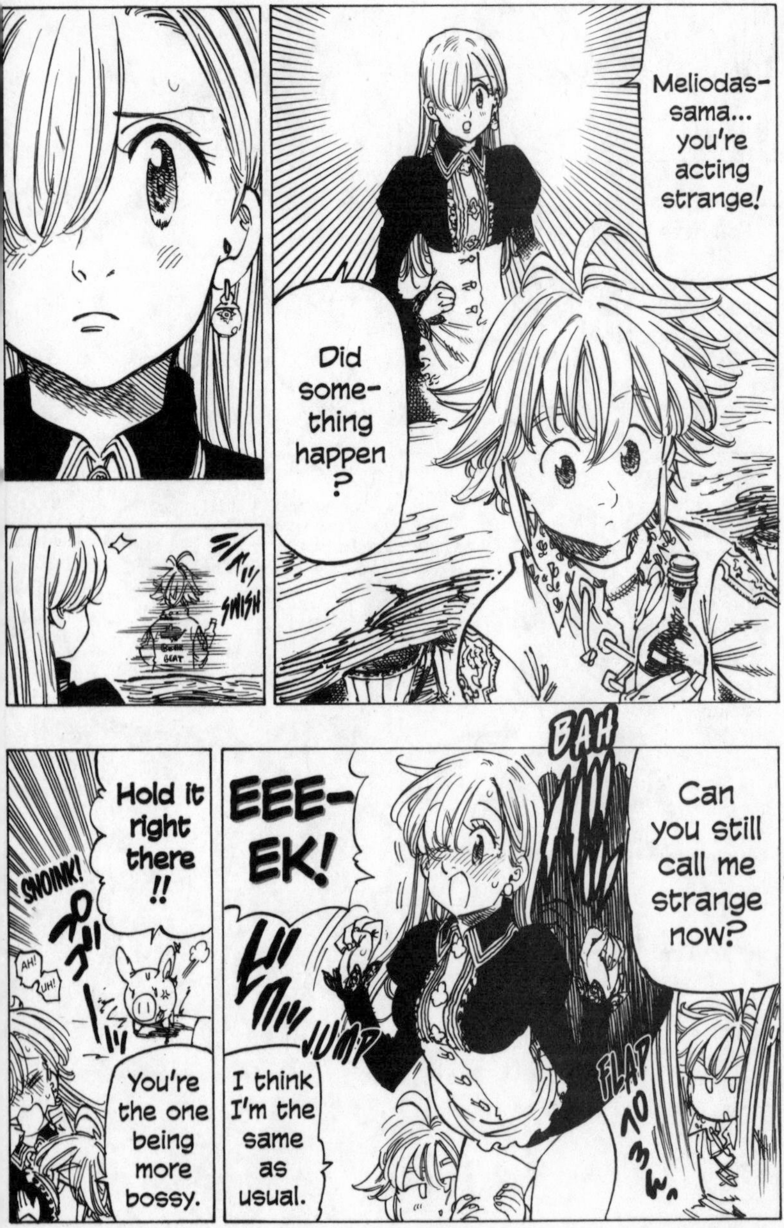
Meliodas-sama... you're acting strange!
Did some-thing happen?
SWISH
BAH
Can you still call me strange now?
EEE-EK!
JUMP
FLAP
I think I'm the same as usual.
Hold it right there!!
SNOINK!
AH!
UH!
You're the one being more bossy.

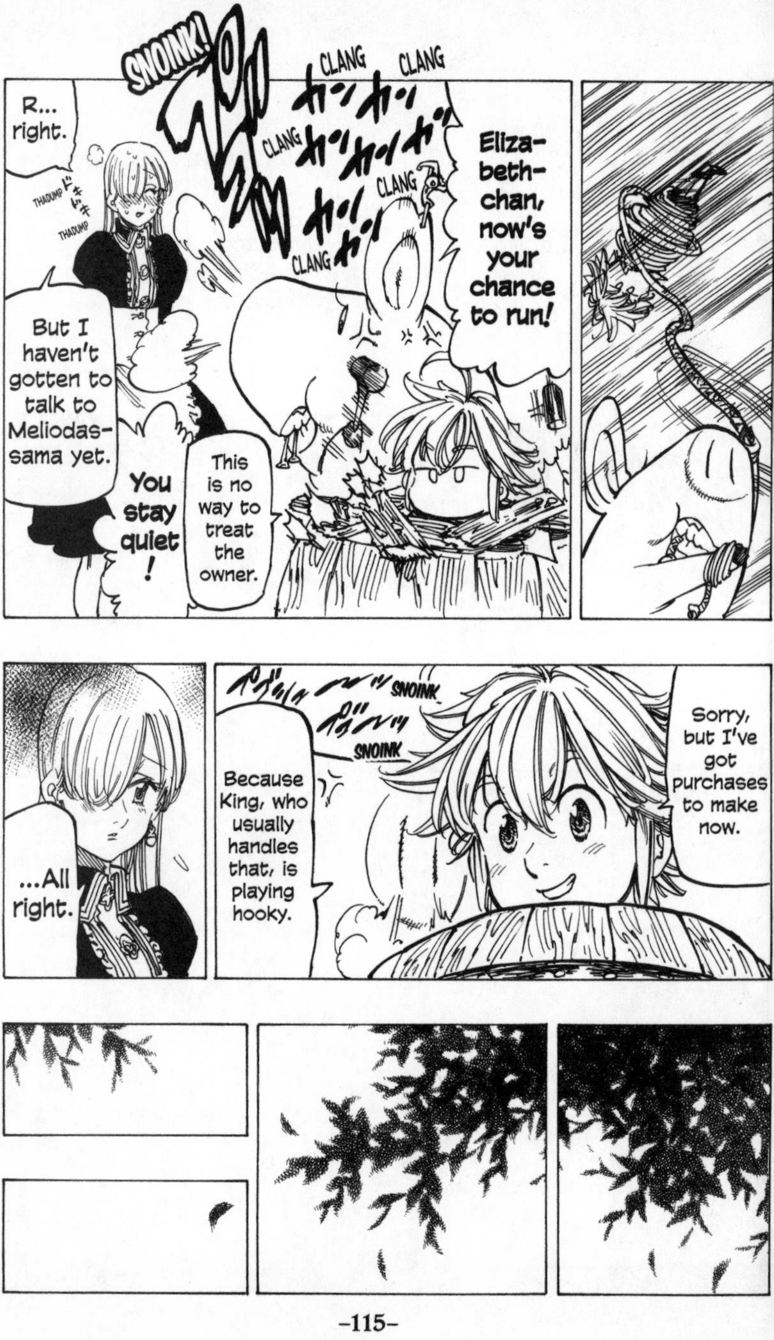
Eliza-beth-chan, now's your chance to run!
CLANG CLANG
CLANG
CLANG
CLANG
SNOINK!
This is no way to treat the owner.
You stay quiet!
R... right.
THADUMP THADUMP
But I haven't gotten to talk to Meliodas-sama yet.
Sorry, but I've got purchases to make now.
SNOINK
SNOINK
Because King, who usually handles that, is playing hooky.
...All right.

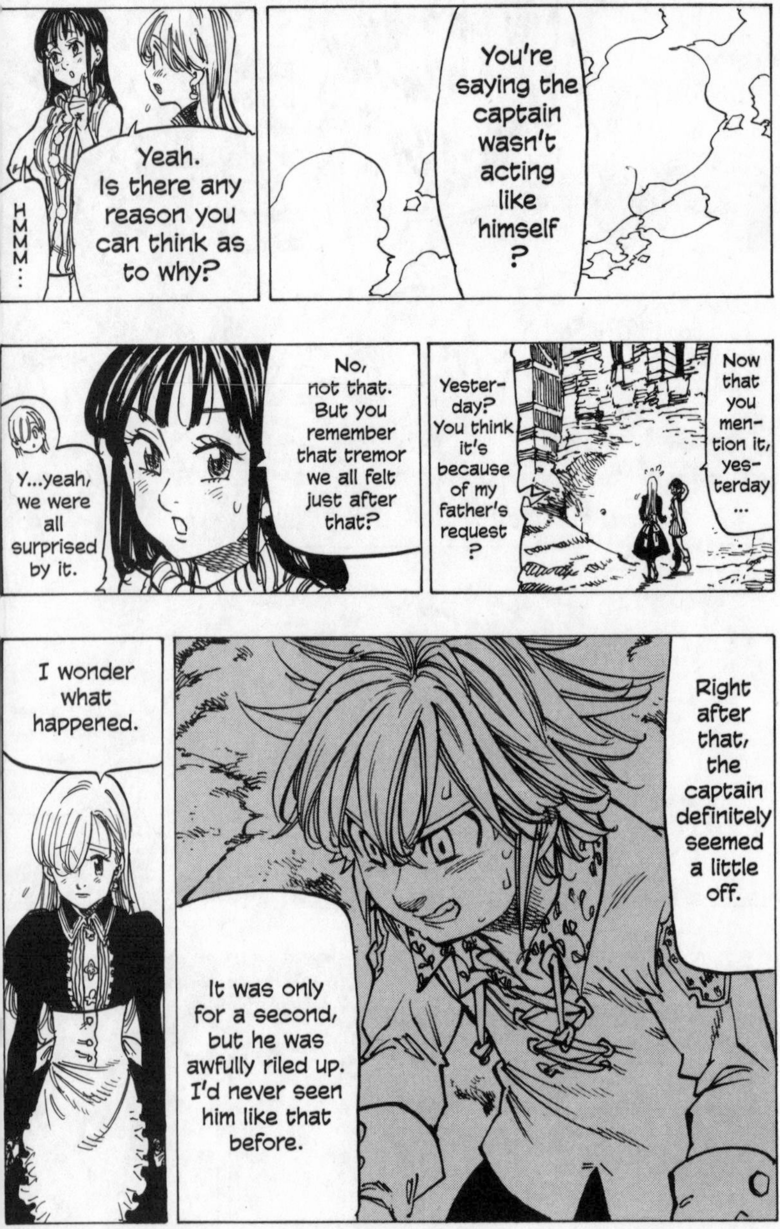
You're saying the captain wasn't acting like himself?
Yeah. Is there any reason you can think as to why?
HMMM...
Now that you mention it, yesterday...
Yesterday? You think it's because of my father's request?
No, not that. But you remember that tremor we all felt just after that?
Y...yeah, we were all surprised by it.
Right after that, the captain definitely seemed a little off.
It was only for a second, but he was awfully riled up. I'd never seen him like that before.
I wonder what happened.

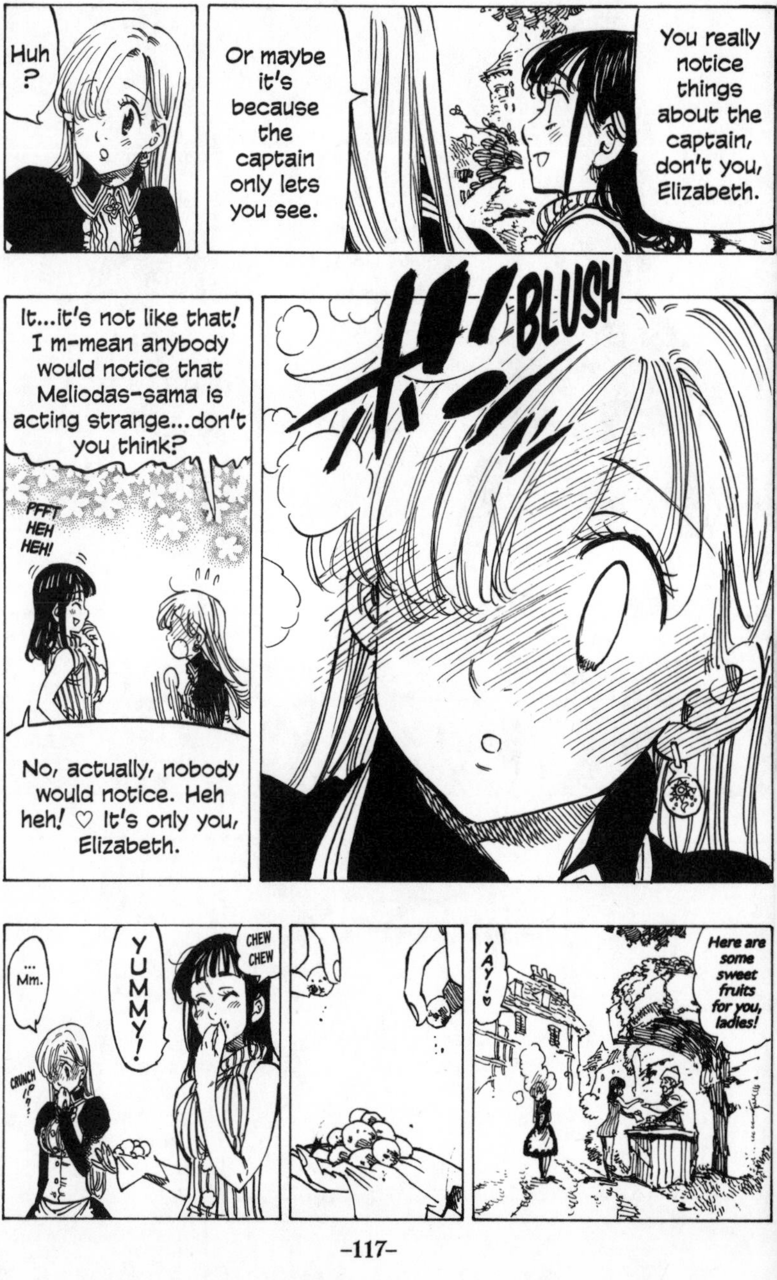
You really notice things about the captain, don't you, Elizabeth.
Or maybe it's because the captain only lets you see.
Huh?
BLUSH
It...it's not like that! I m-mean anybody would notice that Meliodas-sama is acting strange...don't you think?
PFFT HEH HEH!
No, actually, nobody would notice. Heh heh! ♡ It's only you, Elizabeth.
Here are some sweet fruits for you, ladies!
YAY!♡
CHEW CHEW
YUMMY!
... Mm.
CRUNCH
!?

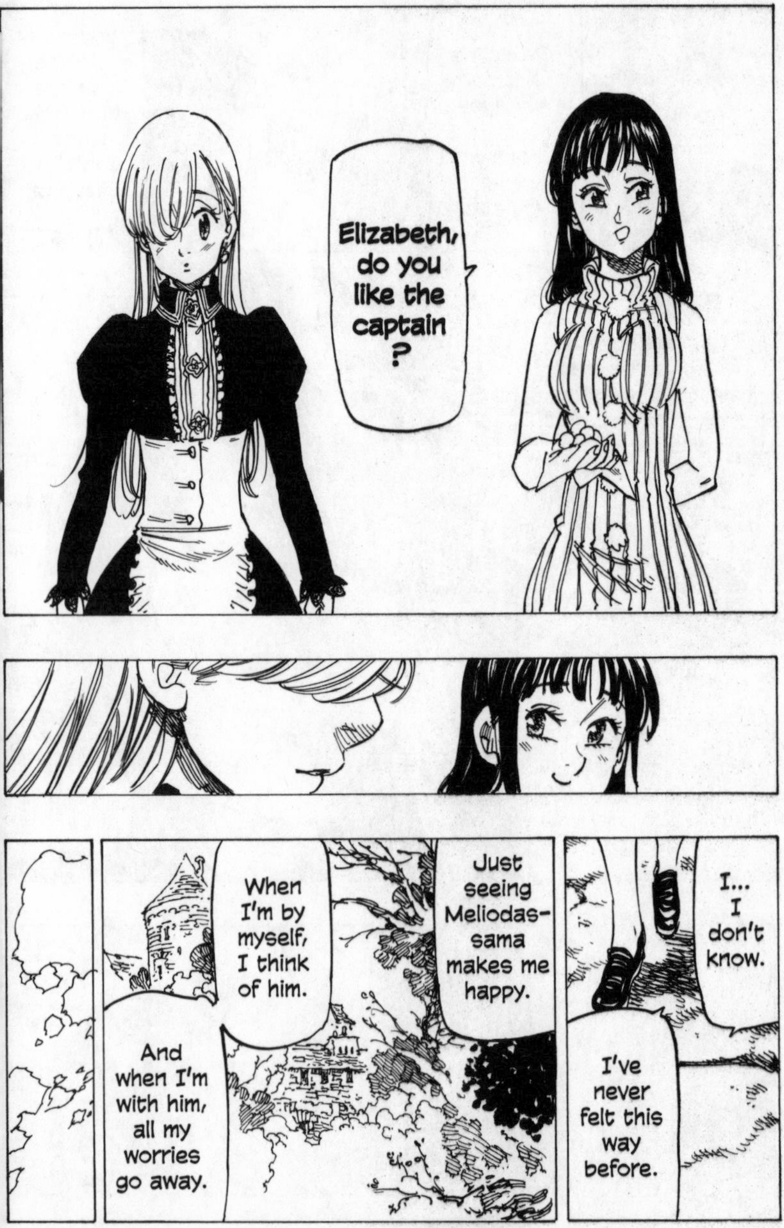
Elizabeth, do you like the captain?
I... I don't know.
I've never felt this way before.
Just seeing Meliodas-sama makes me happy.
When I'm by myself, I think of him.
And when I'm with him, all my worries go away.

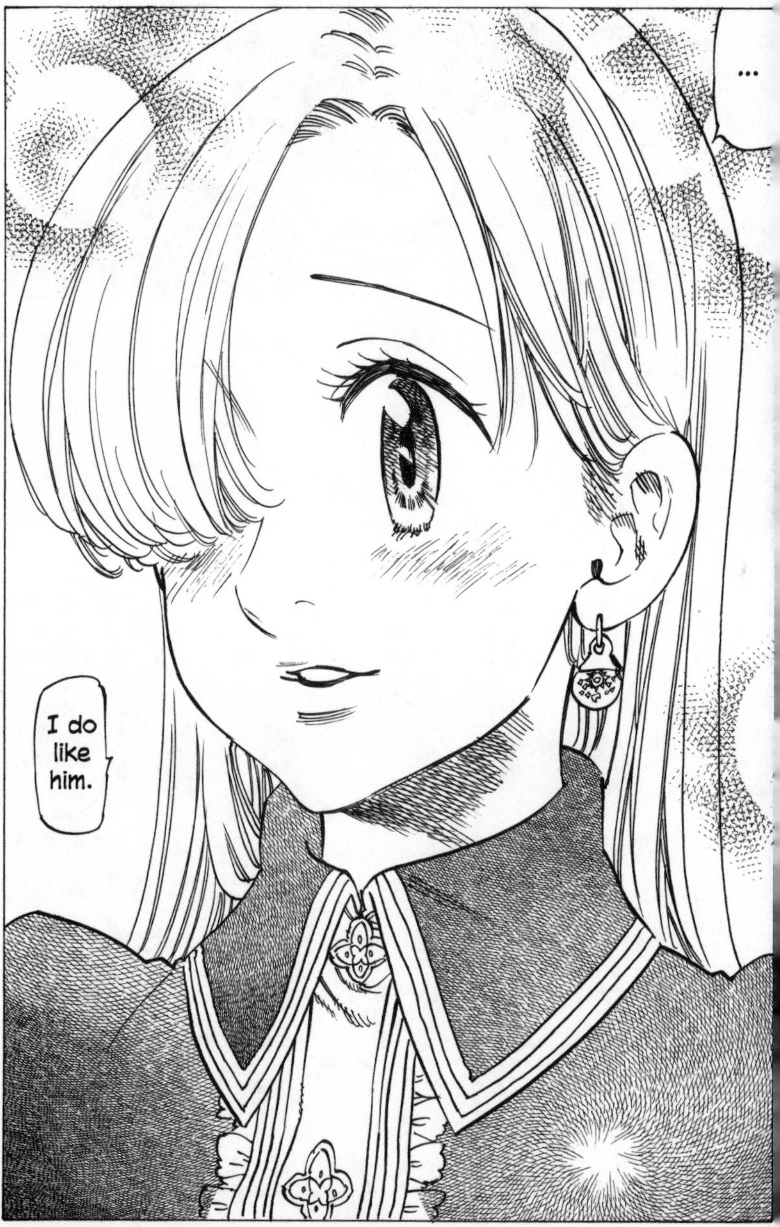
...
I do like him.

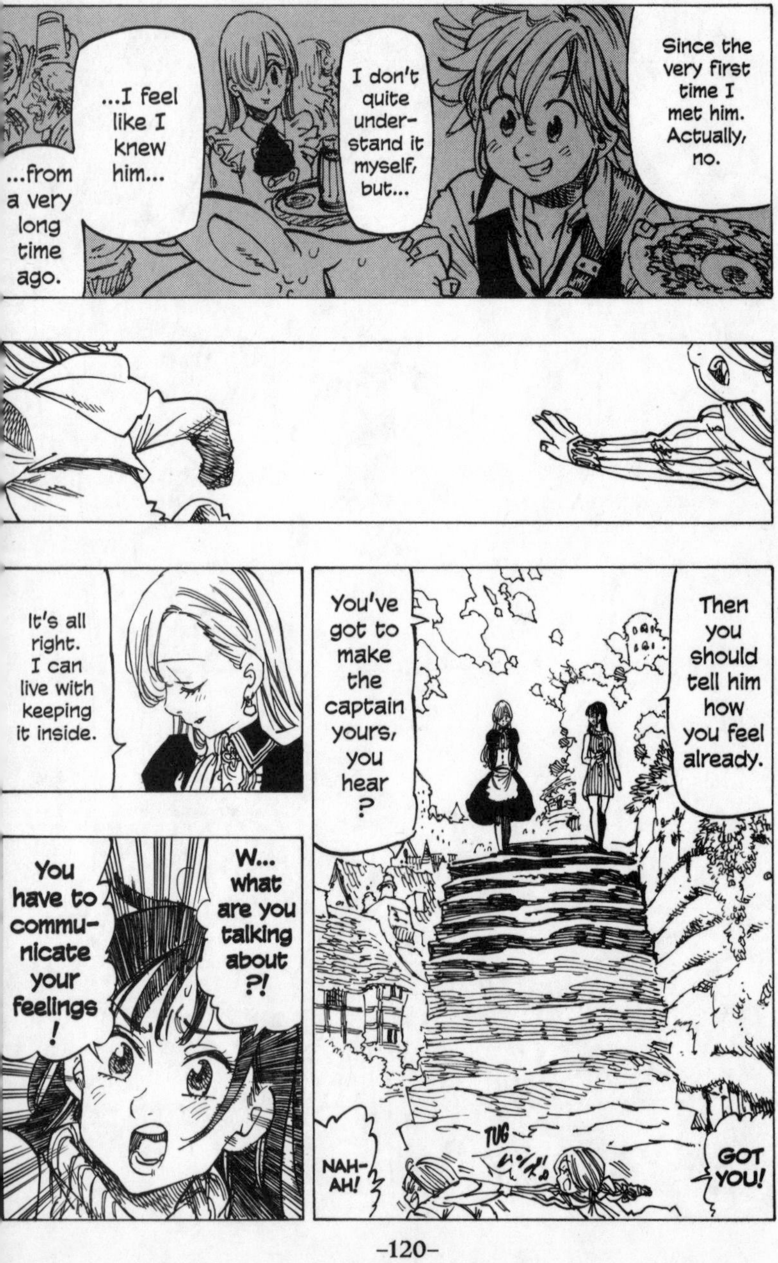
Since the very first time I met him. Actually, no.
I don't quite understand it myself, but...
...I feel like I knew him...
...from a very long time ago.
Then you should tell him how you feel already.
You've got to make the captain yours, you hear?
GOT YOU!
TUG
NAH-AH!
It's all right. I can live with keeping it inside.
W... what are you talking about?!
You have to communicate your feelings!

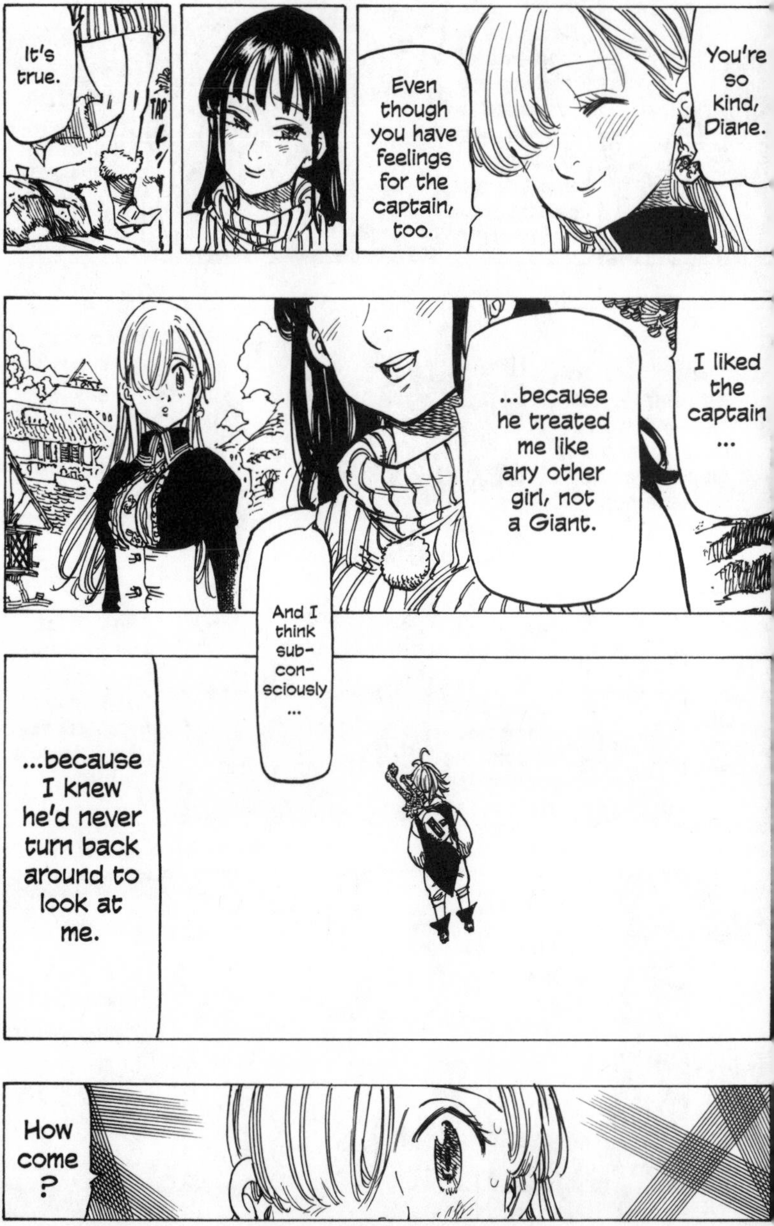
You're so kind, Diane.
Even though you have feelings for the captain, too.
It's true.
TAP
I liked the captain ...
...because he treated me like any other girl, not a Giant.
And I think sub-consciously ...
...because I knew he'd never turn back around to look at me.
How come?

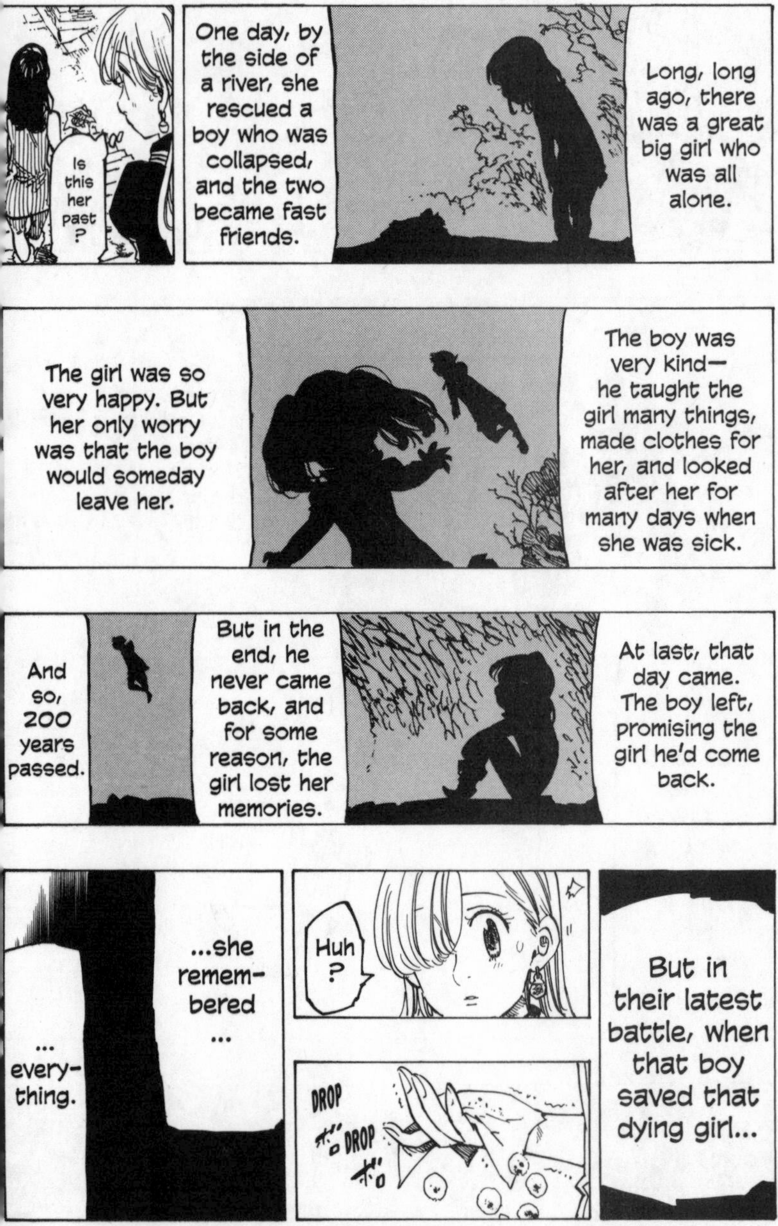

Long, long ago, there was a great big girl who was all alone.
One day, by the side of a river, she rescued a boy who was collapsed, and the two became fast friends.
Is this her past?
The boy was very kind—he taught the girl many things, made clothes for her, and looked after her for many days when she was sick.
The girl was so very happy. But her only worry was that the boy would someday leave her.
At last, that day came. The boy left, promising the girl he'd come back.
But in the end, he never came back, and for some reason, the girl lost her memories.
And so, 200 years passed.
But in their latest battle, when that boy saved that dying girl...
Huh?
DROP
DROP
...she remembered...
...everything.

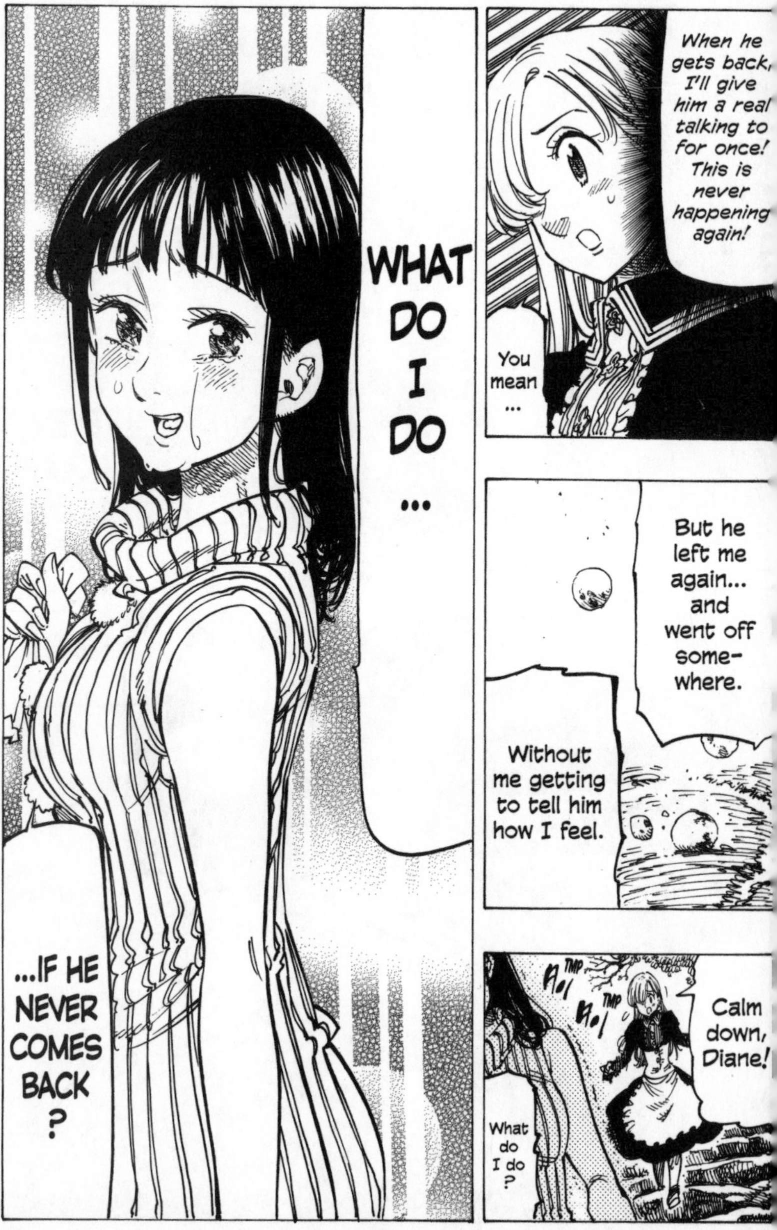
When he gets back, I'll give him a real talking to for once! This is never happening again!
You mean ...
But he left me again... and went off somewhere.
Without me getting to tell him how I feel.
Calm down, Diane!
TMP
TMP
What do I do ?
WHAT DO I DO ...
...IF HE NEVER COMES BACK ?

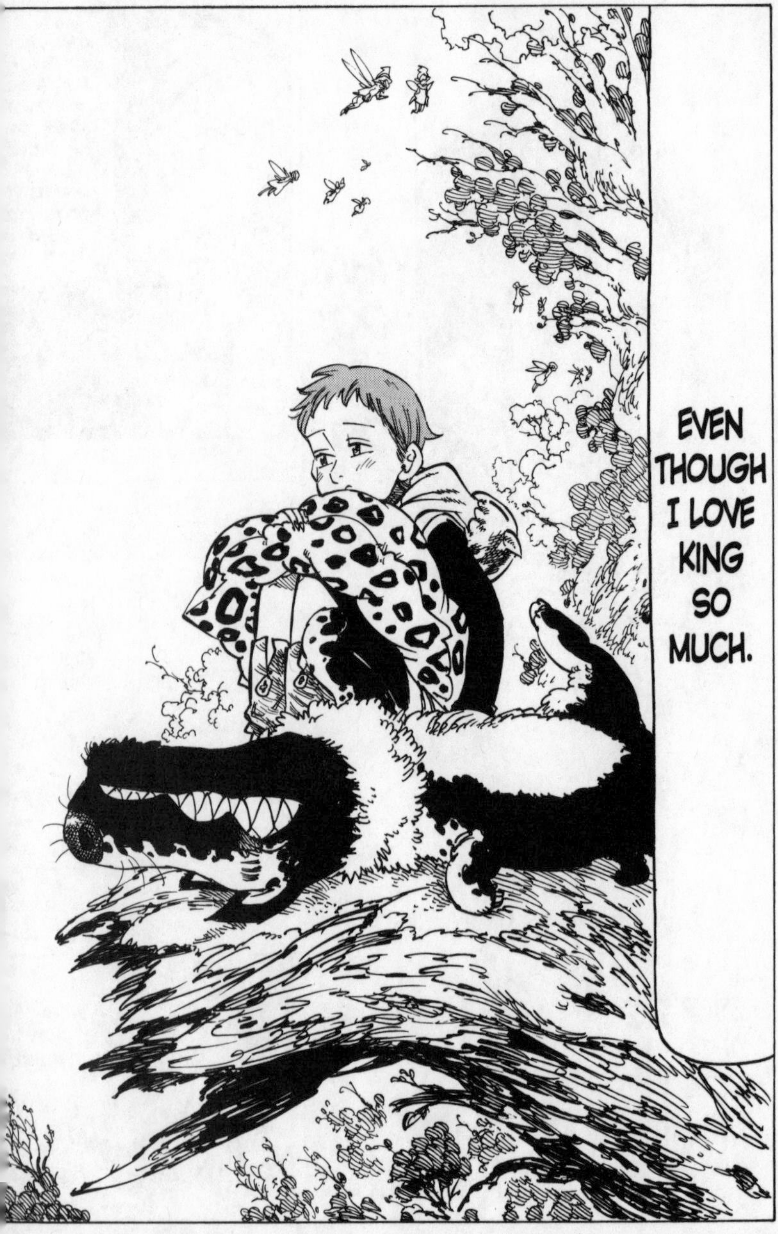
EVEN THOUGH I LOVE KING SO MUCH.

Chapter 111 - The Man Has His Say

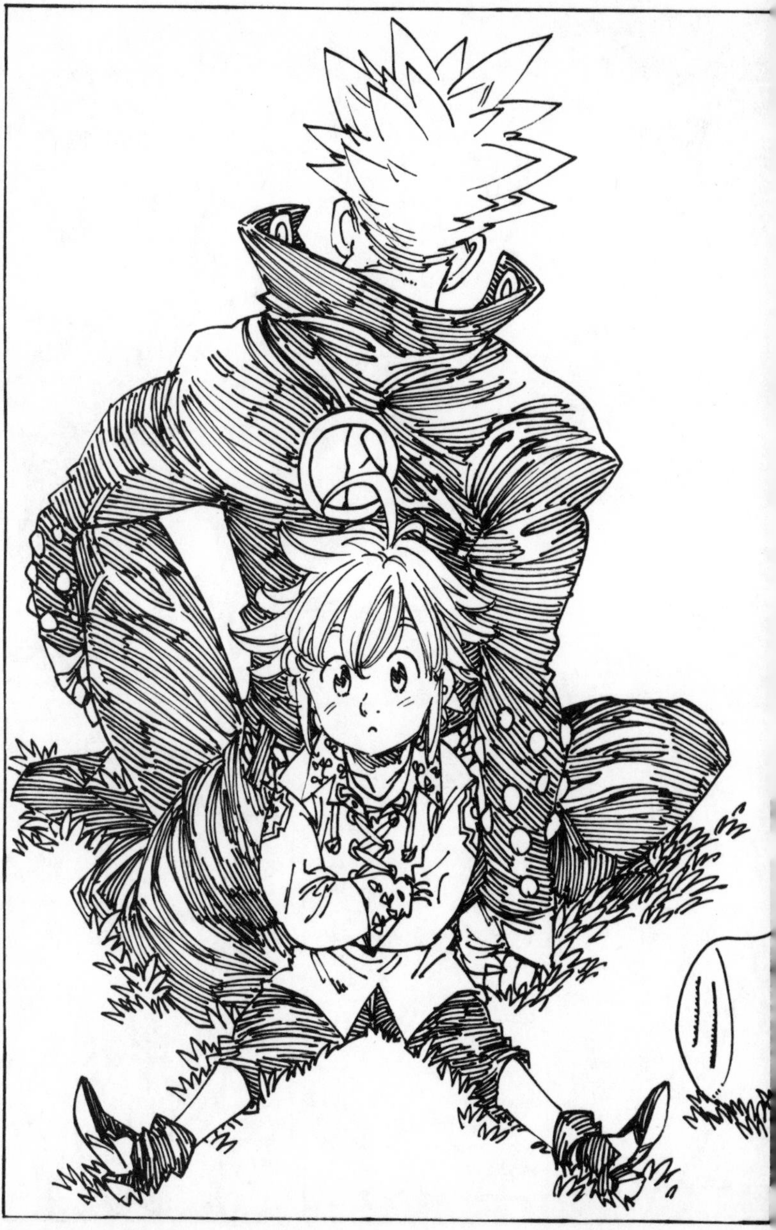

......

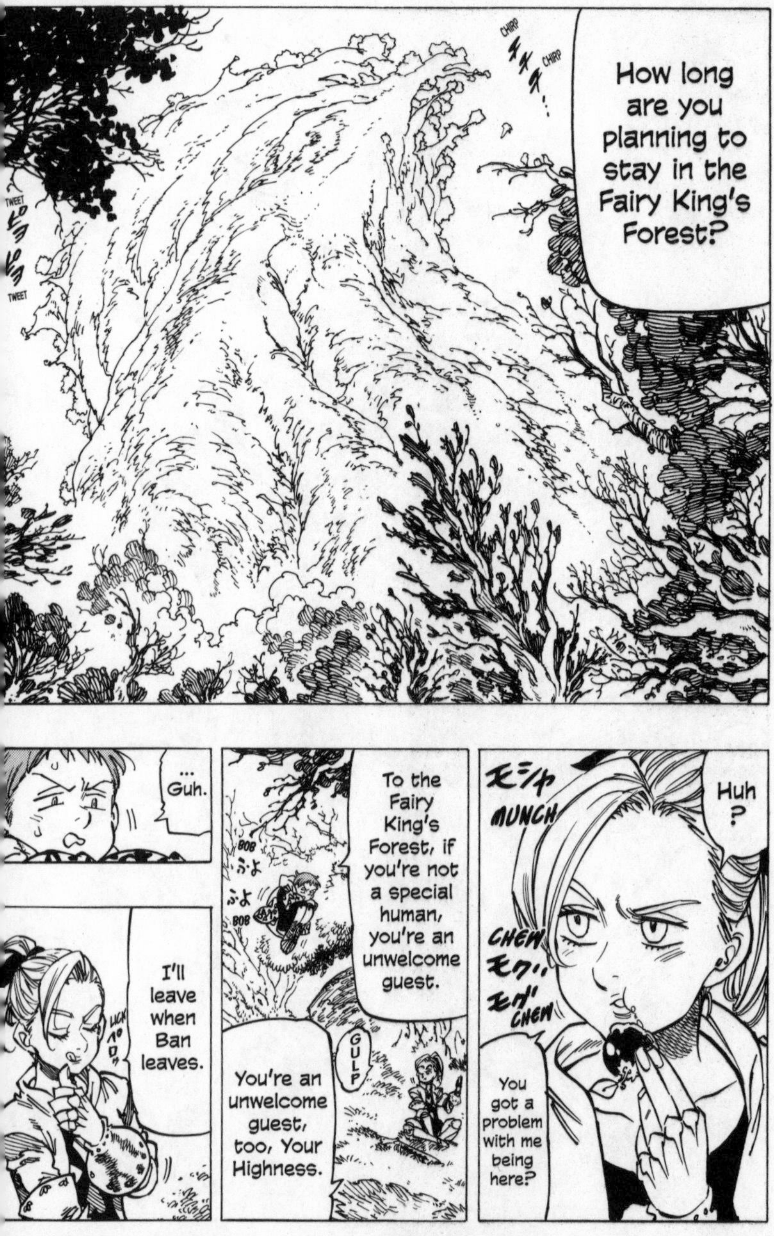
CHIRP
CHIRP
TWEET
TWEET
How long are you planning to stay in the Fairy King's Forest?
MUNCH
Huh?
CHEW
CHEW
You got a problem with me being here?
To the Fairy King's Forest, if you're not a special human, you're an unwelcome guest.
BOB
BOB
GULP
You're an unwelcome guest, too, Your Highness.
... Guh.
LICK
I'll leave when Ban leaves.

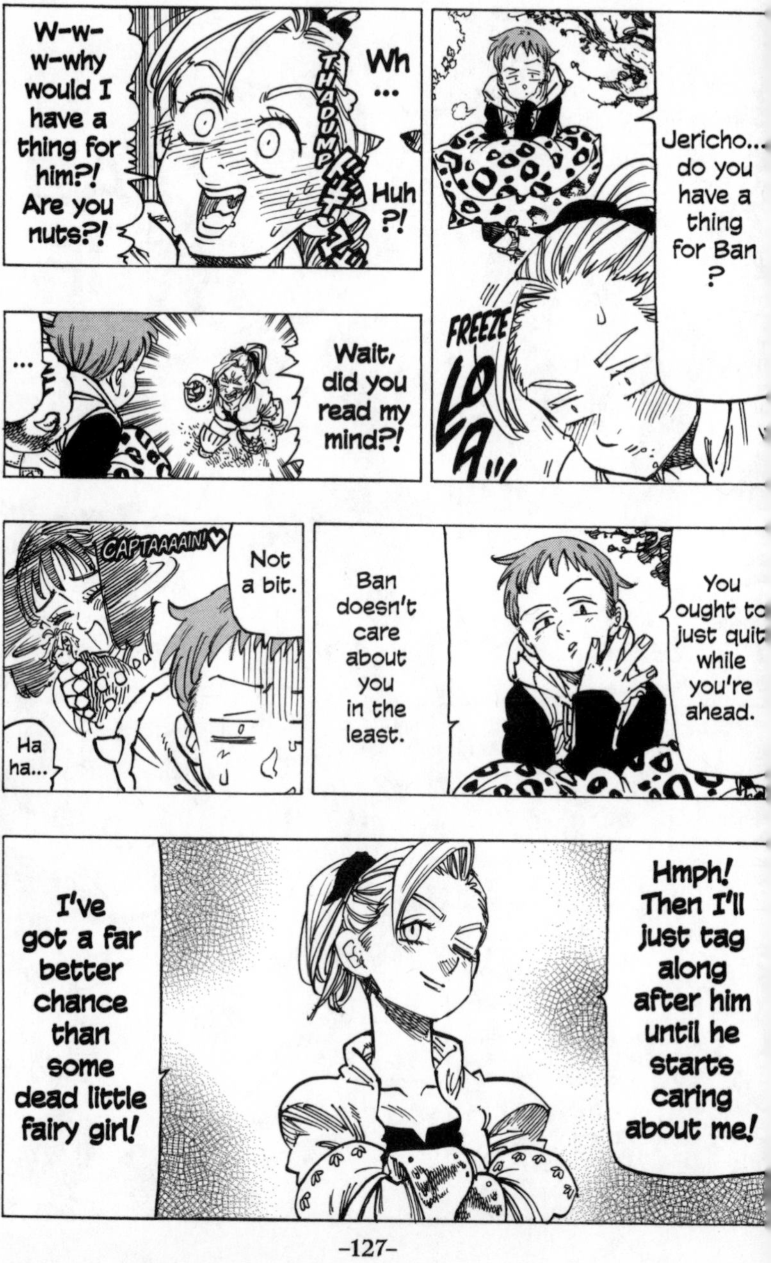
Jericho... do you have a thing for Ban?
FREEZE
Wh...
Huh?!
THADUMP
W-w-w-why would I have a thing for him?! Are you nuts?!
Wait, did you read my mind?!
...
You ought to just quit while you're ahead.
Ban doesn't care about you in the least.
Not a bit.
CAPTAAAAIN!♥
Ha ha...
Hmph! Then I'll just tag along after him until he starts caring about me!
I've got a far better chance than some dead little fairy girl!

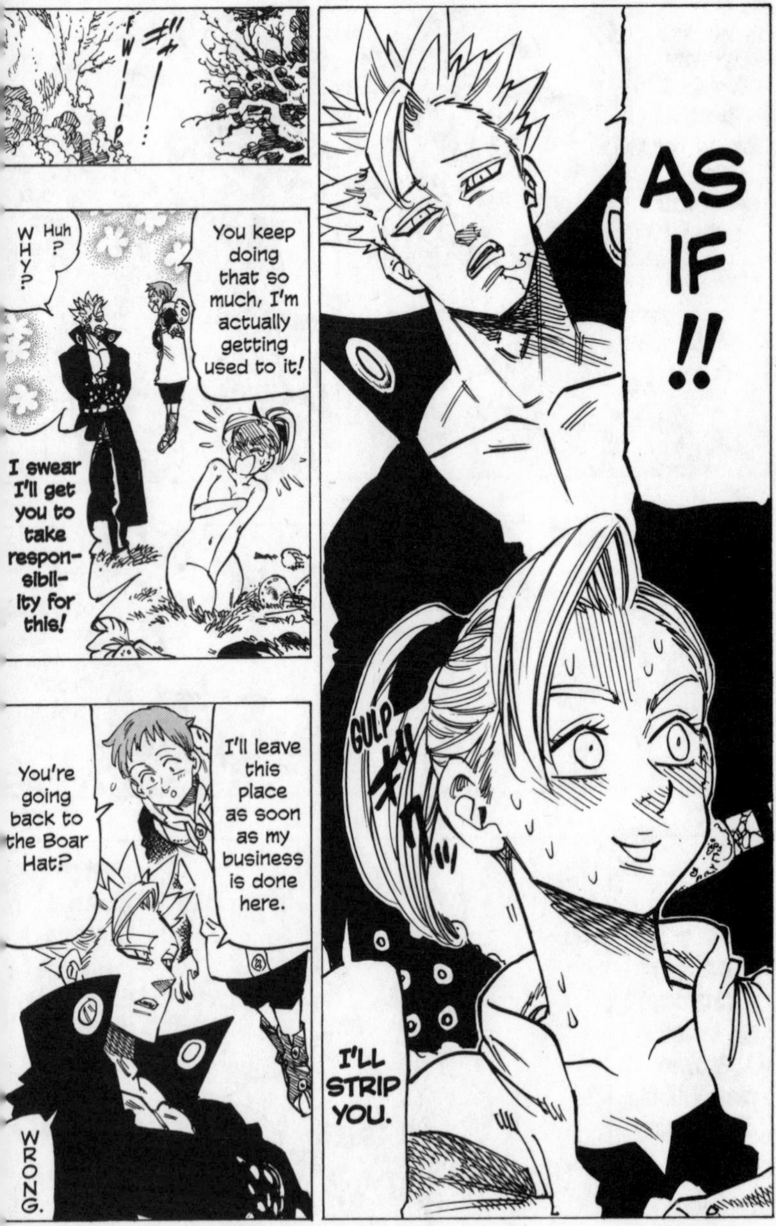
AS IF!!
GULP
I'LL STRIP YOU.
FWI---P
You keep doing that so much, I'm actually getting used to it!
Huh?
WHY?
I swear I'll get you to take responsibility for this!
I'll leave this place as soon as my business is done here.
You're going back to the Boar Hat?
WRONG.

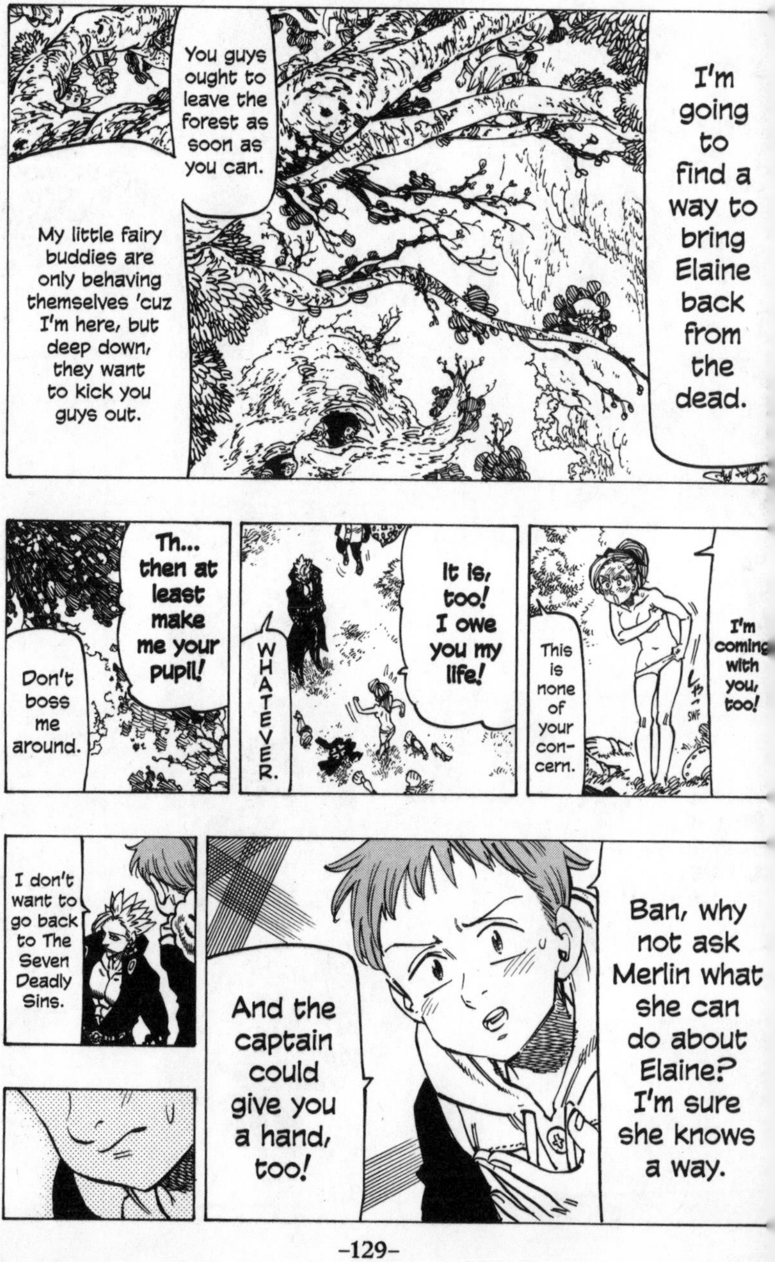
I'm going to find a way to bring Elaine back from the dead.
You guys ought to leave the forest as soon as you can.
My little fairy buddies are only behaving themselves 'cuz I'm here, but deep down, they want to kick you guys out.
I'm coming with you, too!
SWF
This is none of your concern.
It is, too! I owe you my life!
WHATEVER.
Th... then at least make me your pupil!
Don't boss me around.
Ban, why not ask Merlin what she can do about Elaine? I'm sure she knows a way.
And the captain could give you a hand, too!
I don't want to go back to The Seven Deadly Sins.

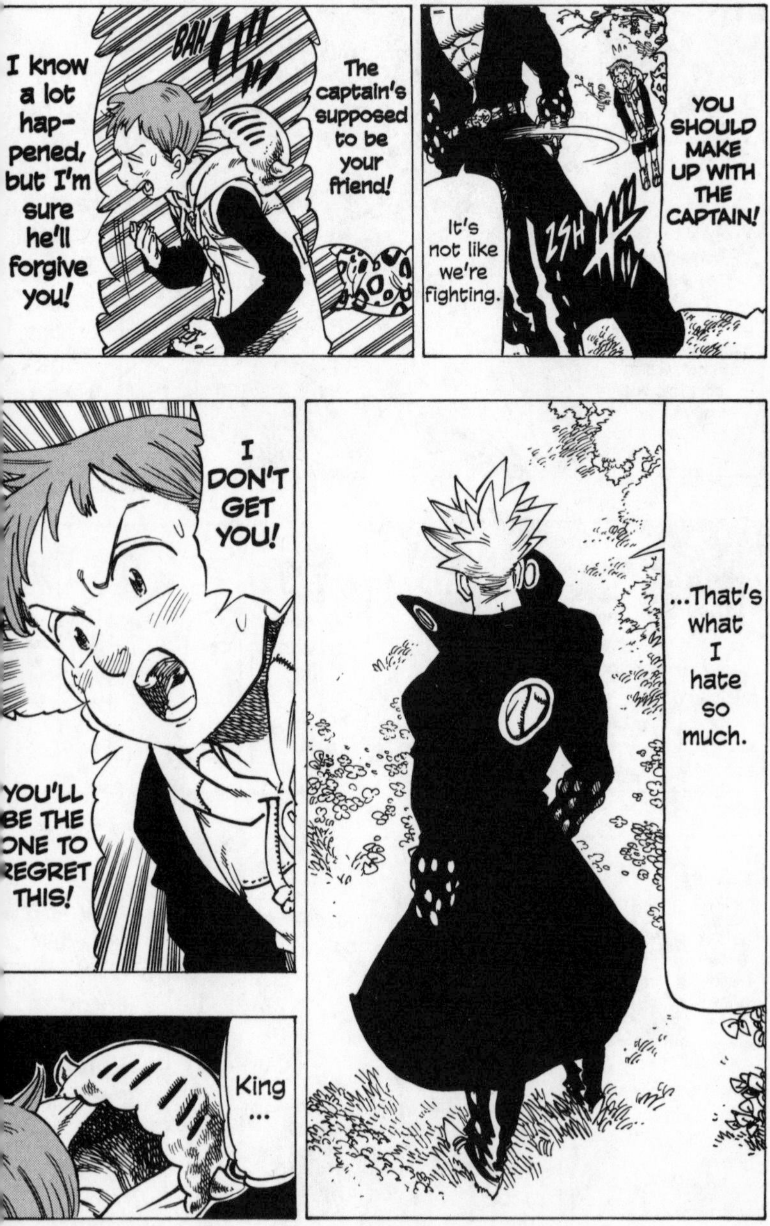
YOU SHOULD MAKE UP WITH THE CAPTAIN!
It's not like we're fighting.
ZSH
The captain's supposed to be your friend!
BAH
I know a lot hap-pened, but I'm sure he'll forgive you!
...That's what I hate so much.
I DON'T GET YOU!
YOU'LL BE THE ONE TO REGRET THIS!
King ...

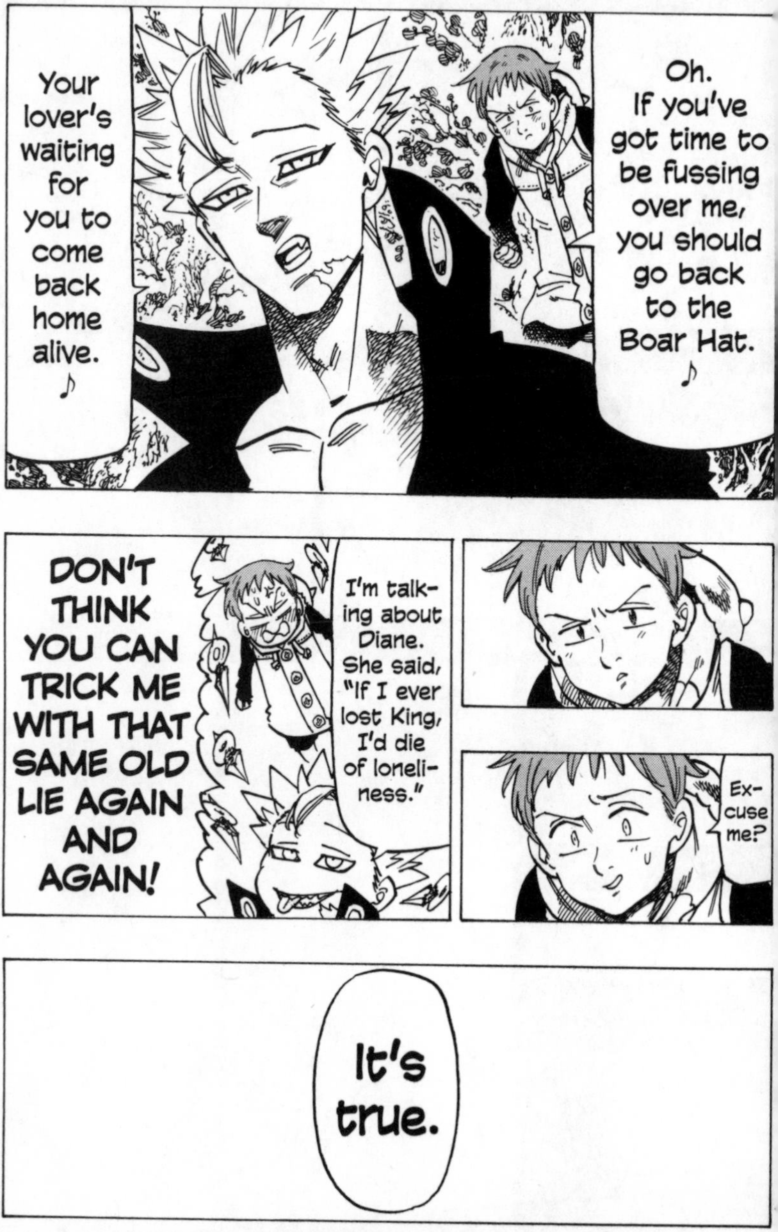
Oh. If you've got time to be fussing over me, you should go back to the Boar Hat. ♪
Your lover's waiting for you to come back home alive. ♪
Excuse me?
I'm talking about Diane. She said, "If I ever lost King, I'd die of loneliness."
DON'T THINK YOU CAN TRICK ME WITH THAT SAME OLD LIE AGAIN AND AGAIN!
It's true.

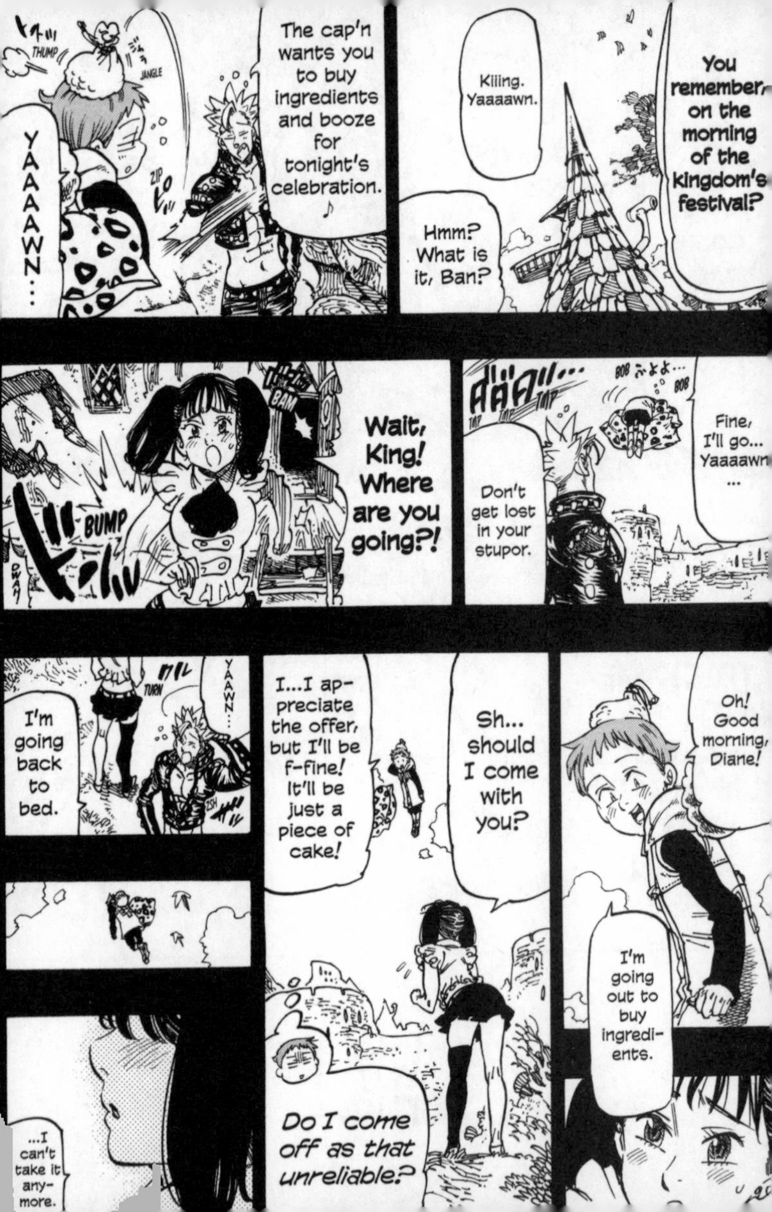
You remember, on the morning of the kingdom's festival?
Kiiing. Yaaaawn.
Hmm? What is it, Ban?
The cap'n wants you to buy ingredients and booze for tonight's celebration. ♪
THUMP
JANGLE
ZIP
YAAAAAWN...
BOB
BOB
TAP TAP TAP
Fine, I'll go... Yaaaawn...
Don't get lost in your stupor.
BAM
Wait, King! Where are you going?!
BUMP
DWAH
Oh! Good morning, Diane!
I'm going out to buy ingredients.
Sh... should I come with you?
I...I appreciate the offer, but I'll be f-fine! It'll be just a piece of cake!
Do I come off as that unreliable?
YAAWN...
TURN
I'm going back to bed.
ZSH
...I can't take it anymore.

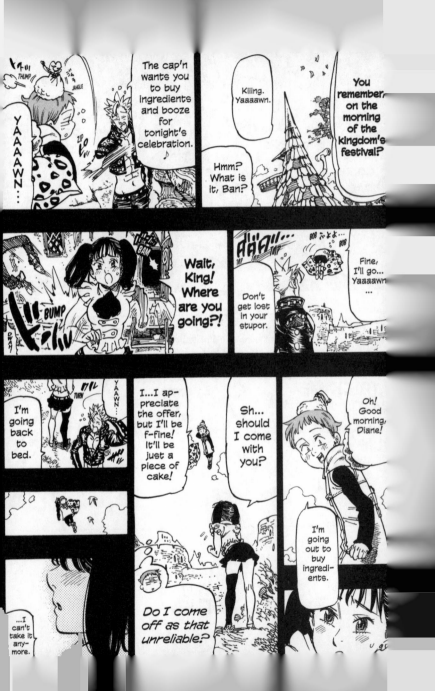

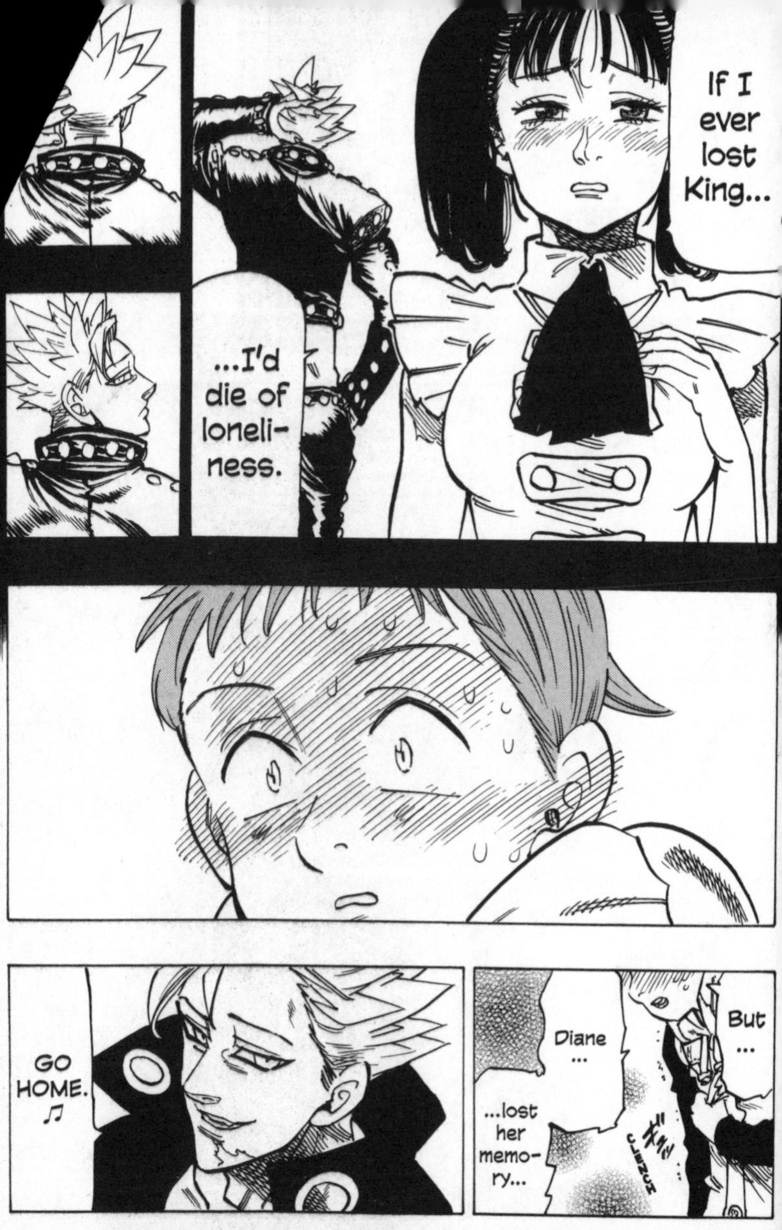
If I ever lost King...
...I'd die of loneli-ness.
But ...
Diane ...
CLENCH
...lost her memo-ry...
GO HOME. ♫

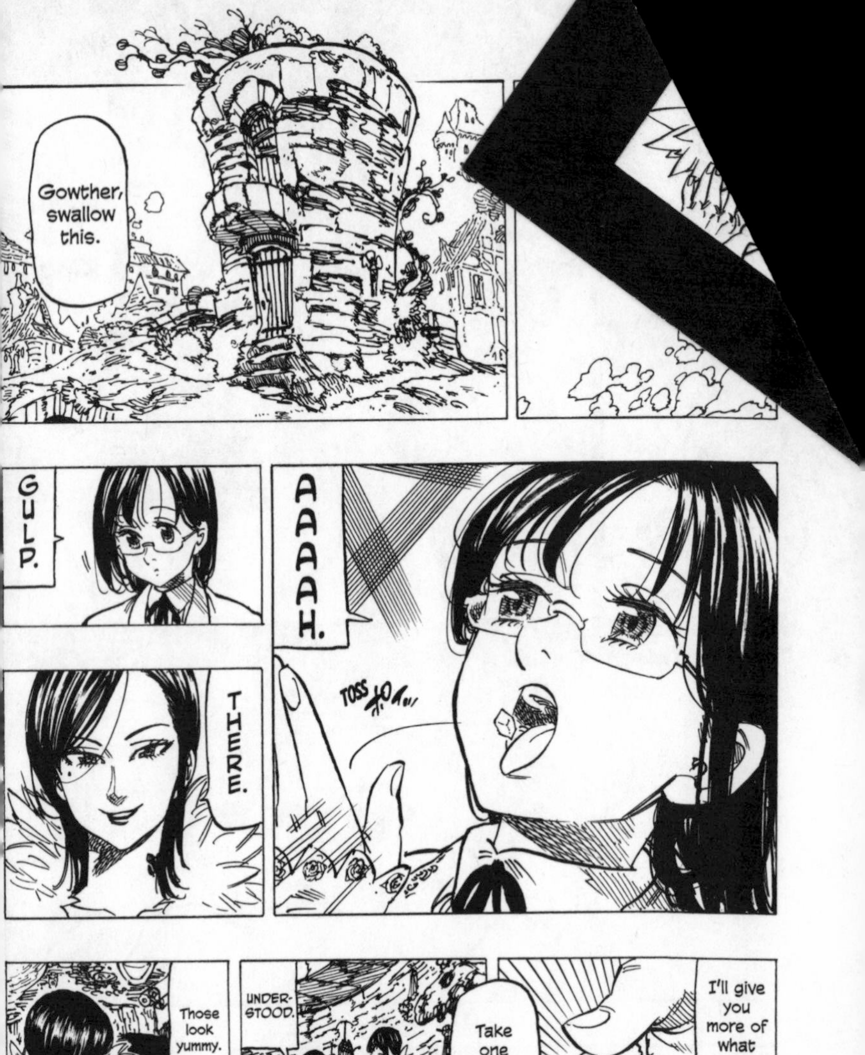
Gowther, swallow this.
AAAAAH.
TOSS
GULP.
THERE.
I'll give you more of what you just had.
JANGLE
Take one every day and never miss a dose.
Your armor will be back in no time.
UNDERSTOOD.
Those look yummy.
It's medicine.

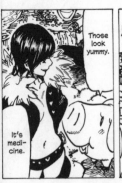

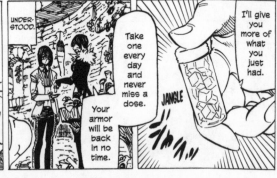

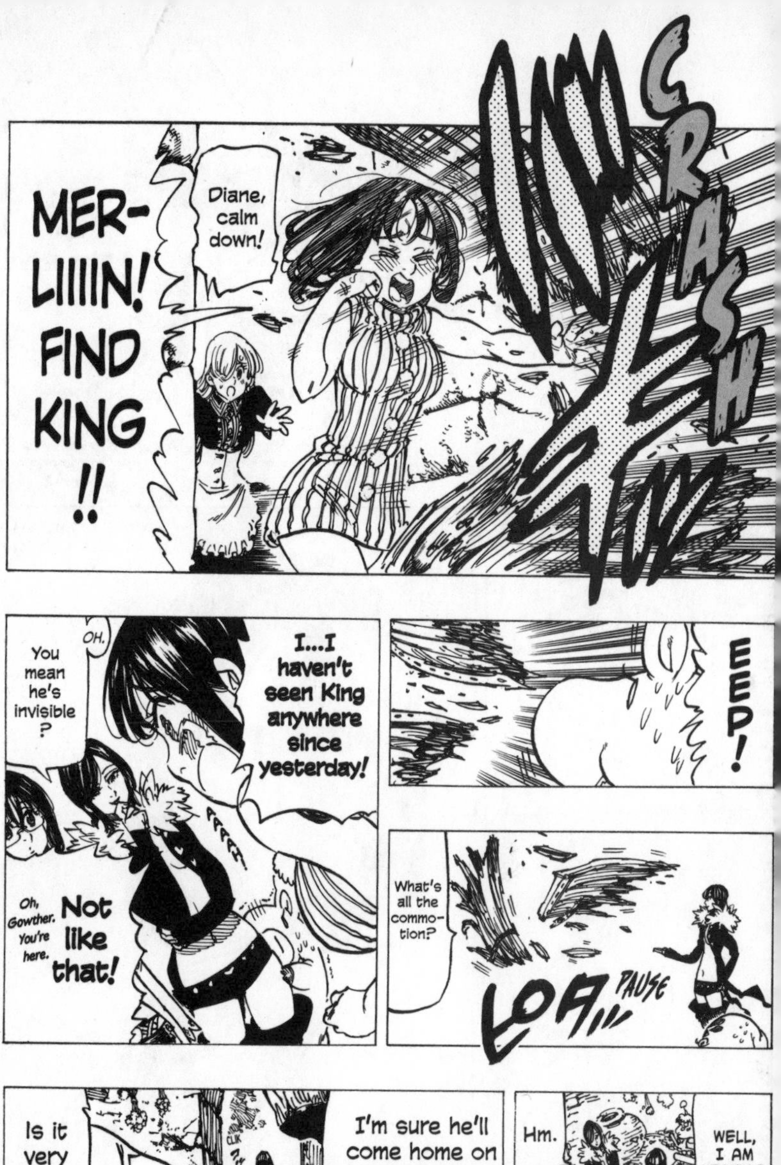
CRASH
Diane, calm down!
MER-LIIIIN! FIND KING!!
EEP!
What's all the commotion?
PAUSE
I...I haven't seen King anywhere since yesterday!
OH.
You mean he's invisible?
Not like that!
Oh, Gowther. You're here.
WELL, I AM LEAVING. BYE-BYYYE.
Hm.
Please! You gotta find him!
I'm sure he'll come home on his own. More importantly, there's something I have to finish up here.
CLIK
CLIK
Is it very impor-tant?
SNOINK!

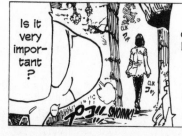

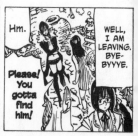

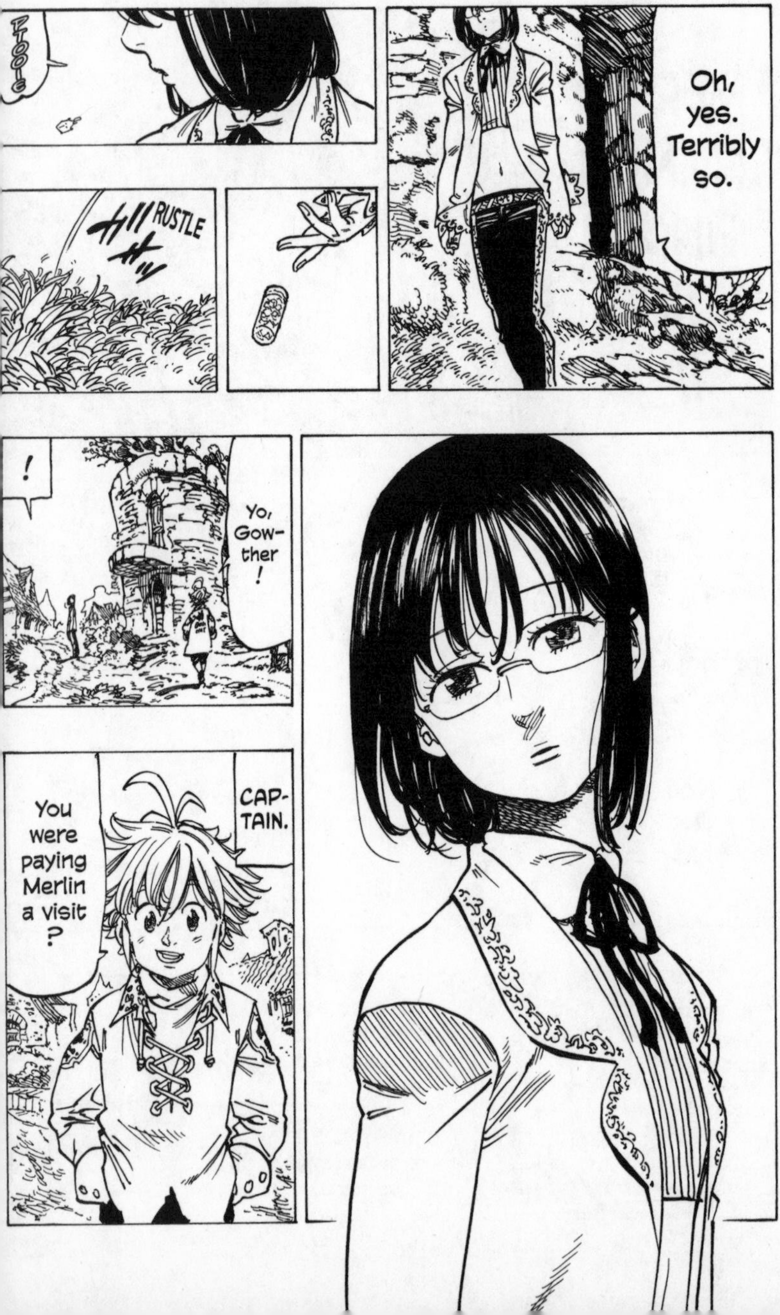
Oh, yes. Terribly so.
PTOOIE
RUSTLE
Yo, Gow-ther!
!
CAP-TAIN.
You were paying Merlin a visit?

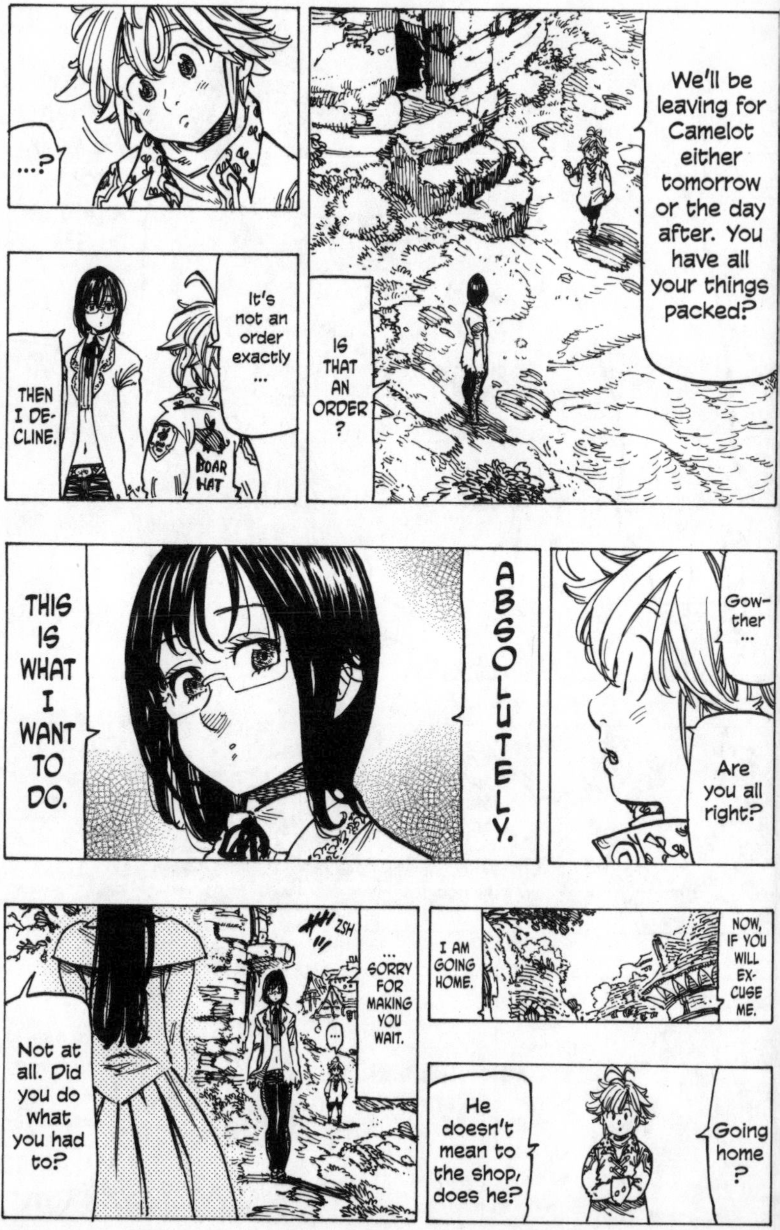
We'll be leaving for Camelot either tomorrow or the day after. You have all your things packed?
IS THAT AN ORDER?
...?
It's not an order exactly...
THEN I DECLINE.
BOAR HAT
Gow-ther...
Are you all right?
ABSOLUTELY.
THIS IS WHAT I WANT TO DO.
NOW, IF YOU WILL EXCUSE ME.
I AM GOING HOME.
Going home?
He doesn't mean to the shop, does he?
ZSH
...SORRY FOR MAKING YOU WAIT.
...
Not at all. Did you do what you had to?

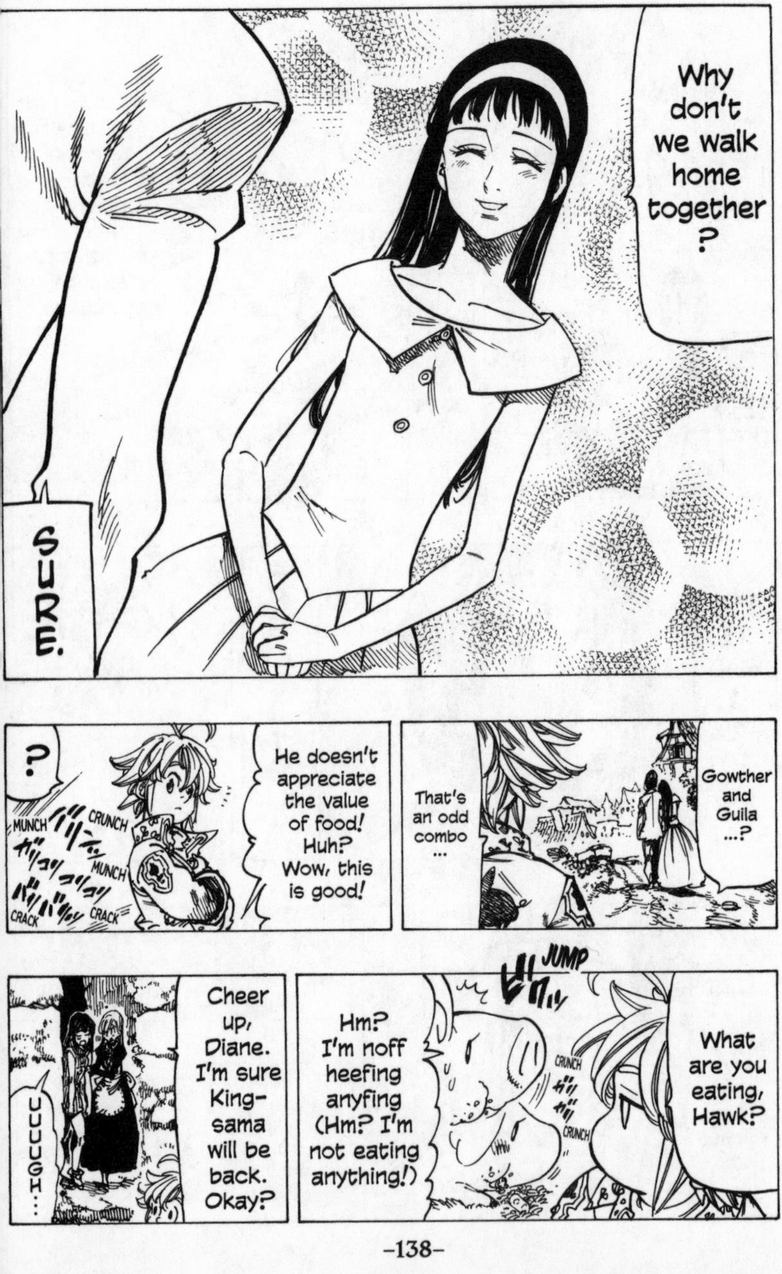
Why don't we walk home together?
SURE.
Gowther and Guila ...?
That's an odd combo ...
He doesn't appreciate the value of food! Huh? Wow, this is good!
?
CRUNCH
MUNCH
MUNCH
CRACK
CRACK
JUMP
What are you eating, Hawk?
CRUNCH
CRUNCH
Hm? I'm noff heefing anyfing (Hm? I'm not eating anything!)
Cheer up, Diane. I'm sure King-sama will be back. Okay?
UUUUGH...

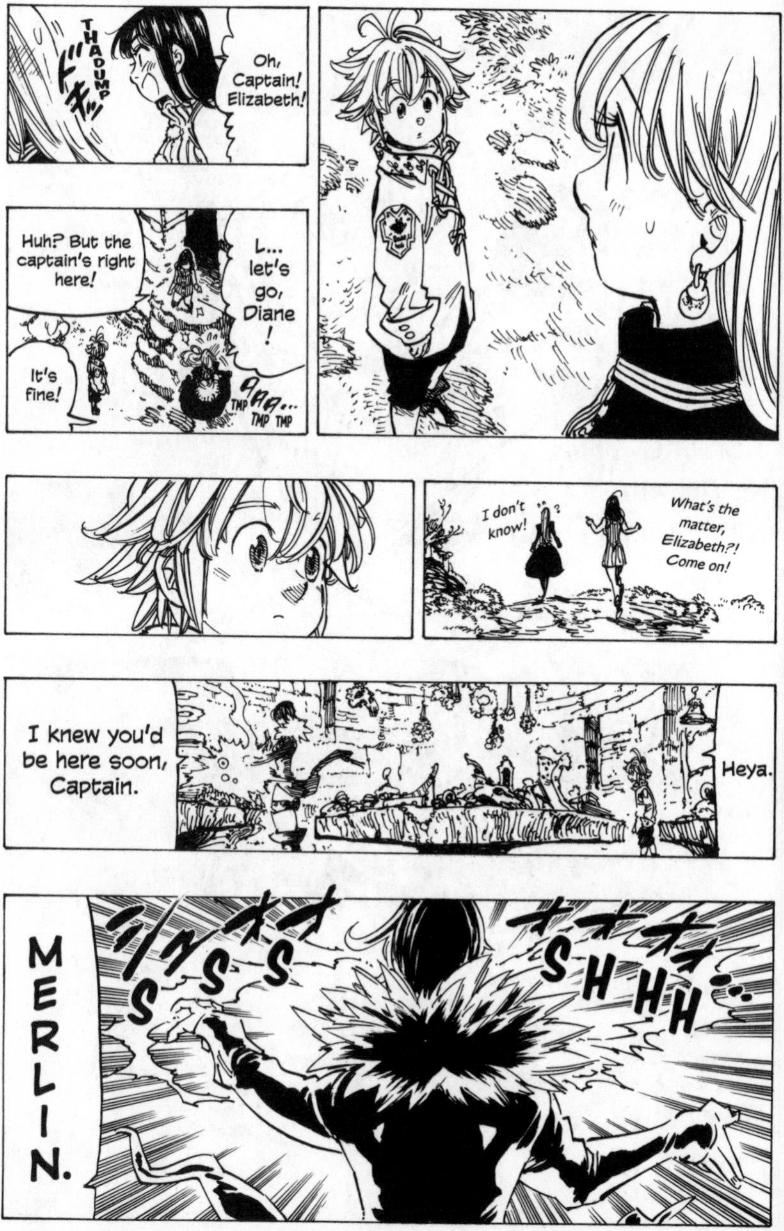
THADUMP
Oh, Captain! Elizabeth!
L... let's go, Diane!
Huh? But the captain's right here!
TMP TMP TMP
It's fine!
What's the matter, Elizabeth?! Come on!
I don't know!
Heya.
I knew you'd be here soon, Captain.
SSS
SHHH
MERLIN.

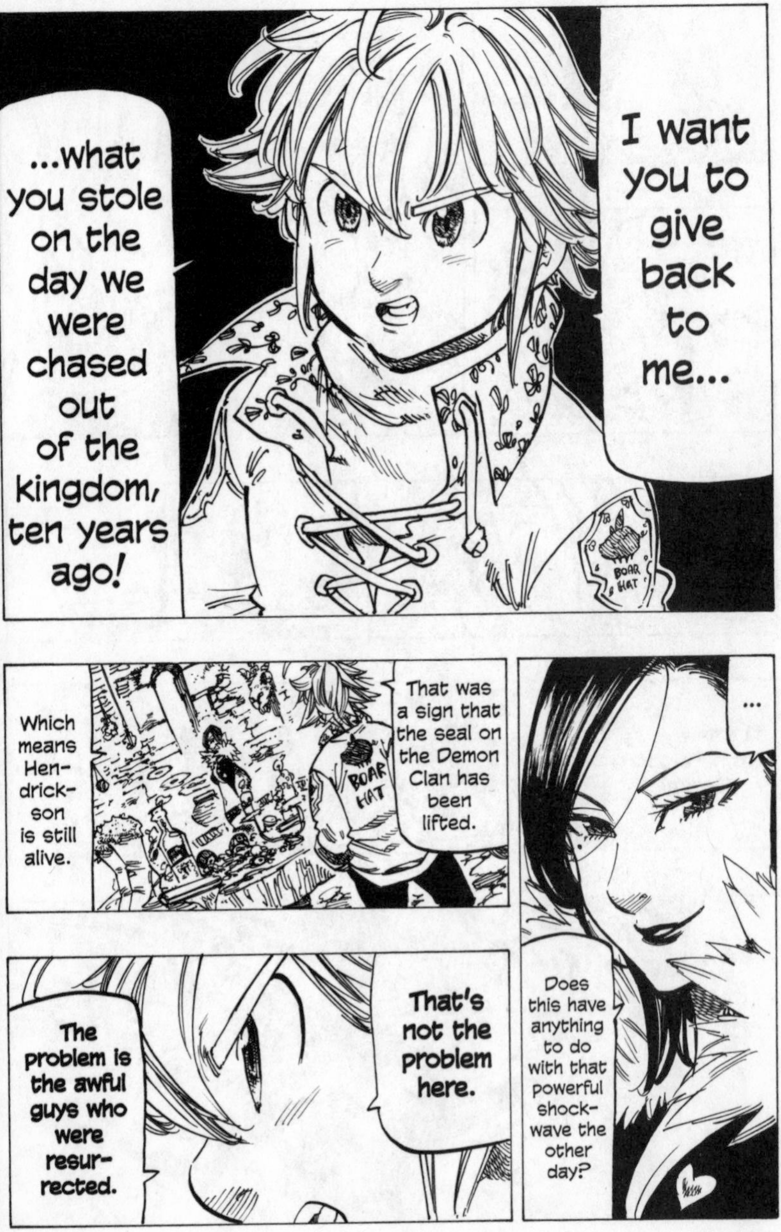
I want you to give back to me...
...what you stole on the day we were chased out of the kingdom, ten years ago!
BOAR HAT
...
Does this have anything to do with that powerful shock-wave the other day?
That was a sign that the seal on the Demon Clan has been lifted.
BOAR HAT
Which means Hendrickson is still alive.
That's not the problem here.
The problem is the awful guys who were resurrected.

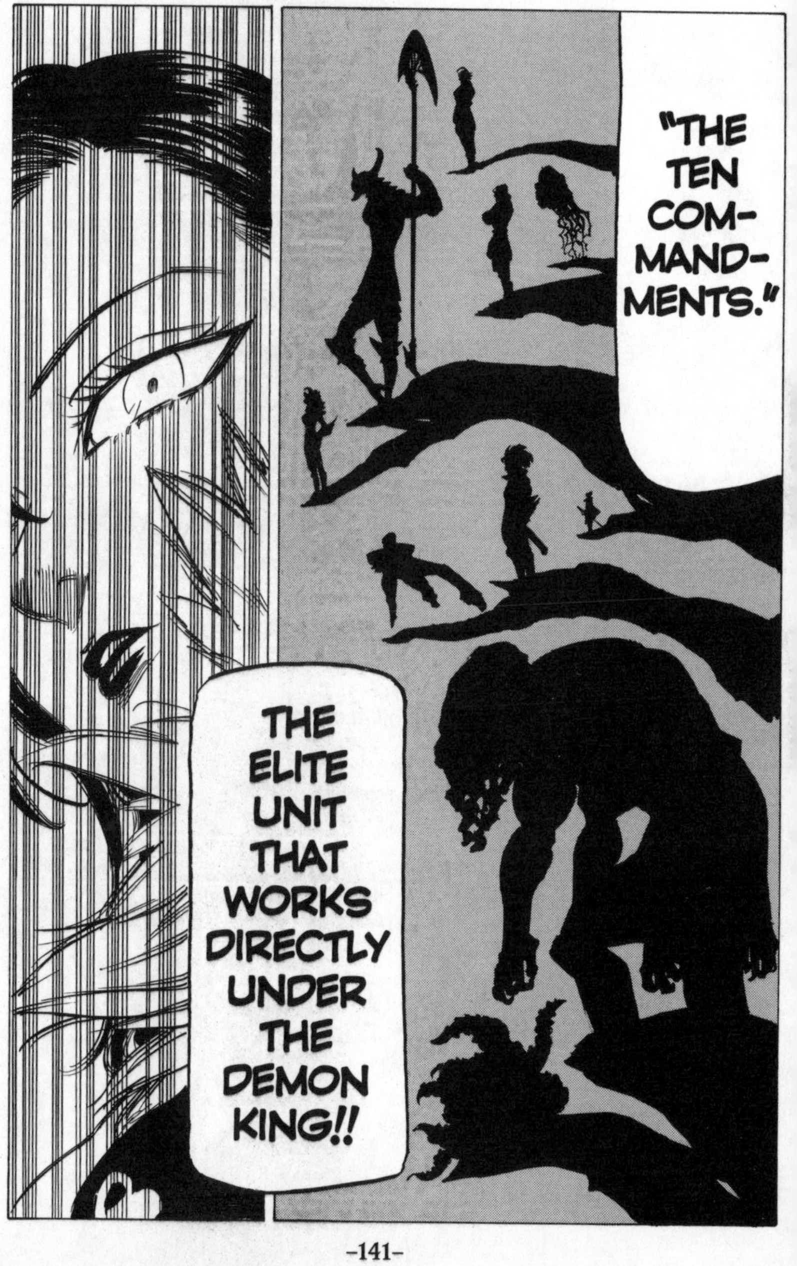
"THE TEN COMMANDMENTS."
THE ELITE UNIT THAT WORKS DIRECTLY UNDER THE DEMON KING!!

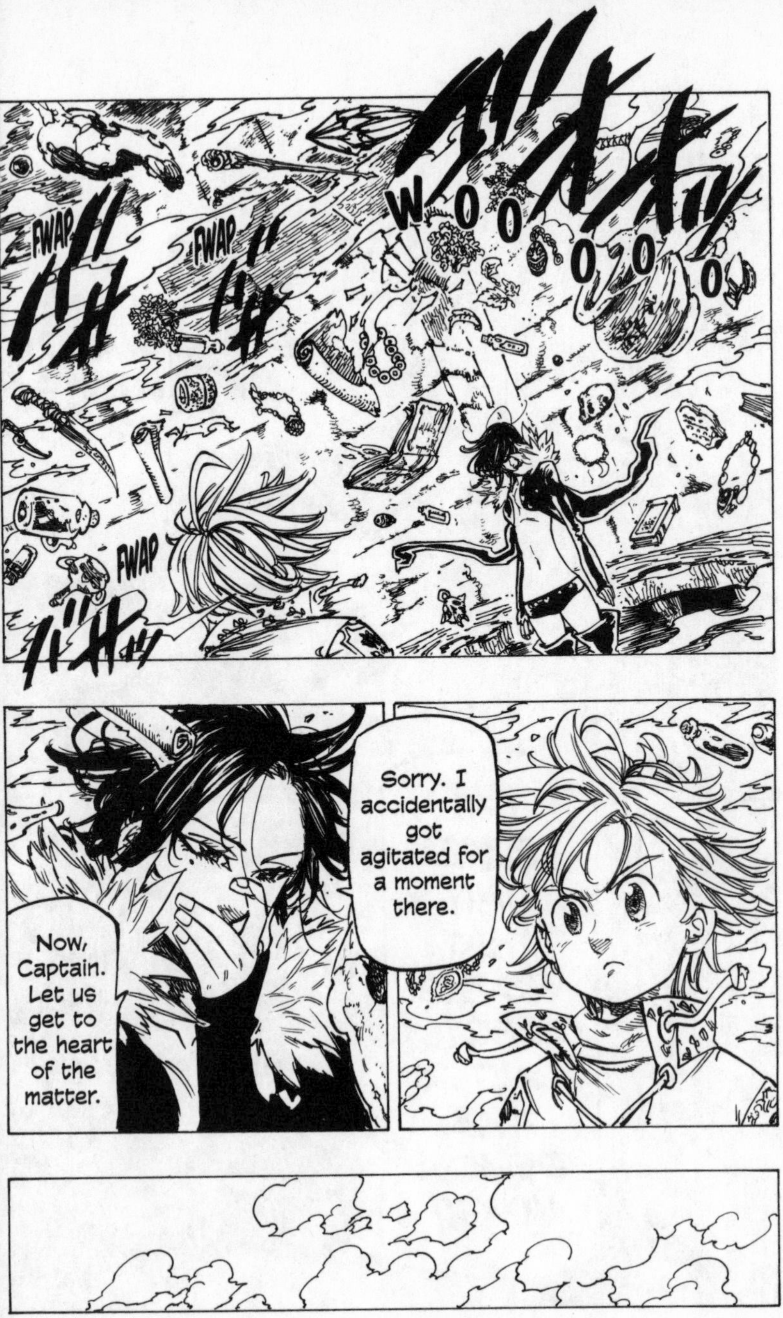
WOOOOO
FWAP
FWAP
FWAP
Sorry. I accidentally got agitated for a moment there.
Now, Captain. Let us get to the heart of the matter.

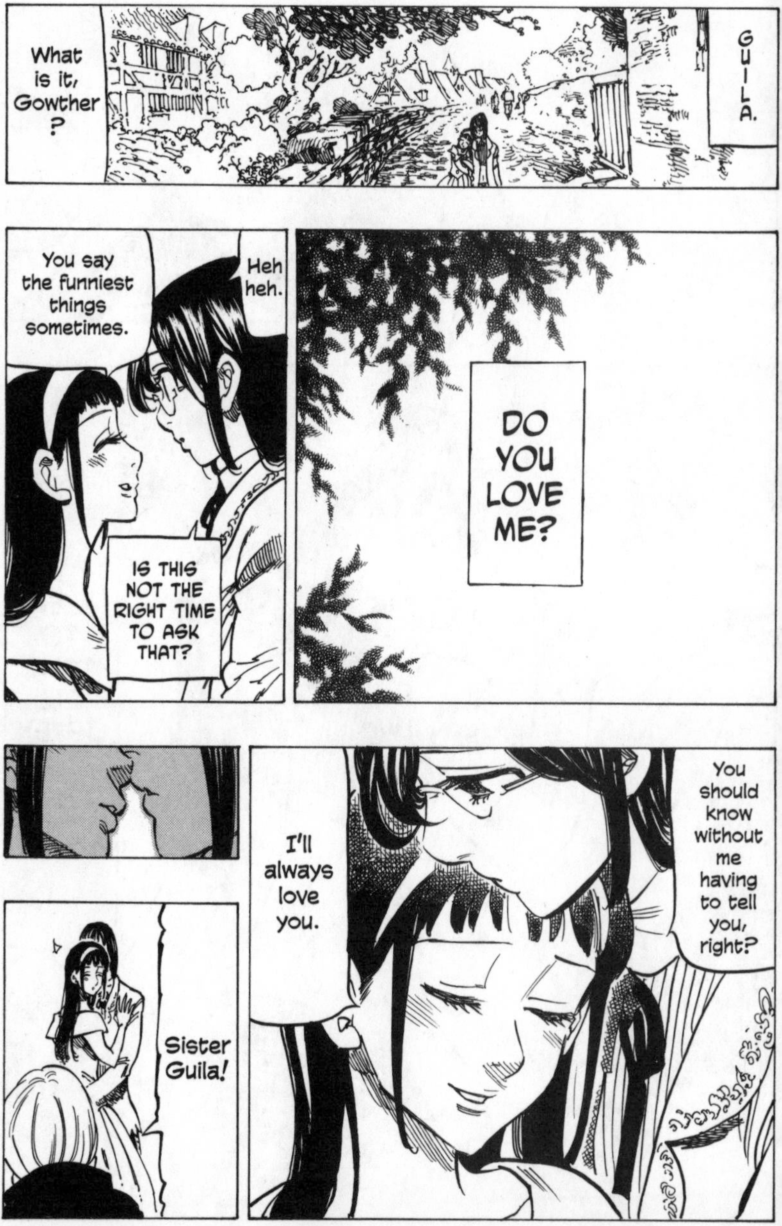
GUILA.
What is it, Gowther?
DO YOU LOVE ME?
Heh heh.
You say the funniest things sometimes.
IS THIS NOT THE RIGHT TIME TO ASK THAT?
You should know without me having to tell you, right?
I'll always love you.
Sister Guila!

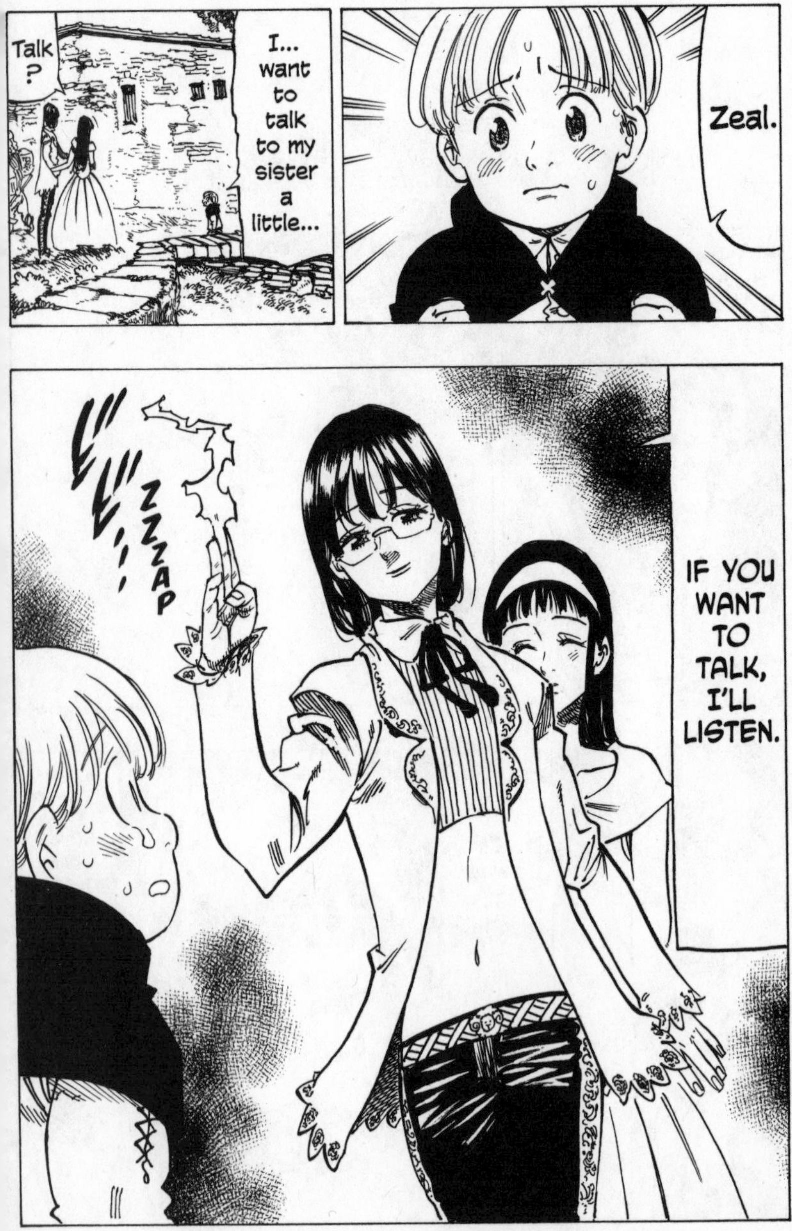
Zeal.
I... want to talk to my sister a little...
Talk?
IF YOU WANT TO TALK, I'LL LISTEN.
ZZZAP

Chapter 112- Existence & Proof

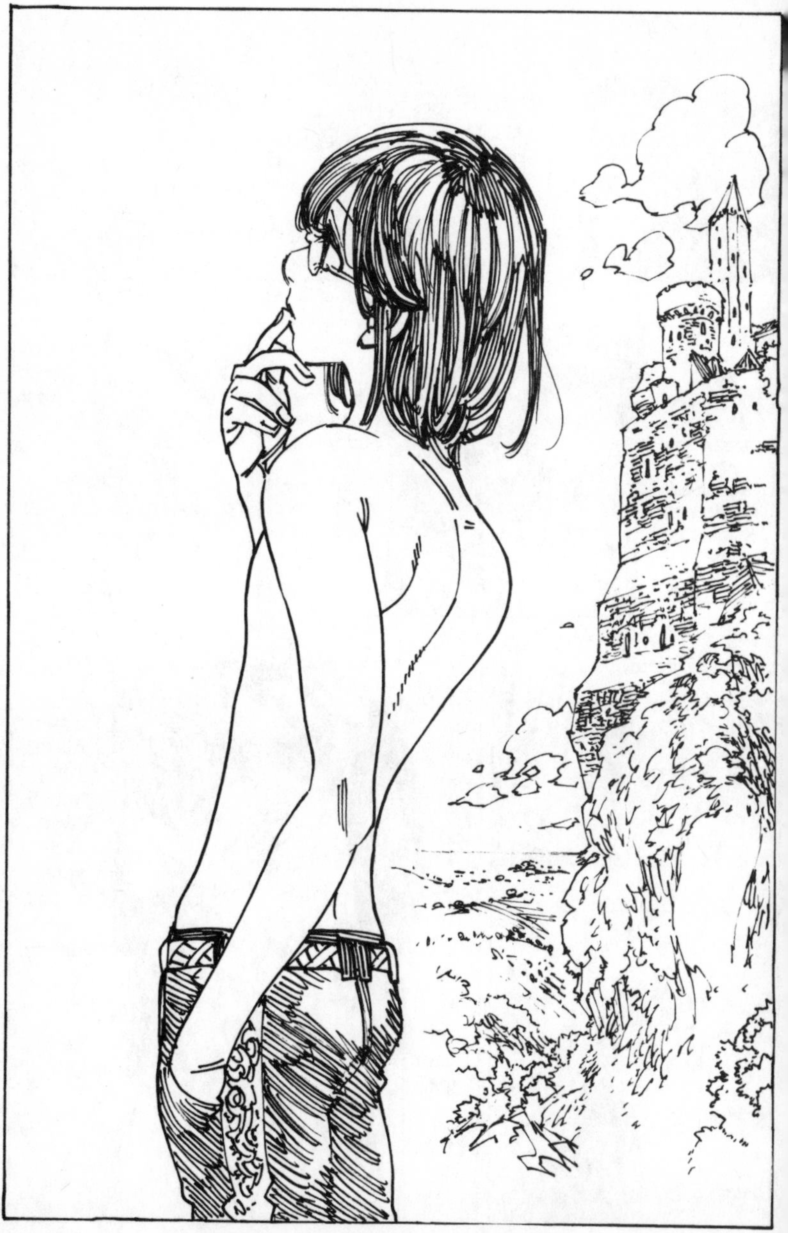

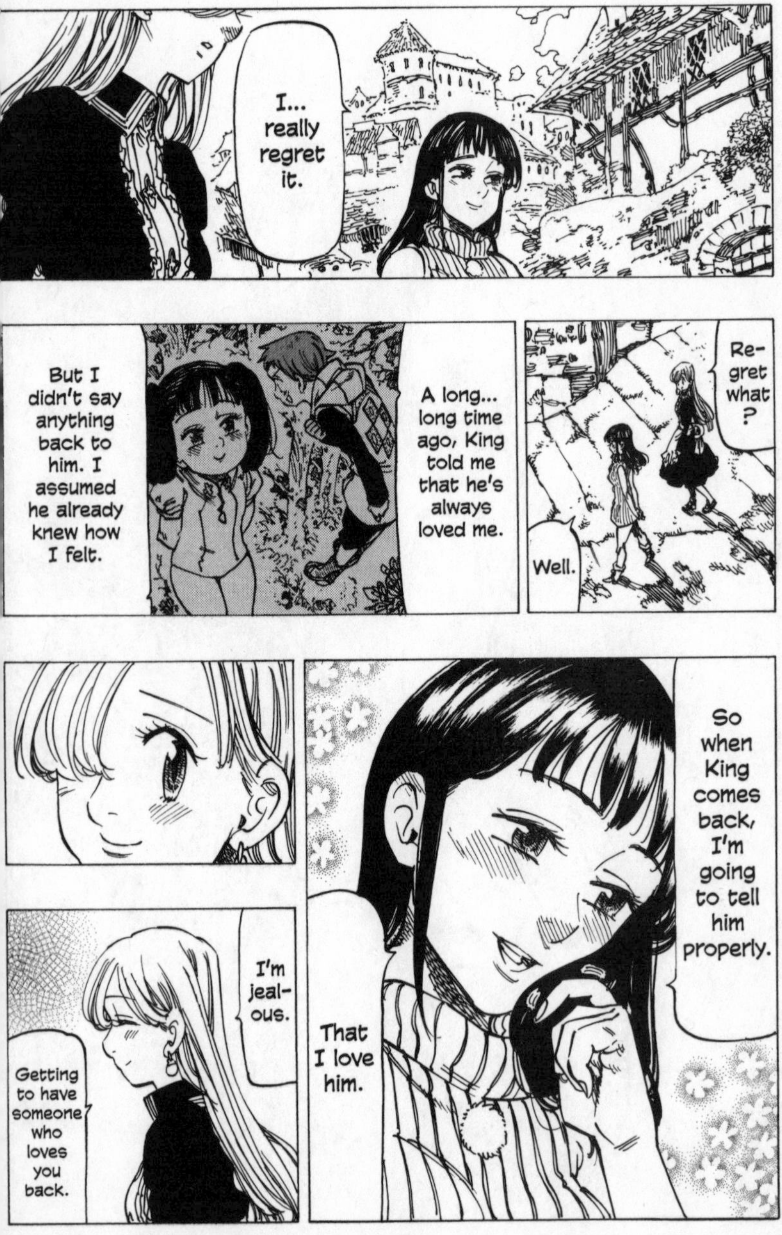
I... really regret it.
Regret what?
Well.
A long... long time ago, King told me that he's always loved me.
But I didn't say anything back to him. I assumed he already knew how I felt.
So when King comes back, I'm going to tell him properly.
That I love him.
I'm jealous.
Getting to have someone who loves you back.

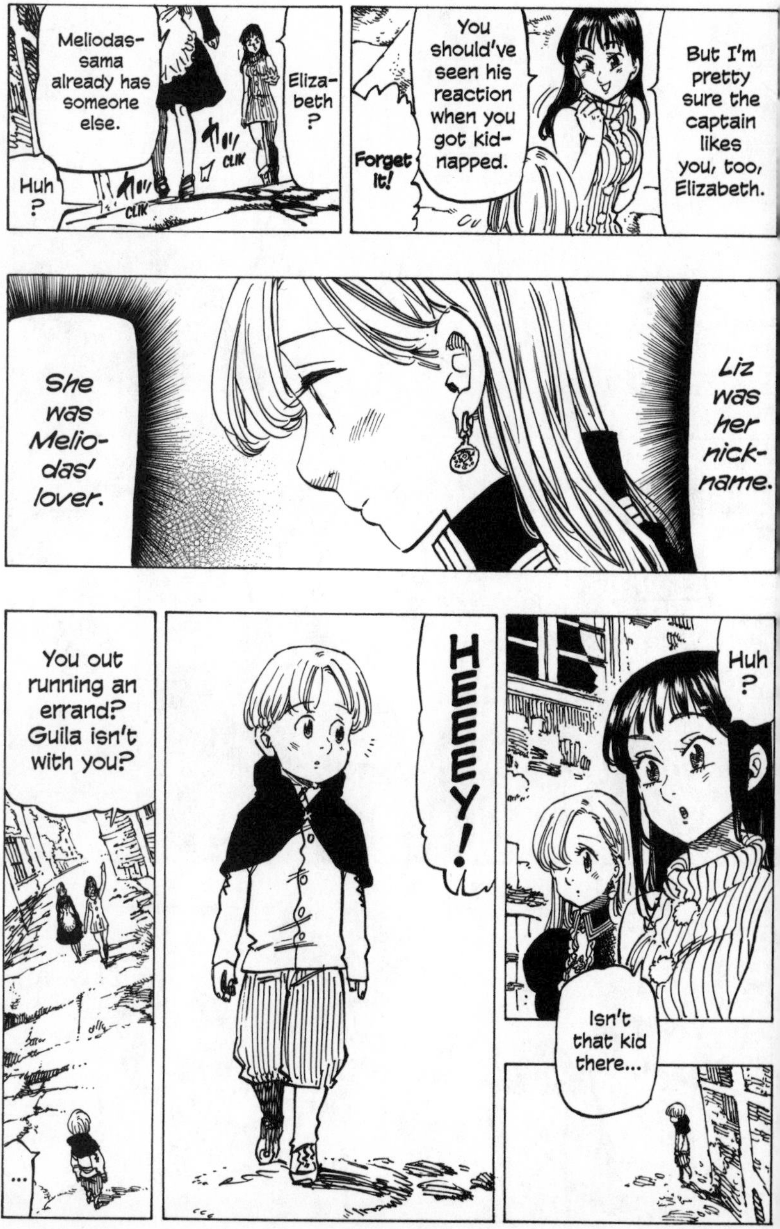
But I'm pretty sure the captain likes you, too, Elizabeth.
You should've seen his reaction when you got kid-napped.
Forget it!
Eliza-beth?
Meliodas-sama already has someone else.
CLIK
CLIK
Huh?
Liz was her nick-name.
She was Melio-das' lover.
Huh?
Isn't that kid there...
HEEEEY!
You out running an errand? Guila isn't with you?
...

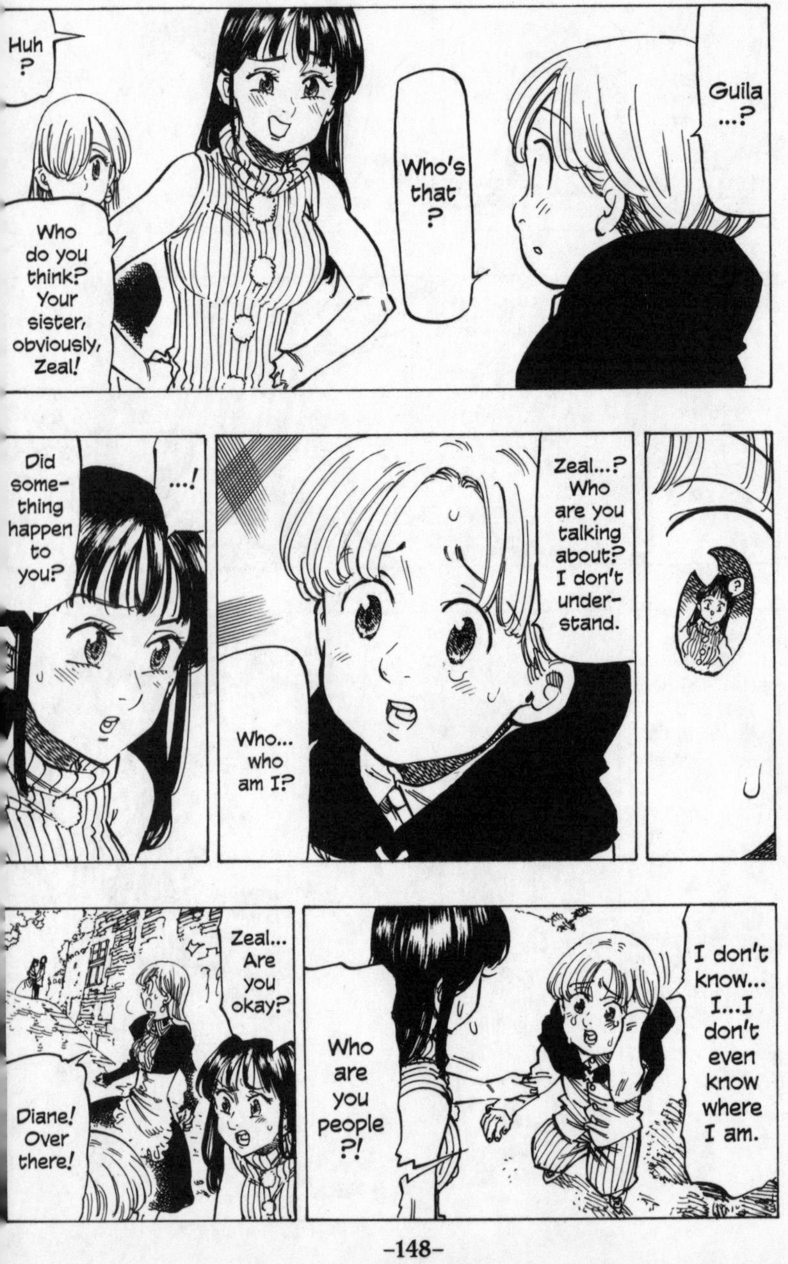
Guila ...?
Who's that ?
Huh ?
Who do you think? Your sister, obviously, Zeal!
Zeal...? Who are you talking about? I don't understand.
Who... who am I?
...!
Did something happen to you?
I don't know... I...I don't even know where I am.
Who are you people ?!
Zeal... Are you okay?
Diane! Over there!

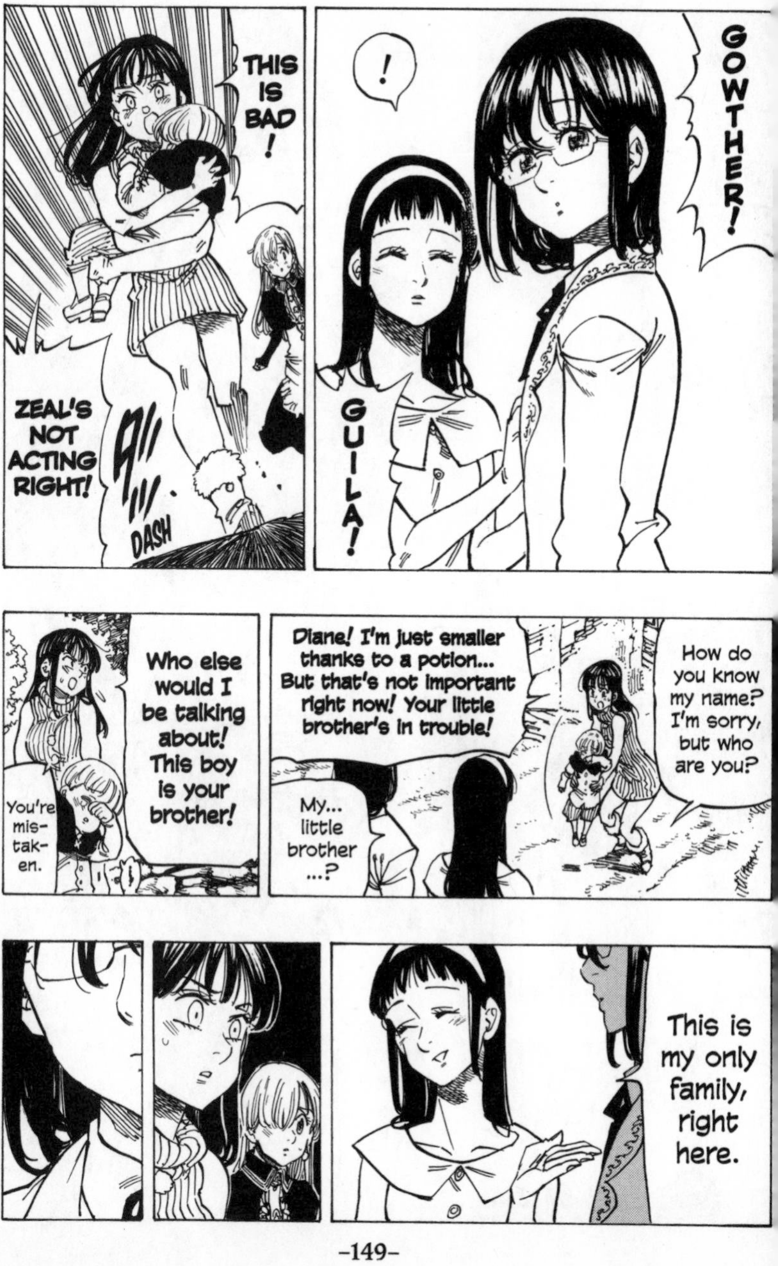
GOWTHER!
!
GUILA!
THIS IS BAD!
ZEAL'S NOT ACTING RIGHT!
DASH
How do you know my name? I'm sorry, but who are you?
Diane! I'm just smaller thanks to a potion... But that's not important right now! Your little brother's in trouble!
My... little brother ...?
Who else would I be talking about! This boy is your brother!
You're mis-tak-en.
This is my only family, right here.

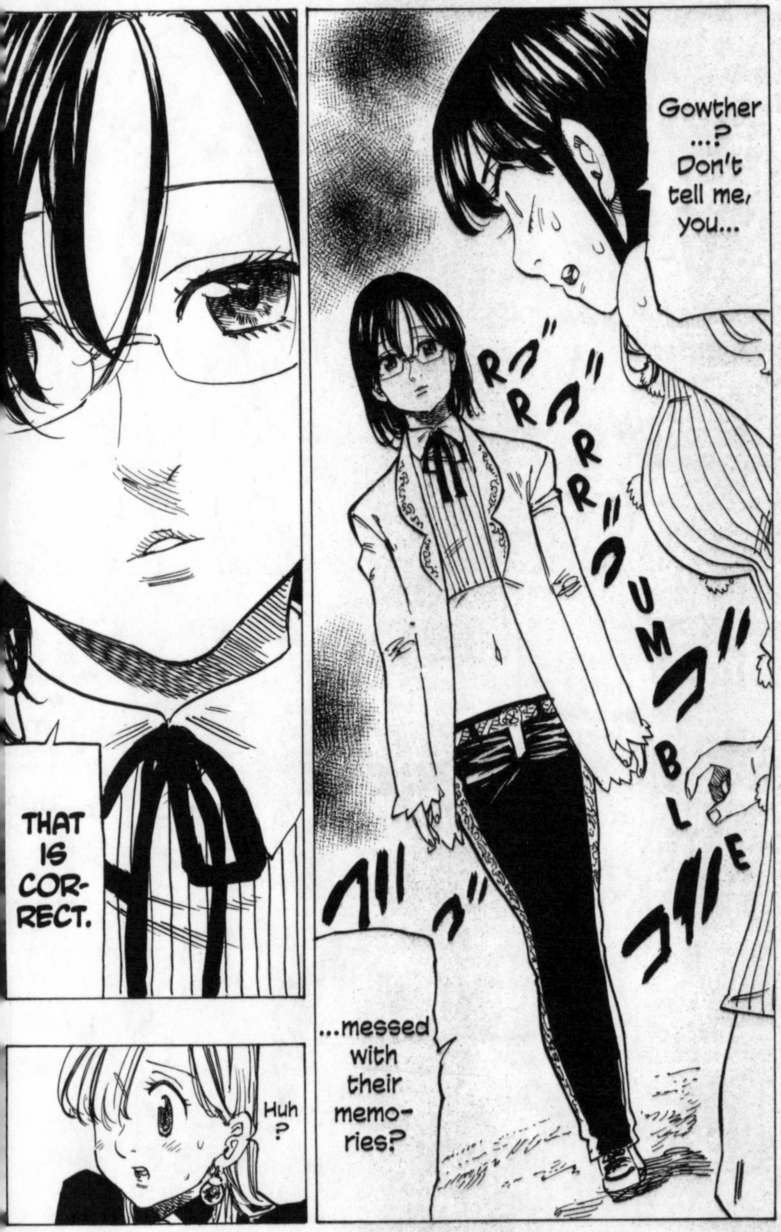
Gowther ...? Don't tell me, you...
RRRRUMBLE
...messed with their memo-ries?
THAT IS COR-RECT.
Huh?

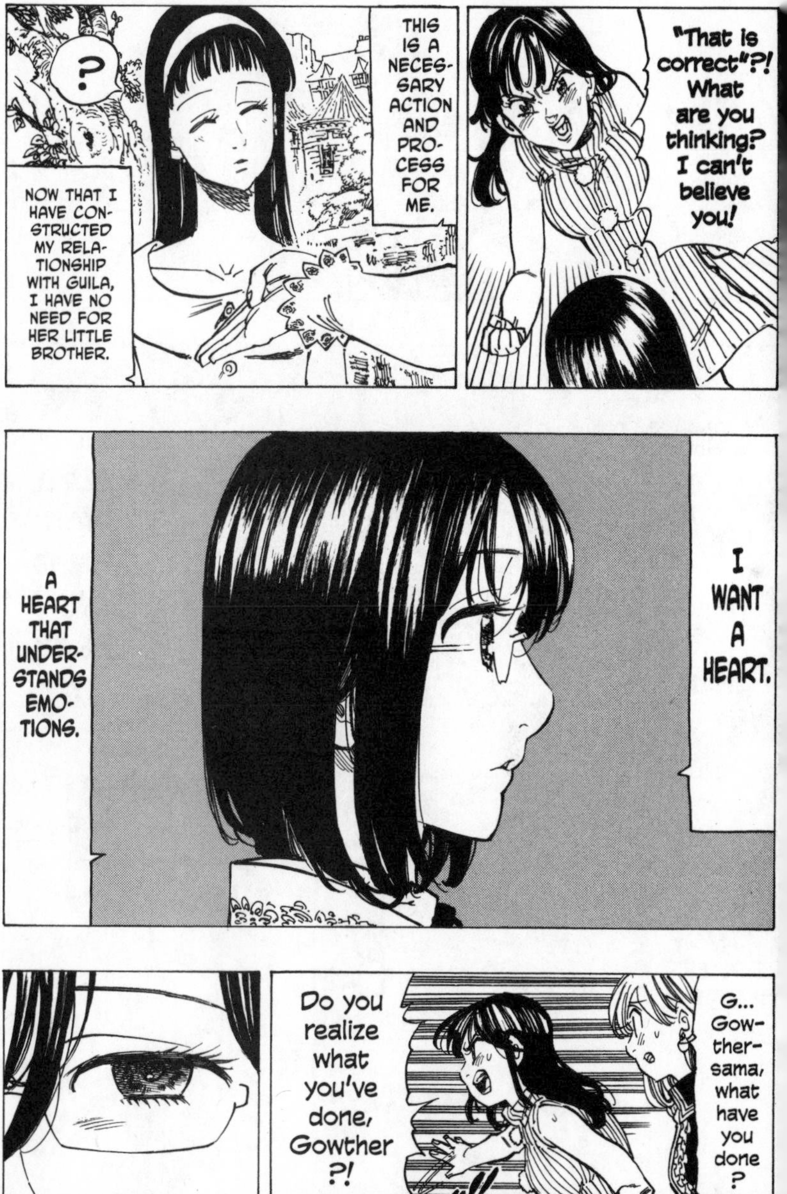
"That is correct"?! What are you thinking? I can't believe you!
THIS IS A NECESSARY ACTION AND PROCESS FOR ME.
?
NOW THAT I HAVE CONSTRUCTED MY RELATIONSHIP WITH GUILA, I HAVE NO NEED FOR HER LITTLE BROTHER.
I WANT A HEART.
A HEART THAT UNDERSTANDS EMOTIONS.
G... Gowther-sama, what have you done?
Do you realize what you've done, Gowther?!
BAH

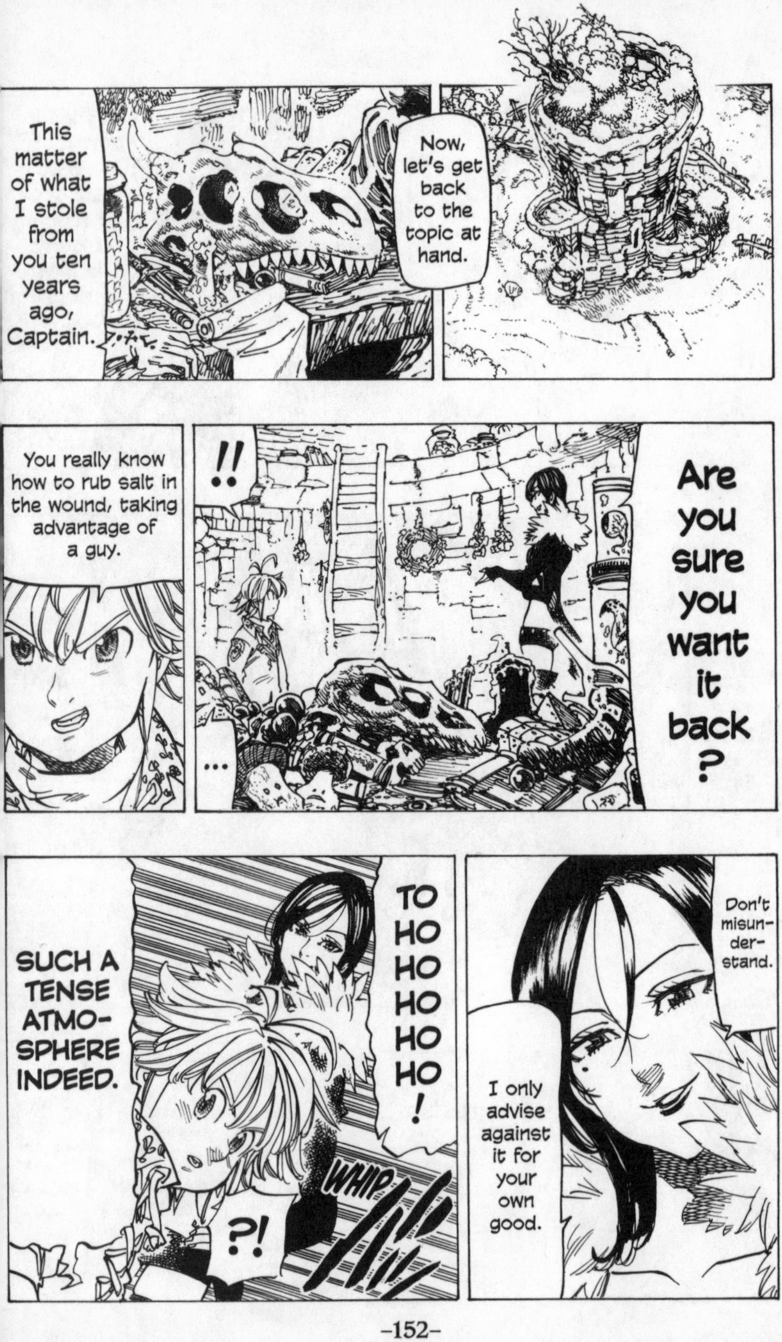
Now, let's get back to the topic at hand.
This matter of what I stole from you ten years ago, Captain.
Are you sure you want it back?
!!
...
You really know how to rub salt in the wound, taking advantage of a guy.
Don't misunderstand.
I only advise against it for your own good.
TO HO HO HO HO HO!
SUCH A TENSE ATMOSPHERE INDEED.
WHIP
?!

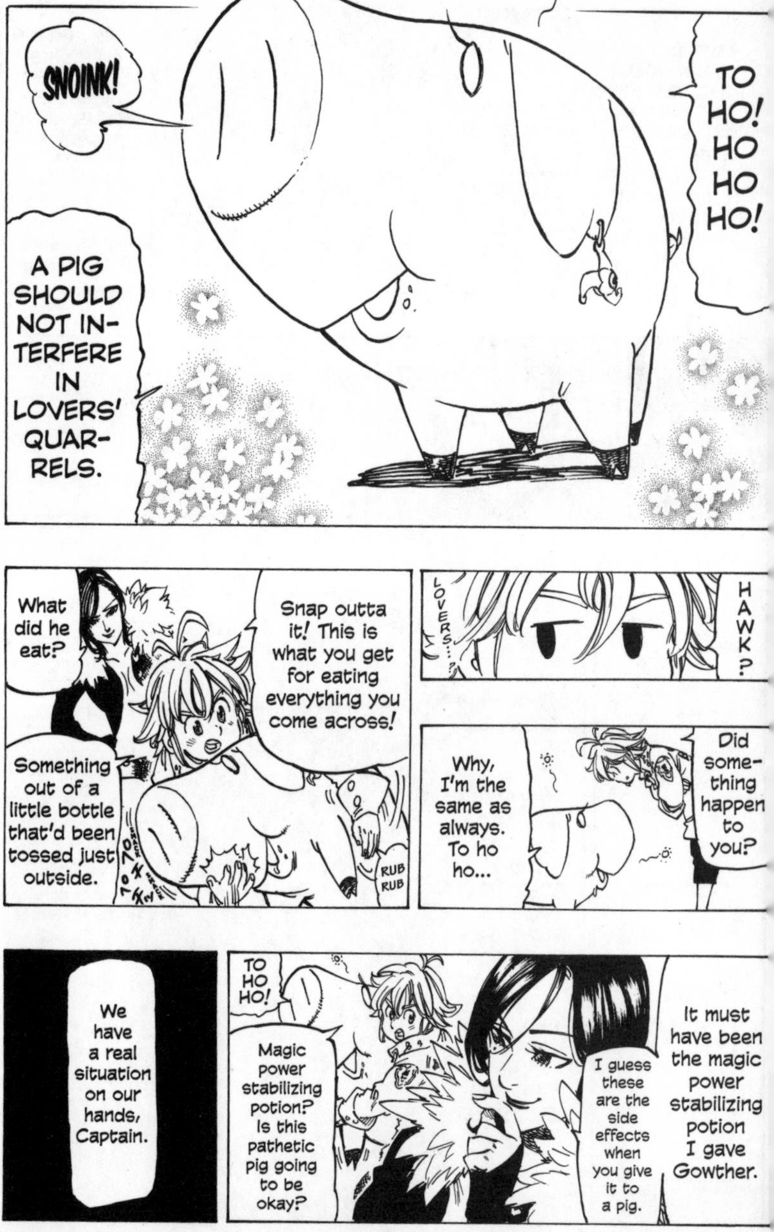
TO HO! HO HO HO!
SNOINK!
A PIG SHOULD NOT INTERFERE IN LOVERS' QUARRELS.
HAWK?
LOVERS...?
Did something happen to you?
Why, I'm the same as always. To ho ho...
Snap outta it! This is what you get for eating everything you come across!
What did he eat?
Something out of a little bottle that'd been tossed just outside.
RUB RUB
It must have been the magic power stabilizing potion I gave Gowther.
I guess these are the side effects when you give it to a pig.
TO HO HO!
Magic power stabilizing potion? Is this pathetic pig going to be okay?
We have a real situation on our hands, Captain.

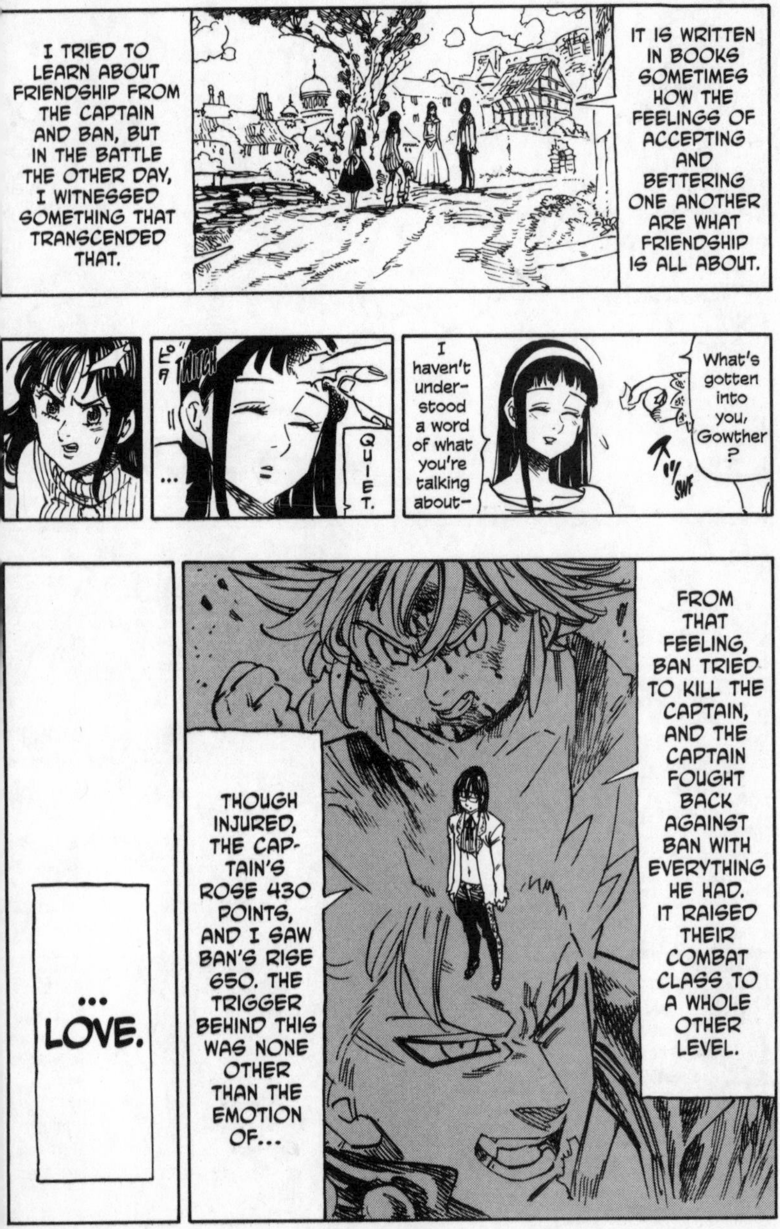
IT IS WRITTEN IN BOOKS SOMETIMES HOW THE FEELINGS OF ACCEPTING AND BETTERING ONE ANOTHER ARE WHAT FRIENDSHIP IS ALL ABOUT.
I TRIED TO LEARN ABOUT FRIENDSHIP FROM THE CAPTAIN AND BAN, BUT IN THE BATTLE THE OTHER DAY, I WITNESSED SOMETHING THAT TRANSCENDED THAT.
What's gotten into you, Gowther?
SWF
I haven't understood a word of what you're talking about-
QUIET.
TWITCH
...
FROM THAT FEELING, BAN TRIED TO KILL THE CAPTAIN, AND THE CAPTAIN FOUGHT BACK AGAINST BAN WITH EVERYTHING HE HAD. IT RAISED THEIR COMBAT CLASS TO A WHOLE OTHER LEVEL.
THOUGH INJURED, THE CAPTAIN'S ROSE 430 POINTS, AND I SAW BAN'S RISE 650. THE TRIGGER BEHIND THIS WAS NONE OTHER THAN THE EMOTION OF...
...LOVE.

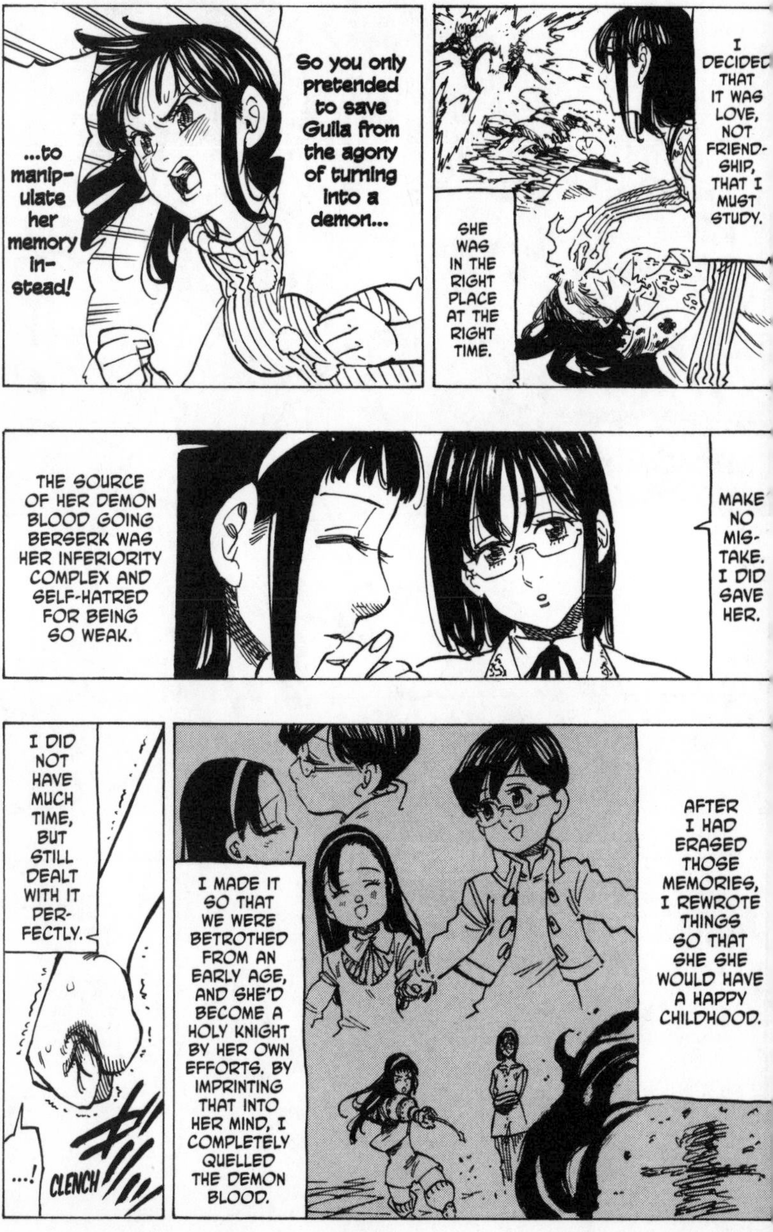
I DECIDED THAT IT WAS LOVE, NOT FRIENDSHIP, THAT I MUST STUDY.
SHE WAS IN THE RIGHT PLACE AT THE RIGHT TIME.
So you only pretended to save Gulla from the agony of turning into a demon...
...to manipulate her memory instead!
MAKE NO MISTAKE. I DID SAVE HER.
THE SOURCE OF HER DEMON BLOOD GOING BERSERK WAS HER INFERIORITY COMPLEX AND SELF-HATRED FOR BEING SO WEAK.
AFTER I HAD ERASED THOSE MEMORIES, I REWROTE THINGS SO THAT SHE SHE WOULD HAVE A HAPPY CHILDHOOD.
I MADE IT SO THAT WE WERE BETROTHED FROM AN EARLY AGE, AND SHE'D BECOME A HOLY KNIGHT BY HER OWN EFFORTS. BY IMPRINTING THAT INTO HER MIND, I COMPLETELY QUELLED THE DEMON BLOOD.
I DID NOT HAVE MUCH TIME, BUT STILL DEALT WITH IT PERFECTLY.
...!
CLENCH

I DON'T CARE WHAT REASON YOU HAVE, YOU CAN'T JUST MESS WITH A PERSON'S MEMORIES LIKE THAT!

AS IF!!

?

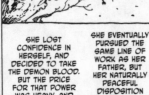

HER FATHER, THE HOLY KNIGHT, WAS SUSPECTED OF KILLING HIS COMRADE, AND THEN DISAPPEARED. SHE HAD TO ENDURE THE JUDGMENT OF OTHERS AS SHE MAINTAINED TRUST IN HER FATHER AND RAISED HER LITTLE BROTHER.

SHE EVENTUALLY PURSUED THE SAME LINE OF WORK AS HER FATHER, BUT HER NATURALLY PEACEFUL DISPOSITION WORKED AGAINST HER, AS IT THWARTED HER MAGIC FROM EVER FULLY BLOSSOMING.

SHE LOST CONFIDENCE IN HERSELF, AND DECIDED TO TAKE THE DEMON BLOOD. BUT THE PRICE FOR THAT POWER WAS HEAVY, AND SHE BORE IN HER HEART A SUFFERING GREATER THAN ANY SHE HAD EVER BEFORE.

RUSTLE

RUSTLE

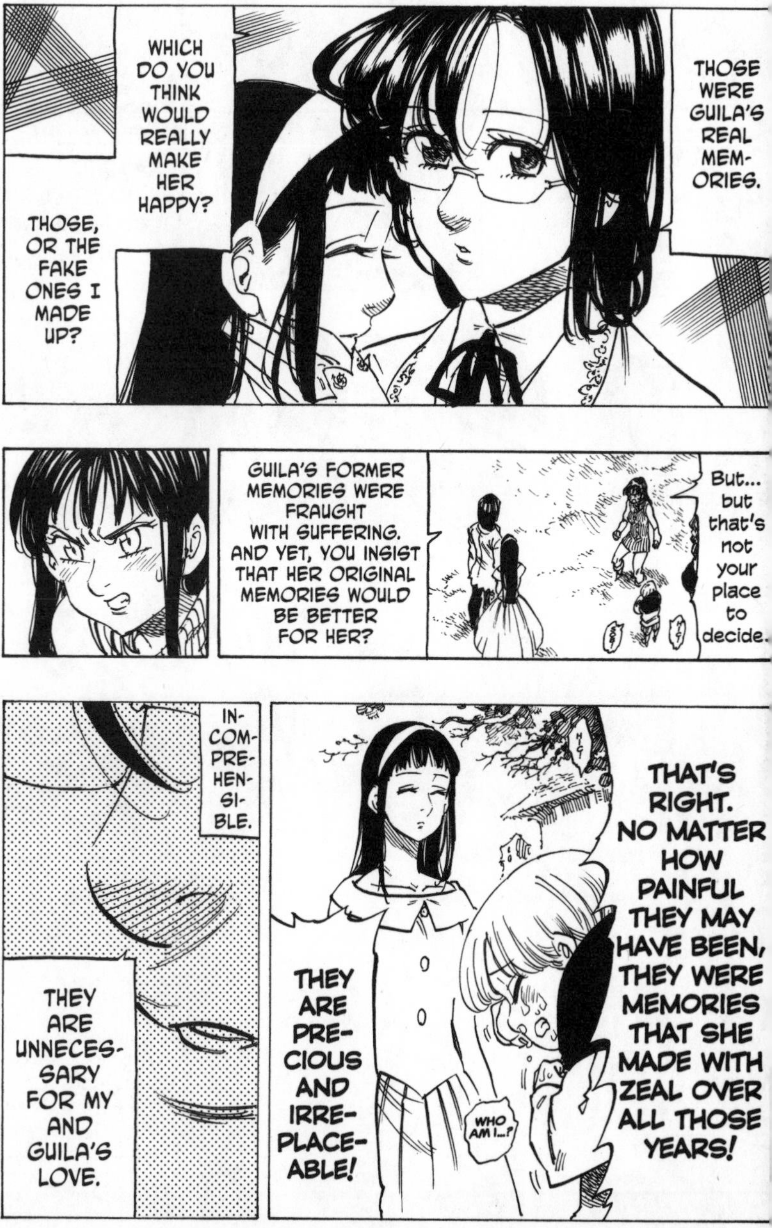
THOSE WERE GUILA'S REAL MEMORIES.
WHICH DO YOU THINK WOULD REALLY MAKE HER HAPPY?
THOSE, OR THE FAKE ONES I MADE UP?
But... but that's not your place to decide.
GUILA'S FORMER MEMORIES WERE FRAUGHT WITH SUFFERING. AND YET, YOU INSIST THAT HER ORIGINAL MEMORIES WOULD BE BETTER FOR HER?
HIC
THAT'S RIGHT. NO MATTER HOW PAINFUL THEY MAY HAVE BEEN, THEY WERE MEMORIES THAT SHE MADE WITH ZEAL OVER ALL THOSE YEARS!
THEY ARE PRECIOUS AND IRREPLACEABLE!
WHO AM I...?
INCOMPREHENSIBLE.
THEY ARE UNNECESSARY FOR MY AND GUILA'S LOVE.

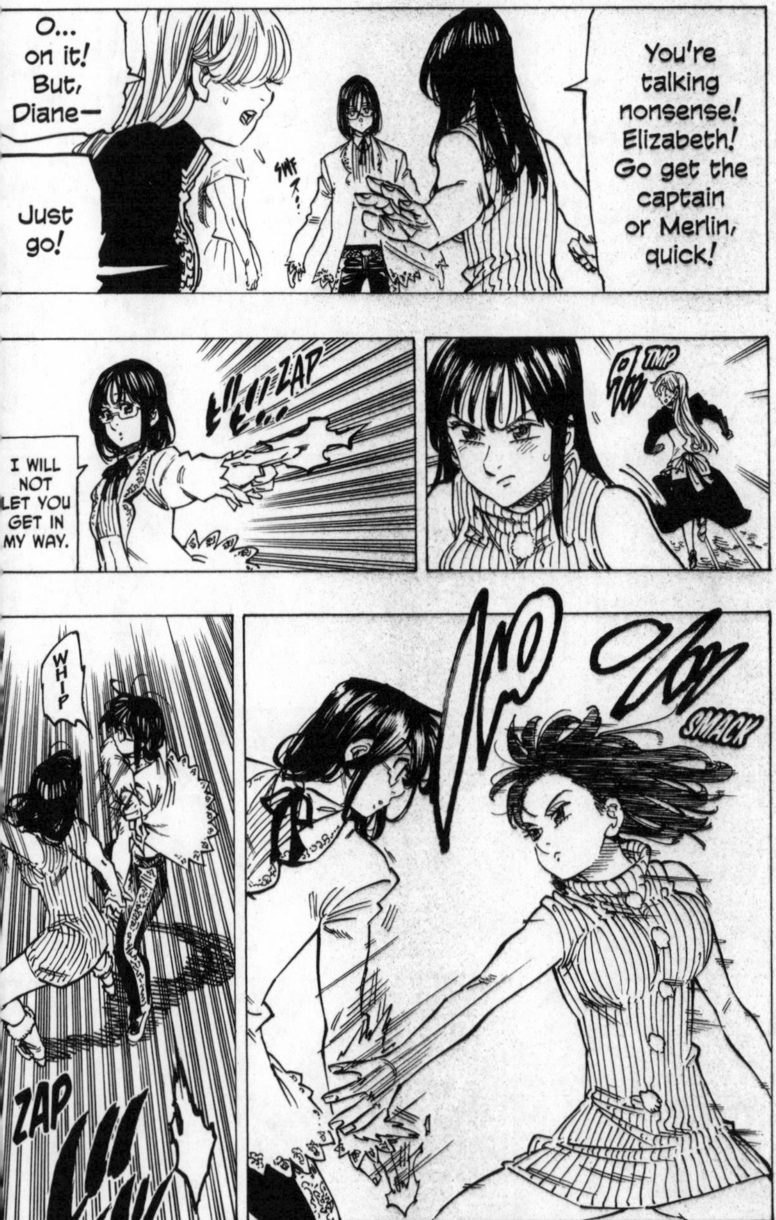
You're talking nonsense! Elizabeth! Go get the captain or Merlin, quick!
O... on it! But, Diane—
Just go!
TMP
ZAP
I WILL NOT LET YOU GET IN MY WAY.
SMACK
WHIP
ZAP

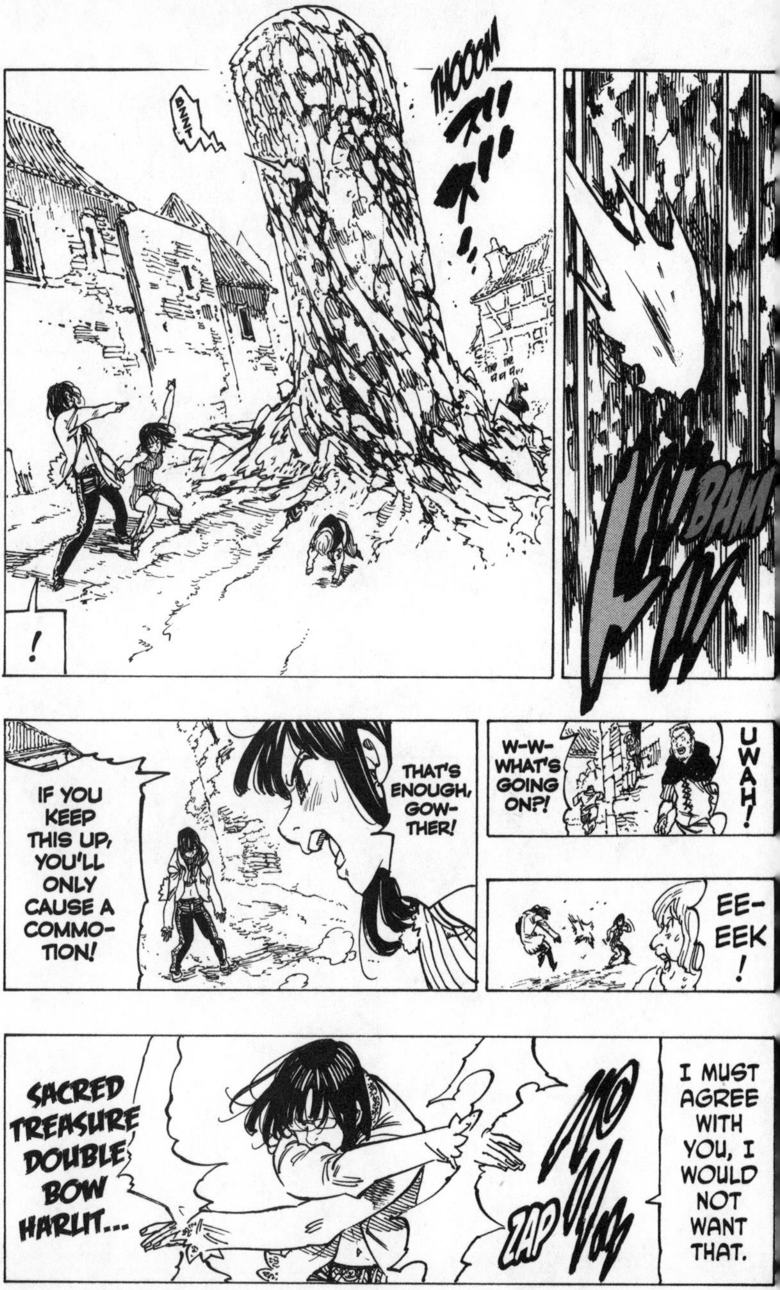
BAM
THOOOM
BZZT
!
UWAH!
W-W-WHAT'S GOING ON?!
EE-EEK!
THAT'S ENOUGH, GOWTHER!
IF YOU KEEP THIS UP, YOU'LL ONLY CAUSE A COMMOTION!
I MUST AGREE WITH YOU, I WOULD NOT WANT THAT.
ZAP
SACRED TREASURE DOUBLE BOW HARLIT...

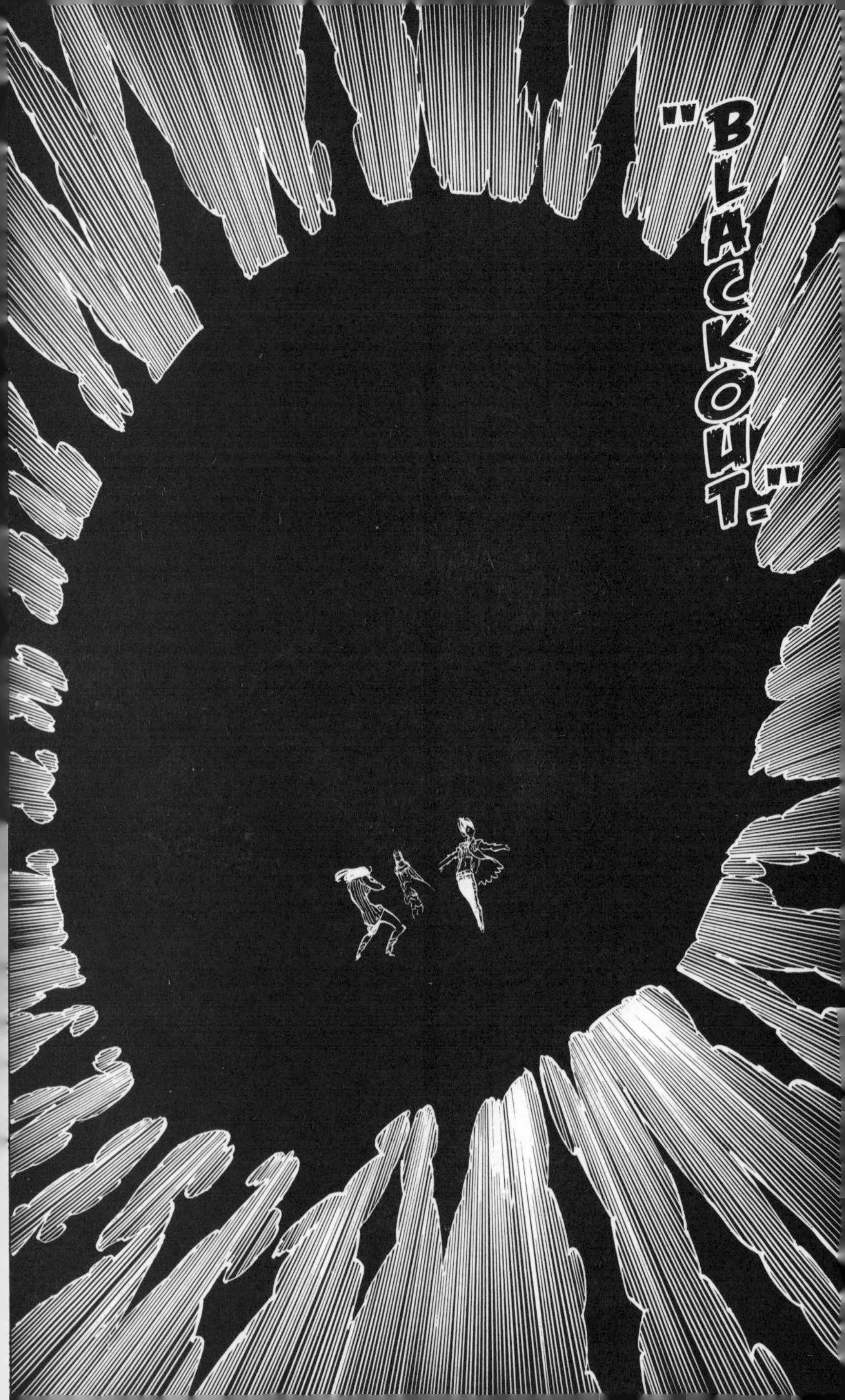
"BLACKOUT-"

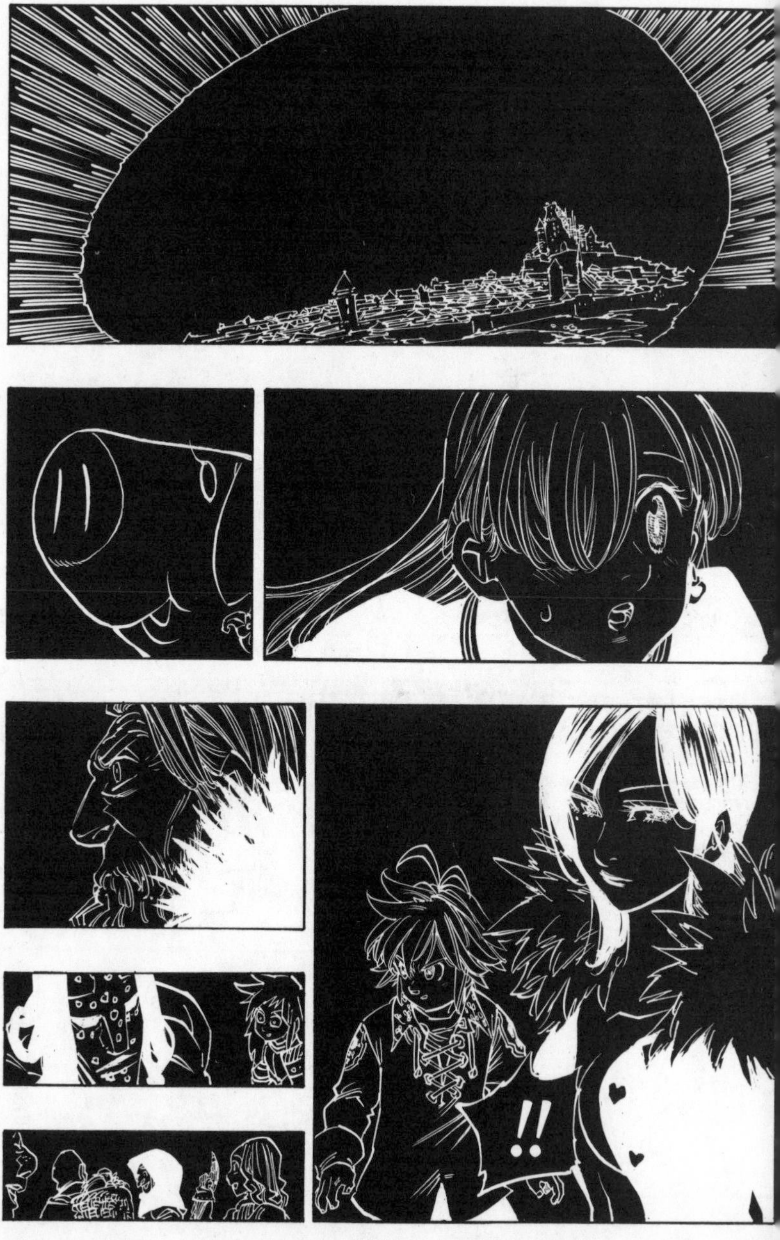
!!

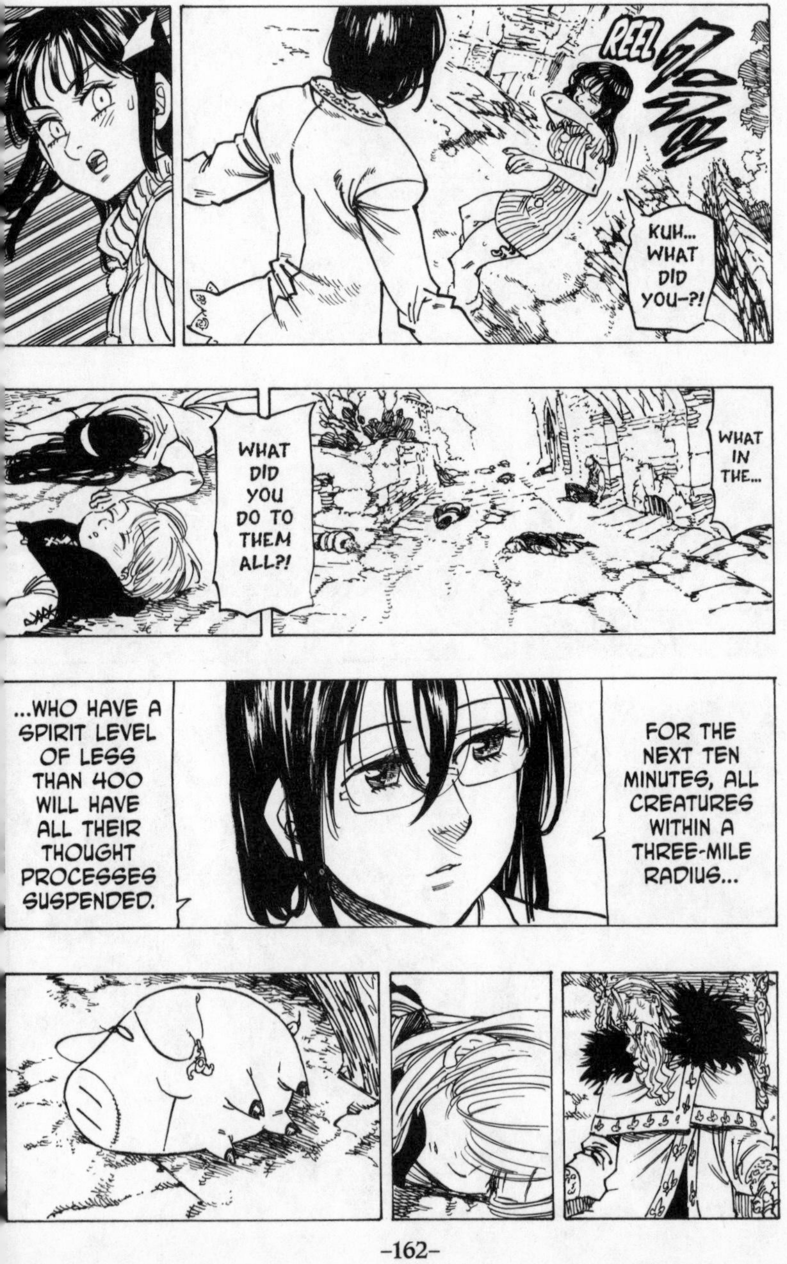
REEL
KUH... WHAT DID YOU-?!
WHAT IN THE...
WHAT DID YOU DO TO THEM ALL?!
FOR THE NEXT TEN MINUTES, ALL CREATURES WITHIN A THREE-MILE RADIUS...
...WHO HAVE A SPIRIT LEVEL OF LESS THAN 400 WILL HAVE ALL THEIR THOUGHT PROCESSES SUSPENDED.

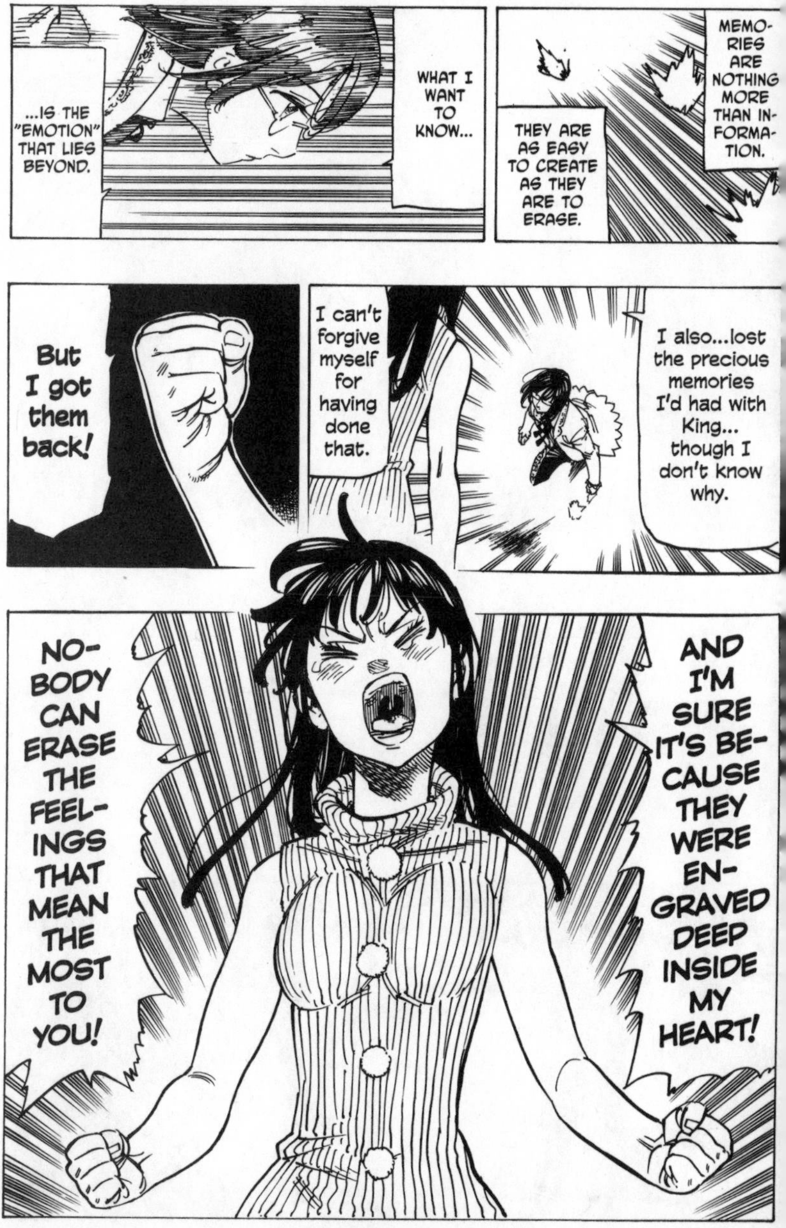
MEMORIES ARE NOTHING MORE THAN INFORMATION.
THEY ARE AS EASY TO CREATE AS THEY ARE TO ERASE.
WHAT I WANT TO KNOW...
...IS THE "EMOTION" THAT LIES BEYOND.
I also...lost the precious memories I'd had with King... though I don't know why.
I can't forgive myself for having done that.
But I got them back!
AND I'M SURE IT'S BECAUSE THEY WERE ENGRAVED DEEP INSIDE MY HEART!
NOBODY CAN ERASE THE FEELINGS THAT MEAN THE MOST TO YOU!

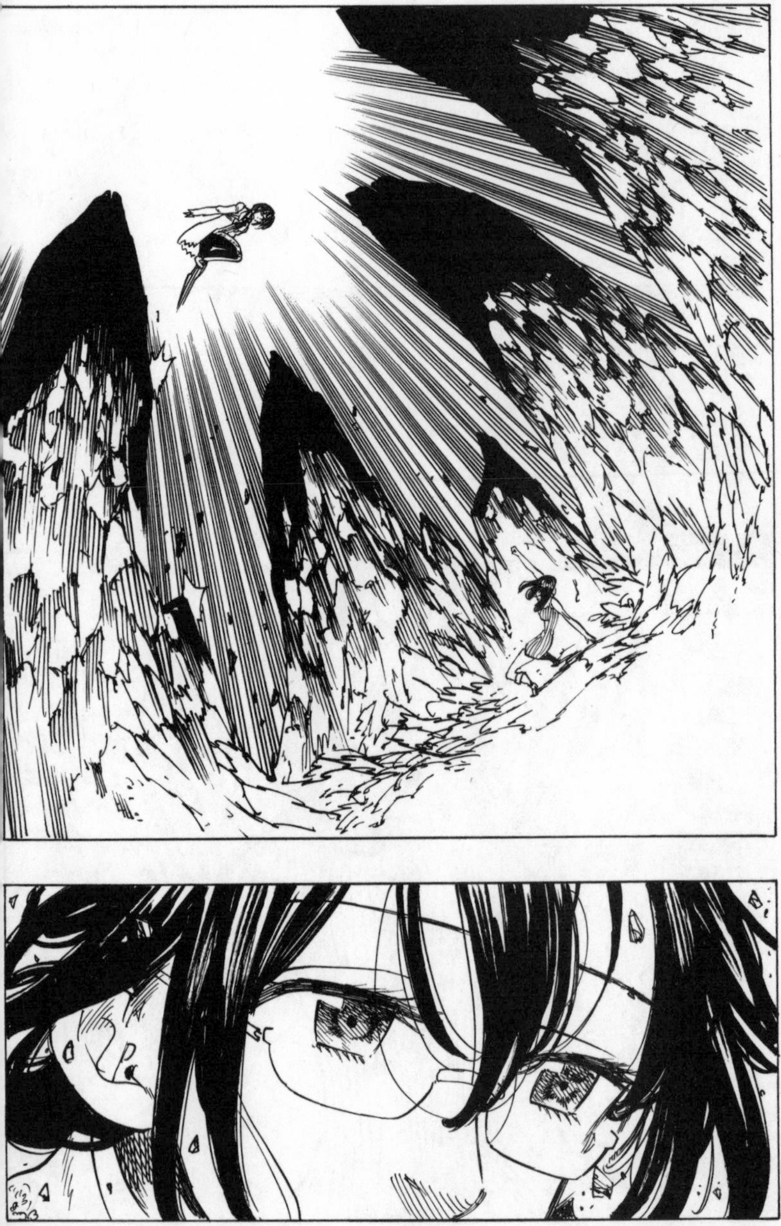

Chapter 113 - Revelation

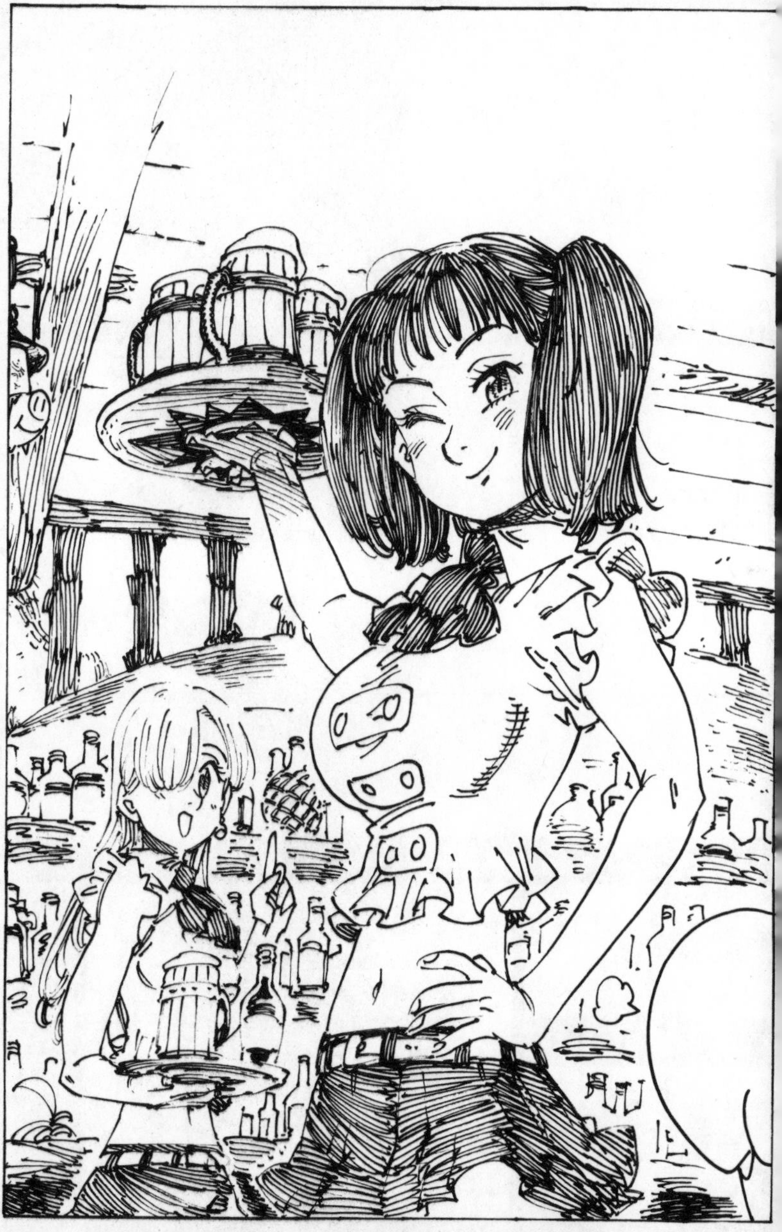

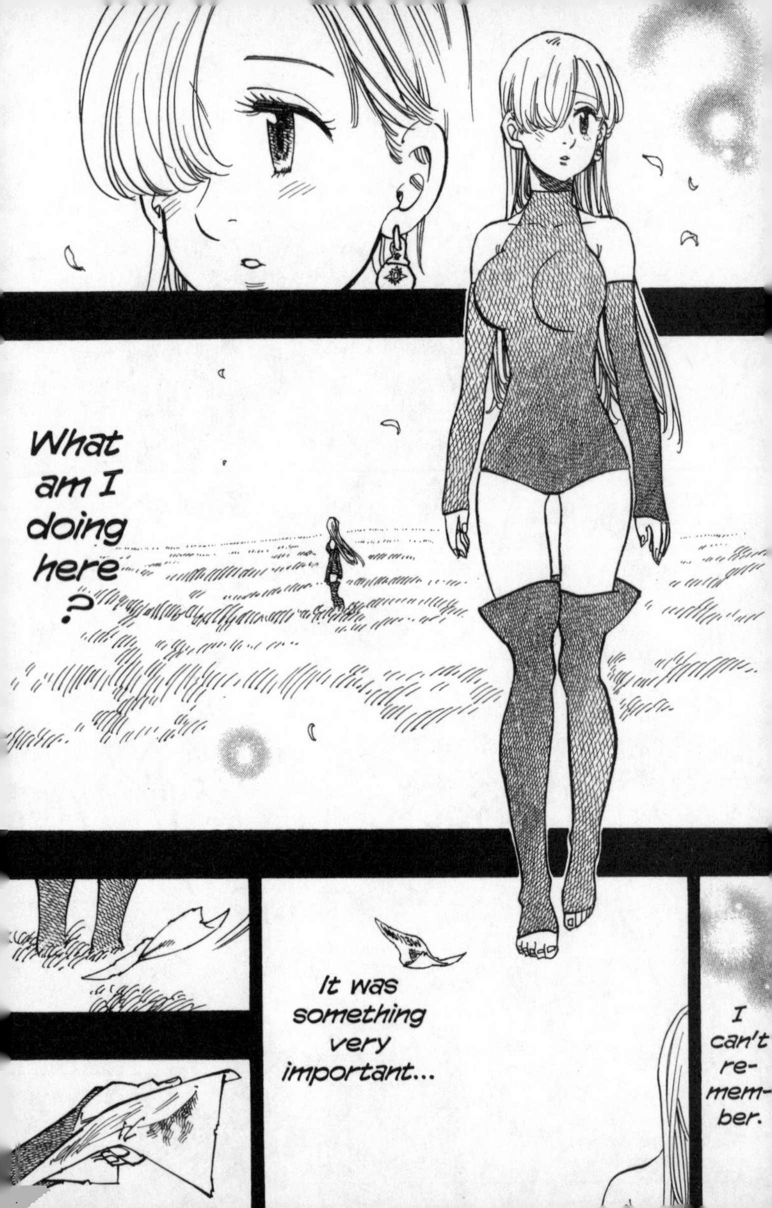
What am I doing here?
I can't re-mem-ber.
It was something very important...

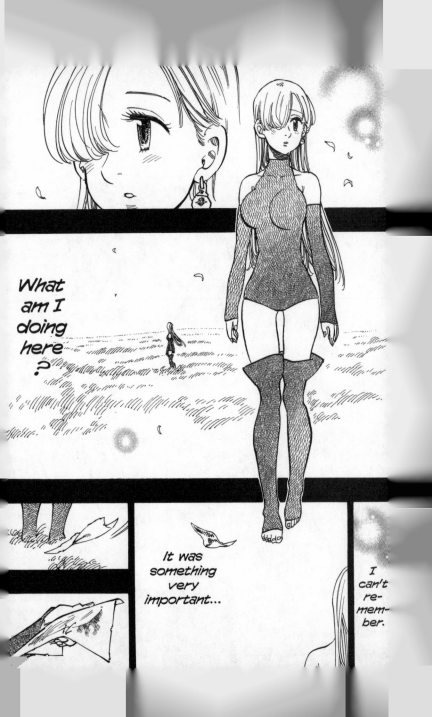

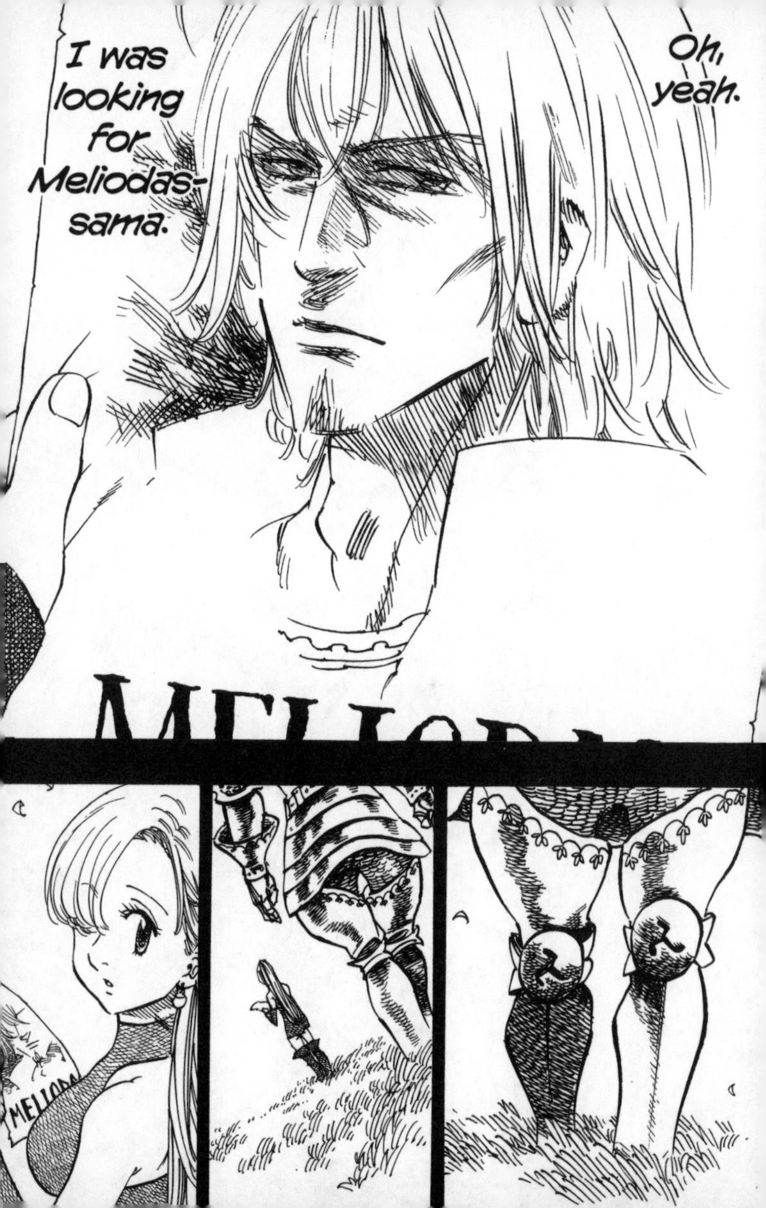
Oh, yeah.
I was looking for Meliodas-sama.

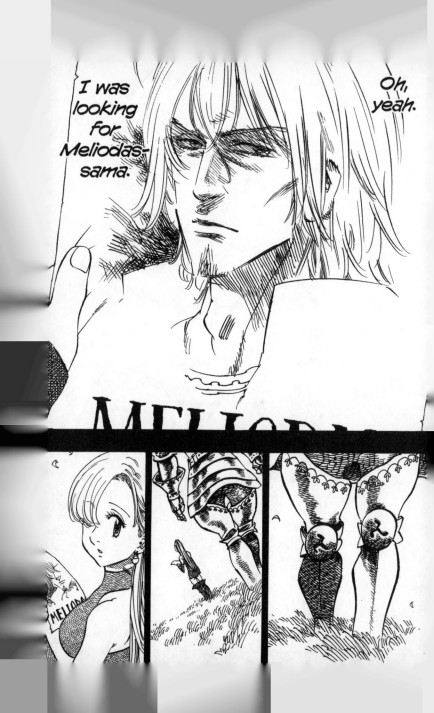

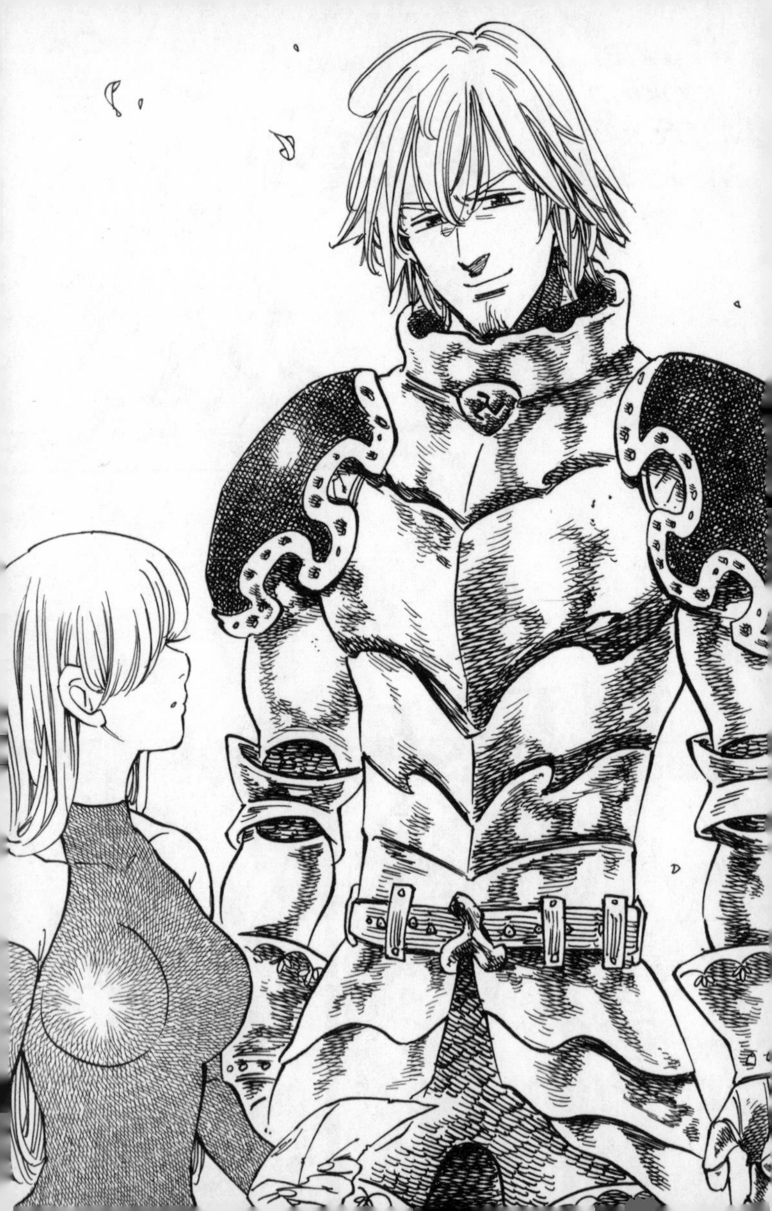

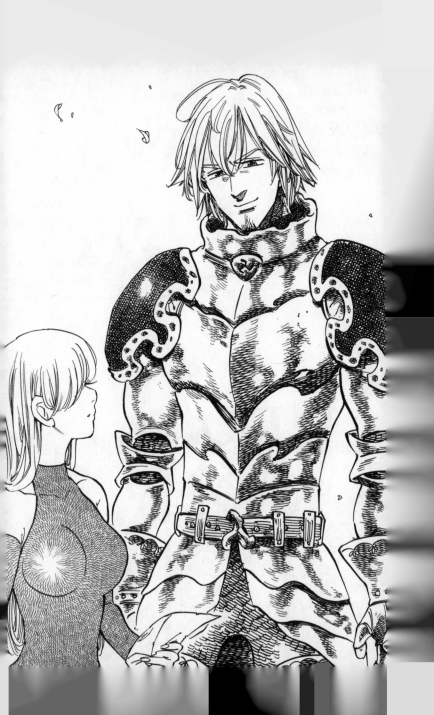

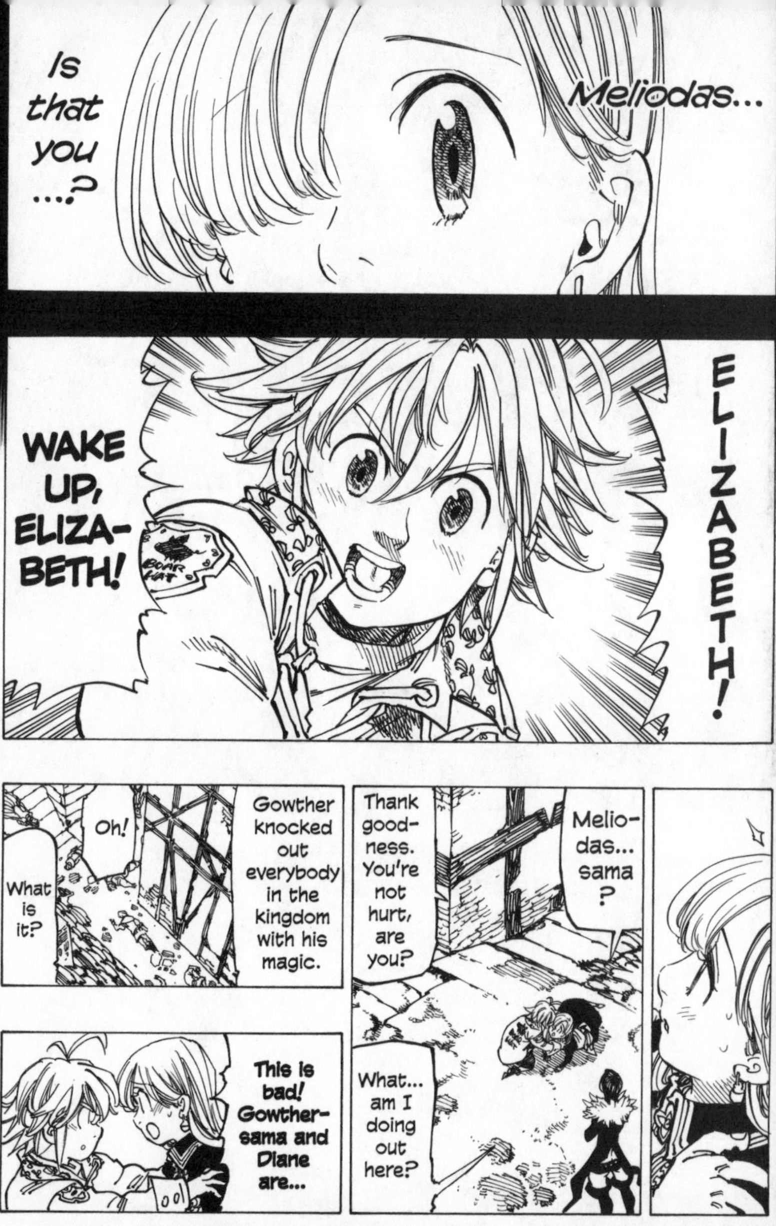
Meliodas...
Is that you ...?
ELIZABETH!
WAKE UP, ELIZABETH!
BOAR HAT
Melio-das... sama?
Thank good-ness. You're not hurt, are you?
What... am I doing out here?
Gowther knocked out everybody in the kingdom with his magic.
Oh!
What is it?
This is bad! Gowther-sama and Diane are...

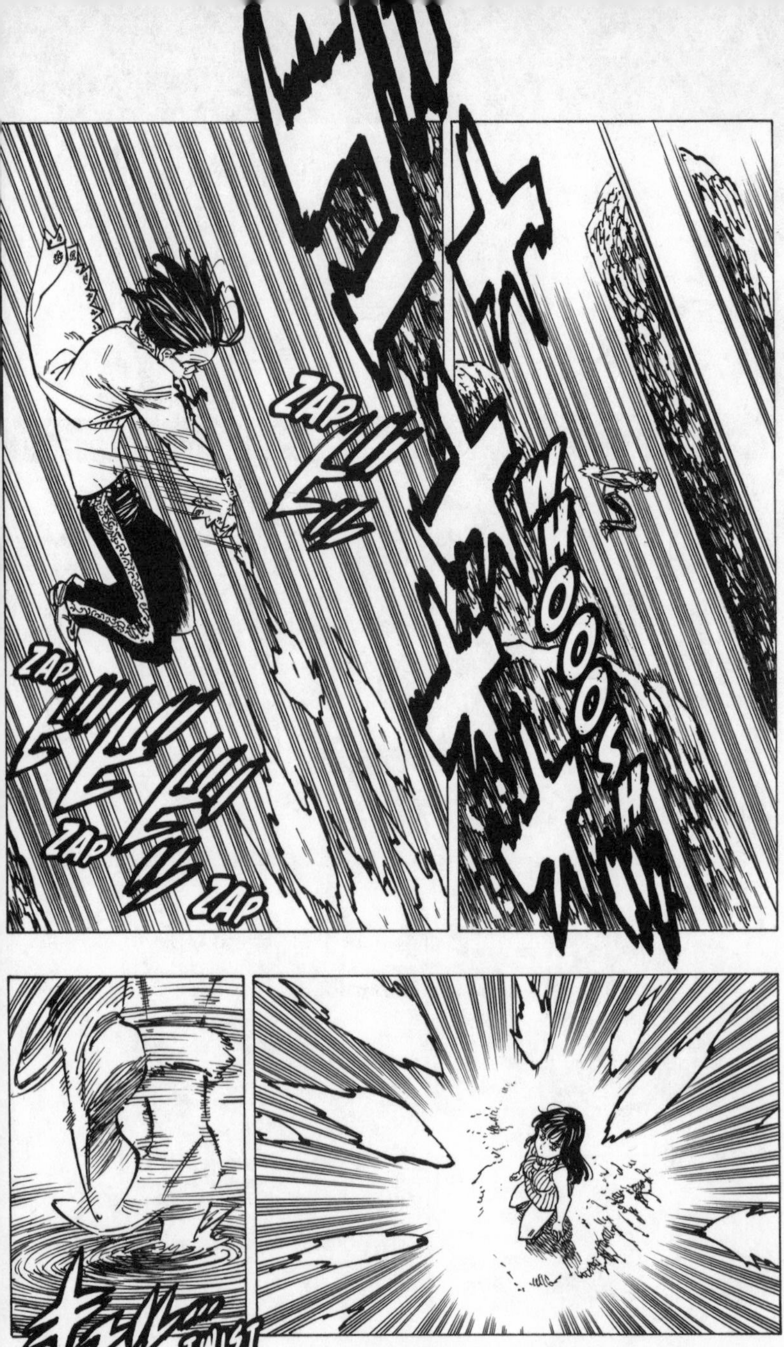
WHOOOOSH
ZAP
ZAP
ZAP
ZAP
TWIST

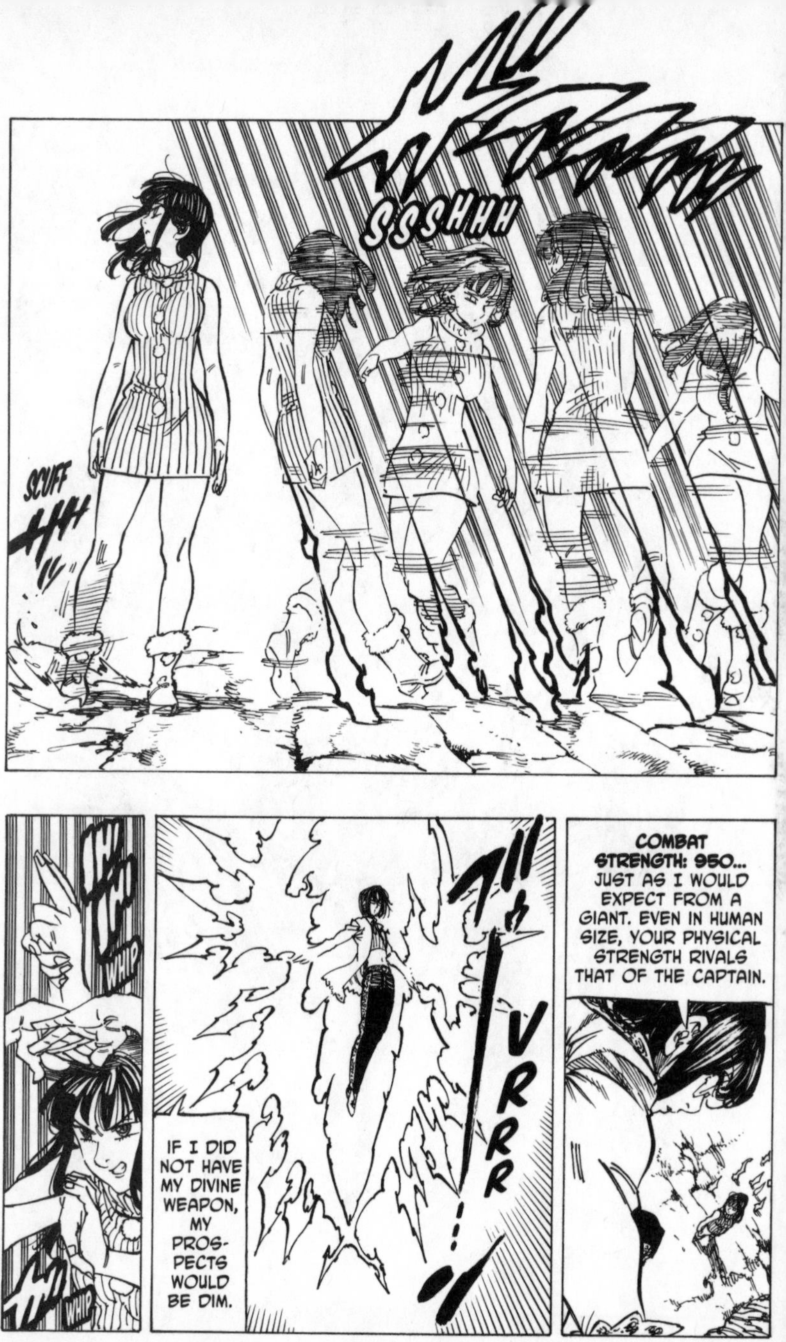
SSSHHH
SCUFF
COMBAT STRENGTH: 950... JUST AS I WOULD EXPECT FROM A GIANT. EVEN IN HUMAN SIZE, YOUR PHYSICAL STRENGTH RIVALS THAT OF THE CAPTAIN.
VRRR!!
IF I DID NOT HAVE MY DIVINE WEAPON, MY PROS-PECTS WOULD BE DIM.
WHIP
WHIP

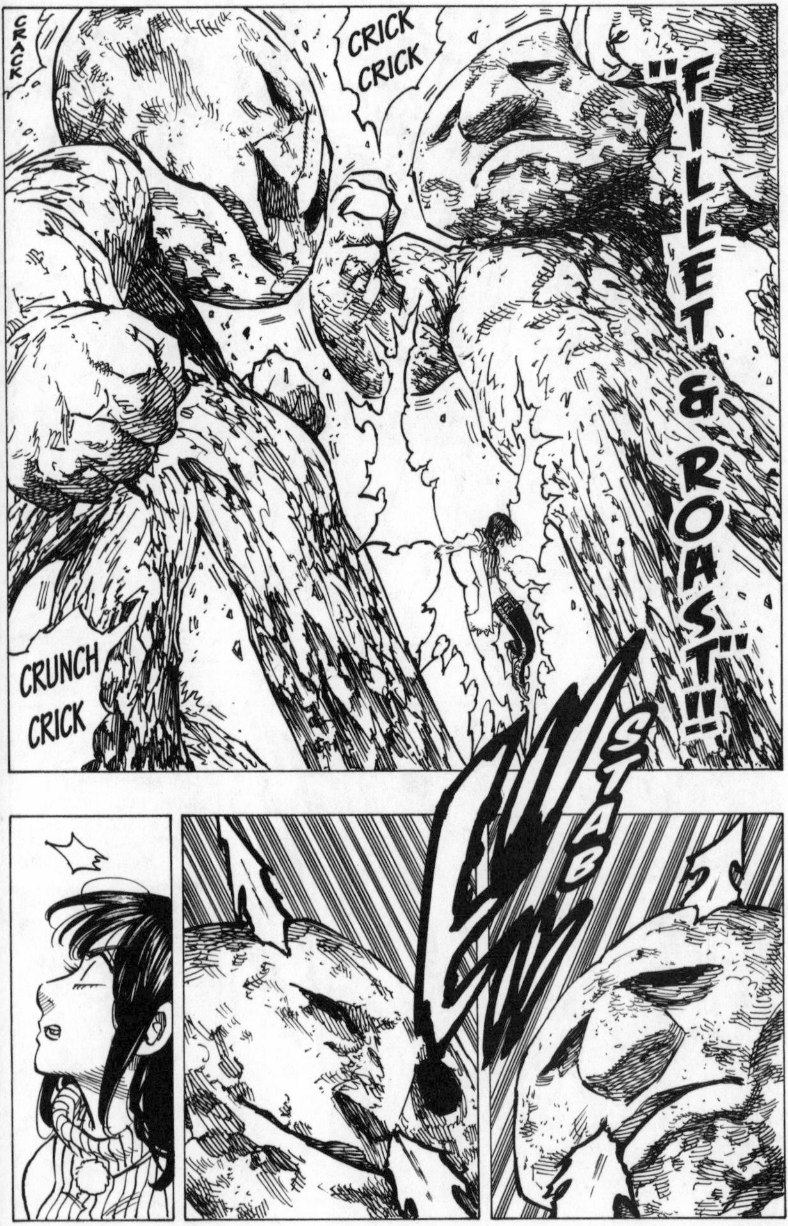
"FILLET & ROAST"!!
CRICK CRICK
CRACK
CRUNCH CRICK
STAB

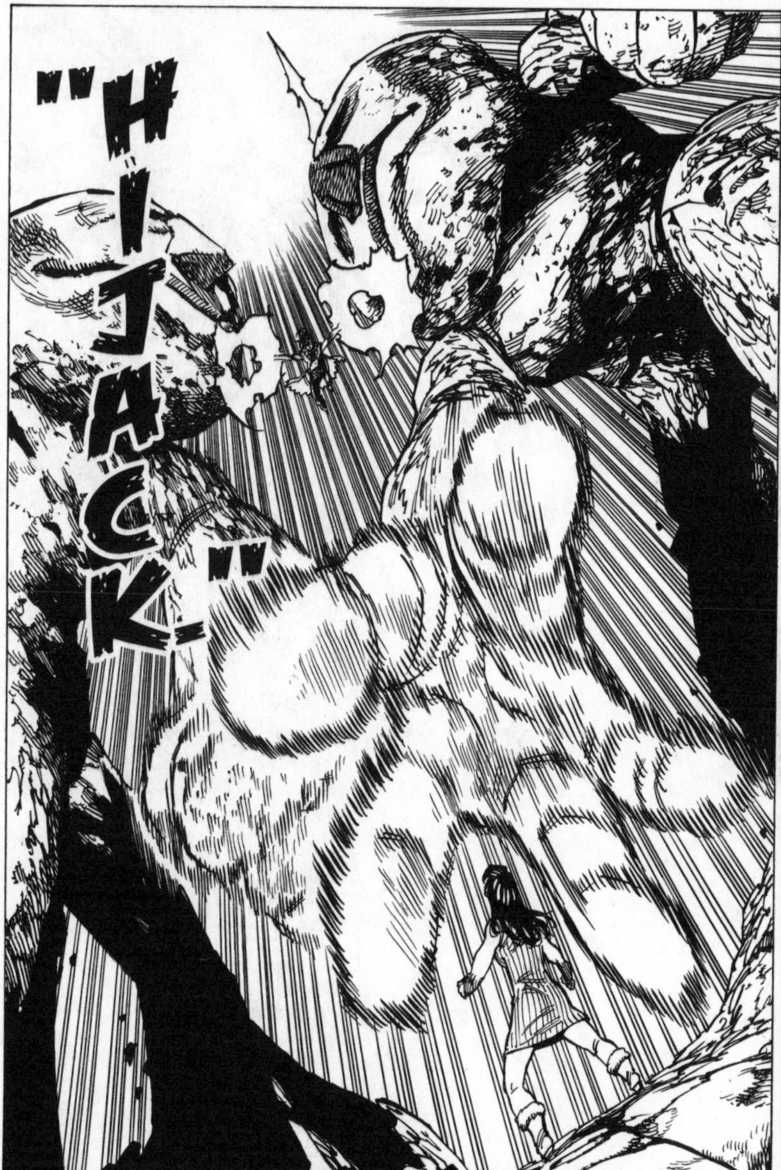
"HIJACK"

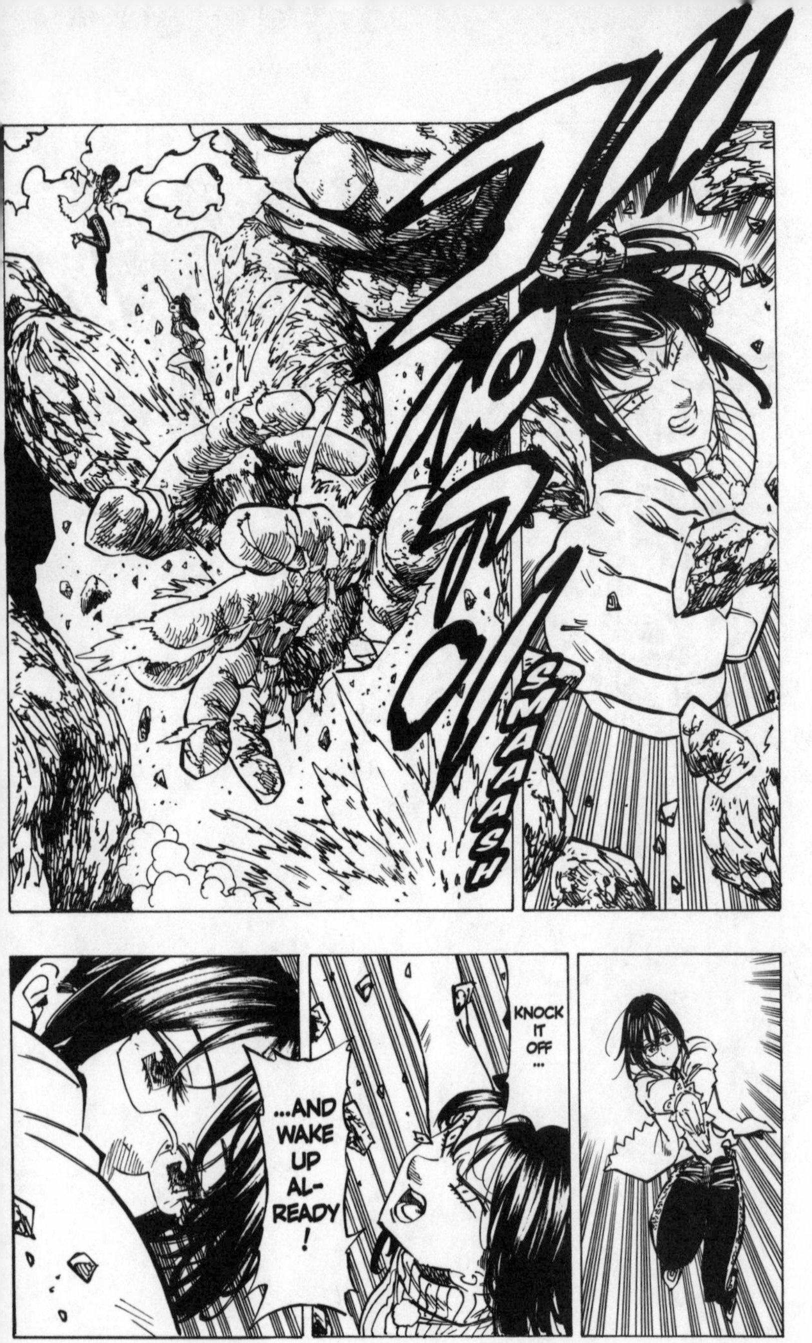
SMAAAASH
KNOCK IT OFF ...
...AND WAKE UP AL-READY!

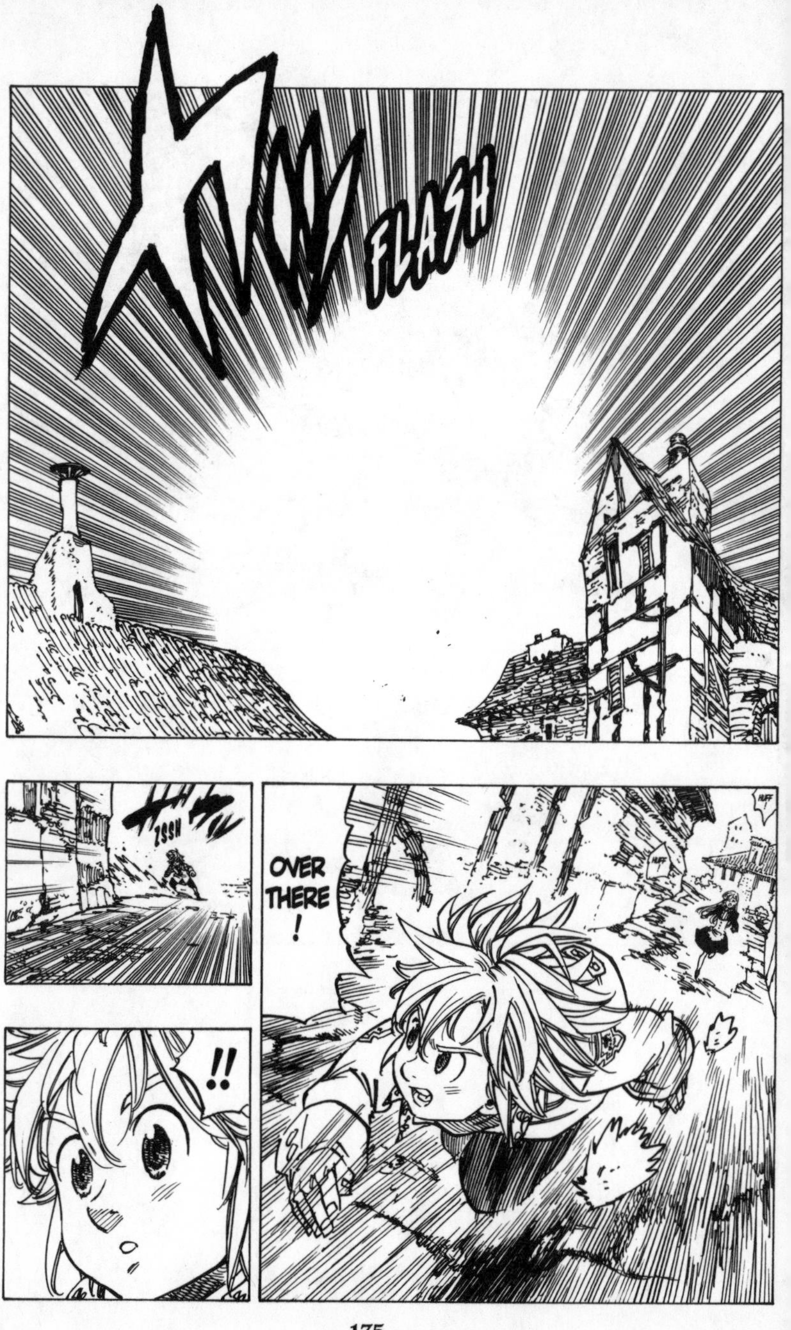
FLASH
HUFF
HUFF
OVER THERE !
ZSSH
!!

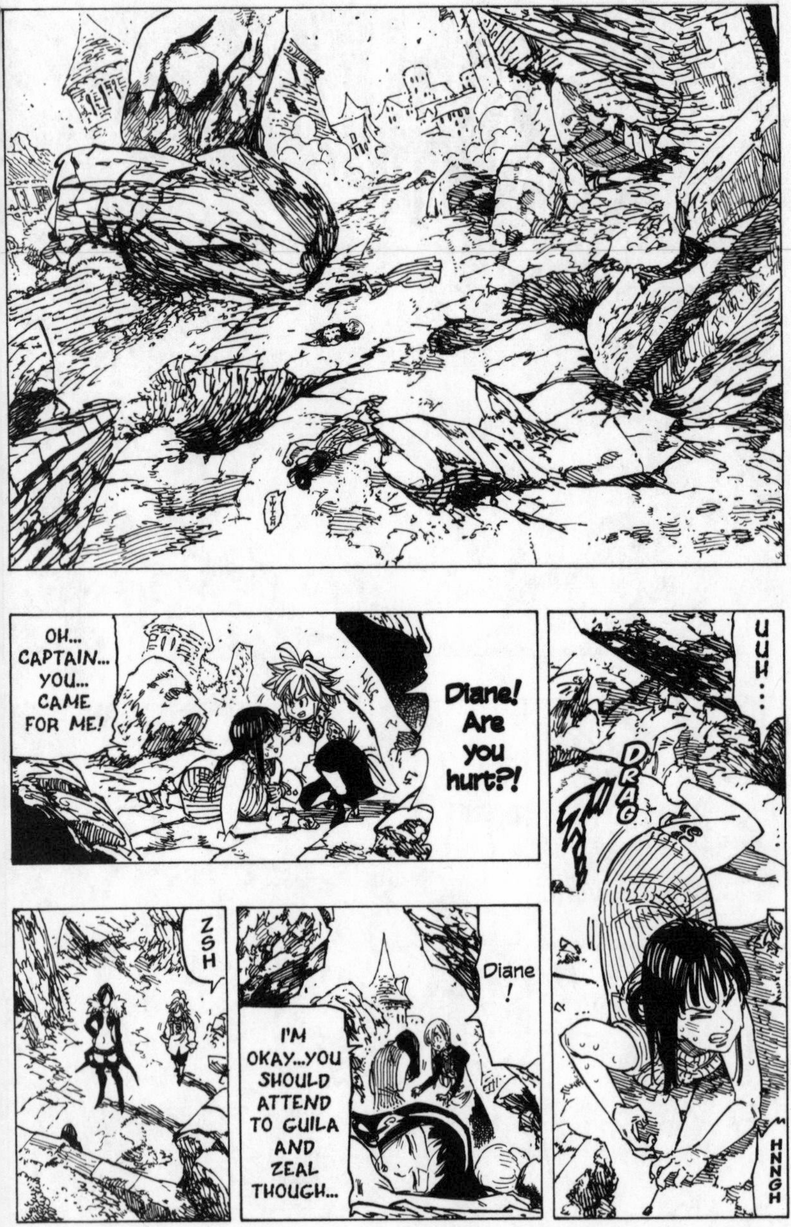
UUH...
DRAG
HNNGH
Diane! Are you hurt?!
OH... CAPTAIN... YOU... CAME FOR ME!
Diane!
I'M OKAY...YOU SHOULD ATTEND TO GUILA AND ZEAL THOUGH...
ZSH

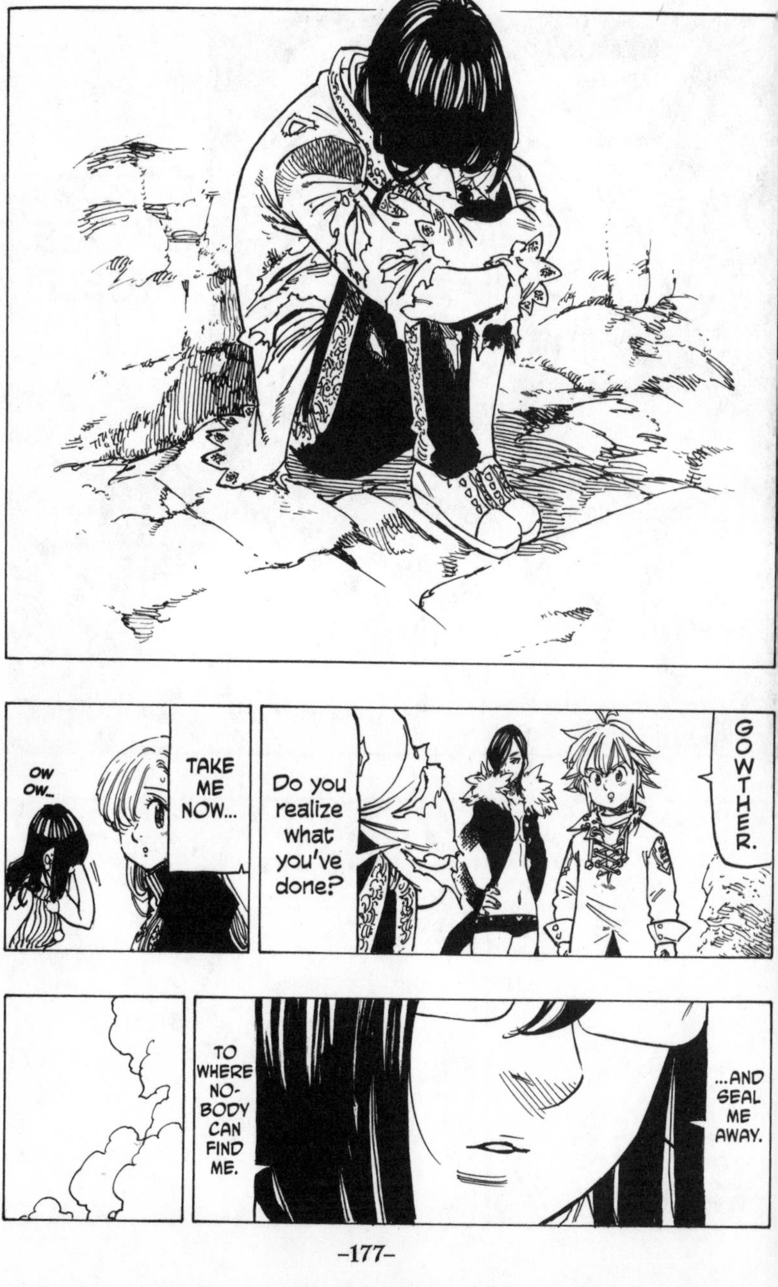
GOWTHER.
Do you realize what you've done?
TAKE ME NOW...
OW OW...
...AND SEAL ME AWAY.
TO WHERE NO-BODY CAN FIND ME.

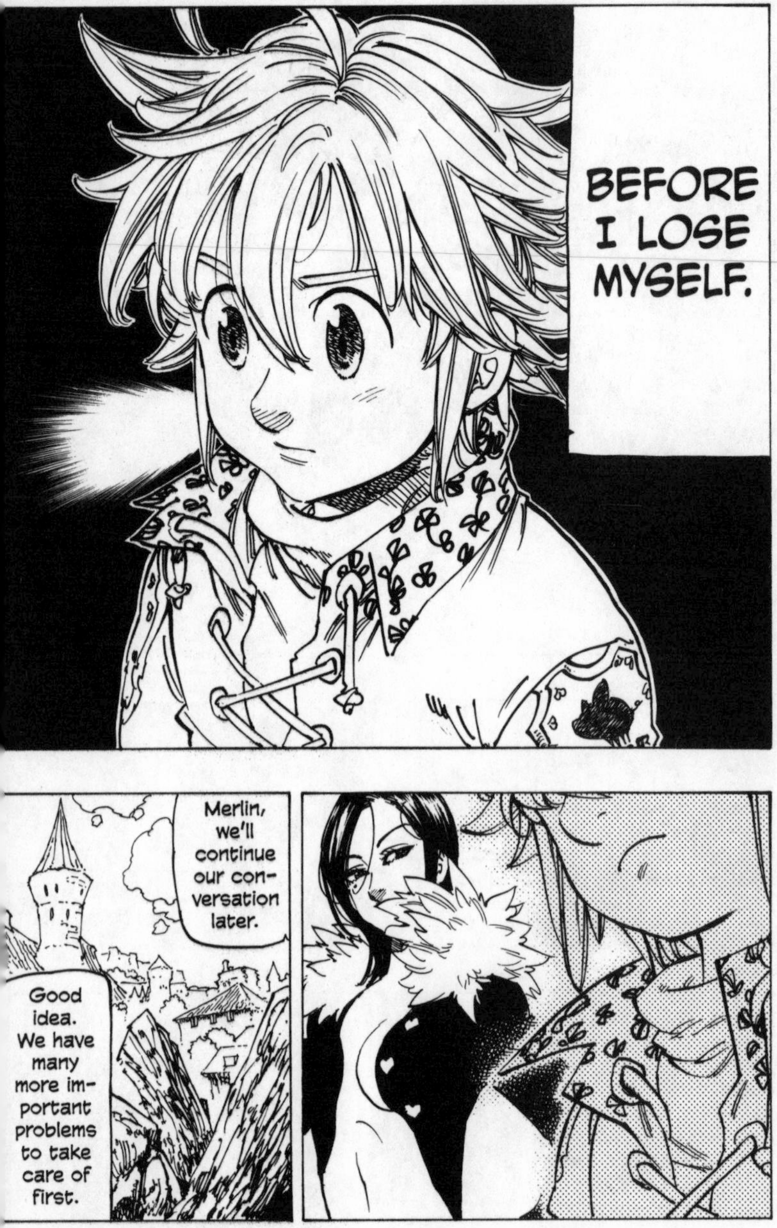
BEFORE I LOSE MYSELF.
Merlin, we'll continue our con-versation later.
Good idea. We have many more im-portant problems to take care of first.

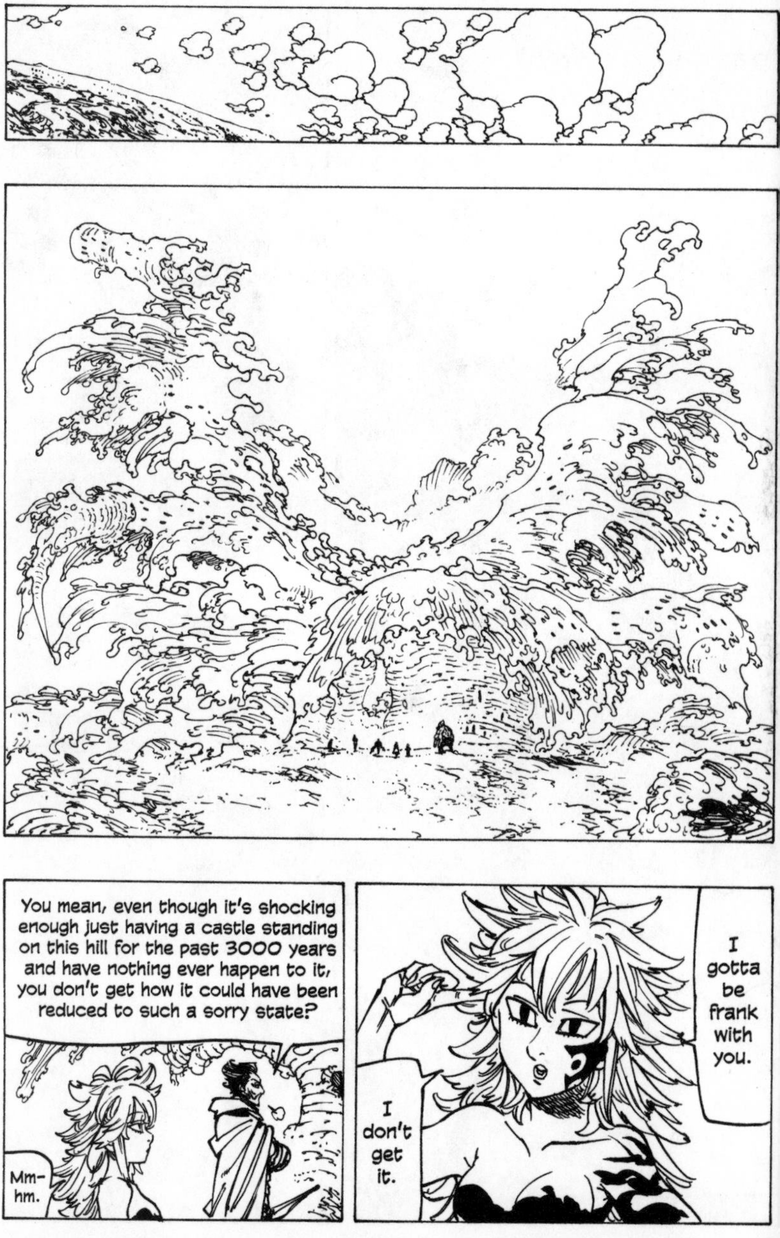
I gotta be frank with you.
I don't get it.
You mean, even though it's shocking enough just having a castle standing on this hill for the past 3000 years and have nothing ever happen to it, you don't get how it could have been reduced to such a sorry state?
Mm-hm.

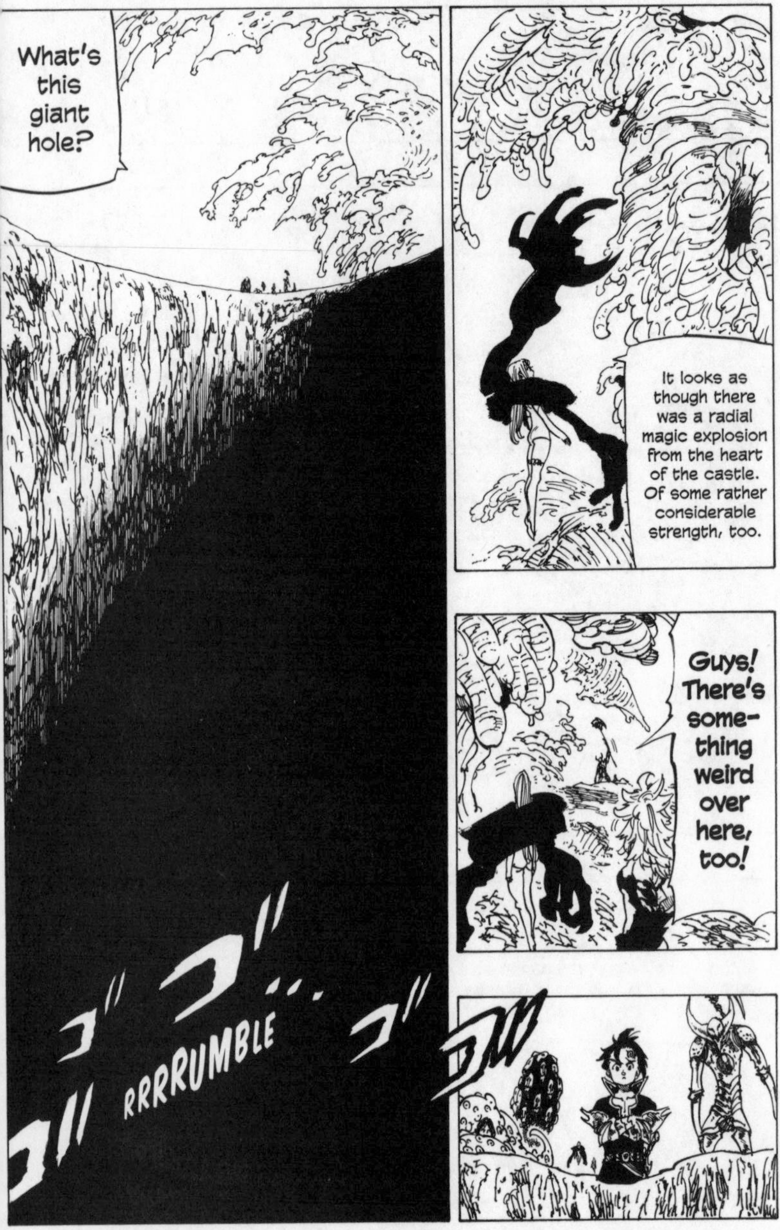
It looks as though there was a radial magic explosion from the heart of the castle. Of some rather considerable strength, too.
Guys! There's some-thing weird over here, too!
What's this giant hole?
RRRRUMBLE

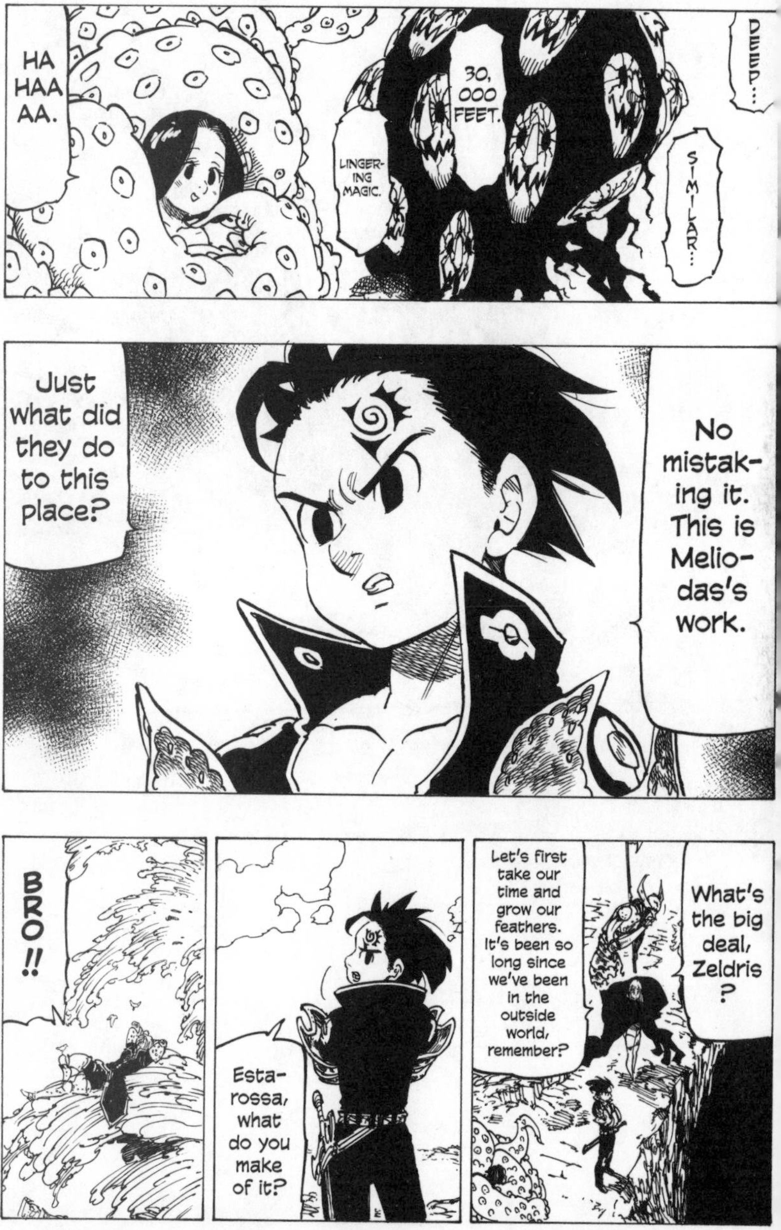
DEEP...
SIMILAR...
30,000 FEET.
LINGERING MAGIC.
HA HAAAA.
No mistaking it. This is Meliodas's work.
Just what did they do to this place?
What's the big deal, Zeldris?
Let's first take our time and grow our feathers. It's been so long since we've been in the outside world, remember?
Estarossa, what do you make of it?
BRO!!

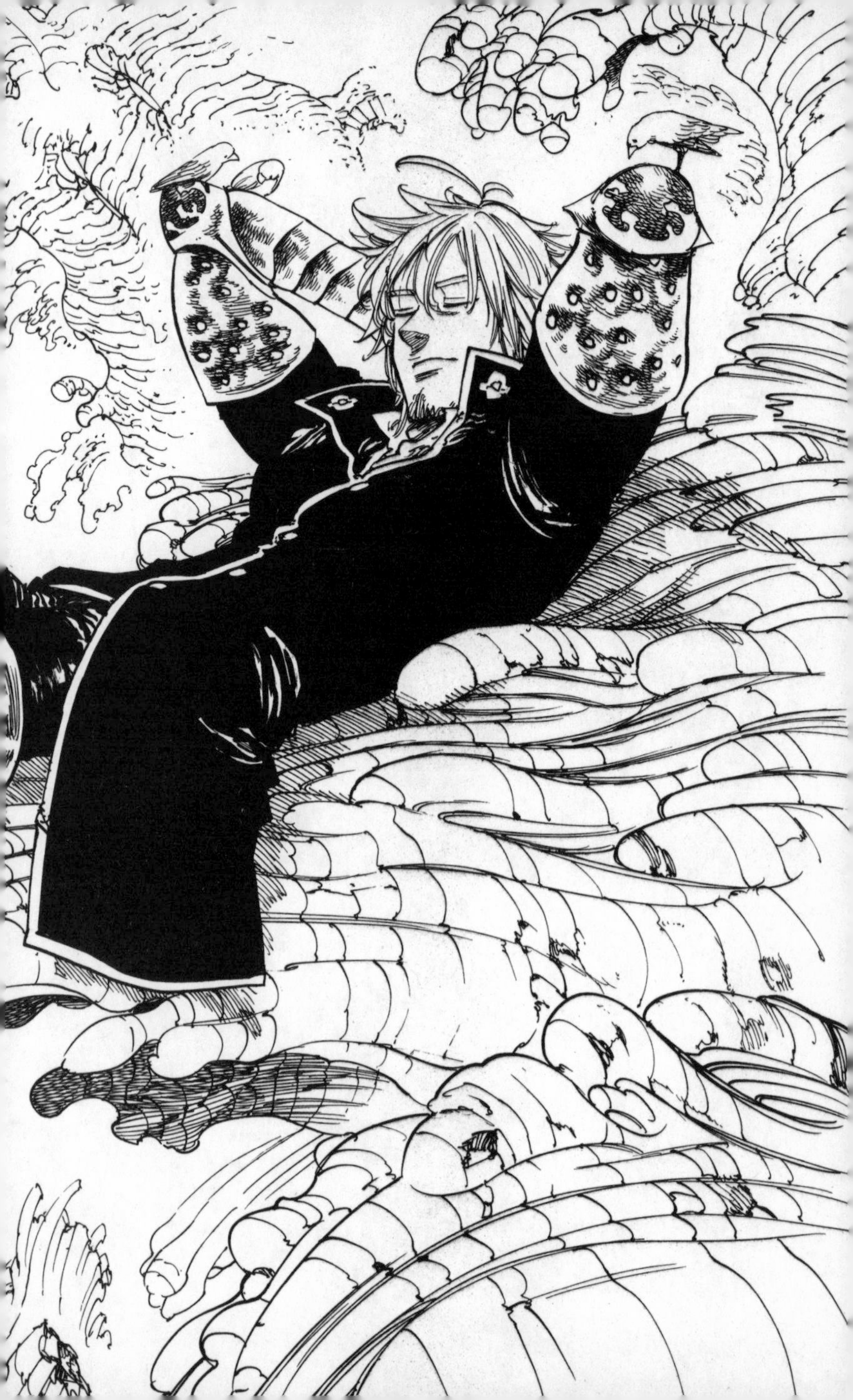

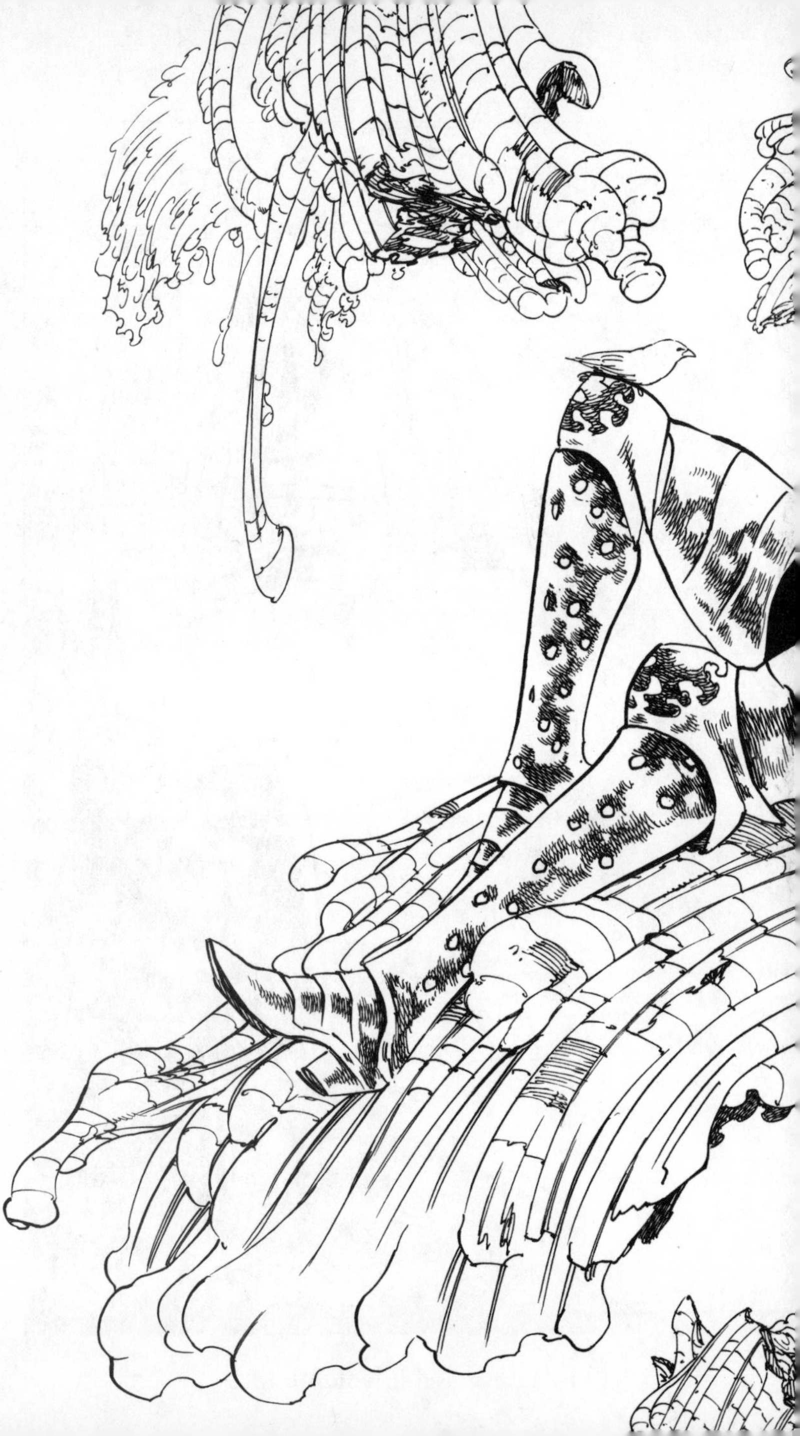

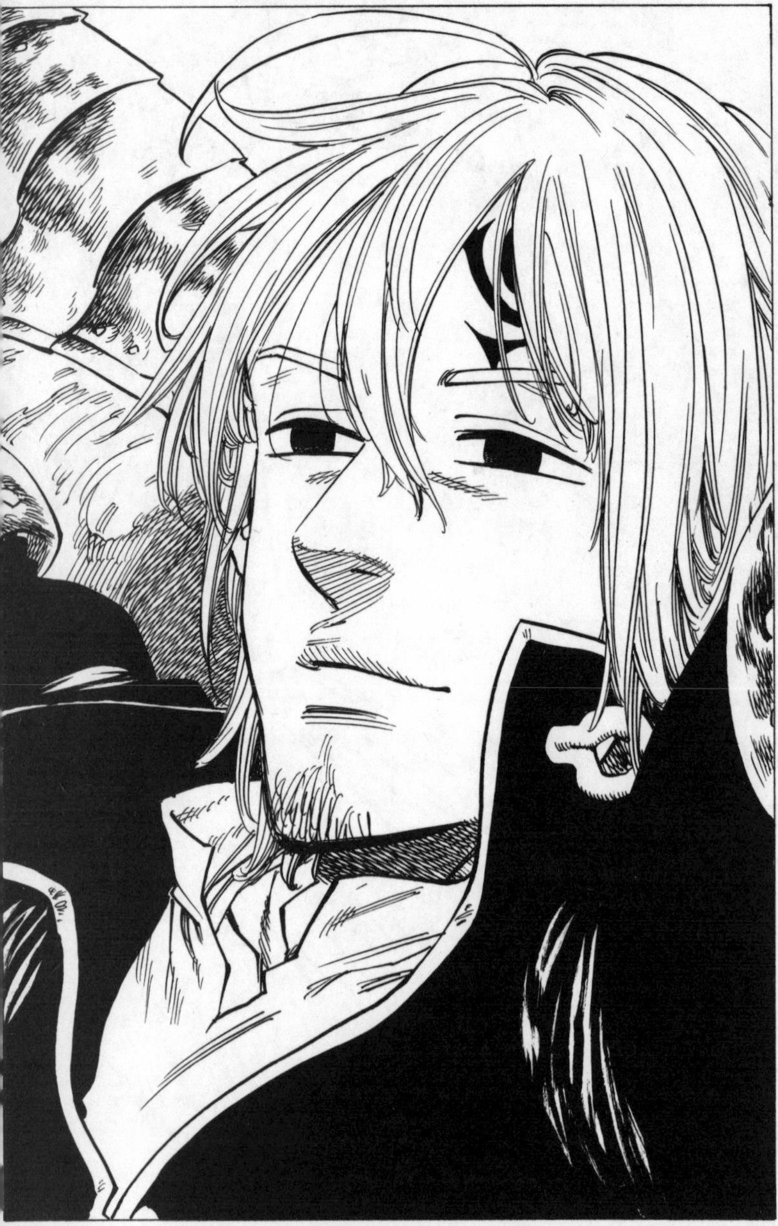

To Be Continued in Volume 15...

"THE SEVEN DEADLY SINS" ILLUSTRATION CORNER

"THE DRAWING KNIGHTHOOD" SPACE

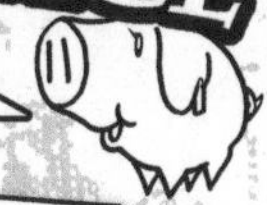
Be sure to include your name and address on your postcard!

M =
H =
E =
D =
B =
K =
G =
MER =

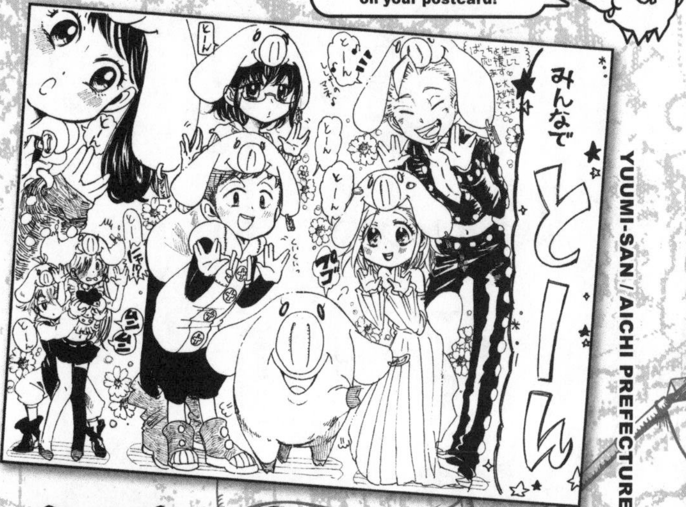
みんなで
と一ん

YUUMI-SAN / AICHI PREFECTURE

SPECIAL PRIZE

"We're all giving Hawk-styled peace signs!"

"How's that for a sign of my popularity?"

"We should make more of these hats and sell them!"

"Listen when I talk!"

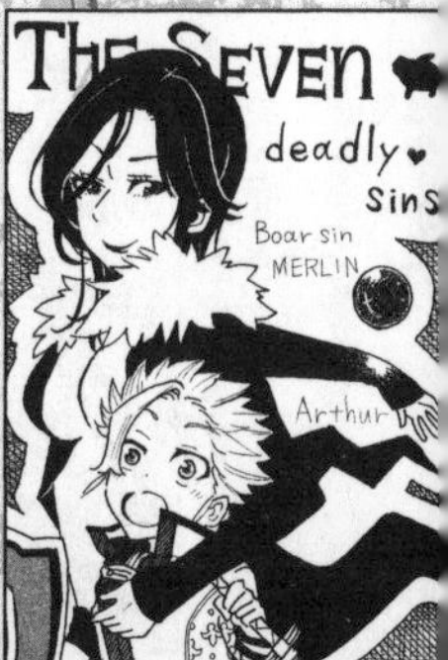
The Seven
deadly
Sins
Boar sin
MERLIN
Arthur

MAYU MATSUNAGA-SAN / AICHI PREFECTURE

E "What does Arthur-sama mean to Merlin-sama?"

M MER "What does he mean to me...? Heh."

"What's with that knowing smile?"

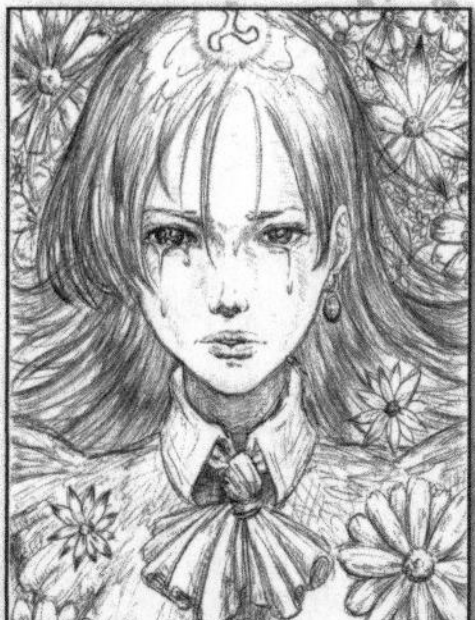

OBOO-SAN / CHIBA PREFECTURE

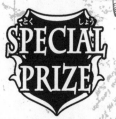

D "I was so shocked that Elizabeth possesses that kind of power!"

E "Huh? ...I honestly don't remember much about it... Hmmm."

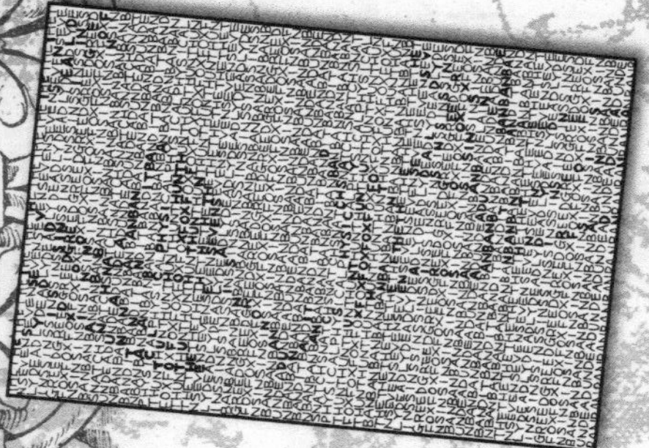

YURIKO-SAN /
AKITA PREFECTURE

"Now this is a piece of work that requires patience and perseverance. Quite impressive."

"I am pretty proficient with such works as this. Shiiiing!"

YUJIRO TONO / TOKYO

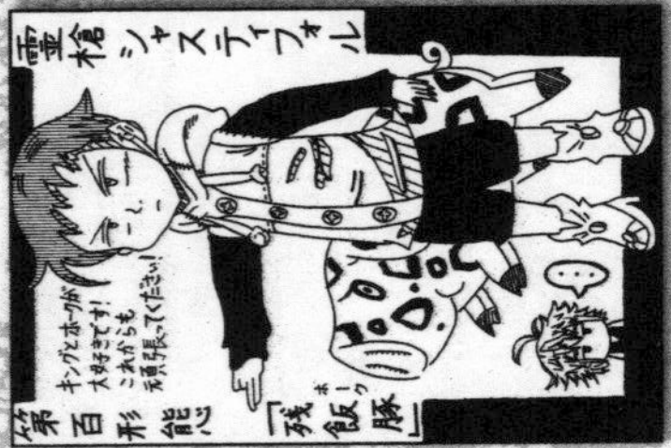
霊槍シャスティフォル
第百形態「残飯豚」
ホーク
キングとホークが大好きです! これからも頑張ってください!

M "All right! Starting today, Hawk's going to be my vehicle of choice!"

K "Actually, you'd better not. You'd just get leftovers all over you."

YASUHA NAGAI-SAN / HOKKAIDO

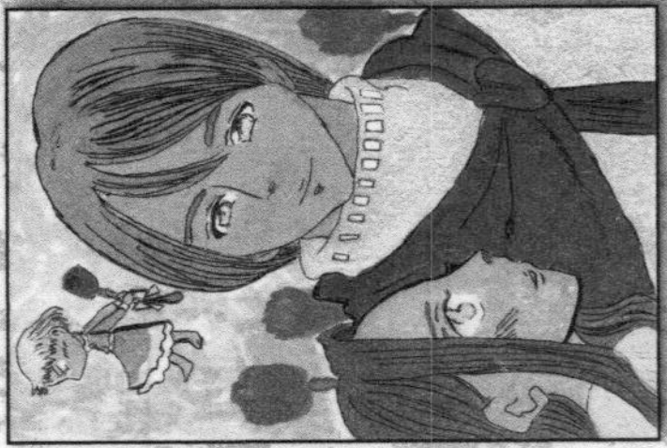

E "I'm glad Sister Margaret looks so happy."

M "He can also be super heartless at the drop of a hat."

TAKEO FUKAZAWA-SAN /
KANAGAWA PREFECTURE

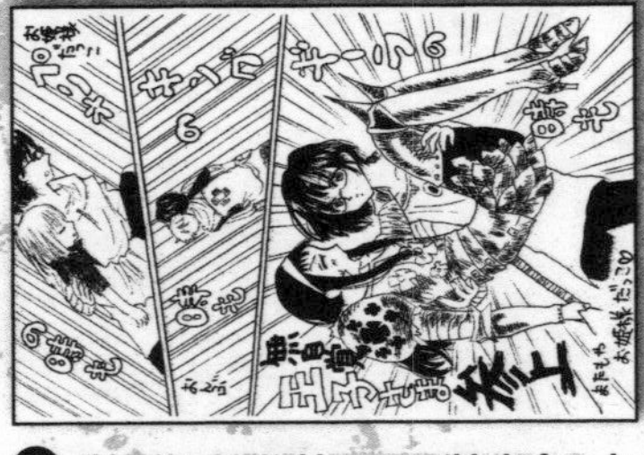
お嬢様だっこ
キングの時も
ギーラの時も
無自覚王子さま参上
またもやお姫様だっこ♡

G "I have never told anyone this before, but I would like to be a booth babe for the tavern as well. At the same time, however, I wish I could be a prince."

K "Y...you don't say. Hmmmm."

MER "I'm also curious about the relationship these two have."

K "Huh? Don't tell me you've got a thing for the captain, too!"

MER "*Smirk*"

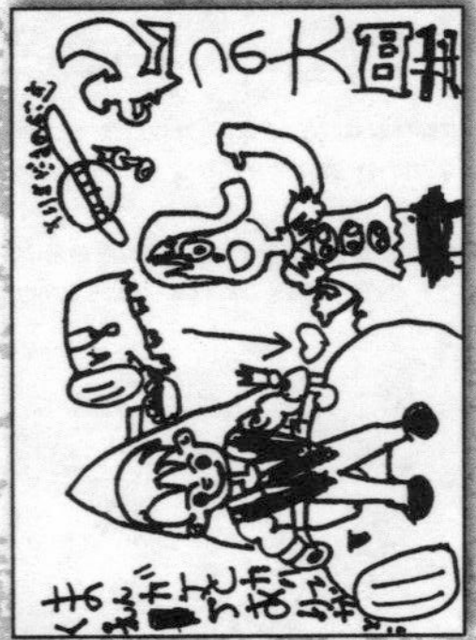

AYANE MAEBARU-SAN /
AICHI PREFECTURE

DAISUKE KURODA-SAN /
WAKAYAMA PREFECTURE

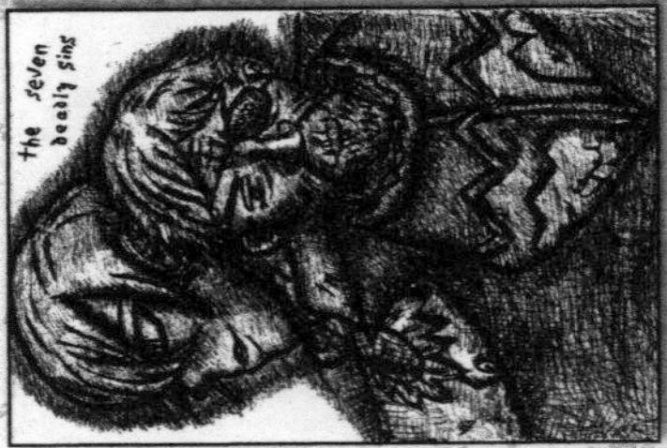
the seven deadly sins

B "What's with the Fairy Folks and having old dude faces?"

K "...Come on, it's sophisticated."

B "I just don't get it."

MAKO KATO-SAN / SAITAMA PREFECTURE

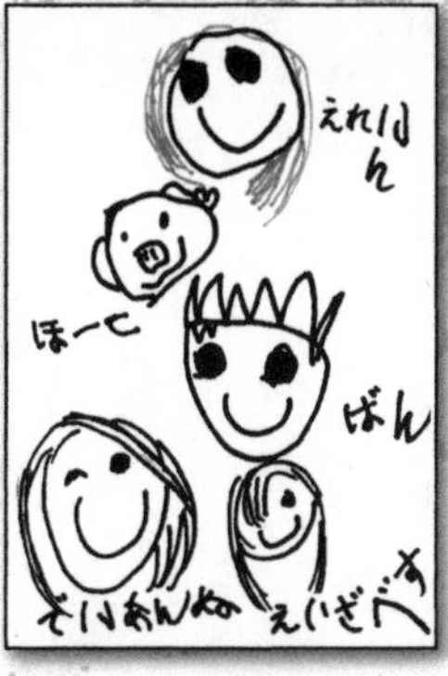
ほーく
ばん

H "Only four years old and already a fan of Ban's."

K "Her mom ought to be concerned! We have to open their eyes to the truth!"

B "Kah kah kah! ♪ Aaw, let her be. ♫"

DEVIL VI-SAN / ISHIKAWA PREFECTURE

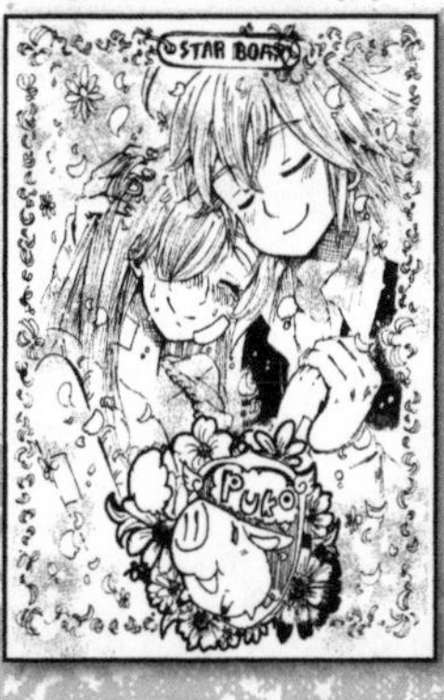
STAR BOAR

E "I want to keep traveling with Meliodas-sama!"

H "Elizabeth-chan... you still hold that dirty pervert in such high regard...? (sob)"

MACHIKO MOMOI-SAN / GUNMA PREFECTURE

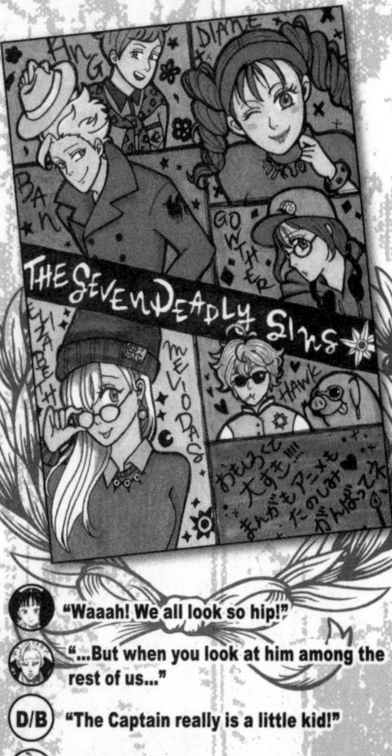
KING
DIANE
BAN
GOWTHER
THE SEVEN DEADLY SINS
ELIZABETH
MELIODAS
HAWK
おもしろくて大すき!!!
まんがもアニメもたのしみ♥
がんばってね

"Waaah! We all look so hip!"

"...But when you look at him among the rest of us..."

D/B "The Captain really is a little kid!"

"Shut up!"

Now Accepting Applicants for "The Drawing Knighthood"!

- **Draw your picture on a postcard, or paper no larger than a postcard, and send it in!**
- **Don't forget to write your name and location on the back of your picture!**
- **You can include comments or not. And colored illustrations will still only be displayed in B&W!**
- **The Drawing Knights whose pictures are particularly noteworthy and run in the print edition will be gifted with a signed specially made pencil board!**
- **And the best overall will be granted the special prize of a signed shikishi!!**

Kodansha Weekly Shonen Magazine
Re: The Seven Deadly Sins Drawing Knighthood
2-12-21 Otowa Bu-kyo-ku, Tokyo 112-8001

*Submitted letters and postcards will be given to the artist. Please be aware that your name, address, and other personal information included will be given as well.

"THE SEVEN DEADLY SINS" Q&A CORNER

"CHATTING KNIGHTHOOD"

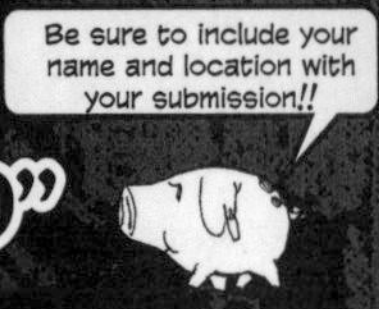
Be sure to include your name and location with your submission!!

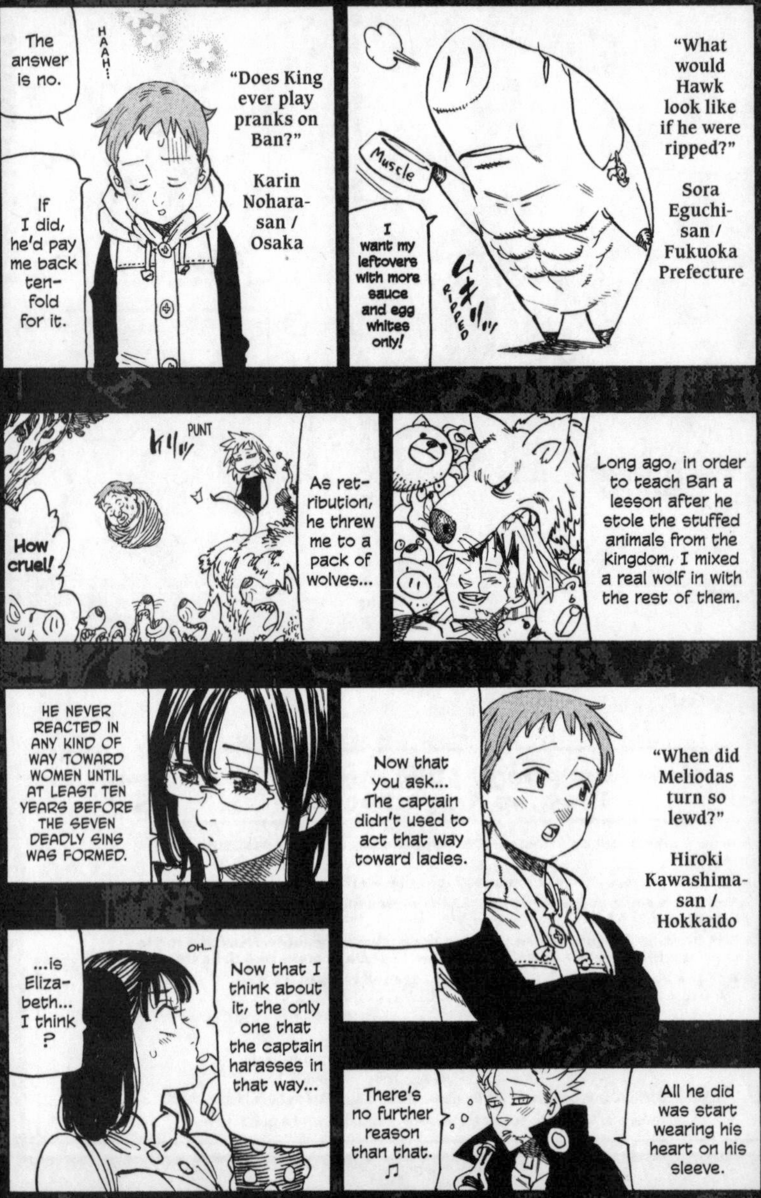
"What would Hawk look like if he were ripped?"
Sora Eguchi-san / Fukuoka Prefecture
Muscle
I want my leftovers with more sauce and egg whites only!
RIPPED
"Does King ever play pranks on Ban?"
Karin Nohara-san / Osaka
HAAH!
The answer is no.
If I did, he'd pay me back ten-fold for it.
Long ago, in order to teach Ban a lesson after he stole the stuffed animals from the kingdom, I mixed a real wolf in with the rest of them.
As retribution, he threw me to a pack of wolves...
PUNT
How cruel!
"When did Meliodas turn so lewd?"
Hiroki Kawashima-san / Hokkaido
Now that you ask... The captain didn't used to act that way toward ladies.
HE NEVER REACTED IN ANY KIND OF WAY TOWARD WOMEN UNTIL AT LEAST TEN YEARS BEFORE THE SEVEN DEADLY SINS WAS FORMED.
Now that I think about it, the only one that the captain harasses in that way...
OH...
...is Elizabeth... I think ?
All he did was start wearing his heart on his sleeve.
There's no further reason than that. ♪

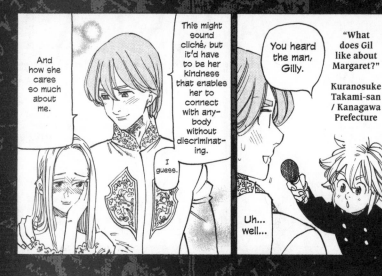

"What does Gil like about Margaret?"
Kuranosuke Takami-san / Kanagawa Prefecture
You heard the man, Gilly.
Uh... well...
This might sound cliché, but it'd have to be her kindness that enables her to connect with anybody without discriminating.
I guess.
And how she cares so much about me.
Then what about me?
SOB SOB
For more than ten years, you were the only one I cared about.

Now Accepting Members to the "Chatting Knighthood"!

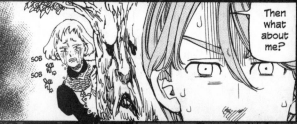

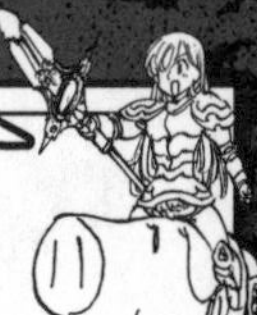

- Send your questions on a postcard!
- You can write as many questions as you like on your postcard
- Don't forget to write your name and location at the end of your question!

Those who get their questions featured in "Chatting Knighthood" will receive a specially signed postcard!

- The Chatting Knights whose questions are particularly noteworthy and run in the print edition will be gifted with a signed, specially-made pencil board!
- And the best overall will be granted the special prize of a signed shikishi!!

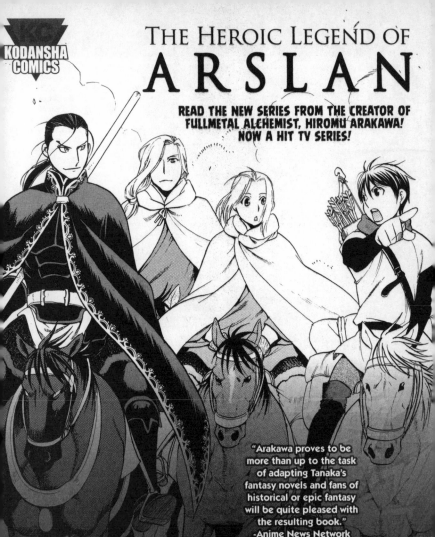

NORAGAMI
STRAY GOD

"A FUN ADVENTURE WITH A COLORFUL AND MEMORABLE CAST OF CHARACTERS IN AN ENGROSSING MODERN-DAY FANTASY SETTING."
—KOTAKU

READ THE SERIES THAT BECAME THE HIT ANIME!

YATO IS A HOMELESS GOD WITHOUT A SHRINE OR ANY WORSHIPPERS! SO TO ACHIEVE HIS AMBITIOUS GOAL OF A LAVISH TEMPLE, HE'S SET UP A SERVICE TO HELP THOSE IN NEED... FOR A SMALL FEE. SINCE HE CAN'T AFFORD TO BE PICKY, YATO ACCEPTS ANY JOB FROM FINDING LOST KITTENS TO HELPING BULLIED STUDENTS. MEANWHILE, HIYORI IKI, AN ORDINARY PRO-WRESTLING-LOVING MIDDLE SCHOOL GIRL, HAS TURNED INTO AN EXISTENCE THAT IS NEITHER HUMAN NOR AYAKASHI! IT'S UP TO YATO'S "DIVINE INTERVENTION" TO TURN HIYORI BACK TO NORMAL, BUT CAN SHE RELY ON THE SPONTANEOUS AND WAYWARD GOD?

AVAILABLE NOW IN PRINT AND DIGITALLY!

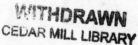

The Seven Deadly Sins volume 14 is a work of fiction. Names, characters, places, and incidents are the products of the author's imagination or are used fictitiously. Any resemblance to actual events, locales, or persons, living or dead, is entirely coincidental.

A Kodansha Comics Trade Paperback Original.

The Seven Deadly Sins volume 14 copyright © 2015 Nakaba Suzuki
English translation copyright © 2016 Nakaba Suzuki

All rights reserved.

Published in the United States by Kodansha Comics, an imprint of Kodansha USA Publishing, LLC, New York.

Publication rights for this English edition arranged through Kodansha Ltd., Tokyo.

First published in Japan in 2015 by Kodansha Ltd., Tokyo.

ISBN 978-1-63236-217-9

Printed in the United States of America.

www.kodansha.us

9 8 7 6 5 4

Translation: Christine Dashiell
Lettering: James Dashiell
Editing: Lauren Scanlan